Redefining Retirement

Redefining Retirement

How Will Boomers Fare?

EDITED BY

Brigitte Madrian, Olivia S. Mitchell, and Beth J. Soldo

OXFORD
UNIVERSITY PRESS

Great Clarendon Street, Oxford OX2 6DP

Oxford University Press is a department of the University of Oxford.
It furthers the University's objective of excellence in research, scholarship,
and education by publishing worldwide in

Oxford New York

Auckland Cape Town Dar es Salaam Hong Kong Karachi
Kuala Lumpur Madrid Melbourne Mexico City Nairobi
New Delhi Shanghai Taipei Toronto

With offices in

Argentina Austria Brazil Chile Czech Republic France Greece
Guatemala Hungary Italy Japan Poland Portugal Singapore
South Korea Switzerland Thailand Turkey Ukraine Vietnam

Oxford is a registered trade mark of Oxford University Press
in the UK and in certain other countries

Published in the United States
by Oxford University Press Inc., New York

British Library Cataloguing in Publication Data

Data available

Library of Congress Cataloging in Publication Data

Data available

Typeset by SPI Publisher Services, Pondicherry, India
Printed in Great Britain
on acid-free paper by
Biddles Ltd., King's Lynn, Norfolk

ISBN 978–0–19–923077–8

1 3 5 7 9 10 8 6 4 2

Preface

The leading edge of the Baby Boom generation, born 1946–66, is now entering its 60s. As this unprecedentedly large and influential cohort moves into what was once known as the 'later life,' Boomers are certain to radically redefine what retirement means. It will surely develop new approaches to work, consumption, and other economic activity, just as it redefined so much else along the way. In turn, Boomer aging represents possibly momentous challenges for the labor market, the health care and pension systems, and national social safety nets.

This volume assesses new evidence about Boomers' prospects for health and income during retirement, drawing on an exciting range of new data-sets and models including the Health and Retirement study. Many contributors find that Boomers will be better off than their predecessors, having benefited from a run-up in housing prices, improvements in health care, and an expanding economy. Yet others argue the generation's sheer size will put potentially dangerous pressure on resources including health care and pensions. Topics covered include an assessment of Boomers' retirement and housing wealth, mental and physical health, and financial literacy as well as preparedness for the later phases of life. Researchers and policymakers concerned with the evolution of the modern economy will find much to interest them in this volume, as will managers, actuaries, and human resource specialists working with Boomers and younger individuals.

This book owes much to its contributors and particularly to my two collegial coeditors, Brigitte Madrian and Beth Soldo. Support for this research and publication were provided by The Wharton School via an Impact Conference grant, The National Institute of Health via a grant to the University of Pennsylvania, and the Pension Research Council as well as the Boettner Center for Pensions and Retirement Research, both of the Wharton School of the University of Pennsylvania. The manuscript was expertly prepared by Mayosha Mendis and Hilary Farrell with help from Caroline Alexander. On behalf of all these institutions and individuals, we thank our collaborators and supporters for their help in making sure that we all work together to redefine retirement.

The Pension Research Council

The Pension Research Council of the Wharton School at the University of Pennsylvania is an organization committed to generating debate on key policy issues affecting pensions and other employee benefits. The Council sponsors interdisciplinary research on the entire range of private and social retirement security and related benefit plans in the United States and around the world. It seeks to broaden understanding of these complex arrangements through basic research into their economic, social, legal, actuarial, and financial foundations. Members of the Advisory Board of the Council, appointed by the Dean of the Wharton School, are leaders in the employee benefits field, and they recognize the essential role of social security and other public sector income maintenance programs while sharing a desire to strengthen private sector approaches to economic security. More information about the Pension Research Council is available on the Internet at http://www.pensionresearchcouncil.org or send email to prc@wharton.upenn.edu.

Contents

List of Figures   ix
List of Tables   xi
Notes on Contributors   xvii
Abbreviations   xxiii

Part I. Prospects for Baby Boomer Retirement

1. Will Boomers Redefine Retirement?   1
   Olivia S. Mitchell

2. Cohort Differences in Retirement Expectations and Realizations   13
   Nicole Maestas

3. The Sufficiency of Retirement Savings: Comparing Cohorts at the
   Time of Retirement   36
   Robert Haveman, Karen Holden, Barbara L. Wolfe, and Andrei Romanov

4. Understanding Baby Boomers' Retirement Prospects   70
   Barbara A. Butrica, Howard M. Iams, and Karen E. Smith

Part II. Changing Health Status and Health Insurance

5. Are Baby Boomers Living Well Longer?   95
   David R. Weir

6. Baby Boomers versus Their Parents: Economic Well-Being and
   Health Status   112
   Joyce Manchester, David Weaver, and Kevin Whitman

7. Cross-Cohort Differences in Health on the Verge of Retirement   138
   Beth J. Soldo, Olivia S. Mitchell, Rania Tfaily, and John F. McCabe

8. Health Insurance Patterns Nearing Retirement   159
   Helen G. Levy

Part III. New Roles for Retirement Assets

 9. The Impact of Pensions on Nonpension Investment Choices   179
    Leora Friedberg and Anthony Webb

10. Measuring Pension Wealth   211
    Chris Cunningham, Gary V. Engelhardt, and Anil Kumar

11. Trends in Pension Values Around Retirement   234
    Michael D. Hurd and Susann Rohwedder

12. Pension Portfolio Choice and Menu Exposure   248
    Anders Karlsson, Massimo Massa, and Andrei Simonov

13. Saving between Cohorts: The Role of Planning   271
    Annamaria Lusardi and Jason Beeler

14. Retiring on the House? Cross-Cohort Differences in
    Housing Wealth   296
    Julia L. Coronado, Dean Maki, and Ben Weitzer

Index   309

List of Figures

2-1	Percent working full-time by age and cohort.	24
2-2	Percent partially retired by age and cohort.	25
2-3	Percent fully retired by age and cohort.	26
2-4	Expected probability of working in future if not currently working by age and cohort.	27
3-1	Age distribution of NBS and HRS samples.	45
3-2	Distribution by annuitized new wealth bins ($000, in $1994).	51
3A-1	Levels of ANW by socioeconomic group.	66
5-1	Health status by age in the cross section: HRS 2004.	97
5-2	Percent working by age and health status: HRS 2004.	98
5-3	Work and health status by age: HRS 2004.	99
5-4	Percent reporting a health problem limits work by age and work/health status: HRS 2004.	100
5-5	Ability to work: objective health and self-reported limits to work.	101
5-6	Subjective probability of survival to age 75 and self-rated health: comparing the original HRS (1992) to Early Boomers (2004).	105
5-7	Comparing health and education for the original HRS (1992) to Early Boomers (2004).	107
6-1	Concentration curve of fair/poor health by welfare ratio for parents.	130
6-2	Concentration index by health measure.	131
7-1	Item characteristic curve for self-reported health: HRS respondents Aged 51–56 in 1992, 1998, and 2004.	148
8-1	Fraction with no health insurance by age and birth cohort: current population survey (1989–2004).	162
8-2	Fraction with private health insurance by age and birth cohort: current population survey (1989–2004).	163
8-3	Fraction with public health insurance by age and birth cohort: current population survey (1989–2004).	163
8-4	Median total net nonpension wealth by cohort, age, and insurance status: health and retirement study (1992–2004).	168
8-5	Median total net nonpension, nonhousing wealth by cohort, age, and insurance status: health and retirement study (1992–2004).	169
9-1	Pension wealth accruals in typical pension plans, 1992 HRS.	182

10-1   Private sector pension plan participation by plan type:
       1977–96.   221
11-1   Conceptual approach to valuing pension entitlements:
       an illustration.   238
12-1   Swedish stock market index.   252
13-1   Ownership of homes and other real estate for original
       HRS and Early Boomer Respondents.   276
13-2   Ownership of stocks and IRAs in 1992 and 2004 across the
       distribution of assets.   277
13-3   Prevalence of retirement planning by demographic
       characteristics.   280
13-4   Estimates of the effect of 'not planning' on net worth by
       percentile of the wealth distribution.   285
14-1   Personal saving as a percentage of disposable income
       between the ages of 28 and 51.   297
14-2   The ratio of net worth to disposable income between the
       ages of 28 and 51.   298
14-3   Real home price appreciation between the ages of 28 and
       51 (% change, year on year).   300
14-4   Home equity appears to be moving into financial assets
       ($ billions, 4-quarter moving average).   302
14-5   Home equity extraction: trend rather than cyclical
       phenomenon.   307

List of Tables

2-1	Cross-Cohort Comparisons at Ages 51–56	16
2-2	Cross-Cohort Comparison at Ages 57–61	20
2-3	Cross-Cohort Comparison at Ages 68–72	23
2-4	OLS Regression Models on Cohort Differences	29
2A-1	Comparison of Current and Alternative Retirement Definitions	34
3-1	Literature Review on Retirement Adequacy: Methods, Data, and Conclusions	38
3-2	Characteristics of New Social Security Benefit Recipients	48
3-3	Net Wealth and Annuitized New Wealth of NBS and HRS Sample by Sample Characteristics	52
3-4	Predictors of Annuitized New Wealth: New Social Security Beneficiaries: OLS Models	56
3-5	Probability of ANW Falling Below Poverty Line Standard: Probit Models	59
4-1	Projected Characteristics of Individuals at Age 67	73
4-2	Mean Family Income per Person at Age 67 (in thousands, $2004)	76
4-3	Percent of Individuals with Family Income at Age 67, by Source	77
4-4	Family Income per Person at Age 67, by Source	78
4-5	Percent of Individuals in Poverty at Age 67	80
4-6	Ratio of Subgroup Income to Cohort Mean Family Income at Age 67	82
4-7	Median Replacement Rates at Age 67	83
4-8	Percent of Individuals at Age 67, by Replacement Rate	84
5-1	Cross-Cohort Comparisons of Health Measures for Respondents Aged 51–56 in Different HRS Cohorts	102
5-2	Health Behaviors for Respondents Aged 51–56: Cross-Cohort Comparisons	103
5-3	Specific Health Conditions for Respondents Aged 51–56: Cross-Cohort Comparison	104
5-4	Determinants of Self-Rated Health for Respondents Aged 51–56: Cross-Cohort Comparisons	105
5-5	Education and Health for Respondents Aged 51–56: Cross-Cohort Comparisons	107

6-1   Demographic Characteristics of Parents' Generation in
1998 and Boomers' Generation in 2022, both at Age 62–72   121

6-2   Percentage in Poverty: Parents' Generation in 1998 and
Boomers' Generation in 2022 both at Age 62–72   122

6-3   Income as a Percentage of Poverty-Level Income: Welfare
Ratios for Parents' Generation in 1998 and Boomers'
Generation in 2022, both at Age 62–72   122

6-4   Per Capita Income as a Percentage of the Average Wage:
Parents' Generation in 1998 and Boomers' Generation
in 2022, both at Age 62–72   123

6-5   Net Non-pension Financial Wealth for Parents'
Generation in 1998 and Boomers' Generation in 2022,
both at Age 62–72: Per Capita Ratio of Wealth to
Average Wage   124

6-6   Home Equity for Parents' Generation in 1998 and
Boomers' Generation in 2022, both at Age 62–72: Per
capita Ratio of Home Equity to Average Wage   124

6-7   Self-Assessed Health Status: Parents' Generation in 1998
and Boomers' Generation in 2022, both at Age 62–72   125

6-8   Work Limitations for Parents' Generation in 1998 and
Boomers' Generation in 2022, both at Age 62–67   126

6-9   Disability Receipt   127

6-10   Life Expectancy for Those Who Survive to at Least Age
62 for Parents' Generation in 1998 and Boomers'
Generation in 2022, both at Age 62–72   128

6-11   Economic Well-Being and Health Status for Parents'
Generation in 1998 and Boomers' Generation in 2022,
both at Age 62–72   129

7-1   Weighted Descriptive Statistics for HRS Sampled Birth
Cohorts: Health-Related Variables, HRS, 1992, 1998,
and 2004   142

7-2   Slope and Threshold IRT Parameters for the Four
Components of Health Index   147

7-3   Fixed Effect Models of Select Demographic and
Socioeconomic Variables on IRT-Derived Health Index:
HRS Birth Cohorts Interviewed in 1992, 1998, and 2004   150

7-4   Determinants of Health and Intraclass Correlation
Coefficient (Standard Errors in Parentheses)   154

8-1   HRS Respondents for Which Health Insurance Data are
Available   161

8-2   Cohort Characteristics: Current Population Surveys,
March 1989–2004   164

8-3	Insurance Histories in the Three Interviews just Prior to Age 65: Original HRS Cohort	166
8-4	Probability of Being Uninsured in at Least One Wave in the Three Interviews just Prior to Age 65 by Sex and Education: Original HRS cohort	166
8-5	Who Loses Insurance and Why?	167
8-6	Probability of any Hospital Stay in the Six Years Prior to Age 65: Original HRS Cohort	170
8A-1	Raw and Regression-adjusted Differences in Health Insurance Coverage: Early Boomers versus War Babies and Original HRS and Current Population Survey, March 1989–2004	173
9-1	Key Characteristics of HRS Sample	194
9-2	Financial Characteristics of Various Subsamples	195
9-3	Estimation Results, Basic Specification	198
9-4	Additional Estimation Results	200
9-5	Pension Wealth at Risk in Defined Benefit Plans, 1992 HRS	204
10-1	Comparing DC Plan Balances at Quit Date for HRS Participants: Results for the Calculator and the Program ($2004; $N = 2,352$)	216
10-2	Comparing DC Plan Balances for HRS Participants at Quit Date and the Expected Present Value of DC Wealth in 1992: Plans 'Hard-Coded' to Replicate the Pension Estimation Program ($2004; $N = 2,383$)	217
10-3	DC Plan Balances for HRS Participants in 1991, Computed Using Calculator and Time-Varying Rates of Return ($2004; $N = 2,306$)	220
10-4	DC Plan Balances for HRS Participants at the Quit Date and the Expected Present Value of DC Wealth in 1992, Computed Using Calculator and Taking into Account Voluntary Contributions ($2004)	222
10-5	DC Plan Balances for HRS Original Cohort and War Babies Cohort: Using Administrative Earnings Records to Measure Earnings, Voluntary Contributions, and Eligibility ($2004)	226
10-6	DC Plan Balances Due to Employee Pre-Tax Voluntary and Employer Matching Contributions: HRS Original Cohort and War Babies Cohort, for Year Prior to Survey Entry ($2004)	227
10A-1	Annual Real Returns and Inflation, 1972–91, in %	232
11-1	Percentage of Workers with Pension Coverage on their Current Job (%)	235

11-2   Distribution of Pension Plans by Type on Current Job, Conditional on Having a Pension (%)   236

11-3   Transition Rates of Plan Types Between Waves among Those Reporting no Change in Plan Type (%)   236

11-4   Distribution of Separations from Employer: Workers 51–56 in 1992   239

11-5   Concordance of 1992 Pension Reports about Current Job with Job Separation Pension Reports (%)   240

11-6   Relationship Between Type of Pension Extracted and Report in 1992 (%)   240

11-7   Present Value of Pension Wealth Extractions: Derived from Lump Sum Amounts (DC and DB) and Annuities (DB), Conditional on Having an Extraction: Workers 51–56 in 1992 (Thousands of $2004)   241

11-8   Average Estimated Present Value of Pension Wealth: Workers 51–56 (Thousands of $2004)   243

11-9   Average Predicted Pension Extractions: Workers 51–56 (Thousands of $2004)   244

12-1   Extract from the PPM Investor Information Folder, for a Specific Fund Example   250

12-2   Descriptive Statistics for PPM Investors   254

12-3   Entry and Exit Rates as Function of PPM Investment Choice   256

12-4   Effect of PPM Choice on Entry Decision   259

12-5   Effect of PPM Choice on Exit Decision   260

12-6   Effect of PPM Choice on Entry Decision: IV Estimates   262

12-7   Effect of PPM Choice on Exit Decision: IV Estimates   264

12-8   Placebo Test: Effect of PPM Choice on Entry Decision before PPM System Introduction: IV Estimates   267

13-1   Distribution of Total Household Income for Original HRS (1992) and Early Boomer (2004) Respondents   273

13-2   Comparing Wealth Distributions for Original HRS (1992) and Early Boomer (2004) Respondents   274

13-3   Distribution of Total Net Worth by Demographic Factors for Original HRS (1992) and Early Boomer (2004) Respondents   275

13-4   Asset Ownership and Percentage of Wealth Accounted for by Each Asset for Original HRS (1992) and Early Boomer (2004) Respondents   276

13-5   Planning and Total Net Worth for Original HRS (1992) and Early Boomer (2004) Respondents ($2004)   278

13-6   Quantile Regressions of Net Worth on Planning for Original HRS (1992) and Early Boomer (2004) Respondents   282

13-7   Median Regression of Non-Housing Wealth on Planning
       for Original HRS (1992) and Early Boomer (2004)
       Respondents ($2004)   284
13-8   OLS and Median Regressions of Net Worth on Planning
       in Pooled Sample ($2004)   284
13-9   OLS Regression of Planning on Total Net Worth ($2004)   287
13-10 First Stage Regressions of IV Estimation of Total Net
       Worth on Housing Price Increases   288
13-11 Instrumental Variables (IV) Estimation of 'Not
       Planning' on Net Worth   289
13A-1 Demographic Characteristics of the Sample: Original
       HRS and Early Boomers (EBB)   292
13A-2 Percentage of Net Worth Accounted for by Not
       Planning, by Wealth Decile ($2004)   293
14-1   Comparing the Wealth and Home Equity Position of the
       Original HRS and Early Baby Boomers at Age 51–56   299
14-2   Comparison of Home Ownership and Values for the
       HRS and Early Baby Boom Generations at Age 51–56, by
       Household Income Quintile   301
14-3   Comparison of Housing and Wealth Measures for the
       HRS Generation as They Transitioned into Retirement   303
14-4   Comparing Changes in Housing and Wealth Variables
       for Original HRS Cohort: Movers versus Nonmovers   304
14-5   The Impact of Moving on Home Equity Extraction:
       Evidence of a Regression of Home Equity Shares Using
       Movers as a Control Group   305

Notes on Contributors

Jason Beeler is a consultant at Mercer Oliver Wyman, where he focuses on risk management. He is a recent graduate of Dartmouth College, where he graduated with high honors in Economics and was awarded the Nelson A. Rockefeller Prize in Economics.

Barbara A. Butrica is a Senior Research Associate in the Income and Benefits Policy Center at The Urban Institute. She is a labor economist with research interests in aging and income dynamics. She previously served as an analyst at Mercer Human Resource Consulting and an economist at the Social Security Administration. Dr Butrica earned the BA in Economics and Political Science from Wellesley College, and the Ph.D. in Economics from Syracuse University.

Julia L. Coronado is a Senior US Economist at Barclays Capital. Her interests include pensions, retirement saving, social security, and pension finance. Previously she was a senior research associate at Watson Wyatt, a consulting firm specializing in pension funds, where she led the retirement and investment research programs. She received the BA from the University of Illinois Urbana-Champaign and the Ph.D. from the University of Texas at Austin.

Chris Cunningham is a research economist and assistant policy adviser at the Federal Reserve Bank of Atlanta. Dr. Cunningham's principal research interests are the economics and political economy of land development. He is a past recipient of the HUD Early Doctoral Student Dissertation Grant, the Homer Hoyt Dissertation Award for work in Real Estate and Urban Economics (AREUEA), and the Syracuse University Doctoral Prize. He worked as graduate research associate at Syracuse University's Center for Policy Research, and also at the Law and Economics Consulting Group (LECG) and the Brookings Institution. He received the BS in Economics from George Washington University and the Ph.D. from Syracuse University.

Gary V. Engelhardt is an Associate Professor of Economics and a Senior Research Associate in the Center for Policy Research in the Maxwell School of Citizenship and Public Affairs at Syracuse University. His research areas include the economics of household saving, employer provided pensions, social security, and housing markets. He previously was on the faculty at Dartmouth College, and he has visited the Wharton School, the University of Minnesota, Tilburg University, and the Federal Reserve Bank of Boston. Dr Engelhardt earned his BA in Economics from Carleton College and the Ph.D. in Economics from the Massachusetts Institute of Technology.

Leora Friedberg is an Assistant Professor of Economics at the University of Virginia. She previously taught at UC-San Diego and MIT, and she has also served as a consultant for the World Bank. She received the Ph.D. in Economics from the Massachusetts Institute of Technology.

Robert Haveman is Professor Emeritus of Economics and Public Affairs at the University of Wisconsin-Madison, where he is also a Research Associate at the Institute for Research on Poverty. He has published widely in the fields of public finance, the economics of environmental and natural resources policy, benefit–cost analysis, and the economics of poverty and social policy. He received the Ph.D. in Economics from Vanderbilt University.

Karen Holden is Associate Director of the La Follette School of Public Affairs, and Professor of Consumer Science and Public Affairs at the University of Wisconsin-Madison. Her research focuses on the effects of social security and pension policy on economic status after retirement and widowhood. She received the BA in Economics from Barnard College, and the MA and Ph.D. degree in Economics from the University of Pennsylvania.

Michael D. Hurd is the Director of the RAND Center for the Study of Aging. He is also a Co-PI of the Health and Retirement Study; a consultant to the English Longitudinal Study of Ageing and to the Survey of Health, Ageing, and Retirement in Europe (SHARE); and a Research Professor with the Mannheim Research Institute for the Economics of Aging. His research interests include the economics of aging, pensions, and Social Security. He earned the MS in Statistics and the Ph.D. in Economics from the University of California, Berkeley.

Howard M. Iams is Division Director in the Office of Policy, Office of Research Evaluation and Statistics, Division of Policy Evaluation, at the Social Security Administration. He received his BA in Sociology from Indiana University and the Ph.D. in Sociology from the University of Michigan-Ann Arbor.

Anders Karlsson is a doctoral student at Stockholm University. Previously he was a financial analyst for Hagströmer & Qviberg, and he also worked as a mine clearance diver for the Royal Swedish Navy. His M.Sc. is from Stockholm University in Finance.

Anil Kumar is an Economist in the regional group of Federal Reserve Bank of Dallas. In addition to analyzing the regional economy, his research focuses on estimating the impact of tax policy on labor market behavior, the measurement of welfare costs of taxation, and the economic effects of 401(k)-type pension plans. He holds a BA in Economics from Delhi University and an MBA from Bombay University, and he earned the MS in Applied Statistics and the Ph.D. in Economics from Syracuse University.

Helen G. Levy is Research Assistant Professor, Institute for Social Research, and Assistant Research Scientist, School of Public Health, at the University of Michigan. Her research interests include the areas of health economics, public finance, and labor economics. She received the BA in Mathematics and History from Yale University and the Ph.D. in Economics from Princeton University.

Annamaria Lusardi is Professor of Economics at Dartmouth College. Her research interests are macroeconomics, economics of aging, and behavioral economics. She has previously visited the University of Chicago, Northwestern University, and the Center for Financial Studies at Frankfurt, as well as the International Center for Economic Research in Turin and several groups at Bocconi University. She received her undergraduate Economics degree from the University of Bocconi and the Ph.D. in Economics from Princeton University.

Brigitte Madrian is Professor of Public Policy and Corporate Management in the Aetna Chair at the Kennedy School of Government at Harvard University. Previously she was on the faculty at the University of Chicago and the Wharton School. Her research focuses on employee benefits and social insurance programs, particularly retirement savings plans and health insurance, and she particularly examines the relationship between 401(k) plan design and employee saving outcomes. Dr. Madrian studied Economics as an undergraduate at Brigham Young University and she received the Ph.D. in Economics from the Massachusetts Institute of Technology.

Nicole Maestas is an Associate Economist at RAND. Her research interests include the economics of aging and health economics; she has published on post-retirement labor supply, portfolio allocation under medical expenditure risk, the effect of the Medicare program on health outcomes, and the market for supplementary health insurance policies (Medigap). She earned the Masters of Public Policy and the Ph.D. in Economics from UC Berkeley.

Dean Maki is Director and Chief US Economist at Barclays Capital where he analyzes the US economy and monetary and fiscal policy. Previously he worked at JP Morgan Chase where he was responsible for forecasts of Federal Reserve policy, the federal budget, and Treasury debt issuance. He also worked at Putnam Investments and at the Federal Reserve Board, where his research examined the relationship between household balance sheets and consumer spending. He earned the Ph.D. in Economics from Stanford University.

Joyce Manchester is Director of Division of Economic Research in the Office of Policy at the Social Security Administration. Previously she was Staff Economist for the Social Security Advisory Board and she also taught economics at Dartmouth College. She earned the BA from Wesleyan University and the Ph.D. in Economics from Harvard University.

Massimo Massa is Assistant Professor of Finance at INSEAD where he teaches international finance, corporate finance, information financial economics, and behavioral finance. His research interests include portfolio theory, theory of information in financial markets, behavioral finance, market microstructure, and mutual funds. He earned the Bachelors' degree in Economics from the LUISS University of Rome; his MBA is from the Yale School of Management; and the Ph.D. in Financial Economics from Yale University.

John F. McCabe is a programmer and research analyst at the Population Studies Center, University of Pennsylvania in Philadelphia. His research is on the demography of health and aging in Mexico and the United States. Previously he was a research analyst at United Behavioral Health, and he also served as research coordinator for the Division of Psychosocial Medicine at the University of California, San Francisco.

Olivia S. Mitchell is the International Foundation of Employee Benefit Plans Professor of Insurance and Risk Management, the Executive Director of the Pension Research Council, and the Director of the Boettner Center on Pensions and Retirement Research at the Wharton School. Concurrently Dr Mitchell is a Research Associate at the National Bureau of Economic Research and a Co-Investigator for the AHEAD/Health and Retirement Studies at the University of Michigan. Dr. Mitchell's main areas of research and teaching are private and public insurance, risk management, public finance and labor markets, and compensation and pensions, with a US and an international focus. She received the BA in Economics from Harvard University and the MA and Ph.D. degrees in Economics from the University of Wisconsin-Madison.

Susann Rohwedder is an Associate Economist at RAND where she researches the economics of aging, household consumption and saving patterns, retirement, and expectations formation. She is actively involved in international research on saving and she is a member of the European Research Training Network on the 'Economics of Ageing in Europe'. She earned the Ph.D. in Economics from University College London.

Andrei Romanov is with the Robert M. La Follette School of Public Affairs at the University of Wisconsin-Madison.

Andrei Simonov is Associate Professor of Finance at Stockholm School of Economics and Research Associate in Stockholm Institute for Financial Research and Stockholm International Corporate Governance Institute. His research interests include asset pricing, individual portfolio decision, and behavioral finance. He earned a doctoral degree in Finance from the European Institute of Business Administration (INSEAD) and a doctoral degree in Theoretical Physics from Moscow State University.

Karen E. Smith is a Senior Research Associate at The Urban Institute. Her research focuses on model building and simulations for health care and tax policy issues. She earned the BA in Computer Science and Economics from the University of Michigan.

Beth J. Soldo is Distinguished Senior Scholar, Department of Sociology, at the University of Pennsylvania. Her research interests include the sociology and demography of aging and health, with a focus on immigration patterns. She received the BA in Sociology from Fordham University, and the MA and Ph.D. degrees in Sociology/Demography from Duke University.

Rania Tfaily is an Assistant Professor of Sociology at Carleton University, Canada. Her research interests include health inequalities, aging, comparability of health measurements and fertility. She received the BS in Biology and MS in Population Studies from the American University of Beirut, and the MA and Ph.D. degrees in Demography from the University of Pennsylvania.

David Weaver is the Deputy Associate Commissioner for Retirement Policy at the Social Security Administration. Most of his research focuses on the economic well-being of the Social Security beneficiary population. He earned the Bachelor's degree from Furman University and the Ph.D. in Economics from Duke University.

Anthony Webb is a Senior Research Analyst at the International Longevity Center-USA. His research interests include pensions, retirement, long-term care, and asset decumulation. Previously he served as economic adviser to the British government on personal savings taxation. He earned the Ph.D. in Economics from the University of California.

David R. Weir is Research Professor in the Institute for Social Research at the University of Michigan, and Co-Director of the Health and Retirement Study. His research interests include the economics of aging and the financial consequences of widowhood. He previously held positions at Yale University and the University of Chicago. He earned the Ph.D. in Economics from Stanford University.

Ben Weitzer is a Research Analyst in the Research and Information Center at Watson Wyatt Worldwide. His research focuses on retirement behavior and defined benefit pension finance. He earned the BS in Economics and also studied at the University of Maryland.

Kevin Whitman is a Social Science Research Analyst for the Social Security Administration's Office of Retirement Policy. His research focuses on best practices in financial education, 401(k) plan design, the characteristics of 'never beneficiaries', and the Railroad Retirement Program. He received the BA in Government from the University of Virginia.

Barbara L. Wolfe is Professor of Economics, Population Health Sciences, and Public Affairs and Faculty Affiliate at the Institute for Research on Poverty at the University of Wisconsin- Madison. Her research focuses on poverty and health issues. She earned the BA in Economics from Cornell University, and the MA and Ph.D. degrees in Economics from the University of Pennsylvania.

Abbreviations

ANW	annuitized net wealth
AIME	Average Indexed Monthly Income
BMI	Body Mass Index
CQR	censored quantile regression
CODA	Children of the Depression Age
CPS	Current Population Survey
DB	defined benefit
DC	defined contribution
DI	disability insurance
EBB	Early Baby Boomer
EBRI	Employee Benefit Research Institute
ESOP	employee stock ownership
ER	employer-reported
FRA	full retirement age
IV	Instrumental Variables
ICI	Investment Company Institute
IRT	Item Response Theory
ME	marginal effects
MINT	Model of Income in the Near Term
NHANES	National Health and Nutrition Examination Study
NIA	National Institute on Aging
NLTCS	National Long-Term Care Survey
NDC	National Defined Contribution
OCACT	Office of the Chief Actuary
OLS	Ordinary Least Square
PBGC	Pension Benefit Guaranty Corporation
PEP	pension estimation program
PIMS	Pension Insurance Modeling System
PARC	Population Aging Research Center
PPM	premium pension
SRH	Self-reported Health
SSA	Social Security Administration
SES	socioeconomic status
SPDs	Summary Plan Descriptions
SCF	Survey of Consumer Finances
SIPP	Survey of Income and Program Participation
WBs	War Babies

Part I
Prospects for Baby Boomer Retirement

Chapter 1

Will Boomers Redefine Retirement?

Olivia S. Mitchell

The number of retirees in the United States will double over the next thirty years, and similar if not larger age waves will also wash over other nations. As the unusually large cohort of individuals born 1946–66 known as 'Baby Boomers' moves into retirement, it is sure to have unprecedented effects on health care systems and private pensions, housing markets, national social safety nets, and indeed the entire economy. This volume provides a detailed and thoughtful assessment of how Baby Boomers will fare in retirement. Our goal is to generate new insights on this keenly important topic to guide future employers, employees, and policymakers, relying on new and never before exploited microeconomic data and modeling techniques developed for the economics of aging.

There is substantial disagreement about how well-off Baby Boomers will be during their 'golden years'. Some compare their financial and physical capital to a fixed consumption standard and deem them fit and ready for retirement. Other analysts assess Boomers as poorly prepared, particularly if one uses community standards such as the average earnings levels or poverty lines. And still others have proffered yet other thresholds such as incomes received by previous retiree cohorts.

The chapters of this book address these and related differences in a systematic and comprehensive manner. First, we take up the question of whether Baby Boomers will remake retirement, and what their financial capital will translate into in terms of later life command over resources. Next, we turn to the question of health capital: whether Boomers are living well longer, or whether they face more years in worse health than previous generations. The answer, as we show below, depends in part on their health insurance coverage. Then we focus on new roles for retirement assets and retirement planning. Of special interest is the way in which the new global economy is remaking pensions, requiring workers to shoulder the responsibility of making sensible portfolio allocation patterns. Finally, we turn to an exploration of how older persons intend to use their homes as a key source of retirement financing.

Will Boomers Remake Retirement?

Some 77 million strong, the leading edge of the Baby Boom generation is now crossing the age-60 threshold. In some very provocative research on past and future work patterns, Nicole Maestas concludes that Boomers are more attached to work than previous generations of workers at the same points in their lives. This change she partly attributes to the fact that Boomers are reaching retirement with markedly different family structures and socioeconomic status (SES) than prior generations of retirees, as well as different attitudes toward work. Her research uses a data-set that many in this volume employ and called the Health and Retirement Study (HRS). This is a nationally representative and very rich survey of individuals over the age of 50, for whom extensive financial, health, and expectations data have been collected and made available for research purposes.[1]

In her analysis, Maestas (Chapter 2, this volume) reviews the experiences of three different generations or birth cohorts, to show that the early members of the Boomer generation are better educated, more ethnically diverse, and less likely to be married than previous cohorts. The Boomers she studies also had significantly higher earnings, housing values, and net worth than their earlier counterparts, and they expect to continue working longer. She then notes a new phenomenon which she terms 'unretiring'; this refers to postretirement employment that Boomers anticipate doing as they move through their 60s. This new perspective on later-life employment cannot be fully attributed to poorer SES, suggesting that Boomers have a growing preference for working longer.

Turning to preparedness for retirement, Robert Haveman, Karen Holden, Andrei Romanov, and Barbara Wolfe (Chapter 3, this volume) compare retirees who retired during the early 1980s with those who left in the mid-1990s. The authors compute for each family annuitized net wealth (ANW) including the equity value of owner-occupied housing, drawing on the Social Security Administration's New Beneficiary Survey (NBS). The team's simulations indicate that mean retiree wealth is projected to rise substantially, for more recent cohorts. Nevertheless, in view of their longer life expectancies, wealth levels will not rise enough to generate more annual (annuitized) income than received by past cohorts. In fact, using the poverty line recommended by the National Academy of Sciences Panel on Poverty Measurement, 4 percent of prior retirees had inadequate resources; for more recent cohorts, they project the figure to rise to 7 percent. In addition, more than one-fifth of these retirees are slated to have ANW below twice the poverty threshold. Accordingly, one theme seen in this and other chapters is that Boomers are better off than their forebears in terms of wealth levels, but this wealth will not be enough to guarantee retirement security.

Another theme which permeates the studies in this volume has to do with the extraordinary diversity of individuals now reaching retirement age. That is, while averages may look attractive, there remain important pockets of vulnerability and these appear to be growing. For instance, Haveman et al. express concern that adequacy targets are less likely to be met by specific groups including women, nonwhites, unmarried persons, and those with less education.

A similar conclusion flows from the work of Barbara Butrica, Howard Iams, and Karen Smith (Chapter 4, this volume), who emphasize the fact that Boomers *on average* will head into retirement in better financial and physical health than prior generations of retirees, but this obscures changes in the *distribution* of income and wealth. These authors rely on a microsimulation model known as the Model of Income in the Near Term (MINT) which projects retirement adequacy at age 67 for cohorts born 1926–35, 1936–45, Early Boomers 1946–55, and Late Boomers born 1956–65. Their analysis concludes that the share of family income from nonretirement income sources is projected to increase due to the increased importance of asset income, which currently represents 4 percent of mean per capita retiree family income but is expected to grow to 20 percent for the Late Boomers. They also evaluate projected retirement replacement rates, comparing per capita family income at age 67 to average household earnings between age 22 and 62. By this measure, median replacement rates are projected to be 93 percent for current retirees, with only 80 percent rates for future retirees. Again, diversity is key: almost half of today's retirees can anticipate incomes that exceed their average lifetime earnings, but the figure drops to around one-third for Boomers. Thus, in absolute terms, Boomers will be better off in terms of higher income and lower poverty rates, but in relative terms, many will be worse off. Of course, all of these projections are tentative, since there is much uncertainty regarding costs of health care and uncertainty regarding the future of Social Security and defined benefit pension plans.

Are Boomers Healthier?

Financial capital is only part of the bundle of resources that older persons look to during retirement. Another resource is health capital, which David Weir (Chapter 5, this volume) compares across cohorts using the HRS. Older workers who are currently on the job tend to say they will work past age 62, but Weir is concerned that their health might not permit it. His data show a mixed picture: that is, for Boomers, smoking is less common than for their predecessors, but obesity is an increasing problem. Overweight persons are defined as having a Body Mass Index (BMI) of 30 or more, where the BMI refers to a calculation of an individual's weight in kilograms divided by height in meters. According to this measure, obesity rose 5 percent from 1992 to 2004; with this, there has also been a rise in the rate of diabetes, up 39 percent for cohorts reporting in 1992 versus in 2004. Some of the increase may be due to better diagnosis, of course. In addition, Weir notes only a slight increase in hypertension and stroke for those on the verge of retirement, but a substantial increase in self-reported pain, of 32 percent. The hypertension finding may be linked to increased use of medication to control the condition, a development he believes may provide insight into the future health of Boomers. He also suggests that there may be a better chance of developing medications or treatments for obesity than there are for smoking. Of course, even if Boomers do have more health problems than prior generations, this may not impact life expectancy; rather, it may presage more disability. Accordingly, Weir concludes that expectations of longer work lives are sustainable for most people, and pessimism about life expectancy is unwarranted.

In their chapter, Joyce Manchester, David Weaver, and Kevin Whitman (Chapter 6, this volume) also assess the relative position of Boomers as they head into retirement. This analysis, which relies on the MINT model, focuses on both the health and wealth of the Boomers. Unlike other analysts, they adopt the US poverty line standard set by the government as the amount of money required to purchase a constant basket of goods, and they compare Boomers to their parents' generations. They forecast a 40 percent more median income relative to the poverty line for Boomers versus older cohorts, and a 35 percent drop in the number of preretirement Boomers living in poverty, compared to their parents. Manchester et al. also find strong evidence of health improvements, noting that only 27 percent of Boomers report being in poor or fair health, 14 percent fewer than the parents' group. Also the fraction of Boomers reporting that it has a work disability fell by 11 percent compared to earlier respondents. The researchers then construct a measure of combined economic well-being and health status, and they conclude that Boomers will fare better than their parents, according to almost all measures of economic and physical well-being.

Health differences across cohorts on the verge of retirement are again the focus of Beth J. Soldo, Olivia Mitchell, Rania Tfaily, and John McCabe (Chapter 7, this volume), who devise a health index using Item Response Theory (IRT). Comparing three HRS cohorts, the authors conclude that Boomers are in poorer health than their counterparts a dozen year ago; in particular, women tend to report worse health (even if they live much longer!) In particular, Boomers indicate they have relatively more difficulty with a range of everyday physical tasks, and they also report having more pain, more chronic conditions, and more drinking and psychiatric problems than their HRS earlier counterparts. This trend suggests that Boomers have poorer self-perceived health than earlier groups.

Another way in which Boomers may differ from earlier retirees includes coverage against health shocks with health insurance. In the United States, of course, health insurance coverage is generally associated with one's workplace, but such insurance is not mandatory. Helen Levy (Chapter 8, this volume) reports that the fraction of Boomers lacking health insurance is slightly higher than for prior generations. Across the three waves of HRS age cohorts leading up to age 65, around 20 percent lacked insurance at some point in the period, which can be deemed substantial risk exposure. Yet only a very small fraction (3%) reported a hospitalization for self or spouse for which insurance paid nothing, and relatively little personal wealth was at stake. According to HRS data, median nonhousing assets of the uninsured totaled only $10,000, while the figure was close to $200,000 for insured persons. Thus median assets of the uninsured would not cover the costs of an average hospital stay of $17,000, suggesting that the uninsured are gambling that, if something happened, they could rely on charity care.

Understanding Retirement Assets

Turning to retirement financing, the discussion coalesces around pensions and private housing equity.[2] In their chapter, Leora Friedberg and Anthony Webb (Chapter 9, this volume) note the long-term shift from defined benefit (DB) to defined contribution (DC) plans over the last two decades, leading to important changes in the risks borne by workers in their retirement accounts. In DB plans, the employer must make investment choices and bear many of the risks associated with those choices; in DC plans, workers bear capital market and longevity risk. Of course, many DB pensions also carry the risk of a substantial loss in pension wealth resulting from an unexpectedly early exit from one's job or from termination and bankruptcy.

Focusing on HRS respondents, the authors assess the impact of these changes in pension structure on workers' investment choices *outside* their pensions. Their main results show significant and substantial differences in stock market investment among workers, depending on their pension characteristics. Specifically, employees covered for a long time in a DB plan holds riskier investments outside the pension. They also find that workers with DC plans invest more in the stock market overall, but there is no change in asset mix with job tenure. The inference is that workers having greater preferences for risk (who would invest more in the stock market anyway) might sort themselves into jobs with DC pensions. This research illustrates another of the consequences of the shift in pension structure that may alter patterns of job mobility at young and older ages, and retirement consumption.

Turning to pension wealth, the chapter by Chris Cunningham, Gary Engelhardt, and Anil Kumar (Chapter 10, this volume) points out that many workers have little or no idea what they can expect in pension benefits during retirement, which makes it difficult for researchers to gauge the adequacy of retirement savings (particularly as retirees move increasingly to DC plans). This team has developed a software tool they call the pension Calculator, which they then use to compute pension wealth measures for HRS respondents. They also compare their results to those produced from an earlier pension estimation program (PEP) developed at the University of Michigan. Based on more flexible assumptions, their model generates somewhat lower DC values than the ones produced by HRS; that is 401(k) pension wealth was some 40 percent lower, and overall DC wealth was 20 percent less. They also show that pension wealth resulting from voluntary saving (and accrued earnings thereon) comprises half of DC pension wealth.

The shift from DB to DC plans also drives analysis by Michael Hurd and Susann Rohwedder (Chapter 11, this volume). A key challenge in this arena is how to measure the value of pension wealth, inasmuch as many workers have no idea what their pension accruals are worth. The researchers rely on HRS data from respondents near retirement when they seem most knowledgeable about what their pension accruals are worth, and what they will have to draw on. The authors find a small increase in the amount of real 'bequeathable' wealth, from a mean of $304,000 for the oldest cohort, to $317,300 for the War Babies (WBs), to $382,300 for the Early Boomers (all in $2004). As a result, and assuming that financial risks in retirement faced by the different cohorts stay the same, they are not concerned that there is a critical pension shortfall facing Boomer near-retirees.

In a very interesting analysis of the Swedish retirement system, Anders Karlsson, Massimo Massa, and Andrei Simonov (Chapter 12, this volume) explore what happened in the year 2000, when Sweden required its workers to invest 2.5 percent of the 18.5 percent total pension tax in their own personal investment accounts. Initially, the government permitted participants to select from about 700 different funds, an unprecedented amount of investment choice. The authors show that having a pension account containing mutual fund investments does change investor incentives to participate directly in the stock market. Specifically, direct equity holding was not a close substitute for equity in the retirement accounts, suggesting that an individual account system will not crowd out direct equity market investment. In sum, they conclude that the new Swedish system helped inform investors of the benefits of stock market participation, boosting participation, and therefore saving.

This discussion dovetails nicely with Annamaria Lusardi and Jason Beeler's (Chapter 13, this volume) study on retirement planning and preparedness, which shows that those who say they plan for retirement do better than those who put little thought into their financial future. In the HRS, they are surprised to find that many Boomers—as many as one-third—had not devoted any thought to retirement prospects, even it is only a few years away. They also note that planning for retirement is positively associated with having more retirement wealth, and the impact is remarkably stable across cohorts. Nonplanners are concentrated disproportionately among the less educated, those with low income, and blacks/Hispanics, households which seem to have been largely unaffected by financial education programs instituted during the 1990s. They conclude that policies to stimulate saving might be best targeted to those groups least likely to plan.

The role of home equity in retirement saving is also crucial, since many older persons own their homes and the homes represent a substantial asset. Julia Coronado, Dean Maki, and Ben Weitzer (Chapter 14, this volume) use the HRS and other data to compare Early Boomers with cohorts older than they, and the authors find that Boomers are both better off and worse off. Thus they have more housing wealth, but they have borrowed more against their homes. As a result, Boomers have not acquired enough net worth to keep constant the replacement ratio of net worth to preretirement household income. Given Boomers' longer life expectancies, the authors conclude that the cohort may be worse off in old age. They also delve into the question of whether older people cash in on home equity to finance retirement. Interestingly, when they follow already-retired cohorts, they find that many who did downsize and therefore decreased their home equity/net worth ratio. In other words, they find evidence that retirees are tapping into their home equity and either spending it or putting it into financial assets. They also find that the decision to move does not appear to be related to changes in health, since both movers and nonmovers report similar health conditions. Boomers then may be expected to follow similar patterns, particularly if financial innovations such as reserve mortgages gain in popularity.

Discussion

The research in this volume offers key lessons for employers, workers, and policymakers looking ahead to the wave of Boomers as it moves into retirement. Evidently, many Boomers plan to keep working, certainly past conventional early retirement. Prolonging one's worklife where possible is a very effective way to add to and preserve retirement assets, which will in turn generate more eventual income for old age. Also, Boomers' expectations about working into retirement may be realistic, inasmuch as they are employed more often in knowledge-based jobs that do not require as much physical stamina as in the case of prior generations.

We also find that Boomer's health capital is about as good as it was for earlier cohorts, though results here are more nuanced. Many researchers conclude that Boomers will fare better than their parents with regard to work limitations and disability patterns. Yet Boomers' own self-reports indicate they have more difficulty with a range of everyday physical tasks, and they also report having more pain, more chronic conditions, and more drinking and psychiatric problems than their HRS earlier counterparts. Women seem particularly at risk, and the dangers of obesity are just beginning to be traced.

In sum, our findings paint a more complex picture than is often afforded by simple warnings of the 'impending retirement crisis' facing Baby Boomers. This is underscored by the fact that, while most Boomers are relatively well-off, there is much dispersion in the data. Some groups, particularly the nonmarried, the least educated, and many blacks and Hispanics, have very little in the way of retirement assets. Thus there will remain a need for a strong safety net in the years to come.

In addition, many people are still not planning adequately for retirement, and as a result, they are failing to save effectively. This could imply that many Boomers will be more vulnerable to old-age shocks and have few resources to cope. A related point is that Boomers have not shown that they can adjust their spending patterns to align these with changing circumstances. Compared to previous cohorts, Boomers have enjoyed lifetime economic prosperity, so that many have never had to scrimp and save as did their parents and grandparents during times of privation. Indeed, for many, the whole idea of retirement risk management is unfamiliar, a point underscored by their lack of retirement planning. This feeds into concerns regarding rising levels of household debt: some in the Boomer generation have shown a tendency to spend now and worry about tomorrow later, whereas retirees who experienced the Great Depression are reluctant to part with their savings.

Despite these cautionary flags, there is much we have learned and reason for excitement. Most importantly, we have confirmed that researcher and policymakers can reap invaluable rewards from long-term investments in rich and detailed data-sets such as the Health and Retirement Study. Indeed the HRS is used by many researchers for the first time here in this book to assess cohorts' retirement preparedness in a variety of new and interesting ways. We have also learned that there are ways to enhance the retirement experience. Innovative pension systems, such as the Swedish plan, are changing the way workers allocate their retirement portfolios. New products are being developed to help workers plan, save, and invest more effectively, manage their funds into retirement, and protect against longevity risk. Ready or not, Baby Boomers are transforming, and being transformed by, retirement.

Notes

[1] The Health and Retirement Study (HRS) is a biannual survey sponsored by the National Institute on Aging (NIA) along with the Social Security Administration (SSA) and administered at the University of Michigan. This survey of some 22,000 individuals has been conducted every 2 years since 1992, and it is an unusually important source for estimating the retirement readiness of prior retirees against Boomers. All the authors books compare distinct HRS cohorts, generally with the earliest termed the 'original HRS' who were aged 51–56 in 1992, the so-called 'War Babies' who were aged 51–56 in 1998, and the Early Boomers who were aged 51–56 in 2004. For more detail, see NIA (forthcoming) and http://hrsonline.isr.umich.edu/

[2] Public pensions and Social Security also are an important element of retirement income security, but are not our focus here. For further information, see Mitchell et al. (1999).

References

Butrica, B. A., Iams, H. M. S., and Smith, K. E. (Chapter 4, this volume). 'Understanding Baby Boomers' Retirement Prospects'.

Coronado, J., Maki, D., and Weitzer, B. (Chapter 14, this volume). 'Retiring on the House? Cross-Cohort Differences in Housing Wealth'.

Cunningham, C., Engelhardt, G. V., and Kumar, A. (Chapter 10, this volume). 'Measuring Pension Wealth'.

Friedberg, L. and Webb, A. (Chapter 9, this volume). 'The Impact of Pensions on Nonpension Investment Choices'.

Haveman, R., Holden, K., Romanov, A., and Wolfe, B. (Chapter 3, this volume). 'The Sufficiency of Retirement Savings: Comparing Cohorts at the Time of Retirement'.

Hurd, M. and Rohwedder, S. (Chapter 11, this volume). 'Trends in Pension Values around Retirement'.

Karlsson, A., Massa, M., and Simonov, A. (Chapter 12, this volume). 'Pension Portfolio Choice and Menu Exposure'.

Levy, H. (Chapter 8, this volume). 'Health Insurance Patterns Nearing Retirement'.

Lusardi, A. and Beeler, J. (Chapter 13, this volume). 'Saving between Cohorts: The Role of Planning'.

Maestas, N. (Chapter 2, this volume). 'Cross-Cohort Differences in Retirement Expectations and Realizations'.

Manchester, J., Weaver, D., and Whitman, K. (Chapter 6, this volume). 'Baby Boomers versus Their Parents: Economic Well-Being and Health Status'.

Mitchell, O. S., Myers, R., and Young, H. (1999). *Prospects for Social Security Reform*. Philadelphia, PA: University of Pennsylvania Press.

National Institute on Aging (NIA) (forthcoming). *Growing Older in America: The Health and Retirement Study*, National Institutes of Health, U.S. Department of Health and Human Services.

Soldo, B. J., Mitchell, O. S., Tfaily, R., and McCabe, J. F. (Chapter 7, this volume). 'Cross-Cohort Differences in Heath on the Verge of Retirement'.

Weir, D. (Chapter 5, this volume). 'Are Boomers Living Well Longer?'

Chapter 2

Cohort Differences in Retirement Expectations and Realizations

Nicole Maestas

Many writers have suggested that retirement patterns among Baby Boomers will differ from those of previous cohorts because of broad social and economic changes in work patterns and family structure. Analysts have already noted several important trends in older workers' employment patterns, including the fact that the long historical trend to earlier retirement among US males came to a halt in the mid-1980s (Quinn 1999; Purcell 2005). Indeed, recent figures suggest even a slight *increase* in men's labor force participation (Purcell 2005), perhaps because of the elimination of mandatory retirement (in 1986), and the weakening of financial incentives to retire under both Social Security and private pension schemes (Burtless and Quinn 2000; Purcell 2005). For older women, labor force participation rates have been rising since 1950, with the most dramatic increases occurring since the mid-1980s (Quinn 1999).

It is also worth noting that many older workers are now choosing retirement paths that depart from the traditional pattern of complete labor force withdrawal following many years of work in a full-time career job. For instance, a half to two-thirds of HRS respondents transition from full-time career jobs to bridge jobs on the way to retirement (Cahill et al. 2005). Partial retirement is also an increasingly important alternative transition path, and some bridge jobs are a form of partial retirement. The prevalence of partial retirement among older workers ranges from 44 percent (Maestas 2005) to half (Ruhm 1990). And even among those who have partially or even completely retired, many people subsequently return to work; if partially retired, many return to full-time work. About a quarter of retirees later returns to work after a period of retirement, with this figure rising to over one-third among younger retirees (Maestas 2005). In sum, recent research suggests that Boomers may be more likely to work longer, transition through a bridge job or partial retirement job, and return to work after a period of labor force withdrawal than earlier cohorts.

This chapter evaluates early data on this hypothesis using the most recent evidence on work and retirement for the leading edge of the Baby Boomers in the Health and Retirement Study (HRS). We compare Boomers with earlier cohorts, to develop insights into current trends in work, retirement, and postretirement work. Thus we examine cross-cohort trends in labor force participation, retirement expectations, retirement transitions to full and partial retirement, and expectations of future work among those who have already retired, and we also consider the role played by cohort differences in socioeconomic status (SES), health, and demographic characteristics. In what follows, we first describe the birth cohorts used and explain our definitions of partial and complete retirement. We then look at age profiles in full-time work, partial retirement, full retirement, and the likelihood of future work to show how trends evolve within a cohort, across cohorts over time, and over the second half of the life cycle. Finally, we present results from several multivariate regression models useful in assessing whether cohort differences in work and retirement behavior are primarily due to changes in SES, or other factors.

Cross-Cohort Comparisons

Our analysis identifies several birth cohorts included in the first seven waves of the Health and Retirement Study (HRS). These cohorts have been denominated according to their birth years as follows: the Children of the Depression Age (CODA, born 1926–30); the original HRS (born 1931–41); the War Babies (WBs) (born 1942–47); and the Early Boomers (born 1948–53). To facilitate comparisons of equal-sized cohorts, we divide the original HRS cohort into two, which we term here the HRS-Early (born 1931–35), and the HRS-Late (born 1936–41) groups. Due to the longitudinal structure of the HRS, we observe each cohort as it ages, and we also observe cohorts at similar ages but at different times. The analysis focuses on four specific age bands, namely 51–56-year olds (which we call the 'preretirement' years); the 57–61-year olds (the 'near-retirement' group); the 62–67-year olds (the 'retirement' group); and the 68–72-year olds (which we term the 'postretirement' group).[1]

Retirement Definitions

There are many ways to define partial and complete retirement, ranging from more objective measures based on hours of work to subjective measures that rely on self-assessed retirement status. Complicating matters is the fact that partial retirement rates are rather sensitive to whether subjective or objective information is used, with subjective responses yielding substantially higher rates. On the other hand, full retirement rates are more stable across alternative definitions. A drawback of relying solely on self-assessed retirement status is that people differ in their retirement definitions. For example, among those who say they are partially retired in the first wave of the HRS, 21 percent were working full-time, 45 percent were working part-time, and 33 percent were not working at all. Similar patterns can be found in the other waves.

Accordingly, in what follows, we combine subjective and objective definitions, classifying a respondent as *partially retired* if he describes himself as retired and working part-time (i.e. working fewer than thirty-five hours per week or fewer than thirty-six weeks per year). We classify a respondent as *completely retired* if he reports himself to be retired and he is not working for pay.[2]

Preretirees (Aged 51–56)

We begin with a cross-cohort comparison of demographic characteristics in Table 2.1, which compares three cohorts of 51–56-year olds, namely the HRS-Late, the WBs, and the Early Boomers. Average ages are similar, as is the fraction female.[3] Not surprisingly, the Early Boomers are more educated than earlier cohorts, with mean years of education rising from 12.5 for the earliest cohort to 13.1 for the middle cohort and to 13.5 for the Early Boomers. The Early Boomers are more ethnically diverse than earlier cohorts, with a significantly higher fraction of Hispanic and Asian cohort members; they are also less likely to be married at age 51–56 and more likely to report they have never married.[4] The evidence also suggests that the cohorts examined here do not differ significantly in terms of the fraction reporting poor health, but there are differences in the mean number of major health conditions reported.[5] It is interesting that the leading edge of the 51–56-year olds is healthier than the Early Boomers, a point taken up elsewhere by Soldo et al. (Chapter 7, this volume) and Weir (Chapter 5, this volume).

The table also indicates that Early Boomers have significantly higher mean labor income, household income, and total net nonpension wealth at ages 51–56 (in constant $2004) than did earlier cohorts at the same ages. And not surprisingly, overall pension coverage rates are similar but pension type has changed, in line with national trends. Some 62 percent of the HRS-Late cohort had a primary defined benefit (DB) pension, but only 39 percent of the Early Boomers do; conversely, defined contribution (DC) coverage rose from 34 percent among the earliest cohort to 56 percent among the Early Boomers. Inasmuch as many DB pension plans have strong age-related retirement incentives largely absent from DC pensions, this difference alone could lead to significant changes in retirement patterns over time.

TABLE 2-1 Cross-Cohort Comparisons at Ages 51–56

Characteristic	HRS-Late (1992)	War Babies (1998)	EBB (2004)	ANOVA p-Value
Demographic				
Age	53.3	53.3	53.3	0.343
Female	52.1	52.5	51.0	0.361
Years of education	12.5	13.1	13.5	0.000
Race/ethnicity				
White	80.6	80.0	75.7	0.000
Black	10.0	9.7	11.0	0.110
Hispanic	7.0	7.4	9.7	0.000
Asian/other	2.3	2.9	3.5	0.011
Marital status				
Married	74.7	71.2	68.5	0.000
Separated/divorced	14.7	18.0	17.4	0.001
Widowed	4.2	3.9	3.5	0.201
Never married	3.5	4.2	5.2	0.002
Health status				
Poor health	6.0	7.0	6.9	0.183
Sum of major health conditions	0.9	1.0	1.2	0.000
Income and wealth				
Labor income ($)	34,208	32,344	38,668	0.000
Household income ($)	74,260	88,694	94,335	0.000
Total net nonpension wealth ($)	307,438	323,580	393,833	0.000
Pension coverage				
Any private pension coverage	58.6	60.2	61.0	0.197
Primary pension is DB	62.2	44.4	39.4	0.000
Primary pension is DC	34.4	44.3	55.6	0.000
Expectations				
Expected retirement age	62.9	62.7	63.8	0.000
Probability of working FT after 62	46.9	47.8	50.5	0.001
Probability of working FT after 65	26.3	28.8	32.8	0.000
Probability of working for pay in future		28.0	37.3	0.000
Probability of living to 75 or more	64.9	66.0	63.7	0.005
Life table probability of living to 75 or more	67.6	69.2	71.3	0.000
Ratio of self-report prob. to life table prob.	0.96	0.95	0.90	0.000
Short financial planning horizon	25.7	21.4	25.1	0.000
Labor force status				
Working FT	61.2	65.3	64.1	0.002
Working PT	10.6	9.4	10.7	0.126

TABLE 2-1 (*continued*)

Characteristic	HRS-Late (1992)	War Babies (1998)	EBB (2004)	ANOVA p-Value
Partly retired	2.2	3.0	2.3	0.072
Completely retired	9.2	8.1	9.2	0.157
Disabled	3.6	5.1	4.0	0.004
Both spouses working if married	52.4	55.3	59.1	0.000
Early retirement transitions				
First retirement within 4 years of baseline	14.8	15.5		0.486
Partial retirement	4.3	4.4		0.918
Full retirement	10.5	11.1		0.461
Unretirement within 2 years of retirement	23.7	27.5		0.200
N	5,325	2,888	3,159	

Source: Author's tabulations.

Notes: Data weighted by survey weights; all $2004. Sample for early retirement transitions includes respondents working for pay (FT or PT) at baseline, which is defined as 1992 for HRS-Late cohort and 1998 for War Babies cohort.

One interesting difference across cohorts is that Early Boomers anticipate retiring later, at age 64 on average, than the age of 63 reported by HRS-Late and WBs. These cross-cohort differences cannot be attributed solely to differences in the Social Security normal retirement age, since nearly all of the WBs and the Early Boomers share a common full retirement age (FRA) of 66 (the FRA for the HRS-Late cohort ranges from 65 to 65 and 8 months).[6] Consistent with their later expected retirement age, the Early Boomers also report higher probabilities of working full-time at ages 62 and 65: they give themselves a 51 percent chance of working full-time at 62, whereas the HRS-Late and WBs cohorts gave themselves a 47 and 48 percent chance, respectively (the differences are statistically significant). Early Boomers also indicate a 33 percent chance of working full-time at age 65, whereas the HRS-Late and WBs reported only a 26 and 29 percent chance, respectively. Similarly, Early Boomers not currently working at ages 51–56 say there is a 37 percent chance they will work again in the future, whereas the WBs gave themselves only a 28 percent chance of doing so.

The HRS respondents are also asked to rate the likelihood they will live to age 75 or beyond; this is particularly interesting since life expectancy is an important input into retirement planning. Strikingly, Early Boomers give themselves a significantly *lower* probability of living to 75 (64%) than the earlier cohorts (65% for HRS-Late and 66% for WBs). In contrast, the life table probability of living to 75 or more is substantially higher for the

Early Boomers (71%) than for earlier cohorts (68% for HRS-Late and 69% for WBs).[7] The ratio of the self-reported over the life table probabilities is about 0.90 and statistically less than 1, indicating the Early Boomers systematically underestimate their probability of surviving to age 75 by about 10 percent.[8] This nontrivial underestimate is also worse for Boomers than earlier cohorts. This finding has implications for retirement planning: those who systematically underestimate their life expectancies may fail to save enough or may dissave too fast. Early Boomers are also more likely than the WBs to report that they have only a short planning horizon (the next few months or next year), though they are about just as likely to have a short planning horizon as the HRS-Late cohort.

We also examine labor force participation rates at ages 51–56. The WBs cohort had the highest fraction working full-time and the lowest fraction completely retired. This is surprising, given the later expected retirement age and higher probabilities of full-time work at 62 and 65 reported by Early Boomers. But in a two-way comparison of means between the WBs and Early Boomers, the differences in full-time work and complete retirement are not statistically significant. Of course, as more respondents implement their retirement plans over time, more pronounced cohort differences may yet emerge. For couples, for instance, the fraction of 51–56-year olds in which both spouses are working has risen over time from 52 percent among the HRS-Late to 59 percent among the Early Boomers. This suggests that joint retirement decisions may become even more important among later cohorts.

The longitudinal structure of the Health and Retirement Study permits us to follow the HRS-Late and WBs forward, to measure early retirement transitions (Early Boomers have not yet been resurveyed). Of the 51–56-year olds working for pay (full- or part-time) at their first interview (1992 for HRS-Late and 1998 for WBs), some 15 percent of both cohorts had retired within four years of their first interview; approximately 70 percent transitioned to full retirement and 30 percent to partial retirement. About 24 percent of the HRS-Late and 28 percent of the WBs later 'unretired' (i.e. returned to work) within two years of their first retirement. Although the unretirement rates are not statistically different, they do suggest the possibility of an increasing trend in early retirement and subsequent unre- tirement. To construct an estimate of the fraction of individuals ever tran- sitioning through partial retirement, we add the fractions transitioning from full-time work to partial retirement, and from complete retirement to partial retirement (i.e. part-time work). Under this definition, about 39 percent of the HRS-Late transitioned through partial retirement com- pared to 43 percent of the more recent WBs cohort. These estimates are suggestive of a rise in partial retirement in later cohorts (see also Maestas 2005).

Near-Retirement (Ages 57–61)

Next, we examine trends among successive cohorts of 57–61-year olds, an analysis limited to the HRS-Early, HRS-Late, and WBs (as the early Boomers are not old enough yet). Table 2.2 shows that age across the cohorts was 59; other trends are as noted for Table 2.1. Later cohorts are more educated, wealthy, more ethnically diverse, and less likely to be married. Although later cohorts are increasingly less likely to report poor health status, they also report having been diagnosed with more major health conditions. With regard to retirement expectations, the HRS-Early cohort is similar to the HRS-Late; many of the significant cross-cohort differences appear to be driven by the WBs cohort (about one-third of whom are the oldest members of the Baby Boom generation born in 1946 and 1947). For example, the expected retirement age is 64 for both HRS-Early and HRS-Late members, compared to 65 for the WBs. Expected retirement ages in Table 2.2 are higher than those in Table 2.1 simply because some of younger people in Table 2.1 already retired. Nonworking persons in their late 50s indicate lower probabilities of working for pay in the future, than nonworkers in their early 50s, probably reflecting the shifting composition of labor force exits away from unemployment spells and toward retirement.

Turning to life expectancy data, it is interesting that people aged 57–61 do not appear to adjust their survival probabilities upward, as they survive additional years. Comparing Table 2.1 with Table 2.2, for example, we note that the WBs at ages 51–56 report a 66 percent chance of surviving to 75 and a 65 percent chance at 57–61. Since the life table survival probability increases with each additional year of survival, the ratio of self-reported and life table probabilities falls substantially below 1 in all cohorts. The underestimation problem gets worse with age for both the WBs and HRS-Late cohorts, the same is likely to be true for the Early Baby Boomers (EBBs).

Another intriguing aspect of Table 2.2 is the sharp rise in reported retirement satisfaction over time. Of the HRS-Early members who had already retired, 31 percent said their retirement years were worse than the years before retirement, compared to 22 percent of the HRS-Late and just 20.3 percent of the WBs. Further study is required to determine whether the differences represent 'real' differences in satisfaction or reflect contextual effects resulting from differences in the survey questionnaires over time.

It is also worth noting that the cohorts look similar in terms of their fractions working full- and part-time at ages 57–61, but partial retirement has risen steadily over time, and the fraction completely retired by these ages is highest among the WBs. We also examine labor force transitions for the subset of 57–61-year olds in each cohort working for pay at baseline (1992 for the HRS-Early and 1998 for the HRS-Late). We then follow each cohort for six years beyond baseline and observe transitions in and out of

TABLE 2-2 Cross-Cohort Comparison at Ages 57–61

Characteristics	HRS-Early (1992)	HRS-Late (1998)	War Babies (2004)	ANOVA p-Value
Demographic				
Age	58.9	58.9	58.9	0.267
Female	52.2	52.7	51.9	0.784
Years of education	12.1	12.5	13.1	0.000
Race				
White	82.0	80.4	79.3	0.018
Black	10.2	9.6	10.4	0.525
Hispanic	5.7	8.0	7.3	0.002
Asian/other	2.1	2.0	3.1	0.004
Marital status				
Married	74.4	71.5	69.5	0.000
Separated/divorced	12.3	13.9	17.0	0.000
Widowed	8.0	7.8	5.5	0.000
Never married	3.6	3.3	4.0	0.257
Health status				
Poor health	9.1	8.2	7.3	0.032
Sum of major health conditions	1.2	1.4	1.7	0.000
Income and wealth				
Labor income ($)	25,846	25,923	28,281	0.102
Household income ($)	62,287	77,861	80,585	0.000
Total net nonpension wealth ($)	337,533	456,010	499,491	0.003
Pension coverage				
Any private pension coverage	51.5	55.9	57.1	0.001
Primary pension is DB	61.0	46.9	41.3	0.000
Primary pension is DC	35.7	45.4	50.5	0.000
Expectations				
Expected retirement age	64.0	64.0	65.1	0.000
Probability of working FT after 62	51.4	51.0	55.0	0.001
Probability of working FT after 65	27.5	28.4	35.3	0.000
Probability of working for pay in future		17.2	21.7	0.001
Probability of living to 75 or more	63.6	65.5	64.5	0.062
Life table probability of living to 75 or more	70.6	72.1	74.2	0.000
Ratio of self-report prob. to life table prob.	0.91	0.91	0.87	0.000
Short financial planning horizon	30.3	25.8	28.9	0.221
Retirement years worse than before	31.3	22.0	20.3	0.000

TABLE 2-2 (*continued*)

Characteristics	HRS-Early (1992)	HRS-Late (1998)	War Babies (2004)	ANOVA p-Value
Labor force status				
Working FT	49.0	49.4	50.4	0.470
Working PT	9.6	8.8	8.3	0.175
Partly retired	4.6	5.9	6.4	0.005
Completely retired	20.6	20.2	22.5	0.039
Disabled	3.6	5.6	4.8	0.001
Retirement transitions				
First retirement within 4 years after baseline	43.8	40.6		0.030
Partial retirement	12.3	11.4		0.356
Full retirement	31.5	29.2		0.093
Unretirement within 2 years of retirement	15.3	16.8		0.386
N	3,955	3,978	2,336	

Source: Author's tabulations.

Notes: Data weighted by survey weights; all $2004. Sample for retirement transitions includes respondents working for pay (FT or PT) at baseline, which is defined as 1992 for HRS-Early cohort and 1998 for HRS-Late cohort.

retirement. The HRS-Late cohort was about 3 percentage points less likely to retire within four years of baseline than the HRS-Early. The HRS-Late were also 2 percentage points more likely to unretire within two years of retirement than the HRS-Early (though the difference is not statistically significant). Comparing Table 2.1 with Table 2.2, the unretirement rates for individuals 57–61 at baseline are approximately 10 percentage points lower than for those who were only 51–56 at baseline. The finding of an age gradient in unretirement has been noted in previous research on unretirement (Maestas 2005). The fractions estimated to ever transition through partial retirement (again combining those who transition from full-time work to partial retirement, and those who transition from complete retirement to partial retirement) yields similar rates for the HRS-Early (37%) and the HRS-Late (38%). These rates are somewhat lower than the rates documented for 51–56-year olds, suggesting that like unretirement, the incidence of partial retirement also declines with age.

At Retirement Comparisons (Ages 62–67)

Comparisons in this age range draw on the HRS-Early and HRS-Late cohorts, using observations from HRS Waves 4 and 7. To avoid redundancies with previous tables, we simply highlight important points. Among those still working at ages 62–67, the HRS-Late cohort has a significantly later expected retirement age, and nonworkers in the HRS-Late cohort are significantly more likely to expect to work in the future than are nonworkers in the HRS-Early cohort (14 vs. 12). The HRS-Late cohort is more likely to underestimate the probability of surviving to age 75— the ratio of self-reported to life table probabilities is 0.87 for the HRS-Early and 0.85 for the HRS-Late—which suggests that the tendency not to update one's survival probability with additional years of life persists through the age distribution. Finally, labor force participation is higher for the HRS-Late, where 23 percent of 62–67-year olds are working full-time, and another 18 percent are either working part-time or partially retired (which is defined by reporting both retirement and part-time work). The comparable figures for the HRS-Early cohort are 20 percent (full-time work) and 16 percent (part-time work/partial retirement).

Postretirement Comparisons (Ages 68–72)

Last, we examine trends in postretirement labor supply by comparing the two cohorts of 68–72-year olds, namely the CODA cohort and the HRS-Early groups.[9] Although these cohorts predate Baby Boomers, they may nevertheless reveal the direction of trends likely to be carried on by the Baby Boomers. Results are summarized in Table 2.3.

Moving directly to the expectations questions, there is again evidence of a rise over time in the likelihood of working for pay in the future. The CODA cohort reports a 6 percent chance of working in the future, whereas this probability rises to 8 percent for the later HRS-Early cohort, an increase of 52 percent. Finally, the rise in partial retirement across cohorts in their late 50s exists at these later ages as well. About 11 percent of 68–72-year olds in the earlier CODA cohort were partially retired, compared to 14 percent of HRS-Early cohort members at the same age.

Age Profiles in Work and Retirement

Next we turn to an examination of work and retirement patterns by single year of age, taking advantage of the longitudinal structure of the HRS. In this process, the length of the observation period varies by cohort, since the cohorts entered the HRS in different calendar years and at different ages.

Patterns of Full-Time Work

Figure 2.1 shows the age pattern of full-time work, using available data by cohort for ages 51–78. We note cohort comparisons in age ranges where two

TABLE 2-3 Cross-Cohort Comparison at Ages 68–72

Characteristics	CODA (1998)	HRS-Early (2004)	t-Ratio
Demographic			
Age	70.0	70.1	−1.56
Female	55.6	54.8	0.54
Years of education	12.0	12.4	−3.97
Race			
White	83.4	84.2	−0.79
Black	9.0	8.8	0.20
Hispanic	5.2	4.9	0.43
Asian/other	2.5	2.1	0.92
Marital status			
Married	65.7	64.8	0.62
Separated/divorced	9.1	10.2	−1.26
Widowed	21.3	18.8	2.14
Never married	2.8	3.8	−1.91
Health status			
Poor health	10.0	8.3	2.05
Sum of major health conditions	1.8	2.3	−12.10
Income and wealth			
Labor income ($)	4,342	4,903	−1.14
Household income ($)	47,400	51,934	−2.50
Total net non-pension wealth ($)	374,631	509,724	−3.20
Expectations			
Probability of working for pay in future	5.7	8.3	−4.01
Short financial planning horizon	33.6	33.5	0.06
Retirement years worse than before	15.0	19.1	−1.74
Labor force status			
Working FT	8.0	9.1	−1.37
Working PT	2.7	3.2	−0.87
Partly retired	10.6	13.9	−3.52
Completely retired	64.0	63.5	0.42
Disabled	1.6	1.0	2.04
N	2,242	2,464	

Source: Author's tabulations.

Notes: Data weighted by the survey weights for each wave; all in $2004. Because the HRS-Early cohort is slightly older than the CODA cohort, we trimmed the very youngest CODA respondents and the very oldest HRS-Early respondents from the sample in Tables 2–3 in order to equalize the age distributions of the two cohorts.

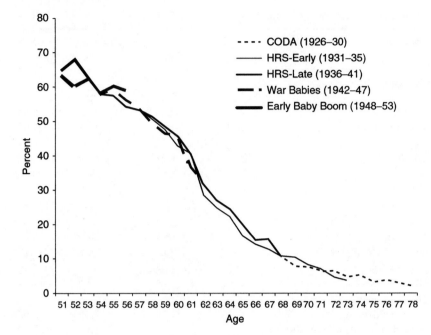

Figure 2-1. Percent working full-time by age and cohort. (*Source*: Author's calculations.)

or more cohorts overlap. This figure confirms the labor force results from Tables 2.1 and 2.2; there are no notable differences across cohorts in rates of full-time work between the ages of 51 and 61. Although Early Boomers have higher participation rates at ages 51 and 52, this differential vanishes by age 53 and the cohort goes on to track the earlier WBs cohort closely. The WBs, in turn, have a higher fraction working full-time during their mid-to-late-50s compared to the HRS-Late cohort, but Table 2.2 showed that on average this difference is not statistically significant. The WBs closely track the HRS-Late over the rest of the age range they share. Between ages 62 and 67, however, cohort differences begin to emerge between the HRS-Late and HRS-Early cohorts. A significantly higher fraction of the HRS-Late cohort works full time (significance tests not reported). Finally, full time work tapers off as individuals enter their 70s, with no statistically significant differences between the CODA and HRS-Early cohorts.

Patterns of Partial Retirement

Figure 2.2 presents age profiles for partial retirement. Here the partial retirement rates rise steadily over ages 51–61, increase sharply just at age

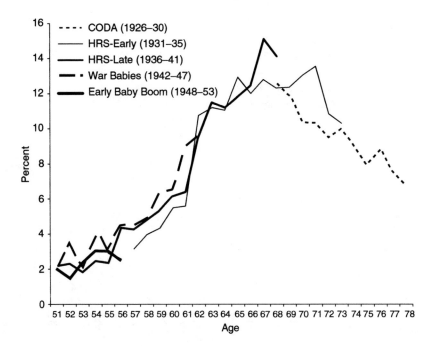

Figure 2-2. Percent partially retired by age and cohort. (*Source*: Author's calculations.)

62 (the Social Security early retirement age), flatten through the late 60s and then decline through the 70s. The near doubling of partial retirement rates at the early retirement age suggests that for many, partial retirement becomes feasible only once they are able to claim old-age retirement benefits.

Partial retirement rates are lower for the Early Boomers than for the WBs through the ages 51–56 (although this difference is not statistically significant). Yet over most of the age range 51–61, WBs had significantly higher partial retirement rates than the earlier cohort. Consistent with the tables, the detailed age profiles in Figure 2.2 suggest a trend toward partial retirement among later cohorts. Although the Early Boomers would seem to be an exception, they are still relatively young and have not moved into the age ranges where partial retirement is most prevalent.

Full Retirement Patterns

Figure 2.3 shows the same analysis for full retirement. Here the age pattern for full retirement steadily rises with age, growing steeper at the Social

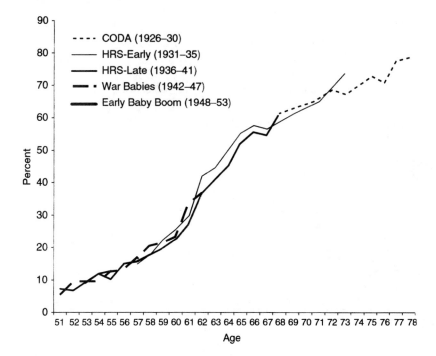

Figure 2-3. Percent fully retired by age and cohort. (*Source*: Author's calculations.)

Security early retirement age. There are few cohort differences in the percentage of fully retired, with an exception for those 62–67 where the HRS-Early have significantly higher full retirement rates than the HRS-Late (significance tests not reported).

Likelihood of Future Work

Finally, Figure 2.4 shows the age profile in respondents' self-assessed percentage of chance of working for pay in the future, a question asked from all those not working. The age profile for the likelihood of future work declines steadily with age, from a high of about 40 percent at age 51 to a low of about 5 percent at age 78. Here we note substantial cohort differences, with a clear upward trend in the likelihood of future work over time. Nonworking Early Boomers in their early 50s are significantly more likely to expect to work in the future than are their counterparts in the earlier WBs cohort. After the late 50s, WBs are more likely to expect future work than the earlier cohorts. This pattern is suggestive of a growing trend toward unretirement among later cohorts.

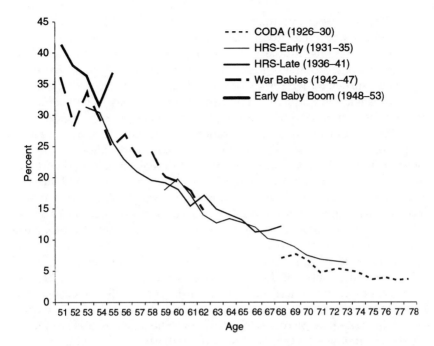

Figure 2-4. Expected probability of working in future if not currently working by age and cohort. (*Source*: Author's calculations.)

Adjusting for Other Cohort Differences: Multivariate Regression Models

Having documented a number of interesting cross-cohort differences with respect to retirement expectations, partial retirement, and the likelihood of future work, we next offer results for a series of multivariate regression models that test for significant differences in a multivariate setting. We estimate equations of the following form:

$$y_{ia} = a_a + \text{DEMOG}_{ia}\beta_a + \text{SES}_{ia}\gamma_a + \text{COHORT}_{ia}\delta_a + \varepsilon_{ia},$$

where y_{ia} represents the outcome of interest for respondent i in age group a; DEMOG_{ia} is a set of demographic variables including gender, race, marital status, and health status and also includes a set of age dummies to control for cross-cohort differences in the distribution of ages within age group a. The term SES_{ia} represents a set of variables measuring SES for person i in age group a, including education, labor income, household income, type of pension coverage, and total net nonpension wealth, and

COHORT$_{ia}$ is a set of dummies for the respondent's birth cohort. Finally, a_a is an intercept for age group a and ε_{ia} is a random error term.

Table 2.4 presents ordinary least squares (OLS) regression results for selected outcome variables in each age group. The first column regresses expected retirement age on socioeconomic factors, health, demographic characteristics, and cohort dummies for 51–56-year olds. The coefficient on the cohort dummy for the Early Boomers implies this cohort expects to retire 0.81 years later than the reference cohort, the HRS-Late, an effect that is highly statistically significant. The unadjusted cohort difference shown in Table 2.1 is about 0.9 years, so the difference is only mildly attenuated once we control for education, labor income, total household income, pension coverage, and total net nonpension wealth. Auxiliary analyses (not shown) suggest that cross-cohort variation in DB pension coverage is the most important attenuating factor in this case. As noted above, Early Boomers are less likely to participate in DB plans than earlier cohorts, and these impose strong disincentives for work beyond key retirement ages.[10]

The second column of Table 2.4 uses as the dependent variable the expected probability of working for pay in the future. Here the reference group is the WBs (this survey question was not asked in the wave during which the HRS-Late were 51–56, Wave 1). The Early Boomer effect is somewhat attenuated, compared to the unadjusted cohort difference in Table 2.1, but it still suggests that those Early Boomers not working at ages 51–56 rate themselves about 6 percentage points (21%) more likely to work in the future than similar WBs. The estimate is economically and statistically significant, even controlling for SES. In sum, at ages 51–56, the Early Boomers appear to be more attached to the labor force than earlier cohorts, even after controlling for variables that also affect labor force attachment, like education, income, and wealth.

Selected outcomes for the 57–61 age group appear in the second panel of Table 2.4. The unadjusted cohort difference in expected retirement age is virtually unchanged once we control for SES, health, and demographic characteristics (Table 2.4, column 3); the WBs expect to retire one year later on average than the HRS-Early and HRS-Late cohorts. This pattern is particularly interesting since the WBs expected to retire nearly half a year *before* the HRS-Late when asked in their early 50s. This reversal likely reflects the greater variance in the retirement plans of later cohorts noted earlier. Cohort differences in the expected probability of working in the future are unaffected by SES, health, and demographic characteristics (column 4), with nonworking WBs reporting they are 5.2 percentage points (30%) more likely to work in the future than nonworking HRS-Late respondents. Of note in this model is the strong effect of last year's labor income on the expected probability of working in the future. The coefficient estimates suggest that the expected probability of future work rises by 4 points for

TABLE 2-4 OLS Regression Models on Cohort Differences

	Ages 51–56		Ages 57–61		Ages 68–72	
	Expected Retirement Age (1)	Prob. of Working in Future (2)	Expected Retirement Age (3)	Prob. of Working in Future (4)	Prob. of Working PT if Retired (5)	Prob. of Working in Future (6)
Cohort dummies						
CODA cohort	—	—	—	—	(ref. group)	(ref. group)
HRS-Early cohort	—	—	(ref. group)	(ref. group)	3.503 (1.207)	2.944 (0.609)
HRS-Late cohort	(ref. group)	(ref. group)	−0.030 (0.133)	—	—	—
War Babies cohort	−0.467 (0.155)	—	1.016 (0.163)	5.216 (1.293)	—	—
Early Baby Boom cohort	0.813 (0.154)	5.848 (1.938)	—	—	—	—
Socioeconomic status						
Years of education	0.119 (0.025)	1.521 (0.339)	0.159 (0.023)	0.977 (0.234)	0.821 (0.206)	0.359 (0.106)
Labor income last year ($10,000)	0.008 (0.016)	1.012 (0.211)	−0.055 (0.022)	4.094 (0.422)	—	8.393 (0.667)
Household income last year ($10,000)	−0.041 (0.011)	−0.225 (0.108)	0.013 (0.012)	−0.262 (0.109)	0.629 (0.128)	0.064 (0.079)
Total net nonpension wealth ($10,000)	−0.002 (0.001)	−0.009 (0.016)	−0.001 (0.001)	−0.011 (0.006)	0.002 (0.004)	−0.012 (0.004)
Primary pension is DB	−2.127 (0.148)	—	−1.638 (0.143)	—	—	—
Primary pension is DC	−0.776 (0.155)	—	−0.858 (0.151)	—	—	—
Demographics						
Female	−0.706 (0.127)	−6.729 (2.122)	−0.666 (0.126)	−1.839 (1.362)	−4.529 (1.215)	−2.303 (0.612)
Black	−0.850 (0.169)	2.641 (2.593)	−0.400 (0.170)	−2.256 (1.744)	−1.345 (1.771)	1.665 (0.918)
Hispanic	−0.152 (0.233)	3.801 (3.012)	0.100 (0.240)	2.409 (2.269)	−5.740 (2.552)	−0.605 (1.182)

(cont.)

TABLE 2-4 (continued)

	Ages 51–56		Ages 57–61		Ages 68–72	
	Expected Retirement Age (1)	Prob. of Working in Future (2)	Expected Retirement Age (3)	Prob. of Working in Future (4)	Prob. of Working PT if Retired (5)	Prob. of Working in Future (6)
Asian/other	-0.427 (0.408)	12.838 (5.114)	0.674 (0.444)	-1.574 (4.233)	-1.618 (4.168)	-1.782 (2.168)
Separated/divorced	0.815 (0.178)	-4.129 (2.591)	0.922 (0.185)	3.437 (1.889)	2.354 (2.076)	2.879 (1.067)
Widowed	-0.032 (0.313)	-0.955 (4.578)	0.495 (0.235)	3.135 (2.265)	1.090 (1.661)	0.116 (0.793)
Never married	0.761 (0.314)	-3.455 (4.187)	0.040 (0.334)	5.710 (3.733)	-6.248 (3.366)	-0.577 (1.689)
Health status						
Poor health	-0.603 (0.459)	-21.377 (2.510)	-0.278 (0.415)	-10.453 (1.794)	-9.175 (2.068)	-2.166 (0.996)
Sum of major health conditions	-0.090 (0.064)	-4.159 (0.697)	-0.051 (0.055)	-2.026 (0.462)	-0.700 (0.437)	-0.661 (0.221)
R^2	0.0816	0.1813	0.0893	0.1133	0.0373	0.0673
N	4,738	1,334	3,345	2,152	3,875	3,559

Source: Author's tabulations.

Notes: All in $2004; labor and household income refer to previous calendar year. In column 5, household income excludes labor income. In models with pension coverage variables, the reference group is respondents with no pension coverage. Pension coverage refers to coverage on the current job. Models also include a constant and age dummies.

every $10,000 earned in the previous calendar year. It makes intuitive sense that nonworkers who had recent labor income would report a higher probability of working again in the future.

Finally, in the last panel of Table 2.4, we offer results for the 68–72-year olds.[11] Column 5 examines partial retirement, and it shows estimates, from a linear probability model, of the percentage working part-time, conditional on having retired. The unadjusted cohort difference is 3.7 percentage points; after adding controls, the difference falls somewhat (to 3.5 percentage points) and remains statistically different from 0. As Figure 2.2 suggested, the fraction of respondents who are partially retired in this part of the life cycle is relatively low, thus the increase over time in the share of retired individuals who are working part-time is quite large—on the order of 33 percent. Since we control for health, marital status, and total net nonpension wealth, the difference is not simply due to later cohorts being in better health or greater financial need. Rather, it is possible that some unobserved component of preferences for work might be driving the difference. Consistent with this possibility, the estimates in column 6 confirm that the HRS-Early cohort reports a 52 percent greater chance of working in the future than the CODA cohort did at the same ages, and that controlling for SES, health and demographic characteristics does not much change the unadjusted differences in means reported in Table 2.3.

Discussion and Conclusion

This study compares Baby Boomers' retirement expectations and patterns of early retirement with those of earlier cohorts. Our analysis of nationally representative data from the Health and Retirement Study suggests that Boomers are, indeed, different. They are characterized by a greater degree of labor force attachment in older age than are earlier cohorts; they expect to retire nearly one full year later than WBs; they are 14 percent more likely to expect to be working full-time at age 65, and they are 21 percent more likely to expect to work again in the future if they are not currently working. A rising unretirement trend among older cohorts supports this finding, and part-time work among the retired may be increasing as well, especially for older retirees in their late 60s.

Our regression models suggest that the greater labor force attachment expressed by more recent cohorts is not simply due to differences in health or SES. These results support those gleaned from an Roper (2002) study of older workers who found that Boomers born between 1946 and 1957 were more likely to report an interest in working part-time during retirement for the sake of interest or enjoyment, compared to an earlier cohort born during 1938–45. In addition, their sense of self-worth was more closely tied to work. Our findings and those suggest that the greater labor force attachment of the Early Boomers may be driven in part by noneconomic factors such as stronger preferences for work or perhaps even a stronger work ethic.[12]

An additional explanation for the observed cohort differences over time might be preferences for joint retirement. We have seen a rise in dual-earner couples over time, and it is possible that older spouses may expect to retire later or even work during retirement, if their younger spouse is still working.[13] Baby Boomers also differ from previous cohorts in other ways. Most notably, they do not face the same strong work disincentives through their employer pension plans as did earlier cohorts; they are more educated; they are wealthier; and they earn more. Yet these differences in SES do not fully explain the cohort differences. It may be that noneconomic factors, such as enjoyment of work, may ultimately distinguish the Boomers from earlier retiree cohorts.

Of some concern is our finding that the Early Boomers are more likely to underestimate their likelihood of survival to age 75 as compared to earlier cohorts. For example, the Early Boomers underestimate their survival probability by about 10 percent, compared to just 5 percent for the WBs. Moreover, this underestimation increases with age, as individuals fail to update their probability of surviving to age 75 with each additional year they live. One possible implication of this finding is that some Boomers may save less, or dissave more rapidly, than their life table survival probability warrants. This is a matter of concern to the extent that Boomers in the bottom half of the wealth distribution have relatively few assets.

Acknowledgments

The author thanks Xiaoyan Li for excellent research assistance and the National Institute on Aging for funding under grant number 1 P01 AG022481-01.

Notes

[1] For cross-cohort analyses of 51–56-year olds, we use data for the Early Boomers from the 2004 survey wave, data for the War Babies from the 1998 wave, and data for the HRS-Late cohort from 1992. For analyses of near-retirement behavior at ages 57–61, we compare the War Babies in 2004 with the HRS-Late cohort in 1998 and the HRS-Early cohort in 1992. For analyses of behavior at 62–67, we compare the HRS-Late in 2004 and the HRS-Early in 1998. For postretirement behavior at 68–72, we compare the HRS-Early in 2004 and the CODA cohort in 1998.

[2] Table 2A-1 shows how the partial and complete retirement rates presented here compare with alternative rates based completely on self-reported retirement data.

Generally, partial retirement is more prevalent under the subjective definition (sometimes two or three times as high) for all cohorts. Accordingly the patterns across cohorts are similar under the two definitions. Rates of complete retirement are also similar under both definitions.

[3] The large p-value from an ANOVA test of differences in means confirms that these cohort differences are not statistically significant. We use a one-way ANOVA test of differences in means is appropriate when there are three or more independent groups being compared. It is analogous to the t-test, which can be used to test for differences in means when there are only two groups.

[4] The War Babies and Early Boomers have significantly higher fractions separated or divorced than the earliest cohort (HRS-Late), but the two cohorts are not statistically different from one another (t-test not reported).

[5] Major health conditions include (a) hypertension, (b) diabetes, (c) cancer (except of skin), (d) chronic lung disease (except asthma), (e) heart attack, coronary heart disease, angina, congestive heart failure, or other heart problem, (f) stroke, (g) emotional, nervous, or psychiatric problems, and (h) arthritis or rheumatism.

[6] Early Boomers also have the highest standard deviation of expected retirement age (not shown), which suggests more variation in retirement plans than for earlier cohorts.

[7] We use the NCHS Life Tables from 1992 for the HRS-Late, 1998 for the War Babies, and 2003 for the Early Boomers (2003 is the most recent Life Table available).

[8] Early Boomers underestimate their probability of surviving to age 80 by an even greater amount: the ratio of self-reported to life table probabilities is 0.86. It is not possible to compare expected survival to 80 across cohorts because the older cohorts were asked about survival to age 85, whereas the Early Boomers were asked about survival to age 80.

[9] The age distribution between 68 and 72 is skewed toward older ages for the HRS-Early relative to the CODA cohort. To equalize the age distributions when comparing cohort means, we trim the very youngest CODA respondents and the very oldest HRS-Early respondents. In the regression models, there is no need to trim as we control for differences in cohort age distributions with age dummies.

[10] We also examine whether the cross-cohort patterns are different for men and women by including a set of sex–cohort interaction terms (not shown). Using an F-test, the null hypothesis that the gender–cohort interaction terms are jointly equal to zero cannot be rejected, and thus cross-cohort patterns appear to be similar for men and women.

[11] As noted in the previous footnote, we use the untrimmed sample and include age dummies to control for cohort differences in the age distribution.

[12] Some recent studies predict that although Boomers will retire later and with higher retirement income than earlier cohorts, they will be less able to maintain their current standard of living (Butrica et al., this volume; Manchester et al., this volume).

[13] In an analysis not reported, we reestimated the model of expected retirement age in column 1 of Table 2.4 using married 51–56-year olds and including an indicator variable for whether both spouses were employed. We found that although married

respondents with working spouses did expect to retire almost a half-year later, the estimated cohort differences remained largely unchanged.

Appendix

TABLE 2A-1 Comparison of Current and Alternative Retirement Definitions

	CODA	HRS-Early	HRS-Late	War Babies	EBB	ANOVA p-value
Ages 51–56						
Current definition (Table 2.1)						
Partly retired			2.2	3.0	2.3	0.072
Completely retired			9.2	8.1	9.2	0.157
Self-assessed retirement status						
Partly retired			5.4	6.5	6.9	0.053
Completely retired			8.6	7.5	7.7	0.255
Ages 57–61						
Current definition (Table 2.2)						
Partly retired		4.6	5.9	6.4		0.005
Completely retired		20.6	20.2	22.5		0.039
Self-assessed retirement status						
Partly retired		9.6	11.2	12.6		0.001
Completely retired		20.9	20.7	22.2		0.303
Ages 68–72						
Current definition (Table 2.3)						
Partly retired	10.6	13.9				0.001
Completely retired	64.0	63.5				0.679
Self-assessed retirement status						
Partly retired	17.3	19.4				0.114
Completely retired	70.1	69.1				0.505

Source: Author's tabulations.

Notes: Under the 'Current Definition' respondents are classified as partially retired if they describe themselves as retired and they are working part-time (i.e. working less than 35 hours per week or less than 36 weeks per year), and completely retired if they describe themselves as retired and they are not working for pay. For the 'Self-Assessed Retirement Status' definition, rates are based on variable RwSAYRET in the RAND HRS data, Version F, where w stands for wave number.

References

Burtless, G. and Quinn, J. (2000). 'Retirement Trends and Policies to Encourage Work among Older Americans', Boston College Department of Economics, Boston College Working Paper in Economics No. 436.

Butrica, B. A., Iams, H. M., and Smith, K. E. (this volume). 'It's All Relative: Understanding the Retirement Prospects of Baby Boomers'.

Cahill, K., Giandrea, M., and Quinn, J. (2005). 'Are Traditional Retirements a Thing of the Past? New Evidence on Retirement Patterns and Bridge Jobs'. US Bureau of Labor Statistics Working Paper No. 384, September.

Maestas, N. (2005). 'Back to Work: Expectations and Realizations of Work after Retirement'. RAND Labor and Population Working Paper No. WR 196-1.

Manchester, J., Weaver, D., and Whitman, K. (this volume). 'Baby Boomers versus Their Parents: Changes in Economic Well-Being and Health Status'.

Purcell, P. J. (2005). 'Older Workers: Employment and Retirement Trends', *Journal of Pension Planning and Compliance*, 30(4): 49–70.

Quinn, J. (1999). 'Has the Early Retirement Trend Reversed?' Boston College Department of Economics, Boston College Working Paper in Economics No. 424.

Roper, A. S. W. (2002). *Staying Ahead of the Curve: The AARP Work and Career Study.* Washington, DC: AARP.

Ruhm, C. J. (1990). 'Bridge Jobs and Partial Retirement', *Journal of Labor Economics*, 8(4): 482–501.

Soldo, B. J., Mitchell, O. S., Tfaily, R., and McCabe, J. (this volume). 'Cross-Cohort Differences in Retirement Preparedness: A Multi-Level Analysis'.

Weir, D. (this volume). 'Are Boomers Living Well Longer?'

Chapter 3

The Sufficiency of Retirement Savings: Comparing Cohorts at the Time of Retirement

Robert Haveman, Karen Holden, Barbara L. Wolfe, and Andrei Romanov

Social Security benefits provide nearly all US retirees with a base level of support, but for many, postretirement consumption above that base level requires privately accumulated financial wealth, housing equity, and pensions.[1] Policymakers are concerned that resources available at the time of retirement may be insufficient to maintain economic well-being during the remaining years of life, and researchers arrive at rather different conclusions regarding the adequacy of available retirement resources.[2] This chapter explores saving sufficiency using data on two cohorts of individuals at the time they retired, one in the early 1980s and a second in the mid-1990s. We use data from the Health and Retirement Survey (HRS) and also the New Beneficiary Survey (NBS) to evaluate the adequacy of saving across these two cohorts. Our comparison of resource sufficiency across these two cohorts enables us to assess time-series changes in the overall level of retirement resources, and also to appraise the impact on saving adequacy of changes in financial wealth and especially the concentration of wealth increments among the wealthy (Wolff 2004).

After a brief survey of prior studies, we go on to discuss our methodology and summarize results. We conclude that mean levels of both new retiree wealth and annuitized net wealth (ANW) increased substantially from the earlier to later cohort, yet social adequacy targets are less well met over time. Our results further indicate that the failure to meet the poverty and near-poverty thresholds is increasingly concentrated among singles and among those with the lowest human capital and low labor force attachment; vulnerability to inadequate resources in working life appears to persist into retirement.

Previous Literature

A growing literature analyzes the 'adequacy of savings' of people at or near to retirement, using a variety of approaches. These studies generally fall into two categories: those that assess savings behavior of individuals prior to retirement and, hence, the likely adequacy of resources at retirement, and those that assess how well individuals fare during retirement, given the retirement resources they have accumulated. Both types of studies require a standard against which to judge resource adequacy, as well as an estimate of the number of years (and family members) over which these resources must be allocated.

The first set of studies asks whether individuals approaching retirement—but not yet retired—are saving 'enough' to attain some standard of adequacy as of an assumed retirement age. The availability of longitudinal data with rich financial data, including the Health and Retirement Survey (HRS), has enabled the study of individuals' preretirement savings and asset accumulation patterns as they approach retirement. These studies of prospective savings adequacy at retirement reach quite disparate conclusions. Some conclude that modest pockets of inadequacy mar a generally optimistic overall situation, while others find a serious shortfall in savings. The disparate results of prospective saving adequacy studies arise from different methods of estimating future savings and assumptions about adequacy, life expectancy, and retirement age. In what follows we focus on a subset of past studies; a wide range of prior research and their conclusions appear in Table 3-1.

Some models, including Bernheim (1997), construct a simulation model to calculate 'optimal' savings behavior over the life cycle for families of different sizes, educational levels, ages (and hence, life expectancies), earnings, Social Security, and pension benefits. Bernheim's 'Baby Boomer Retirement Index' is the ratio of the actual level of older persons' accumulated financial and housing savings and the simulated target level of savings minus Social Security and pension savings. Low levels of this index support his conclusion that the financial and housing wealth of 'Baby Boomers' is only about one-third of the target level of savings. Mitchell et al. (2000) and Moore and Mitchell (2000) also take this tack, simulating saving required by the initial HRS sample that would be necessary to maintain living conditions after assumed retirement. Assuming continued earnings up to the early (62) or normal (65) retirement age, and historical returns on financial wealth, they find a median *required* savings rate of 16 percent if retirement is at age 62, dropping to only 7 percent if retirement were delayed to age 65. There is substantial heterogeneity in required saving rates, with required saving rising with earnings. Compared to actual saving patterns, these figures imply substantial under saving as people approach retirement, especially if retirement were slated for the modal retirement age of 62. A similar analysis by Gustman and Steinmeier (1998) also uses the HRS, and calculates the annuitized value of household wealth for respondents age 51–61, projecting to their expected retirement ages. As in Moore and Mitchell, this annuitized value is computed as the sum of

TABLE 3-1 Literature Review on Retirement Adequacy: Methods, Data, and Conclusions

Study	Data	Measure of adequacy	Estimation approach	Conclusions
Bernheim (1992–97)	Annual surveys of 2000 households	Financial saving relative to simulated target saving needed to maintain preretirement living standards.	Simulation model calculating 'optimal' savings over the life cycle for heterogeneous families.	About one-third of households are projected to have sufficient financial savings to meet objective.
Moore and Mitchell (2000); Mitchell et al. (2000)	HRS (1992)	Ability to maintain preretirement consumption, assuming retirement at ages 62 and 65.	Estimation of required savings rates over remaining work years to maintain current consumption.	30–40 percent of households have sufficient savings; median wealth household needs to save 9–18 percent of income in remaining work years; between one quarter and one-third of households have actual savings rates equal to prescribed rates.
Gustman and Steinmeier (1998)	HRS (1992)	Annuitized wealth relative to current earnings at expected retirement age.	Estimation of ability to purchase a two-thirds joint-and-survivors benefit annuity at assumed retirement age based on assumed work/earnings/savings behavior.	Real replacement rate of household at median of lifetime earnings distribution is about two-thirds. Low earnings and wealth households have lower rates.
Engen et al. (1999)	HRS (1992); SCF (1983–98)	Distribution of actual wealth relative to simulated utility maximizing target wealth, assuming optimizing behavior in the face of uncertainty.	Stochastic life-cycle model of utility maximizing families optimizing consumption, to estimate attainment of target wealth at retirement.	Over 60 percent of families meet the target replacement rate; with substantially lower percentages among lower income and wealth families.

Scholz et al. (2004)	HRS (1992)	Actual wealth relative to simulated utility maximizing target wealth, assuming optimizing behavior in the face of uncertainty.	Comparison of actual household with simulated household maximizing wealth to estimate extent to which wealth is sufficient to maintain preretirement consumption.	More than 80 percent of households have sufficient expected wealth at retirement.
Wolff (2002)	SCF (1983–98)	A projection of annuitized wealth at retirement (age 65) relative to the poverty line and to income in the survey year.	Estimation of income-replacement rates and ratios of annuitized wealth relative to the poverty line, from 1983–98, for age group 47–64 years.	Percentage with expected retirement income below a half of *current* income increased from 30 percent to 43 percent over the period—an increasingly serious shortfall in retirement income.
Butrica et al. (2003)	SIPP; Social Security Administration Earnings and Benefit Records	A projection of income at age 67 relative to average shared income over ages 22 to 62 and to poverty line.	Uses Social Security Administration MINT data system to project income and demographic characteristics of 'Baby Boom' generation into retirement years, and compares this income to preretirement living standards.	Median replacement rates are projected to be 93 percent for current retirees, decreasing to about 80 percent for future cohorts of retirees; poverty rates decline from about 8 percent for current retirees to 4 percent for 'Baby Boomers'.

(*cont.*)

TABLE 3-1 (continued)

Study	Data	Measure of adequacy	Estimation approach	Conclusions
Haveman et al. (2006)	NBS	Annuitized wealth relative to permanent preretirement earnings and consumption and poverty line, for new Social Security beneficiaries in 1980–81.	Uses survey data and linked administrative records to calculate annuitized wealth of new beneficiaries, permanent preretirement earnings and consumption.	Approximately 30 percent of new retirees have insufficient resources to replace 70 percent of preretirement consumption. Fewer than 2 percent of couples and about 10 percent of singles are in poverty; this problem is concentrated among the lowest earners.
Munnell and Soto (2006a, 2006b, 2006c)	HRS (Waves 1–6)	Social Security benefits (and benefits plus employer pensions/401k, and this definition plus annuitized financial assets) relative to average indexed monthly income (AIME) (plus AIME plus returns on financial assets and to top five years of recent ten of inflation-adjusted preretirement earnings).	Uses administrative records and survey information to calculate alternative measures of retirement resources and income requirements.	Regardless of how retirement income and preretirement income are defined, the two-thirds of households with pensions approximate the 65–75 percent threshold of adequacy; households without pensions fare less well.

Source: Authors' analysis.

Notes: HRS = Health and Retirement Survey; SCF = Survey of Consumer Finances; SIPP = Survey of Income and Program Participation; and NBS = New Beneficiary Survey.

Social Security wealth (obtained by projecting covered earnings until the expected age of retirement), pension wealth, financial assets, and housing assets. These annuitized values as of 1992 are then compared with the 1992 earnings of the household, yielding a replacement rate at each individual's expected age of retirement. The authors report nominal replacement rates when the average respondent was 56 years for the median household at 97 percent, while the real replacement rate was 66 percent (see also Montalto 2001).

A similar accounting approach is followed by Wolff (2002) who relies on repeated cross-sectional Surveys of Consumer Finance (for 1983, 1985, 1989, and 1998). He reaches a gloomy conclusion by calculating 'expected retirement income'—a crude estimate of annuitized wealth at the expected age of retirement—for households in each of the annual surveys. He finds that average expected retirement income grew from 1989 to 1998, but the percentage of households' age 47–64 who would have expected retirement income below the poverty line rose from 17 to 19 percent. He also concludes that an unequal distribution of financial market gains during this period implies a rising percentage of people with expected retirement income below a half of *current* income, growing from 30 to 43 percent. For these reasons, Wolfe concludes that there is an increasingly serious shortfall in retirement income.[3]

Our own prior related research looks wealth and measures of adequacy using the New Beneficiary Survey (NBS) sample of individuals who first received Social Security retired-worker benefits in 1980–81 (Haveman et al. 2006). Below we discuss this in more detail; here we simply note that we estimate a comprehensive measure of annuitized wealth in 1982 and ask what level of potential consumption could be maintained over the remaining lifetime of the individual (and spouse, if married) if assets were annuitized and all sources of retirement income were counted. Our results suggest a modest resource adequacy problem: if the income replacement target is 70 percent of preretirement pay, we find that approximately 30 percent of new retirees have insufficient resources.

A different set of authors has taken a different modeling tack, developing a stochastic life-cycle model to compute retirement preparedness. For instance, Engen et al. (1999) posit that married two-child families maximize lifetime utility by optimizing consumption and savings both for retirement (assumed to occur at age 62) and as a precaution against uncertainty.[4] Optimal wealth accumulation is defined as that which enables smoothing of the marginal utility of consumption over the life cycle. The authors then compare the distribution of simulated results (for couples differentiated by age–education–pension coverage) with actual wealth/earnings distributions for working couples (taken from both the HRS and selected Surveys of Consumer Finance). Assuming a 3 percent rate of time preference, they find that over 60 percent of married couples exceed the median target wealth/earnings ratio (relative to an expected 50 percent in a stochastic model), suggesting that overall savings are more than 'optimal' at the median of the distribution. But comparisons at other points in the distribution suggest that about a quarter of couple households are under saving. Based on these results, the authors calculate replacement rates (defined as the ratio of Social Security and pension benefits plus income, but no principal, from wealth to final earnings), and find a median value of 72 percent. The authors argue that, considering lower consumption needs in retirement, 'even without saving a large share of income in terms of financial assets, households can easily achieve replacement rates that are within the range recommended by financial planners and by the simulation model.'

This stochastic approach was extended by Scholz et al. (2005) whose life-cycle model reflects uncertainty regarding life expectancy, the uninsurability of certain future income and expense flows, and the characteristics of tax, transfer, social, and private pension arrangements. That model also assumes that each household can solve the optimal consumption/savings decision problem over the remaining years of its life. This solution, together with earnings histories, enables a prediction of optimum wealth holdings for a representative sample of HRS observations. Their model 'explains' over 80 percent of the variation in wealth holdings, so the authors conclude that fewer than 20 percent of households have less actual wealth than their estimated target level. Even for them, the shortfall from optimal wealth levels is deemed small.

Yet a third strand of the adequacy literature uses microsimulation models to project cohort well-being in retirement. For instance, Butrica et al. (Chapter 4, this volume) simulate using Social Security's Model of Income in the Near Term (MINT) how well Baby Boomers will do in retirement. Their assessment is that Boomer retirees will have higher real income and lower poverty rates; their replacement rates will be lower.

A fourth strand in the adequacy literature is asking how well-off individuals seem to be as they age, and what influences their ability to weather shocks in the process. Munnell and Soto (2005a, 2005b, 2005c) have exploited the longitudinal nature of the HRS surveys to trace the evolution of replacement rates and compare them to target replacement rates of 65–75 percent of preretirement earnings. They conclude that households without company pensions fare poorly, whereas those with pensions do better.

Clearly there are many reasons for the different conclusions across prior studies, including differences in data, assumptions, estimation procedures, and the definition of adequacy. For example, Mitchell et al. (2000), Moore and Mitchell (2000), and Engen et al. (1999) focus on consumption smoothing, where potential consumption targets are inferred based on preretirement pay, or income net of retirement savings. Instead, Wolff (2002) focuses on wealth accumulation at retirement and its ability to generate income (and implied consumption) above the poverty threshold. And even when the main conclusions differ, all prior studies agree that there is wide heterogeneity in saving adequacy. Indeed, when comparing differences across studies, Engen et al. (1999) suggest that there may be less disagreement regarding the overall adequacy of retirement savings than is generally recognized, after when adjustments are made for differences in assumptions and estimating procedures.

Methodology: Savings Sufficiency for Two Cohorts

In our prior work we estimated accumulated retirement saving for single individuals and married couples first observed at retirement in the early 1980s, and we also computed the ANW that this saving implied over their remaining lifetimes. Retirement was defined as first receipt of Social Security benefits. In what follows, we extend this research by comparing our prior results to those for a new group, one which retired about a decade later. To do so, we compare estimated ANW to two alternative criteria of minimum-acceptable consumption adequacy, namely the national poverty standard, and the 'near-poverty' standard, which we set at twice the poverty standard. We distinguish changes in overall sufficiency over time, and also intertemporal changes for particular groups of new retirees focusing on patterns among groups with high and low levels of preretirement earnings and retirement wealth.

To do so, we draw on two data-sets on individuals entering retirement, each linked to Social Security administrative records. With these comparably constructed retirement cohorts we are able to examine whether, as hypothesized by Delorme et al. (2006), later cohorts of retirees are more vulnerable than were early cohorts to inadequate retirement resources due to longer life expectancy, changes in the prevalence of defined benefit (DB) plans, and uncertainties tied to growth in financial assets of defined contribution (DC) plans and own financial portfolios.

The Early and Later Cohorts

For the early cohort, we use the New Beneficiary Survey (NBS) to assess the adequacy of economic resources available at the time of retirement as defined by the first receipt of Social Security retired-worker benefits. The NBS contains information on a sample of individuals who first received Social Security benefits in 1980–81 (Ycas 1992); they were interviewed first in 1982 and again in 1991. Our sample is drawn from the retired-worker sample and includes individuals age 62–72 at time of first benefit receipt and who were interviewed in both years.[5]

For the later cohort we take respondents to the Health and Retirement Study (HRS) from the 1931–41 birth cohort. This original HRS sample was aged 51–61 when first interviewed in 1992 and was revisited every two years after that. In 1998, additional cohorts were added to the HRS interview sequence, including a cohort born between 1924 and 1930, labeled the Children of the Depression Age (CODA), which we include in our sample frame.[6] Our HRS sample, therefore, consists of individuals who report initial Social Security receipt in the two years prior to each interview.[7] This setup mimics the NBS data selection on first Social Security receipt in 1980–81 and the initial interview up to two years later, in 1982. The HRS respondents must be at least 62 years of age at the first benefit receipt (the minimum age at which retired-worker benefits can be received) and no older than age 72 (the maximum age we selected for our NBS analysis sample).[8] By selecting our HRS sample through the 1998 interview, all of the observations report receiving Social Security benefits by 1998.[9]

Individuals in both samples are observed as they first enter Social Security recipiency status, the point in the retirement cycle at which they choose to first draw on this important retirement asset. The NBS is of individuals who first receive Social Security during a specific one-year period. The HRS sample also observes individuals at the point of first Social Security receipt, but this event can occur over a six-year period, between 1992 and 1998. Our HRS new beneficiary sample is a younger sample than is the NBS because it is drawn largely from the original HRS cohort whom we can observe only over the early retirement-ages rather than from all new Social Security beneficiaries.[10] We adjust for this unequal age distribution (see Figure 3-1) by standardizing our HRS cohort to the NBS age distribution.[11]

The NBS and HRS Data-Sets

The NBS and HRS share features important to the study of retirement adequacy across cohorts. Both the NBS and the HRS gathered detailed information from individuals on their (and their spouse/partner's) health, retirement, and economic status, including demographic information and data on family structure, work history and current employment, health status, housing, income and assets, health and life insurance coverage, and Social Security receipt and benefits. Most important is the matching of both data-sets to Social Security administrative benefits and earnings records.[12]

Because both data-sets provide comparably detailed financial information for each spouse in married-couple households, we are able to

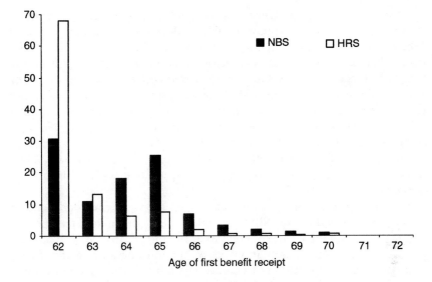

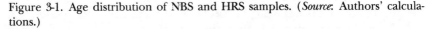

Figure 3-1. Age distribution of NBS and HRS samples. (*Source*: Authors' calculations.)

accurately estimate financial, housing, pension, and Social Security wealth for all respondents (including the period during which only one spouse in a married couple survives).[13] Asset and housing information is provided at the household level in both surveys. Our samples are of two (age-standardized) cohorts that first accepted Social Security benefits (i.e. retired) approximately a decade apart. Adopting this definition of retirement avoids the need to estimate unobserved preretirement earnings, savings, and pension and asset accretion of individuals.

Net Wealth

For respondents in both the NBS and the HRS, we calculate for each unmarried individual and married couple the present value (in $2004) of all retirement resources currently held and expected over their retired lifetimes. Net wealth, so defined, is the sum of nonpension financial wealth, the net value of own home (home value less outstanding mortgage), other property including business property, the present value of currently received and expected DB pensions, the value of all DC pension accounts [including IRA and 401(k)], and the present value of currently received and expected Social Security benefits.[14] In both data-sets, respondents report directly the value of their financial, property, and net home equity wealth. For the NBS cohort, we estimate Social Security wealth using the monthly inflation-adjusted benefits to which each individual is entitled (from the linked Master Beneficiary File), calculating the present value (in 1982 but in $2004) of these benefits over the individual's expected remaining lifetime including, if married, the probable widow(er)hood years of the longer lived spouse. We include for a married couple spouse and survivor benefits, if greater than own retired-worker benefits. Survival probabilities to each year are drawn from 1982 race- and gender-specific life tables (US Department of Health and Human Services, Public Health Service, National Center for Health Statistics 1985). We discount this expected stream of Social Security benefits to 1982 using a 2.75 percent rate, taken to be the individual rate of time preference, yielding the wealth value of Social Security benefits.[15]

The value of current (or future expected) employer-provided pension benefits is provided by the NBS respondent (and, if married, the spouse) and reflects a nominal value of benefits at the time of interview. While few pension plans are fully price indexed, we incorporate a price adjustment estimated from the NBS data. The average annual growth rate of mean pension benefits from 1982 to 1991 for those fully retired and receiving benefits in both years was 3.25 percent between 1982 and 1991, a value that is 0.75 percentage points less than the actual 4 percent rate of inflation between those years. We thus use a 3.50 percent rate to discount pension benefit streams to 1982 [2.75 percent for individual time preference plus 0.75 (4.00 − 3.25) to capture the average erosion in the value of pensions due to inflation]. In calculating couples' pension wealth, we use survey responses that indicate whether a pensioner chose a single-life or some form of survivor benefit that would continue to be paid to a surviving spouse and adjust our pension wealth estimates for that choice.

For the HRS sample, data on pension wealth are obtained primarily from the HRS 'pension estimation program', which uses plan descriptions provided by employers, along with specific data from respondents to estimate pension entitlements held by respondents. Using assumptions on macroeconomic variables consistent with the NBS study (e.g. nominal discount rate of 3.5 percent), we estimate the present value of each respondent's or couple's stock of pension wealth. We used survey responses to questions about pension income to construct pension wealth for the CODA cohort, which was not represented in the 'pension estimation program'. For the HRS sample, we use the 'Mitchell Social Security Wealth' estimates available in the restricted version of the data. For those observations for which this value is not available (28% of our sample), we substitute calculated Social Security wealth based on the respondent's own estimate of Social Security benefits, using the same algorithm as used in the NBS estimate. For the missing (nonmatched) Social Security wealth estimates, we follow a procedure similar to those of the NBS and Mitchell, using survey responses on current or expected retired-worker benefits amounts for both respondent and the spouse, as well as expected date of receipt if relevant. For single respondents, the estimate of Social Security wealth is the present discounted value of the stream of projected benefits taking into account his or her probability to survive until that age. We again use a 2.75 percent discount rate (reflecting a nominal rate of 3.5%) and survival probabilities based on US Decennial Life Tables for 1989–91 (US Department of Health and Human Services, Public Health Service, National Center for Health Statistics 1997).

For married couples in both the NBS and the HRS samples, Social Security plus pension wealth estimates are the expected stream of benefits of both spouses over their expected lifetimes, including that of the lone survivor who will claim survivor benefits whenever they exceed their own work-based benefits.[16]

Annuitized Net Wealth

Wealth estimates do not account for the number of remaining years of life, or the two lives of couples, over which resources must be spread. Our primary measure of well-being is the annuitized value of total assets over the remaining expected lifetime of respondents and, if married, of surviving spouses (again using race- and sex-specific life tables). Because our wealth estimates already reflect differences in inflation indexing, we use a uniform interest rate of 2.75 percent, taken to be the individual rate of time preference. The annuitized value we report is the single-person equivalent annual income that could be consumed if an individual or couple maintained a steady level of consumption potential over their remaining lifetimes, including, for couples, the period when only one is expected to survive. All wealth is annuitized assuming couples require 1.66 of the income of a single individual to maintain equivalent consumption.[17] This single-person equivalent permits easy comparison between singles and couples. It diverges from the income a couple might actually report from pensions or annuitized wealth (e.g. if an annuity were actually purchased) because we force a couple to take an annuity that preserves equivalent consumption over the survival of only one of them. This, for example, could result in lower estimated than actually reported annual pension income for a couple in which the retired worker selected a single-life pension.[18]

Characteristics of the Early (NBS) and Later (HRS) Samples

Table 3-2 summarizes key characteristics of the two samples of new Social Security retired-worker beneficiaries; all dollar values are in $2004. The

TABLE 3-2 Characteristics of New Social Security Benefit Recipients

Variable Means	Characteristics of NBS Sample			Age Standardized HRS Characteristics		
	Married Couples	Single Men	Single Women	Married Couples	Single Men	Single Women
Number of observations	5,783	702	1,381	1,447	196	309
Age	65.64	65.93	66.48	64.56	66.22	65.12
Male	0.66			0.56		
Nonwhite	0.08	0.19	0.15	0.10	0.15	0.23
Widowed		0.33	0.50		0.29	0.42
Separated or divorced		0.40	0.29		0.51	0.43
Respondent high school only	0.32	0.22	0.30	0.34	0.29	0.25
Respondent some college	0.14	0.10	0.19	0.19	0.22	0.24
Respondent college or higher	0.12	0.10	0.12	0.24	0.18	0.17
Spouse high school only	0.35			0.37		
Spouse some college	0.13			0.19		
Spouse college or higher	0.09			0.20		
Number of children	2.69	1.93	1.89	3.10	3.07	2.84
Respondent health condition	0.24	0.26	0.24	0.19	0.19	0.24
Spouse health condition	0.42			0.24		
Private health insurance (resp.)	0.84	0.69	0.77	0.65	0.62	0.60
Private health insurance (spouse.)				0.66		

Has a pension	0.57	0.43	0.46	0.56	0.42	0.37
Home ownership	0.87	0.46	0.57	0.92	0.66	0.68
Years worked	32.23	34.66	28.36			
Longest job uncovered	0.19	0.18	0.10	0.20	0.18	0.16
ANW	29,202	27,719	23,452	46,912	37,515	32,145
Standard deviation	26,587	26,900	18,357	58,379	39,173	44,533
Minimum	2,567	3,919	3,426	856	1,833	293
Maximum	881,687	356,590	201,494	545,456	291,385	377,839
Replacement rate (PovLine)	3.67	3.48	2.95	5.89	4.71	4.04
Standard deviation	3.34	3.38	2.31	7.33	4.92	5.59
Minimum	0.32	0.49	0.43	0.11	0.23	0.04
Maximum	110.75	44.79	25.31	68.51	36.60	47.46

Source: Authors' calculations.

Notes: NBS age is in 1982; HRS age is at first interview as recipient Health Condition: indicating poor or fair health, estimated from number of health conditions in NBS, from specific question in HRS. Pension: current or future expected pension receipt.

HRS sample is age-standardized by age of first benefit receipt to match the NBS sample (unadjusted data are available on request). The age reported in this table and that is used in our analysis is age at first post-benefit-receipt interview rather than 'retirement' age since that is the age at which financial data are reported.

Differences in the characteristics of the two beneficiary cohorts reflect changes in both overall population characteristics and the probability of subgroups achieving eligibility for retired-worker benefits. The later HRS beneficiary cohort contains a higher proportion of nonwhite respondents, reflecting both the growth in the share of the American population that is nonwhite and the increase in Social Security eligibility of the nonwhite population. Similarly, the greater percentage of new beneficiaries in higher education categories in the HRS cohort reflects the time-series rise in schooling among the population, as well as the long-term increase in women's labor force participation. Because of somewhat different health status definitions in the two data-sets, the means in respondent and spouse health conditions are not precisely comparable, though the means imply there has been no change in the overall probability of poor health among beneficiaries.[19] Comparing the early 1980s to mid-1990s retirees, private health insurance coverage has fallen somewhat, consistent with overall national patterns of declining employer-provided health care coverage and its continuation into retirement. While family size has fallen overall, the increasing labor force participation of women with children is reflected in the higher number of children among female new beneficiaries. The percentage with current or expected pension income, and the percentage, whose longest job was uncovered by Social Security, are comparable between the two data-sets.

The bottom panel of Table 3-2 summarizes our ANW estimates (in $2004) for the early and late cohorts; Figure 3-2 summarizes changes in distribution of ANW across the two cohorts. For married couples, mean ANW grew by 60 percent between the cohorts (from $29,200 to $46,900). For single men and women, the increases were 35 and 37 percent, respectively.

A striking finding is the rising dispersion in ANW across the cohorts. Across all households, the standard deviation of ANW rises by more than 140 percent, reflecting the increased inequality in financial wealth holdings over this period. The minimum value of ANW is much lower in the later sample for all HRS marital/gender groups, perhaps because of the increased likelihood of low income/wealth spouse-only individuals being included in the HRS sample. The relatively high variance of ANW in the HRS sample is likely contributing to the high standard errors in our multivariate estimates reported below.

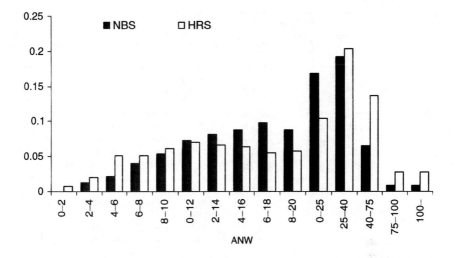

Figure 3-2. Distribution by annuitized new wealth bins ($000, in $1994). *Note*: HRS not age-weighted. (*Source*: Authors' calculations.)

Estimates of Wealth and ANW

The first panel of Table 3-3 summarizes mean wealth values at retirement for the early and later beneficiary cohorts ($2004).[20] The mean level of wealth over all individuals and couples in the samples grew by 60 percent, from the early cohort ($554,000) to the later one ($891,000). Much of this was due to rising financial wealth; for the NBS cohort, for instance, average financial wealth was nearly $125,000; a decade later, the mean level of financial/property wealth for new beneficiaries tripled. During the period, financial wealth also grew from 22 to 42 percent of total wealth. The increase in pension wealth between the cohorts is also substantial, from less than $80,000 to $194,000. Social Security wealth fell by almost 25 percent, from $263,000 in the early cohort, to $207,000 for the later cohort.[21]

We also see that, for both the early and later cohorts, the level of wealth varies substantially by race, marital status, sex, education, and the age of retirement. For both cohorts, the mean level of wealth for white households is about twice that for nonwhite households, though the difference is somewhat larger for the HRS cohort (2.4 times vs. 1.93 times for the NBS cohort). White households tend to hold a far larger share of their wealth in financial wealth than do nonwhite households (23% vs. 8.6%), although the share was larger for both groups in the HRS cohort of retirees (to 44% and 16.8%, respectively). Mean wealth for retirees in both cohorts is less

TABLE 3-3 Net Wealth and Annuitized New Wealth of NBS and HRS Sample by Sample Characteristics

| | All Households | Distribution of Wealth (%) | Race | | Marital Status | | | Age at |
			White	Nonwhite	Single	Married	62–64	65
New Beneficiary Survey								
Number of households	7,866		7,059	807	2,083	5,783	2,544	771
Net wealth, means								
Total net Wealth	$553,967	100.0	$582,786	$301,873	$322,244	$637,431	$522,459	$555,553
Financial/property	124,276	22.4	135,526	25,870	64,603	145,770	94,194	124,897
Housing	86,715	15.7	92,050	40,047	50,127	99,894	81,135	87,135
Pensions	79,447	14.3	83,492	44,065	49,305	90,304	90,444	79,433
Social Security	263,528	47.6	271,718	191,890	158,208	301,464	256,685	264,087
ANW, means								
Total ANW	$28,060	100.0	$29,279	$17,404	$24,890	$29,202	$24,116	$27,124
Financial/property	6,067	21.6	6,609	1,323	4,933	6,475	4,176	5,981
Housing	4,229	15.1	4,470	2,122	3,723	4,412	3,644	4,039
Pensions	4,191	14.9	4,366	2,662	3,862	4,310	4,349	4,041
Social security	13,573	48.4	13,833	11,296	12,372	14,005	11,947	13,062
Social poverty indicators, means								
ANW/poverty standard	3.52		3.68	2.19	3.13	3.67	3.03	3.41
ANW/twice poverty standard	1.76		1.84	1.09	1.56	1.83	1.51	1.70
ANW < poverty standard	0.04		0.03	0.16	0.10	0.02	0.06	0.04
ANW < 2 × poverty standard	0.23		0.19	0.54	0.37	0.18	0.31	0.25
Health and Retirement Survey								
Number of households	1,952		1,543	409	505	1,447	1,588	180
Net wealth, means								
Total net wealth	$890,918	100.0	$962,547	$402,290	$459,569	$1,095,624	$875,203	$992,265
Financial/property	376,068	42.2	421,311	67,431	172,856	472,506	342,160	489,329
Housing	113,961	12.8	122,995	52,328	72,016	133,866	108,319	113,988
Pensions	194,019	21.8	204,133	125,025	82,949	246,729	212,237	188,852
Social Security	206,871	23.2	214,107	157,506	131,748	242,522	212,487	200,096
ANW, means								
Total ANW	$42,971	100.0	$46,044	$22,006	$34,666	$46,912	$39,313	$45,405
Financial/property	17,918	41.7	19,997	3,735	12,976	20,263	15,252	22,260
Housing	5,689	13.2	6,104	2,859	5,446	5,805	4,957	5,249
Pensions	8,929	20.8	9,266	6,625	6,070	10,285	9,361	8,318
Social Security	10,435	24.3	10,676	8,787	10,173	10,559	9,743	9,579
Social poverty indicators, means								
ANW/poverty standard	5.40		5.78	2.76	4.35	5.89	4.94	5.70
ANW/twice poverty standard	2.70		2.89	1.38	2.18	2.95	2.47	2.85
ANW < poverty standard	0.08		0.06	0.25	0.17	0.04	0.07	0.09
ANW < 2 × poverty standard	0.23		0.20	0.52	0.36	0.19	0.27	0.24

Source: Authors' calculations.

Note: HRS data are age standardized (see text).

Retirement		Marital Status/Sex				Education			
66–69	70–72	Single Women	Single Men	Married Women	Married Men	No High School	High School	Some College	College+
4,206	345	1,381	702	1,952	3,831	3,406	2,420	1,130	910
$567,267	$620,608	$322,287	$322,160	$623,931	$644,310	$423,752	$582,800	$629,980	$870,273
135,367	209,499	58,569	76,474	125,866	155,912	70,212	130,862	155,064	270,885
88,703	102,682	54,491	41,541	93,042	103,385	64,785	90,697	104,021	136,717
74,065	63,999	48,398	51,091	85,954	92,520	47,240	81,853	94,744	174,598
269,131	244,427	160,829	153,054	319,069	292,493	241,515	279,387	276,150	288,073
$29,861	$37,284	$23,452	$27,719	$27,824	$29,905	$21,584	$28,948	$32,419	$44,527
6,752	11,853	4,168	6,437	5,841	6,799	3,418	6,309	7,810	13,171
4,477	5,943	3,850	3,471	4,270	4,484	3,144	4,386	5,153	6,728
4,137	4,027	3,571	4,436	3,820	4,559	2,518	4,203	5,047	9,361
14,495	15,462	11,863	13,374	13,893	14,063	12,504	14,050	14,409	15,267
3.75	4.68	2.95	3.48	3.49	3.76	2.71	3.64	4.07	5.59
1.88	2.34	1.47	1.74	1.75	1.88	1.36	1.82	2.04	2.80
0.03	0.05	0.10	0.09	0.02	0.02	0.07	0.02	0.01	0.02
0.18	0.14	0.37	0.36	0.20	0.16	0.36	0.14	0.12	0.07
152	32	309	196	671	776	550	704	364	334
$844,261	$808,216	$467,052	$451,113	$963,984	$1,199,169	$473,598	$845,986	$968,496	$1,373,199
333,290	388,109	168,054	178,283	359,714	561,226	149,511	387,215	382,867	618,895
115,933	158,633	77,876	65,394	125,594	140,373	73,939	113,380	112,923	162,658
191,709	50,087	85,328	80,262	220,353	267,476	69,712	137,940	257,043	362,830
203,329	211,387	135,795	127,174	258,323	230,093	180,435	207,452	215,663	228,816
$44,383	$57,396	$32,145	$37,515	$42,915	$50,056	$25,190	$39,491	$47,489	$64,673
17,244	25,842	11,625	14,504	16,194	23,464	8,534	17,867	18,334	28,600
6,182	12,342	5,333	5,574	5,640	5,934	3,898	5,345	5,961	8,036
9,511	3,825	5,711	6,476	9,735	10,718	3,182	6,168	12,020	16,813
11,447	15,387	9,476	10,961	11,346	9,940	9,576	10,111	11,174	11,225
5.57	7.21	4.04	4.71	5.39	6.29	3.16	4.96	5.96	8.12
2.79	3.60	2.02	2.36	2.70	3.14	1.58	2.48	2.98	4.06
0.10	0.00	0.19	0.14	0.02	0.05	0.20	0.05	0.03	0.02
0.24	0.07	0.39	0.33	0.18	0.19	0.47	0.24	0.15	0.07

for those who first received benefits at ages 62–64 than those who did so at later ages.[22] In both cohorts, total wealth (unadjusted for household size) was about twice as great for married compared to single respondents, and for those with more schooling. Differences for men and women by marital status are not substantial, though a higher percentage of men's wealth is in financial assets.

The second panel of Table 3-3 presents estimates of the single-person equivalent ANW values for our samples of new beneficiaries. Couples' mean ANW rise by almost two-thirds (60 percent) from the early to the later cohort, while for singles it rose by about 40 percent.[23] As was true for total wealth, ANW is positively related to the age at first benefit receipt. However, the disparity in ANW values between early (<age 65) and late retirees is greater than for wealth, as the shorter expected lifetimes of older retirees reduces the period over which retirement resources must be annuitized.[24] Furthermore, as in the case of the wealth estimates, levels of ANW vary by socioeconomic group (shown in Appendix Figure 3A-1). Between the early 1980s and the mid-1990s, ANW increased for all of the age groups, but the relative position of nonwhites, single individuals, early retirees (62–64-year olds) and those with less education eroded as their ANW grew more slowly. While ANW for whites in the HRS cohort was 57 percent larger than for whites in the NBS cohort, ANW for nonwhites increased by only 26 percent from the early to the later cohort. Among the marital status gender groups, smaller increases in ANW are seen for single men and women (35% and 37%, respectively), compared to married men (67%). The pattern seems clear; wealth (and hence, ANW) gains between the early 1980s and the mid-1990s were greatest for those groups with the greatest human capital and the strongest attachment to the labor force. The wealth advantage for whites relative to nonwhites increased substantially, expanding an already substantial racial disparity in resources at retirement.

Retirement Resource Adequacy for Newly Retired Workers

There is no universally accepted definition of retirement resource adequacy, and no consensus on the means of achieving this goal.[25] Nevertheless, we are able to address the question: 'Do newly retired workers have resources sufficient to enable them to escape poverty or near poverty during retirement?' This adequacy criterion reflects a social norm—the meeting of basic needs—irrespective of individual preretirement living standards. We also study the relative importance of public and private resources in supporting retirement and the effects of individual characteristics in individuals' ability to meet these adequacy criteria. Specifically, we posit two absolute standards, namely a *family-size-conditioned poverty threshold*, and a threshold equal to *twice the poverty threshold*; the latter is commonly referred to as a near-poverty standard.[26] A ratio of ANW to the poverty line (or twice the poverty line) of one or more is interpreted as a level of retirement resources sufficient to avoid poverty (or near poverty) throughout the retirement period.

The final panel of Table 3-3 indicates households' position relative to the social minimum consumption ratios. For the early and late cohorts, respectively, the poverty line ratios are 3.5 and nearly 5.5; for the near-poverty standard the ratios are 1.8 and 2.7, respectively. The increase in the mean ratio reflects the increase in ANW across the two cohorts. Table 3-3 also shows the percentage of respondents in the various groups who fail to meet the poverty and near-poverty standards. In contrast to the large increase in mean ANW, but consistent with the increase in the standard deviation of the ANW distribution, the percentage of new beneficiaries who fail to meet the poverty standard rises from the early to the later cohort. In the early 1980s, about 4 percent of new retirees failed to have ANW in excess of the poverty threshold; by the mid-1990s, this had increased to 8 percent; the percentage of failing to meet the near-poverty standard remained stable at 23 percent.

These patterns persist generally across the more detailed demographic groups. In general, groups with lower human capital or labor force attachment (those with low education, women, singles, nonwhites, and those retired at an earlier age) have substantially lower poverty and near-poverty ratios than do those with higher levels of human capital and labor force attachment. For the early and the late cohort, those groups with low levels of human capital or labor force attachment— those with low levels of schooling, nonwhites, singles, and females—have the highest percentages failing to meet the poverty and near-poverty standards. These same disadvantaged groups experienced the largest increases in the percentage that fail to meet the poverty and near-poverty standards.

Correlates of Retirement Resource Adequacy

To describe the predictors of individual resources and resource adequacy, we next estimate multivariate regression models of ANW and indicators of falling below the poverty threshold, relating these outcomes to socioeconomic characteristics. Table 3-4 presents the ANW results for married

TABLE 3-4 Predictors of Annuitized New Wealth: New Social Security Beneficiaries: OLS Models

	Married Couples		Single Men		Single Women	
	Coefficient	t-Value	Coefficient	t-Value	Coefficient	t-Value
New Beneficiary Survey						
Intercept	−74.50	−7.77	−72.97	−3.11	−88.03	−6.82
Age at retirement	1.31	9.04	1.23	3.47	1.46	7.54
Nonwhite	−4.72	−4.50	−4.65	−2.41	−4.04	−3.74
Widowed			5.41	2.53	0.09	0.09
Separated or divorced			0.15	0.08	−0.49	−0.43
Respondent high school	2.84	4.12	2.30	1.23	3.84	4.25
Respondent some college	4.42	4.80	8.27	3.25	6.07	5.82
Respondent college or higher	12.00	11.35	15.94	6.27	11.66	9.27
Spouse high school	2.25	3.31				
Spouse some college	4.11	4.39				
Spouse college or higher	10.12	8.79				
Number of children	−0.20	−1.38	−0.18	−0.48	−0.50	−2.45
Longest job uncovered	3.80	5.19	4.35	2.21	3.85	3.13
Respondent health condition	−1.76	−2.71	−0.75	−0.45	−1.12	−1.29
Spouse health condition	−1.71	−3.02				
Private health insurance	4.08	5.26	4.87	2.89	2.09	2.25
Pension	6.31	10.83	11.20	7.08	9.06	11.99
Home ownership	5.98	7.23	11.68	7.57	8.38	11.08
Number of observations	5,783		702		1,381	
F-value (p-value)	71.7	<.0001	26.28	<.0001	55.33	<.0001
Adjusted R^2	0.1550		0.3192		0.3385	
Mean ANW ($000)	29.20		27.72		23.45	

Health and Retirement Study

	Coef.	t	Coef.	t	Coef.	t
Intercept	−137.15	−3.23	68.58	0.83	−219.01	−3.15
Age at retirement	2.23	3.35	−0.83	−0.65	3.80	3.51
Nonwhite	−7.15	−2.50	−6.62	−0.94	−8.89	−2.18
Widowed			−22.92	−2.74	−6.85	−1.22
Separated or divorced			−16.46	−2.37	−6.66	−1.23
Respondent high school	5.82	2.12	3.97	0.53	−2.41	−0.49
Respondent some college	8.92	2.66	7.26	0.83	4.53	0.82
Respondent college or higher	22.40	6.07	21.35	2.36	31.04	4.53
Spouse high school	3.75	1.39				
Spouse some college	6.47	1.93				
Spouse college or higher	22.99	6.27				
Number of children	0.08	0.16	−0.23	−0.16	−1.27	−1.40
Longest job uncovered	0.67	0.26	2.99	0.46	−6.32	−1.23
Respondent health condition	−2.68	−1.00	2.39	0.33	−2.62	−0.59
Spouse health condition	−4.16	−1.65				
Private health insurance	7.22	3.35	11.76	2.02	3.32	0.82
Pension	4.82	2.27	19.50	3.31	7.46	1.76
Home ownership	16.98	4.50	27.02	4.34	13.42	3.11
Number of observations	1,447		196		309	
F-value (p-value)	20.97	<.0001	6.65	<.0001	8.65	<.0001
Adjusted R^2	0.1716		0.2736		0.2441	
Mean ANW ($000)	46.91		37.51		32.15	

Source: Authors' calculations.

Note: HRS data are age standardized (see text).

couples as well as for single men and women. Results for the early (NBS) cohort are shown in the top panel of the table. Respondents who are white, with more than a high school degree (and, if married, those with a more educated spouse), who first received retired-worker benefits at an older age, and whose longest job was uncovered by Social Security tend to have higher ANW than respondents without these characteristics. These characteristics are likely associated with higher savings propensities or more generous pensions in noncovered work. Respondents with a health condition and those who have a spouse with a health condition have lower ANW, though respondent health is statistically significant only for married couples. Two variables that directly capture the presence of components of ANW—having a private pension and owning a home—are positively and significantly related to the ANW. Finally, those with private health insurance coverage have greater ANW than those who lack private health insurance coverage. The significance of these wealth components indicate that individuals do not compensate with greater savings in other forms for the absence of an employer-provided pension or probable absence of retiree health insurance coverage. Nor is investment in housing merely an asset allocation decision; housing is either associated with or enables greater retirement resource accumulation.

The bottom panel of Table 3-4 presents results for the later (HRS) cohort. With only a few exceptions, patterns are similar, especially for married couples. In general, the size of the coefficients is larger in the regressions for the later cohort though levels of statistical significance are somewhat lower.[27] The coefficient of working in an uncovered job is substantially smaller and statistically insignificant for married couples in this cohort, most likely due to the difference in the definition of this variable between the NBS and the HRS coupled with the expansion of Social Security coverage to federal employment in the 1980s.[28] Being widowed or divorced rather than never-married suggests substantially lower ANW for the later HRS cohort than for the NBS cohort.[29] This may reflect the better labor force prospects of never-married women in the later cohort (and consequently their ability to accumulate their own retirement resources), and the financial losses among women among the larger share of women who become divorced or widowed at an early age in the later cohort.

Table 3-5 links the failure to meet the poverty standard (ANW/poverty line ≤ 1) to the same socioeconomic characteristics as above. For the early (NBS) cohort, several factors are negatively related to the probability of resource failures, including later retirement age, schooling, coverage by private health insurance, and the owning of a pension and a home. Vulnerability to poverty is higher for nonwhites, having more children, and poor

TABLE 3-5 Probability of ANW Falling Below Poverty Line Standard: Probit Models

	Married Couples				Single Women				Single Men			
	Coefficient	S.E.	χ²	Prob.	Coefficient	S.E.	χ²	Prob.	Coefficient	S.E.	χ²	Prob.
New Beneficiary Survey												
Intercept	4.36	1.85	5.56	0.02	8.85	3.12	8.07	0.00	9.47	2.20	18.44	0.00
Age at retirement	-0.09	0.03	9.15	0.00	-0.14	0.05	8.57	0.00	-0.14	0.03	19.08	0.00
Nonwhite	0.72	0.12	33.25	0.00	0.33	0.20	2.79	0.09	0.63	0.15	18.02	0.00
Widowed					-0.75	0.28	7.09	0.01	-0.06	0.19	0.11	0.74
Separated or divorced					-0.49	0.22	4.88	0.03	-0.21	0.20	1.18	0.28
Respondent high school	-0.28	0.15	3.4	0.07	-0.43	0.27	2.52	0.11	-0.56	0.16	12.52	0.00
Respondent some college	-0.30	0.24	1.55	0.21	-0.27	0.41	0.42	0.52	-0.76	0.23	11.16	0.00
Respondent college or higher	-0.71	0.44	2.57	0.11	-0.24	0.38	0.40	0.52	0.17	0.24	0.48	0.49
Spouse high school	-0.49	0.15	10.48	0.00								
Spouse some college	-0.70	0.31	4.95	0.03								
Spouse college or higher	-0.54	0.45	1.44	0.23								
Number of children	0.05	0.02	8.15	0.00	0.01	0.05	0.07	0.79	0.07	0.03	5.49	0.02
Longest job uncovered	0.40	0.11	11.91	0.00	0.34	0.21	2.61	0.11	0.42	0.19	4.87	0.03
Respondent health condition	0.38	0.11	11.72	0.00	0.28	0.19	2.18	0.14	0.21	0.14	2.30	0.13
Spouse health condition	0.09	0.11	0.6	0.44								
Private health insurance	-0.45	0.11	15.89	0.00	-0.57	0.18	9.46	0.00	-0.60	0.13	19.67	0.00
Pension	-1.87	0.38	24.27	0.00	-6.54		0.00	1.00	-1.91	0.26	55.76	0.00
Home ownership	-0.80	0.11	51.63	0.00	-1.28	0.26	25.05	0.00	-1.26	0.15	73.07	0.00
Number of observations	5,783				702				1,381			
Log-likelihood	-327.10				-136.25				-256.35			

(cont.)

TABLE 3-5 (continued)

	Married Couples				Single Women				Single Men			
	Coefficient	S.E.	χ^2	Prob.	Coefficient	S.E.	χ^2	Prob.	Coefficient	S.E.	χ^2	Prob.
Health and Retirement Study												
Intercept	0.04	3.54	0	0.99	5.26	5.80	0.82	0.36	3.69	3.88	0.9	0.34
Age at retirement	0.00	0.06	0	0.97	−0.08	0.09	0.76	0.38	−0.06	0.06	0.97	0.33
Nonwhite	0.33	0.18	3.56	0.06	0.73	0.36	4.01	0.05	0.18	0.22	0.67	0.41
Widowed					−1.33	0.62	4.64	0.03	−0.07	0.31	0.04	0.83
Separated or divorced					−0.93	0.42	4.89	0.03	0.38	0.30	1.61	0.20
Respondent high school	−0.47	0.20	5.41	0.02	−0.52	0.37	1.97	0.16	−0.34	0.25	1.86	0.17
Respondent some college	−0.28	0.28	1.03	0.31	−0.93	0.63	2.18	0.14	−0.52	0.30	2.98	0.08
Respondent college or higher	−0.39	0.37	1.11	0.29	−1.64	0.74	4.89	0.03	−0.62	0.55	1.28	0.26
Spouse high school	−0.38	0.20	3.73	0.05								
Spouse some college	−0.25	0.28	0.79	0.38								
Spouse college or higher	−1.44	0.64	5.13	0.02								
Number of children	0.09	0.03	9.6	0.00	0.01	0.07	0.03	0.86	0.02	0.05	0.29	0.59
Longest job uncovered	0.33	0.20	2.72	0.10	0.65	0.39	2.82	0.09	0.34	0.28	1.44	0.23
Respondent health condition	0.00	0.18	0	0.98	0.72	0.34	4.53	0.03	0.65	0.22	8.82	0.00
Spouse health condition	0.36	0.17	4.47	0.03								
Private health insurance	−0.53	0.16	10.44	0.00	−0.16	0.32	0.24	0.62	−0.08	0.22	0.14	0.71
Pension	−1.32	0.24	29.32	0.00	−1.21	0.45	7.29	0.01	−1.34	0.33	16.63	0.00
Home ownership	−1.37	0.18	57.41	0.00	−1.38	0.38	12.97	0.00	−1.32	0.22	36.86	0.00
Number of observations	1,447				197				311			
Log-likelihood	−156.41				−42.83				−96.08			

Source: Authors' calculations.

Note: HRS data are age standardized (see text).

health conditions. The pattern of coefficients is similar for the later (HRS) cohort, though again statistical significance is somewhat less. An exception to this is the loss of any association between coverage by private health insurance and having ANW less than the poverty line among single men and women.

Since our results suggest that the most disadvantaged among the retirees do not fare well, we conduct some further exploration of the predictors of the distribution of well-being among retirees at the time of retirement. We also run quantile regressions for the married sample,[30] and these indicate the influence of a set of explanatory variables on ANW, conditional on the position in the distribution of the dependent variable. The distinct points of the ANW distribution that we use are percentiles 20, 40, 50, 60, and 80.[31] The age of retirement, which was significantly related to ANW for both cohorts, has a greater effect at high levels of ANW for the NBS sample than for the HRS sample (where age has its largest effect over the middle of the ANW distribution).[32] The negative effect of nonwhite on ANW is greater at the top of the ANW distribution for both the early and the later cohorts, although the pattern is somewhat different between the samples. The effect of education on ANW is increasing over the ANW distribution, and is especially large for those with some college and for college graduates.[33] The results for spouse schooling mimic those of the respondent for both samples. The negative influence of respondent health problems is greater for those higher in the ANW distribution, and this also is consistent across samples; the pattern is less clear for spouse health. For both cohorts, the importance of private health insurance in protecting ANW is greatest higher in the distribution of ANW. The composition of ANW in terms of pensions and home ownership appears to be more important for those higher in the distribution of ANW for the early (NBS) cohort, although the general pattern holds for the HRS sample as well. Having more children seems to have a constant effect over the ANW distribution.

Conclusions and Discussion

Our results contribute to the growing literature on the adequacy of resources of older Americans. In particular, we explore how resources have changed for two cohorts that entered retirement, defined by Social Security benefit receipt, nearly two decades apart. The rich data-sets we use permit comprehensive estimates of the wealth individuals bring into retirement, avoiding the need to forecast either wealth accumulation or earnings or the retirement age to which savings may be targeted. With these data-sets we estimate the ANW of all members of our sample, considering the age and life expectancy of the respondent (and spouse, if married). We take into account the effect of increasing life expectancy on retirement security of successive cohorts, and we compare wealth to national standards of basic needs adequacy. The data may not be representative of all current retirees, they do provide a picture of the resources individuals deem adequate as they make a key retirement decision.[34]

We find that only about 4 percent of new retirees in the early cohort have inadequate resources; for the later cohort, about 8 percent of the respondent living units have ANW below the poverty line. This rise in exposure to poverty occurs despite wealth increases of more than 50 percent for the more recent cohort. In both cohorts, more than one-fifth of the sample has ANW less than twice the poverty threshold. Respondents failing to meet these standards are concentrated among those groups with lower levels of human capital, and/or labor force attachment (nonwhites, women, single individuals, those with low education levels, and those who retired at an early age). We also show that failure to meet social adequacy targets is increasingly concentrated among those who fared least well during their working years, with the least human capital and most modest employment patterns. In other words, vulnerability during the work life appears to persist into retirement, and this is particularly true for nonmarried men and women.

Future work can elaborate our findings in more detail, by following HRS respondents into retirement to evaluate whether anticipated saving adequacy proved sufficient. In addition, some argue that including the equity value of owner-occupied housing overstates ANW; alternative estimates can be derived. Finally, the adequacy standards we use reflect national norms of minimal acceptable consumption, but these are crude indicators of retirement resources. Future work can do more by accounting for alternative standards, as well as possible income flows from postretirement employment, intrafamily transfers, and public cash and in-kind benefits.

Acknowledgments

This research was supported by grants from the US Social Security Administration; funding was also received from the Institute for Research on Poverty, the Graduate School, and the Center for Demography and Ecology, all at the University of Wisconsin, Madison.

Notes

[1] Concern with *expost* adequacy of individual wealth holdings at the time of retirement complements that regarding the motivation and pattern of

consumption-savings choices made prior to retirement. This literature includes Modigliani and Brumberg (1954) and Kotlikoff and Summers (1981); more recent contributions include Banks et al. (1998), Bernheim et al. (2001), Hurd and Rohwedder (2003), and Venti and Wise (2000); see also Bloom et al. (2002).

[2] The Congressional Budget Office (2003) provides an extensive review of these studies and a summary of their results.

[3] For several reasons, Wolff's conclusion seems overstated. First, he assumes people aged 47–64 will accrue no additional savings between their current age and the age of their retirement. Second, he assumes that the financial and housing assets that they currently hold will not grow in real value over the years from their current age to the age of retirement. Third, his replacement rate uses 'current' earnings as the denominator.

[4] To incorporate uncertainty of earnings in preretirement years, heterogeneous earnings shocks over the preretirement years are introduced. When this stochastic pattern is recognized, some households who have optimal savings will have wealth-earnings ratios below (above) the median and hence be seen as having inadequate (adequate) savings.

[5] Our NBS sample consists of respondents who were interviewed in both years; we do not require that their spouses survive. We require a 1991 interview since data on earnings and on Social Security and pension benefits are available for many spouses of retired workers only in the later survey. We exclude from our sample individuals who have fewer than ten years of recorded Social Security earnings data after the age of 50. For details on those who attrited see Antonovics et al. (2000).

[6] With the CODA sample added to our sample, the older HRS spouses in the original HRS cohort, approximately age 68–74 when first interview in 1998, now become part of the individual sample.

[7] For a married couple, the first person to be identified determines the timing of 'retirement' for the couple.

[8] Both data-sets have age of benefit receipt. The first interview occurs up to two years after initial benefit receipt in both data-sets. Financial variables are identified as at that age. The NBS sample was truncated at age 72 since at the time of the NBS that was the age at which the earnings test was lifted. We use that same age limit in selecting the HRS sample.

[9] The 1998 cutoff is because the primary purpose of the project from which this paper derives is to track well-being over the years after this retirement point. We have done this in the NBS for the 1982–91 periods (Haveman et al. 2005). Our HRS sample is intended as one that can be followed for a minimum of six years, up to the latest 2004 interview.

[10] This is the case even though we include members of the CODA sample in our analysis. For the CODA sample, we only include those who retired in the two years prior to 1998, the period of observation that is both available and consistent with our selection for the HRS more generally.

[11] Descriptive data are weighted by the HRS weights and by the age-standardizing 'weight'. The standardization adjusts for the differential 'population sampling' of new beneficiaries from the younger HRS sample. In other words, we must observe a lower proportion of retirements at later ages among the HRS cohort because of the

younger age of the original HRS sample. Differential patterns of retirement timing by racial groups or by gender are reflected in the data, but these represent 'true' changes over time in population composition and retirement timing rather than sample selection procedures.

[12] The NBS is fully matched to Social Security Earnings History and Master Beneficiary records. The HRS is also linked to Social Security Administration (SSA) administrative data, but only for respondents who granted permission for the link; we estimate Social Security wealth from reported Social Security benefit amounts for individuals who refused permission.

[13] We use the RAND HRS data file (Version F). See http://hrsonline.isr.umich.edu/ for more information on this file.

[14] Because the NBS does not include an estimate of nonhousing debt, we subtracted the value of nonhousing debt from the HRS financial wealth estimate for consistency. The resulting overstatement of net wealth is modest as older households hold very small amount of nonhousing debt. Gist and Figueiredo (2002) report median 1989 nonhousing debt (in $1998) for those in the lowest quarter of the income distribution of $850, rising to about $2,900 for those in the middle two quartiles and to about $12,000 for those in the top quartile.

[15] We selected this rate for comparability with Smith (1995). The rate used in other studies, including those discussed above, typically ranges between 2.5 and 3.0 percent.

[16] Social Security and pension wealth for married couples is the sum of spousal wealth values. The value of Social Security benefits are estimated conditional on remaining married or being a sole survivor, using Social Security survivorship rules. If a pensioner indicated continuation of benefits to his or her surviving spouse, a joint and two-thirds (67%) survivor benefit is assumed.

[17] This equivalence scale, based on the National Academy of Sciences study of poverty measurement (Citro and Michael 1995), is used to allocate wealth—and achieve equivalent consumption—over the married and widow(er)ed lifetimes of couples.

[18] It is interesting that our annuitized values are remarkably close to the inflation-indexed annuity estimated by the Social Security Office of the Actuary (NASI 2005). The Office estimated a single unisex life annuity of approximately $741 paid to a 65-year old for a $10,000 payment. Our estimates imply on average (across our race and sex groups) a $737 annual annuity for the same payment.

[19] In the HRS, we use a self-reported health (SRH) status variable, and assign a value of 1 to those reporting fair/poor health status. For NBS, those with the four or more limitations on daily living are assigned a value of 1. Note that both samples exclude disabled workers who had received benefits prior to age 62: the NBS does so explicitly and our HRS sample by our selection criteria.

[20] Our estimates of asset values for the NBS and HRS samples tend to be greater than those based on the Survey of Income and Program Participation, but smaller than estimates of asset holdings for households headed by persons aged 62–70 years in the Survey of Consumer Finances (SCF). This latter difference is likely to be due to the higher proportion of older persons in this age range in the SCF, as well as the substantial efforts of the SCF in collecting wealth

data, especially among high-wealth individuals (available from the authors on request).

[21] This is not due to increased early retirement since all descriptive statistics are age standardized. This may still reflect differences in the probability of Social Security eligibility by gender, marital status, and other characteristics.

[22] Given the age of the initial HRS and the shorter period we observe the CODA sample we have a smaller number who retired at 66+ and so we can say less about the relative economic position of older retirees.

[23] This difference is much smaller than the marital status difference in total wealth, a result of both allocating wealth over the remaining lifetime of the longer surviving spouse and accounting for the greater consumption needs of married couples when both spouses are alive.

[24] Because our samples include only new beneficiaries, this age effect is not a measure of the effect of delaying retirement on the economic well-being of early retirees. It only indicates that those who delay retirement have both higher wealth and greater ANW.

[25] The 1965 Older Americans Act stipulates the following objective: 'An adequate income in retirement in accordance with the American standard of living'.

[26] We use the revised poverty lines suggested by the National Research Council study of poverty (Citro and Michael 1995). In 2000, the absolute poverty line for single individuals was $7961 in $2004; for married couples we used the single-person equivalent ANW.

[27] Our bootstrap estimates indicate that this is not wholly a consequence of the smaller HRS sample to test whether the difference between HRS and NBS coefficients and standard errors were attributable to differences in sample size, we simulated NBS bootstrap estimates of standard errors for an NBS sample of a size comparable to the HRS. Using this smaller NBS sample yields standard errors approximately double those in the original NBS regressions, but only about one-half of the standard errors in the HRS regressions. The higher variance of the dependent variable (ANW) in the HRS relative to the NBS could account for the remainder of the difference.

[28] The NBS asks directly about longest job coverage. The HRS asks if the respondent ever worked in an uncovered job.

[29] Note indicates the effect of marital status among single individuals at the time they retire and does not describe the effect of becoming widowed or divorced compared to being married.

[30] See Buchinsky (1998).

[31] Full results are available on request from the authors.

[32] This difference in samples may be tied to the slightly different sample structure of the two data-sets.

[33] For the earlier HRS cohort, this pattern is pronounced for college graduates only.

[34] Virtually all US citizens become new Social Security beneficiaries at some age. For some, that age may reflect retirement-age adjustments in response to the adequacy of savings; for others unexpected events may lead to unexpectedly early retirement.

Appendix

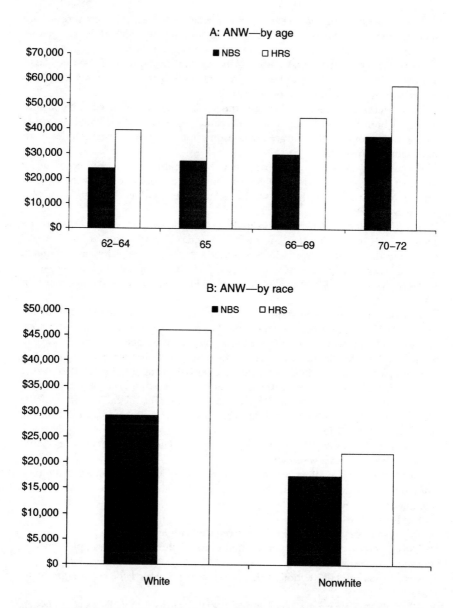

Figure 3-A1. Levels of ANW by socioeconomic group. (*Source*: Authors' calculations.)

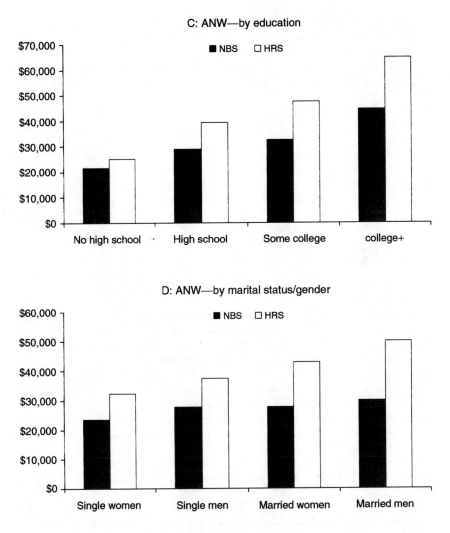

Figure 3-A1. (*continued*)

References

Antonovics, K., Haveman, R., Holden, K., and Wolfe, B. (2000). 'Attrition in the National Beneficiary Survey and Follow-Up, and Its Correlates', *Social Security Bulletin*, 1(1): 1–7.

Banks, J., Blundell, R., and Tanner, S. (1998). 'Is There a Retirement-Savings Puzzle?', *American Economic Review*, 88(4): 769–88.

Bernheim, B. D. (1997). 'The Adequacy of Personal Retirement Saving: Issues and Options', in D. A. Wise (ed.), *Facing the Age Wave*, Publication No. 440. Stanford, CA: Hoover Institution Press, pp. 30–56.

—— Skinner, J., and Weinberg, S. (2001). 'What Accounts for the Variation in Retirement Wealth among U.S. Households?', *American Economic Review*, 91(4): 832–57.

Bloom, D., Canning, D., and Graham, B. (2002). 'Longevity and Life Cycle Savings', NBER Working Paper No. 8808. Cambridge, MA: National Bureau of Economic Research.

Buchinsky, M. (1998). 'Recent Advances in Quantile Regression Models: A Practical Guideline for Empirical Research', *Journal of Human Resources*, 33: 88–126.

Butrica, B. A., Smith, K. E., and Iams, H. (this volume). 'It's All Relative: Understanding the Retirement Prospects of Baby-Boomers'.

Citro, C. and Michael, R. (1995). *Measuring Poverty: A New Approach*. Washington, DC: National Academy Press.

Congressional Budget Office (2003). *Baby Boomers' Retirement Prospects: An Overview*. Washington, DC: USGPO, November.

Delorme, L., Munnell, A. H., and Webb, A. (2006). 'Empirical Regularity Suggests Retirement Risks', *Issue in Brief*, No 41. Chestnut Hill, MA: Center for Retirement Research at Boston College.

Engen, E. M., Gale, W. G., and Uccello, C. E. (1999). 'The Adequacy of Household Saving', *Brookings Papers on Economic Activity*, 2: 65–187.

Gist, J. and Figueiredo, C. (2002). *Deeper in Debt: Trends among Midlife and Older Americans*. Research Report. Washington, DC: AARP Public Policy Institute.

Gustman, A. L. and Steinmeier, T. L. (1998). 'Effects of Pensions on Saving: Analysis with Data from the Health and Retirement Study', NBER Working Paper No. 6681, Cambridge, MA: National Bureau of Economic Research.

Haveman, R., Holden, K., Wolfe, B., and Romanov, A. (2005). 'Assessing the Maintenance of Savings Sufficiency over the First Decade of Retirement', CESinfo Working Paper, Munich, DE.

—— —— —— and Sherlund, S. (2006). 'Do Newly Retired Workers in the U.S. Have Sufficient Resources to Maintain Well-Being?', *Economic Inquiry*, 44(2): 249–64.

Hurd, M. and Rohwedder, S. (2003). 'The Retirement–Consumption Puzzle: Anticipated and Actual Declines in Spending at Retirement', NBER Working Paper No. 9586, Cambridge, MA: National Bureau of Economic Research.

Kotlikoff, L. J. and Summers, L. (1981). 'The Role of Intergenerational Transfers in Aggregate Capital Accumulation', *Journal of Political Economy*, 89(4): 706–32.

Mitchell, O., Moore, J., and Phillips, J. (2000). 'Explaining Retirement Saving Shortfalls', in O. S. Mitchell, B. Hammond, and A. Rappaport (eds.), *Forecasting Retirement Needs and Retirement Wealth*. Philadelphia, PA: University of Pennsylvania Press, pp. 139–66.

Modigliani, F. and Brumberg, R. (1954). 'Utility Analysis and the Consumption Function: An Interpretation of Cross-section Data', in K. K. Kurihara (ed.), *Post-Keynesian Economics*. New Brunswick, NJ: Rutgers University Press: 128–97.

Montalto, C. P. (2001). 'Retirement Wealth and Its Adequacy: Assessing the Impact of Changes in the Age of Eligibility for Full Social Security Benefits', Working Paper 2001–07, Chestnut Hill, MA: Center for Retirement Research at Boston College, September.

Moore, J. and Mitchell, O. S. (2000). 'Projected Retirement Wealth and Saving Adequacy', in O. S. Mitchell, P. B. Hammond, and A. Rappaport (eds.), *Forecasting Retirement Needs and Retirement Wealth.* Philadelphia, PA: University of Pennsylvania Press, pp. 68–94.

Munnell, A. H. and Soto, M. (2005*a*). 'How Much Pre-Retirement Income Does Social Security Replace?', *Issue in Brief*, No 35. Chestnut Hill, MA: Center for Retirement Research at Boston College.

—— —— (2005*b*). 'How Do Pensions Affect Replacement Rates?', *Issue in Brief,* No 37. Chestnut Hill, MA: Center for Retirement Research at Boston College.

—— —— (2005*c*). 'The House and Living Standards in Retirement', *Issue in Brief,* No 39. Chestnut Hill, MA: Center for Retirement Research at Boston College.

National Academy on Social Insurance (NASI). (2005). *Unchartered Waters.* Washington, DC: NASI.

Scholz, J. K., Sheshadri, A., and Khitatrakun, S. (2005). 'Are Americans Saving "Optimally" for Retirement?', *Journal of Political Economy,* (December): 607–43.

Smith, J. P. (1995). 'Racial and Ethnic Differences in Wealth in the Health and Retirement Study', *Journal of Human Resources,* 30(Supplement): S158–83.

U.S. Department of Health and Human Services, Public Health Service, National Center for Health Statistics (1985). *Vital Statistics of the United States, 1982.* Life Tables Volume 11, Section 6. Hyattsville, MD.

—— (1997). *U.S. Decennial Life Tables for 1989–91.* Volume 1, Number 1. Hyattsville, MD.

Venti, S. and Wise, D. (2000). 'Choice, Chance, and Wealth Dispersion at Retirement', NBER Working Paper No. 7521, Cambridge, MA: National Bureau of Economic Research.

Wolff, E. N. (2002). *Retirement Insecurity: The Income Shortfalls Awaiting the Soon-to-Retire.* Washington, DC: Economic Policy Institute.

—— (2004). 'Changes in Household Wealth in the 1080s and 1990s in the U.S.', Levy Institute Working Paper No. 407.

Ycas, M. A. (1992). 'The New Beneficiary Data System: The First Phase', *Social Security Bulletin,* 55(2): 20–35.

Chapter 4

Understanding Baby Boomers' Retirement Prospects

Barbara A. Butrica, Howard M. Iams, and Karen E. Smith

The economic well-being of future retirees in the Baby Boom cohort—the 76 million people born 1946–64—is of concern to many policymakers, particularly those concerned with the US Social Security system (Board of Trustees 2006). Yet relatively little is known about how this birth cohort will fare in retirement. This chapter compares the US Baby Boom cohort with previous generations along several dimensions, focusing specifically on the level, distribution, and composition of expected retirement income, and also on the adequacy of this income in maintaining their economic well-being.

An analysis of the retirement security of future generations requires techniques to simulate the aging of a population into the future (cf. Butrica, Iams, and Smith 2003). Accordingly, we rely on the Social Security's Model of Income in the Near Term (MINT), a micro simulation model that projects lifetime demographics and labor force activity, and ultimately retirement incomes, for a representative group of individuals born between 1926 and 1965.[1] Using MINT, we assess the distribution of individual outcomes for retirement, the 'notable advantage' of micro simulation models (Burtless 1996: 255). In so doing, we begin with background information on some of the salient historic trends likely to influence the demographic characteristics and well-being of the future retired population. Next, we discuss previous research, followed by a discussion of methodology for projecting retirement incomes. Our results focus on characteristics of current and future retirees, their projected family incomes and poverty rates, and their relative incomes and replacement rates.

Cohort Patterns Over Time

Baby Boomers grew up in a very different social and economic environment from that experienced by current retirees, as it was marked by changes in marriage patterns, earnings and work patterns, retirement policy, and economic fluctuations. Boomers have been more likely to never marry and divorce; women were more likely to work for pay and to have higher earnings when they did. These developments will translate into different Social Security benefits, as these are programmatically linked to marital and earnings histories, and to corporate pension benefits as well. Of course, the retirement income system has also changed in the last twenty years, with the erosion of defined benefit (DB) plans and the emergence of defined contribution (DC) plans, particularly 401(k) s and IRAs. As a result, Boomers will be less likely to have DB pensions and more likely to have contributed to DC plans or IRAs over their working careers, as compared to earlier cohorts. Boomers also face different Social Security regimes, compared to their parents. Currently, many retirees took 'full' or unreduced benefits at age 65, but the age for full benefits is rising to age 67 over time. Finally, compared to previous birth cohorts, Boomers have become accustomed to economic prosperity where real earnings have grown about 2–3 percent per year between 1947 and 1973, less from the mid-1970s to the early 1990s, and then again averaging 2.7 percent per year from 1995 to 2000 (Levy and Murnane 1992; Levy 1998; United States Board of Trustees 2006).

Previous studies have attempted to determine how these factors have influenced Boomers' prospects for retirement. Many of these have focused on the already retired or those on the verge of retirement, rather than Boomers per se (Gustman and Steinmeier 1999; Moore and Mitchell 2000; Haveman et al. 2003). Others compared Boomers in middle age with the situation of their parents at the same age (Easterlin et al. 1990, 1993; Sabelhaus and Manchester 1995). In other words, those studies ask whether Boomers are *on track* to an affordable retirement, but they do not actually analyze their expected retirement incomes. In some related work, Wolff (2002) does project expected retirement income for households with some Boomers; nevertheless, he potentially understates economic well-being at retirement as he excludes several key income sources. These include additional saving from the survey date to retirement, postretirement earnings, and income received from transfer programs (such as SSI, the means-tested Supplemental Security Income program). Work by Munnell et al. (2006) also excludes postretirement earnings from their measures of Boomer income at older ages. This flies in the face of recent evidence indicating that many adults age 65+ continue to work and earn (Butrica et al. 2006). Additionally, Munnell et al. presume that Boomers' lifetime earnings will replicate the age-earnings profiles of persons born much earlier (1931–41). This assumption likely underestimates women's lifetime earnings, as well as their earned pensions and Social Security benefits, since lifetime earnings are quite different for Boomer women than for those born in the Depression (Goldin 1990).

Methodology

Our analysis addresses the shortcomings of prior studies because we project the economic well-being of the entire Baby Boom cohort (born 1946–64) in retirement, using a comprehensive measure of retirement resources. This allows us to more accurately measure total income at retirement, to examine how each component's share of income changes over time, and to assess the adequacy of retirement resources. In particular, we project retirement income sources using a micro simulation model which takes into account many of the structural changes expected to impact the aged population.

The work draws on projections of the major sources of retirement income from the Social Security Administration's (SSA) (MINT).[2] MINT starts with data from the 1990–93 US Census Bureau's Survey of Income and Program Participation (SIPP), matched to the SSA's earnings and benefit records through the year 2000. For persons born 1926–65, MINT independently projects each person's marital changes, mortality, entry to and exit from Social Security disability insurance (DI) rolls, and age of first receipt of Social Security retirement benefits. It also projects family income to include Social Security benefits, pension income, asset income, earnings, SSI benefits, income from no spouse coresident family members, and imputed rental income.[3] This definition of income differs slightly from that used by other researchers in this volume, due to differences in data sources available to us.

MINT is ideal for this analysis because it directly measures the experiences of survey respondents as of the early 1990s—representing the first third to the first half of the lives of the Boomer cohort—and it statistically projects their income and characteristics into the future, adjusting for expected demographic and socioeconomic changes. The model also accounts for the growth of economywide real earnings, the distribution of earnings between and within birth cohorts, and the composition of the retiree population.[4]

Distinct from other researchers in this volume, we separate our analyses into ten-year birth cohorts representing current retirees (born 1926–35), near retirees (1936–45), leading Boomers (born 1946–55), and trailing Boomers (1956–65).[5] We analyze the characteristics and family income of individuals born in these cohorts when they reach age 67 (the age by which most people will have retired). We also test whether the differences between Baby Boomer retirees and current retirees are statistically significant. Because our sample sizes are large (over 100,000 records), we highlight results only where differences are not statistically significant. All reported income projections are in $2004.

Characteristics of Current and Future Retirees

Characteristics of projected retirees in each of the ten-year cohorts arepresented in Table 4-1, where it is clear that shifts in the marital status across generations are expected, reflecting the historical marriage trends discussed earlier. Just over one in four current retirees is nonmarried, compared with about one in three Boomers. Not only will the share of nonmarried retirees increase for the Baby Boom cohorts, but their composition will also change dramatically. All Boomer retirees are more

TABLE 4-1 Projected Characteristics of Individuals at Age 67

	Current Retirees (1926–35)	Near Retirees (1936–45)	Leading Boomers (1946–55)	Trailing Boomers (1956–65)
Total	100%	100%	100%	100%
Sex and marital status				
Female: never married	2	3	3	4
Female: married	33	32	31	30
Female: widowed	13	10	8	9
Female: divorced	6	9	10	10
Male: never married	2	2*	2	3
Male: married	38	36	36	34
Male: widowed	2	2*	2*	2*
Male: divorced	4	6	7	7
Race/ethnicity				
Non-Hispanic white	82	79	76	72
Non-Hispanic black	8	8*	9	10
Hispanic	7	8	9	12
Asian and Native American	4	5*	6*	7*
Education				
High school dropout	28	19	11	12
High school graduate	54	58	58	60
College graduate	18	24	31	28
Mean values				
Years in the labor force	26	29	32	32
Shared lifetime earnings ($2004)	24,000	33,000	42,000	46,000

*Indicates not significantly different (p < .01) from current retirees.

Source: Authors' computations of MINT3 (see text for details).

Notes: Shared lifetime earnings is the average of wage-indexed shared earnings between ages 22 and 62, where shared earnings are computed by assigning each individual half the total earnings of the couple in the years when the individual is married and his or her own earnings in years when unmarried.

likely than current retirees to never marry or to be divorced, and women in the Baby Boom generation are less likely than current retirees to be widowed.

The differences between men and women are pronounced. Nonmarried men will represent 17 percent of all men in the current retiree population $[= (2+2+4)/(2+38+2+4)]$ but 22 percent of those in the near retiree population, 23 percent of leading Boomers, and 26 percent of trailing Boomers. While the compositional change between cohorts is much smaller for women, their numbers are much higher: 39 percent of current retirees, 41 percent of near retirees, 40 percent of leading Boomers, and 43 percent of trailing Boomers are projected to be nonmarried at retirement. This is important since among current retirees age 65 or older, the never married have the highest poverty rates, followed by the divorced, widowed, and married. In addition, within marital groups, female poverty rates are significantly higher than for males (Koenig 2002). Since women are more likely than men to be non-married in retirement, and this proportion is projected to increase for Baby Boomers, a larger share of the future retiree population will face the risk of poverty.

The racial and educational composition of retirees will also change. Boomer retirees are significantly more likely than current retirees to be Black and Hispanic; for instance, about one-in-six current retirees are in a racial/ethnic minority, compared with one-in-four Boomer retirees. The shift in minority group representation is also expected to influence the retirement income and economic well-being of future retirees, since among current retirees age 65+, Blacks are 2.5 times more likely to be poor, and Hispanics are about twice as likely to be poor as whites (Koenig 2002). Boomer retirees are about 1.5 times more likely than current retirees to be college educated, and about half as likely to be high school dropouts. Nevertheless, the educational gains between current retirees and leading Boomers dissipate somewhat for trailing Boomers; that is, fewer trailing Boomer retirees will have completed college than leading Boomer retirees.

These projections also indicate rising labor force experience across cohorts, from an average of twenty-six years among current retirees, to twenty-nine years among near retirees, and thirty-two years among Boomers.[6] Increased time spent in the labor force, in turn, leads to higher average lifetime earnings among Baby Boomers. Our measure of 'shared' lifetime earnings is the average of wage-indexed 'shared' earnings between ages 22 and 62, where 'shared' earnings are computed by assigning each individual in a couple half the total earnings of the couple in the years when the individual is married, and his or her own earnings in years when nonmarried. We find that shared lifetime earnings are projected to increase with each successive cohort, though at a decreasing rate.

Absolute Measures of Well-Being

Next we compare the economic well-being of current and future retirees using two absolute well-being measures: family income and poverty. Poverty is an absolute concept because in the United States, individuals are considered poor if they have family incomes below an absolute minimum level— the official poverty thresholds of the US census bureau.[7]

Projected Income

Average family income per person is projected to be higher for future retirees than for current retirees. It is worth noting that much of this difference is attributable to large increases in family income between the first three ten-year cohorts (see Table 4-2). That is, comparing current and near retirees, average annual income per person increases 21 percent (from $30,000 to $36,000). Between near retirees and leading Boomers, average income is projected to increase another 26 percent (from $36,000 to $46,000). Finally, between leading and trailing Boomers, average income is again projected to increase but by only 9 percent (from $46,000 to $49,000).[8]

Both earnings and income inequality will likely be higher for Baby Boomer retirees than for current retirees. Thus average income per person at the top of the earnings and income distribution is growing faster than income at the bottom of the distribution. For current retirees, family income in the fifth quintile of the shared lifetime earnings distribution is about three times higher than that in the first quintile. For Baby Boomers, this is projected to increase to more than four times higher. Among current retirees, family income in the fifth quintile of the income distribution is about eight times higher than that in the first quintile; for Boomers, this is projected to increase to ten times higher.[9] Average family income per person is highest for men, those who are widowed, non-Hispanic whites, those who are college educated, those with more work experience, and those with earnings and income in the highest quintile, if we focus on current retirees. These patterns will also hold for future retirees, according to the projections, except that never married Baby Boomer women will have higher incomes than widows.

Our projections also show that most retirees can anticipate income from several sources, including from assets, earnings, SSI benefits, imputed rental income, and coresident income (Table 4-3). Among current retirees, 90 percent have asset income, 29 percent have own earnings, 23 percent have spouse earnings, 5 percent have own SSI benefits, 1 percent have spouse SSI benefits, 80 percent have imputed rent, and 17 percent have coresident income. The prevalence of asset income, earnings, and imputed

TABLE 4-2 Mean Family Income per Person at Age 67 (in thousands, $2004)

	Current Retirees (1926–35)	Near Retirees (1936–45)	Leading Boomers (1946–55)	Trailing Boomers (1956–65)
Total	$30	$36	$46	$49
Sex and marital status				
Female: never married	27	36	49	53
Female: married	28	34	43	47
Female: widowed	32	38	46	48
Female: divorced	28	36	43	47
Male: never married	30	36	44	53
Male: married	29	35	45	48
Male: widowed	39	51	61	68
Male: divorced	38	48	53	62
Race/ethnicity				
Non-Hispanic white	31	38	49	53
Non-Hispanic black	24	27	33	37
Hispanic	21	27	32	35
Asian and Native American	28	35	43	54
Education				
High school dropout	20	24	24	27
High school graduate	29	33	38	40
College graduate	47	54	68	80
Labor force experience				
Less than 20 years	26	27	28	30
20–29 years	29	35	36	38
30 or more year	32	40	51	55
Shared lifetime earnings				
1st quintile	17	20	21	23
2nd quintile	23	27	29	31
3rd quintile	27	33	38	39
4th quintile	31	40	51	52
5th quintile	50	61	88	102
Income quintile				
1st quintile	8	10	12	12
2nd quintile	16	20	23	23
3rd quintile	23	29	34	35
4th quintile	33	42	51	54
5th quintile	67	81	108	122

Note: See Table 4-1.

TABLE 4-3 Percent of Individuals with Family Income at Age 67, by Source

	Current Retirees (1926–35)	Near Retirees (1936–45)	Leading Boomers (1946–55)	Trailing Boomers (1956–65)
Total income	100%	100%	100%	100%
Nonretirement income	98	99	99	99
Income from assets	90	91	93	94
Earnings	29	31	33	33
Spouse earnings	23	25	26	26
SSI benefits	5	3	2	2
Spouse SSI benefits	1	1	1	1
Imputed rental income	80	82	85	84
Co resident income	17	16	14	14
Retirement income	95	95*	96	97
Social security benefits	88	92	93	94
Spouse social security benefits	53	53*	52*	49
DB pension benefits	38	31	31	29
Spouse DB pension benefits	23	21	20	17
Retirement accounts	38	43	45	46
Spouse retirement accounts	24	29	29	28

Note: See Table 4-1.

*Indicates not significantly different (p < .01) from current retirees.

rental income is projected to rise for the Baby Boom cohort, while a smaller percent is projected to have SSI benefits and coresident income.

Nearly all retirees will also receive income from retirement income sources, that is Social Security benefits, DB pension benefits, and income from retirement accounts (i.e. DC pensions, and IRA and Keogh plans). Among current retirees, 88 percent will collect own Social Security benefits, 53 percent have spouse Social Security benefits, 38 percent have own DB pension income, 23 percent have spouse DB pension income, 38 percent have own retirement account income, and 24 percent have spouse retirement account income. Reflecting the shift in employer pensions from DB to DC, retirees with retirement accounts are projected to increase and those with DB pensions are projected to fall for Boomers. The share with own Social Security benefits is projected to increase across all cohorts, while the share with spousal benefits will decrease among only the trailing Boomers. The share of retirees with any Social Security benefits is projected to increase from 91 percent among current retirees to 94 percent among Boomers.

Table 4-4 shows each income source's contribution to average family income per person and how these vary by cohort. The top half of the table

TABLE 4-4 Family Income per Person at Age 67, by Source

	Current Retirees (1926–35)	Near Retirees (1936–45)	Leading Boomers (1946–55)	Trailing Boomers (1956–65)
A. Mean family income per person at age 67 (in thousands, $2004)				
Total income	$30	$36	$46	$49
Nonretirement income	16	20	25	28
Income from assets	4	6	9	10
Earnings	4	4	6	6
Spouse earnings	3	3*	4	5
SSI benefits	0	0	0	0
Spouse SSI benefits	0	0	0	0
Imputed rental income	2	2	3	3
Coresident income	3	4	3	4
Retirement income	14	16	20	22
Social security benefits	6	8	9	10
Spouse social security benefits	3	3	4	4
DB pension benefits	3	2	3	3
Spouse DB pension benefits	2	1	1*	1
Retirement accounts	1	1	2	3
Spouse retirement accounts	0	1	1	1
B. Share of mean family income per person at age 67				
Total income	100%	100%	100%	100%
Nonretirement income	53	55	55	56
Income from assets	14	17	19	20
Earnings	12	12	13	13
Spouse earnings	10	9*	9	10
SSI benefits	0	0	0	0
Spouse SSI benefits	0	0	0	0
Imputed rental income	6	6	6	5
Coresident income	10	10	8	8
Retirement income	47	45	45	44
SS benefits	19	21	20	20
Spouse SS benefits	9	9	8	7
DB pension benefits	11	7	6	6
Spouse DB pension benefits	5	4	3*	3
Retirement accounts	2	3	5	6
Spouse retirement accounts	1	2	2	2

Note: See Table 4-3.

shows average income by source, and the bottom half presents the share of income held by each source. Focusing first on current retirees, some $16,000 (53 % of family income comes from nonretirement income, including $4,000 from asset income (14%), $7,000 from own and spouse earnings

(22%), $2,000 from imputed rental income (6 percent), and $3,000 from coresident income (10%). Own and spouse SSI benefits account for less than $1,000 and less than 1 percent of family income. The remaining $14,000 (47%) of family income is derived from retirement income. Own and spousal Social Security benefits averaging $9,000 make up the bulk of retirement income and constitute 28 percent of family income. The DB pension benefits and retirement accounts average $5,000 and $1,000, respectively, or 16 and 3 percent of family income. Looking ahead, however, there will be an increasing importance of asset income. This is evident in that asset income represents 14 percent of average family income per person for current retirees, 17 percent for near retirees, 19 percent for leading Boomers, and 20 percent for trailing Boomers. The relative role of family earnings, family SSI benefits, and imputed rental income remains fairly constant across cohorts, while the importance of coresident income decreases slightly from 10 percent among current retirees to 8 percent among Boomers.

The declining role of DB pension benefits is clear, in that this income source makes up 16 percent of average family income per person for current retirees, and only 9 percent of average family income per person for trailing Boomers. Although the contribution of retirement accounts to family income nearly triples between cohorts (from 3% among current retirees to 8% among trailing Boomers), the growth is not large enough to completely offset the decreased importance of DB pension benefits.[10] The significance of Social Security benefits, on the other hand, remains largely unchanged across cohorts.

Projected Poverty

These projected rises in real incomes over time will reduce poverty rates for most future retirees (Table 4-5). As with increases in income, declines in poverty rates are projected to occur largely between the first three ten-year cohorts. Eight percent of current retirees are expected to be poor at age 67, compared with 6 percent of near retirees, and 4 percent of Boomers. This halving of the poverty rate is largely the effect of rising real earnings, translating into higher real Social Security benefits, and other retirement income.

While most demographic and economic subgroups will experience declines in poverty rates over time, Boomers with weak labor force attachment are projected to have higher poverty rates than current retirees. Among Boomers, poverty rates will be highest for never-married men and women, Hispanics, high school dropouts, those with weak labor force attachments, and those with shared lifetime earnings in the lowest quintiles.

TABLE 4-5 Percent of Individuals in Poverty at Age 67

	Current Retirees (1926–35)	Near Retirees (1936–45)	Leading Boomers (1946–55)	Trailing Boomers (1956–65)
Total	8%	6%	4%	4%
Sex and marital status				
Female: never married	25	21*	11	10
Female: married	6	3	2	2
Female: widowed	10	9*	7	6
Female: divorced	21	13	10	9
Male: never married	18	13*	15*	10
Male: married	5	3	3	3
Male: widowed	11	7	6	6
Male: divorced	12	6	6	5
Race/ethnicity				
Non-Hispanic white	6	4	3	3
Non-Hispanic black	14	10	8	8
Hispanic	20	15	12	9
Asian and native American	23	11	8	7
Education				
High school dropout	17	15*	16*	14
High school graduate	5	4	4	4
College graduate	3	2*	1	2
Labor force experience				
Less than 20 years	17	18	22	23
20–29 years	8	5	5	5
30 or more years	2	1	1	1
Shared lifetime earnings				
1st quintile	31	25	21	20
2nd quintile	7	3	1	1
3rd quintile	2	1	0	0
4th quintile	1	0	0	0
5th quintile	0	0	0	0

Note: See Tables 4-1 and 4-3.

In contrast, poverty rates are lowest for married men and women, non-Hispanic whites, those with college educations, those with many years of work experience, and those with shared lifetime earnings in the highest quintiles.

Relative Measures of Well-Being

While Boomer retirees are projected to enjoy higher incomes and lower poverty rates than current retirees, we next ask whether Baby Boomer retirees will be *relatively* better off than current retirees. More precisely, we are interested whether Boomers will maintain their relative economic position in retirement, relative to others in their birth cohort and relative to their own pre-retirement standard of living. To do this we examine their relative family incomes and replacement rates.

Projected Relative Incomes

Although average family income per person is projected to increase across cohorts for all subgroups, not all Boomers will be as well-off. To illustrate the relative economic well-being of various subgroups, we next present the ratio of average income in a subgroup to average income of the entire cohort (see Table 4-6). This gauge of retirement security shows that many Boomers will have lower relative incomes than current retirees. The specific groups in question are widowed women, high school dropouts and graduates, those with less than thirty years of work experience, and those with earnings and income in the lowest quintiles.

As an illustration, a high school dropout who is currently retired has family income per person only 68 percent of the overall average. For leading Boomers, the comparable statistic is only 53 percent, and 55 percent for trailing Boomers. This is because average income is slated to rise by 52 percent over the period, but average income for high school dropouts rises by less, only 20 percent. So even though Boomer high school dropouts have higher family incomes than current retirees, they are relatively worse off compared with others in their cohort. Other subgroups are expected to be relatively better off. For instance, Boomer widowed men, non-Hispanic whites, those with strong labor force attachments, and those with earnings and income in the highest quintiles will have higher relative incomes than do current retirees. Never-married Boomer women will also have higher relative incomes than current retirees. For these women, the growth in average family income per person between current retirees and Baby Boomers (78% for the leading and 89% for the trailing Boomers) far exceeds the growth in overall average income across the generations (66%).

Projected Replacement Rates

Replacement rates are useful in informing us about retirement well-being relative to well-being during preretirement years. Our replacement rates are computed as the ratio of average family income per person at age 67, to average shared earnings between ages 22 and 62.[11] Not surprisingly, most retirees are not likely to have as much income during retirement as during the working years (Table 4-7). For current retirees, the median replacement rate stands at about 93 percent; replacement rates are anticipated to

TABLE 4-6 Ratio of Subgroup Income to Cohort Mean Family Income at Age 67

	Current Retirees (1926–35)	Near Retirees (1936–45)	Leading Boomers (1946–55)	Trailing Boomers (1956–65)
Total	100%	100%	100%	100%
Sex and marital status				
Female: never married	92	99	108	107
Female: married	94	94	95	95
Female: widowed	110	105	102	98
Female: divorced	94	98	94	96
Male: never married	102	100	98	107
Male: married	98	97	100	97
Male: widowed	132	142	134	138
Male: divorced	128	131	116	125
Race/ethnicity				
Non-Hispanic white	104	105	107	108
Non-Hispanic black	80	75	73	74
Hispanic	72	75	70	71
Asian and native American	96	96	96	109
Education				
High school dropout	68	65	53	55
High school graduate	97	91	83	81
College graduate	160	149	149	162
Labor force experience				
Less than 20 years	87	75	62	60
20–29 years	98	98	79	76
30 or more years	110	110	112	112
Shared lifetime earnings				
1st quintile	59	55	46	47
2nd quintile	77	74	65	62
3rd quintile	90	91	84	79
4th quintile	105	111	111	106
5th quintile	169	169	194	206
Income quintile				
1st quintile	29	28	26	24
2nd quintile	55	54	51	47
3rd quintile	79	79	75	71
4th quintile	111	115	112	109
5th quintile	226	224	238	248

Notes: See Table 4-1. This statistic is the ratio of mean income in a subgroup to mean income of the entire cohort.

TABLE 4-7 Median Replacement Rates at Age 67

	Current Retirees (1926–35)	Near Retirees (1936–45)	Leading Boomers (1946–55)	Trailing Boomers (1956–65)
Total	93%	82%	81%	81%
Sex and marital status				
Female: never married	114	96	85	85
Female: married	92	84	80	79
Female: widowed	105	89	89	90
Female: divorced	87	76	72	75
Male: never married	97	79	81	78
Male: married	90	78	80	81
Male: widowed	109	94	97	102
Male: divorced	88	83	80	80
Race/ethnicity				
Non-Hispanic white	91	81	80	80
Non-Hispanic black	97	76	74	78
Hispanic	92	91*	86	87
Asian and native American	90	83	78	85
Education				
High school dropout	86	86*	93	97
High school graduate	92	79	77	78
College graduate	114	88	85	84
Labor force experience				
Less than 20 years	115	113	120	122
20–29 years	99	87	81	86
30 or more years	84	75	77	76
Shared lifetime earnings				
1st quintile	178	136	115	117
2nd quintile	97	82	77	78
3rd quintile	85	76	74	73
4th quintile	81	74	75	73
5th quintile	83	72	78	79
Income quintile				
1st quintile	66	63	64	63
2nd quintile	73	65	63	65
3rd quintile	84	75	74	75
4th quintile	106	94	91	94
5th quintile	146	126	128	124

*Indicates not significantly different (p < .01) from current retirees.

Notes: See Tables 4-1 and 4-3. Replacement rates refer to ratio of income at age 67 to shared lifetime earnings; income includes SS and DB pension benefits, annuitized income from nonpension, nonhousing assets and retirement accounts, earnings, and SSI income. It excludes coresident and imputed rental income. Median is measured as the mean value between the 45th and 55th percentiles of the distribution.

decrease to 81 percent for future retirees. Indeed, except for high school dropouts and those with less than twenty years of work experience, we find that all subgroups of Baby Boomers will have lower replacement rates than current retirees.

To disaggregate the results somewhat, we find that replacement rates for current retirees are highest for never-married women, widowed men, non-Hispanic blacks, college graduates, those with weak labor force attachment, those in the lowest quintiles of shared lifetime earnings, and those in the highest quintile of total income. Replacement rates are lowest for divorced men and women, non-Hispanic whites, Asians, and Native Americans, high school dropouts, those with many years of work experience, those in the highest quintile of shared lifetime earnings, and those in the lowest quintile of total income. Because of the Social Security progressive payment formula, individuals with low earnings typically have relatively higher replacement rates and those with high earnings typically have relatively lower replacement rates. Looking ahead, therefore, the same patterns will generally hold across all cohorts of retirees, except Boomers will have higher replacement rates for widowed women, Hispanics, and high school dropouts, and lower ones for never married men, non-Hispanic blacks, and high school graduates. Family income replaces less than 25 percent of shared lifetime earnings for 2 percent of current retirees, less than 50 percent of shared lifetime earnings for 12 percent of current retirees, less than 75 percent of shared lifetime earnings for 35 percent of current retirees, and less than 100% of shared lifetime earnings for 55 percent of current retirees (Table 4-8). In other words, only 45 percent (100% − 55% of current retirees will have higher average family incomes at age 67 than average shared earnings between ages 22 and 62. About 15 percent (100% − 85%) of current retirees will have average family incomes at age 67 that are at least twice as high as their average shared earnings between

TABLE 4-8 Percent of Individuals at Age 67, by Replacement Rate

Replacement Rate (%)	Current Retirees (1926–35)	Near Retirees (1936–45)	Leading Boomers (1946–55)	Trailing Boomers (1956–65)
<25	2%	2%*	2%*	2%*
<50	12	17	17	17
<75	35	44	45	44
<100	55	63	65	64
<200	85	89	91	91

*Indicates not significantly different (p < .01) from current retirees.
Note. See Tables 4-1 and 4-3.

ages 22 and 62. Boomers will be less likely than current retirees to have enough income to maintain their preretirement living standards. That is, only 35–36 percent of Boomer retirees will have more than enough income at age 67 to maintain their preretirement standard of living. Further, only about 9 percent of Boomer retirees will have average family income at age 67 that is at least twice as high as their average shared earnings between ages 22 and 62.

Conclusions

Many recent analyses predict that future cohorts and Baby Boomer retirees, in particular, confront a markedly unattractive retirement period. Munnell et al. (2006) project that 43 percent of current retirees will have inadequate retirement income even if they retire at age 65 and exhaust all their assets. Wolff (2002) also projects that future retirees face a future with markedly less household income. These prophets of gloom receive a great deal of attention in the popular press. By contrast, our analysis is more nuanced and more balanced. We suggest that Baby Boomers can expect to have higher incomes in retirement than current retirees. As a result, Boomer poverty rates are projected to be much lower than for current retirees. Thus using *absolute* measures of well-being, Boomer retirees will be better off than current retirees.

The story is rather different when we use *relative* well-being measures, because the gains in family income across cohorts are not equally distributed. Many Baby Boom retirees will be worse off than their peers, compared to earlier cohorts, and we anticipate that some subgroups will do better than others. Women's career earnings will rise over time, though their improved earnings often offset rather than add to the couple's Social Security benefit because of the spouse benefit and progressive payment formula in Social Security. Incomes for never-married women will rise by much more than incomes for the overall population, but incomes for high school dropouts will rise much less than the overall population. As a result, never-married Boomer women will be relatively better off, and high school Boomer dropouts will be relatively worse, than current retirees. We also find that many Baby Boomer retirees will be worse off than current retirees, when we compare their relative position—their income versus their own preretirement living standards. This is because postretirement incomes are not predicted to rise as much as preretirement incomes. In particular, Social Security benefits, DB pensions, and retirement accounts are expected to contribute less to Boomers' retirement income than they do for current retirees. Income from DC pensions, IRAs, and Keogh plans will comprise a larger share of family income for future retirees than for current retirees; their increased importance is not projected to offset the falling importance of DB pensions. Regardless of the measure of well-being, certain Baby Boomer subgroups will remain economically vulnerable, including divorced women, never-married men, Hispanics, high school dropouts, those with weak labor force attachments, and those with the lowest lifetime earnings. While these economically vulnerable subgroups typically have higher than average replacement rates, high replacement rates do not ensure economic well-being.

In sum, our prognosis for future retirees is not as starkly grim as those often reported in the popular press. Our micro simulation results depart from earlier, more ominous, predictions because they are based on the lifetime experiences and earnings of survey respondents, including the entire Baby Boom cohort, and because they use a comprehensive measure of retirement income that includes not only Social Security and private pension income, but also income from earnings and annuitized income from financial assets. Accordingly, our replacement rates are generally higher and do not exhibit the substantial deterioration between leading and trailing Boomers that others have reported using less complete measures. We do acknowledge that our conclusions may be somewhat optimistic as we do not account for the uncertainty of promised Social Security benefits, rising health care costs, and increasing long-term care costs.

Acknowledgments

The research reported herein was supported by the Center for Retirement Research at Boston College pursuant to a grant from the US SSA funded as part of the Retirement Research Consortium. The opinions and conclusions are solely those of the authors and should not be construed as representing the opinions or policy of the SSA or any agency of the Federal Government, the Center for Retirement Research at Boston College, or the Urban Institute, its board, or its funders. The authors are grateful to Rich Johnson and Sheila Zedlewski for valuable comments on earlier versions of this paper.

Notes

[1] Manchester et al. (this volume) also use MINT but they focus on a subset of Baby Boomers between age 62 and 72. By contrast, this analysis focuses on the economic security of the entire Baby Boom cohort at age 67.

[2] This model was developed by SSA's Office of Research, Evaluation, and Statistics, with substantial assistance from the Brookings Institution, the RAND Corporation, and the Urban Institute.

[3] Imputed rental income is 3 percent of the difference between the house value and the remaining mortgage principal. There is debate over whether to include housing in income measures and replacement rates. Proponents argue that home-owners with identical financial resources as renters are better off because they do not have to pay additional income for housing. Critics argue that only actual income flows should be included. Although we include imputed rent in the income measure we use to describe the overall levels and composition of family income, we do not include imputed rent in the income measure we use to determine replacement rates and poverty rates.

[4] The projections in this paper are based on MINT3 (Toder et al. 2002), which uses projections of disability prevalence and mortality through age 65 and of the growth of average economy-wide wages and the consumer price index (CPI). For further detail see the Technical Appendix.

[5] The Baby Boom cohort is typically represented as those born between 1946 through 1964 but for the present discussion, we include in the Boomer cohort all those born 1946–65.

[6] Labor force experience represents the number of years with positive earnings. Historical earnings in MINT come from two administrative data sources: earnings for 1951–81 come from the Summary Earnings Record (SER) and include only Social Security taxable or 'covered' earnings; while earnings between 1982 and 1999 come from the Detailed Earnings Record (DER) and include earnings from both covered and uncovered jobs as well as pay over the taxable maximum. Projected earnings in MINT are based on the DER. We tested the sensitivity of results to different earnings data and conclude they produce similar patterns over time.

[7] Like the US Census Bureau, we do not include imputed rent in the income measure we use to determine poverty rates.

[8] Because average family income can be skewed by high outliers, we also report median family income in Butrica et al. (2003). Although lower than average income, median income exhibits similar patterns across cohorts and within subgroups.

[9] Again, we tested the sensitivity of our results to different sources of earnings data. Because it captures total earnings, not just social security covered earnings; the DER has fewer years of zero earnings and higher earnings on average than the SER. However, SER data sources exhibit similar earnings patterns over time. That is, average SER earnings are projected to increase over time (although earnings growth is higher using DER earnings) and earnings inequality is projected to increase over time (although inequality is somewhat higher using DER earnings). Using either data source, Baby Boomer retirees are projected to have higher lifetime earnings and higher earnings and income inequality than current retirees.

[10] There are statutory limits on the amount individuals can contribute to retirement accounts. MINT assumes these limits remain fixed at current levels.

[11] We exclude imputed rent and coresident income from per capita household income since these income flows, unlike social security and pensions (e.g.), are not derived from preretirement earnings. In Butrica et al. (2003), we test the sensitivity of our replacement rates to alternative measures of pre- and postretirement income, while the specific numbers differ, our general findings hold up to these alternative measures.

Technical Appendix

MINT projects the wealth and income of individuals born between 1926 and 1965 from the early 1990s until 2032. It was developed by SSA's Office of Research, Evaluation, and Statistics, with substantial assistance from the Brookings Institution, the RAND Corporation, and the Urban Institute (for more information, see Panis and Lillard 1999; Toder et al. 1999; Butrica et al. 2001). The projections in this paper are based on MINT3 (Toder et al. 2002).

For persons born between 1926 and 1965, MINT independently projects each person's marital changes, mortality, entry to and exit from Social Security DI rolls, and age of first receipt of Social Security retirement benefits. It also projects lifetime earnings, Social Security benefits, and other sources of income after age 49 from the early 1990s through the year 2032 or death. These other sources of income include income from pension plans, retirement accounts, no pension, no housing assets, SSI, and income of no spouse coresidents. It also calculates a rate of return on owner-occupied housing to reflect that homeowners are better off than non-homeowners. The base data for these projections are the 1990–93 panels of the SIPP, matched to SSA administrative records through year 2000 on earnings, benefits, and mortality.

MINT projects future marital histories and estimates characteristics of future and former spouses. It estimates marital transitions from the reported marital status in the SIPP panels, using gender-specific continuous time hazard models for marriage and divorce. Explanatory variables that predict marital transitions in the equations are age, education, year's unmarried, whether widowed, and calendar year after 1980. The last variable captures the stabilization of divorce rates at a relatively high level in the early 1980s (Goldstein 1999).

MINT also identifies characteristics of spouses, in particular their earnings histories, for all married individuals. Individuals who were married in the 1990–93 SIPP panels and remain married throughout the projection period are exactly matched with their spouses from the survey. Former and future spouses are statistically assigned from a MINT observation with similar characteristics, or a 'nearest neighbor.' Thus MINT contains observed and estimated marital histories with the linkages to the characteristics of current, former, and future spouses that are necessary for calculation of spousal and survivors benefits.

MINT imputes earnings histories and disability onset through age 67 using a 'nearest neighbor' matching procedure. MINT starts with a person's own SSA-recorded earnings from 1951 through 1999. The nearest neighbor procedure statistically assigns to each 'recipient' worker the next five years of earnings and Social Security DI entitlement status, based on the earnings and DI status of a 'donor' MINT observation born five years earlier with similar characteristics. The splicing of five-year blocks of earnings from donors to recipients continues until earnings projections reach age 67. A number of criteria are used to match recipients with donors in the same age interval. These criteria include gender, minority group status, education level, DI entitlement status, average earnings over the five-year period, presence of earnings in the fourth and fifth years of the five-year period, and age-gender group quintile of average prematch period earnings. An advantage of this approach is that it preserves the observed heterogeneity in age-earnings profiles for earlier birth cohorts in projecting earnings of later cohorts.

In a subsequent process, for all individuals who never become DI recipients, MINT projects earnings, retirement, and benefit take-up from age 50 until death. These earnings replace the earnings generated from the splicing method after age 50. This postprocess allows the model to project behavioral changes in earnings, retirement, and benefit take-up in response to policy changes. MINT then calculates Social Security benefits based on earnings histories and past DI entitlement status of workers, marital histories, and earnings histories of current and former spouses.

MINT projects DB pension coverage and benefits starting with the self-reported pension coverage information in the SIPP. MINT then links individuals to pension plans and simulates new pension plans along with job changes. Pension accruals depend on the characteristics of individuals' specific pension plan parameters. MINT also projects wealth from retirement accounts (i.e. DC, IRA, and Keogh plans) by accumulating account balances to the retirement date, along with any new contributions and interest earnings.

MINT also projects housing equity and nonpension, no housing wealth (i.e. vehicle, other real estate, farm and business equity, stock, mutual fund and bond values, checking, saving, money market, certificate of deposit account balances, and less unsecured debt). These projections are based on random-effects models estimated from the Panel Survey of Income Dynamics (PSID), Health and Retirement Study (HRS), and the SIPP. Explanatory variables include age, recent earnings and present value of earnings, number of years with earnings above the Social Security taxable maximum, marital status, gender, number and age of children, education, race, health and disability status, pension coverage, self-employment, and last year of life.

In each year from retirement until death, MINT takes the stock of wealth in retirement accounts and nonpension, no housing assets and: (*a*) decays it based on age-wealth patterns in the SIPP to represent the spend-down of assets in retirement; and (*b*) converts it into income by calculating the fair market annuity a couple or individual could buy if they annuitized 80 percent of their total wealth. Thus asset income is derived from a series of annuity estimates based on a declining stock of wealth in retirement.

MINT also projects living arrangements, SSI income, and income of no spouse coresidents from age 62 until death. Living arrangements depend on the marital status, age, gender, race, ethnicity, nativity, number of children ever born, education, income and assets of the individual, and date of death. For those projected to coreside, MINT uses a 'nearest neighbor' match to assign the income and characteristics of the other family members from a donor file of coresident families from the 1990–93 SIPP panels. After all incomes and assets are calculated, MINT calculates SSI eligibility and projects participation and benefits for eligible participants.

Finally, MINT projects immigration to represent people who immigrated after the SIPP survey and those who will immigrate in future years. Because immigrants have lower average income than native-born Americans, omitting them from the projection period and analyses of well-being would understate true poverty.

References

Board of Trustees of the Federal Old-Age and Survivors Insurance and Disability Insurance Trust Funds (2006). *Annual Report*. Washington, DC: United States Government Printing Office.

Burtless, G. (1996). 'A Framework For Analyzing Future Retirement Income Security', in E. A. Hanushek and N. L. Maritato (eds.), *Assessing Knowledge of Retirement Behavior*. Washington, DC: National Academy Press, pp. 244–72.

Butrica, B. A. and Iams, H. M. (2000). 'Divorced Women at Retirement: Projections of Economic Well-Being in the Near Future', *Social Security Bulletin*, 63(3): 3–12.

—— —— and Smith, K. E. (2003). 'It's All Relative: Understanding the Retirement Prospects of Baby Boomers', Social Security Administration, available at http://www.urban.org/UploadedPDF/411127_all_relative.pdf

—— —— Moore, J., and Waid, M. (2001). 'Methods in Modeling Income in the Near Term (MINT)', ORES Working Paper No. 93, Office of Policy, Social Security Administration.

—— Schaner, S. G., and Zedlewski, S. R. (2006). 'Enjoying the Golden Work Years', *Perspectives on Productive Aging*, No. 6. Washington, DC: The Urban Institute.

Easterlin, R. A., MacDonald, C., and Macunovich, D. J. (1990). 'Retirement Prospects of the Baby Boom Generation: A Different Perspective', *The Gerontologist*, 30(6): 776–83.

—— Schaeffer, C. M., and Macunovich, D. J. (1993). 'Will the Baby Boomers be Less Well Off Than Their Parents? Income, Wealth, and Family Circumstances Over the Life Cycle in the United States', *Population and Development Review*, 19(3): 497–522.

Goldin, C. (1990). *Understanding the Gender Gap: An Economic History of American Women.* New York: Oxford University Press.

Goldstein, J. R. (1999). 'The Leveling of Divorce in the United States', *Demography*, 36(3): 409–14.

Gustman, A. L. and Steinmeier, T. L. (1999). 'Effects of Pensions on Savings: Analysis with Data from the Health and Retirement Study', *Carnegie-Rochester Conference Series*, 50(July): 271–326.

Haveman, R., Holden, K., Wolfe, B., and Sherlund, S. (2003). 'Have Newly Retired Workers in the U.S. Saved Enough to Maintain Well-Being Through Retirement Years?, Paper presented at 2003 Annual APPAM Research Conference. Available at http://www.appam.org/conferences/fall/dc03/sessions/downloads/3491.pdf

Koenig, M. (2002). *Income of the Population 55 or Older, 2000.* Social Security Administration, Office of Policy, Office of Research and Statistics, Washington, DC: United States Government Printing Office.

Levy, F. (1998). *The New Dollars and Dreams: American Incomes and Economic Change.* New York: The Russell Sage Foundation.

—— and Murnane, R. J. (1992). 'U.S. Earnings Levels and Earnings Inequality: A Review of Recent Trends and Proposed Explanations', *Journal of Economic Literature*, 30(3): 1333–81.

Manchester, J., Weaver, D., and Whitman, K. (this volume). 'Changes in Economic Well-Being and Health Status: Baby Boomers and Their Parents'.

Moore, J. F. and Mitchell, O. S. (2000). 'Projected Retirement Wealth and Savings Adequacy in the Health and Retirement Study', in O. S. Mitchell, P. B. Hammond, and A. M. Rappaport (eds.), *Forecasting Retirement Needs and Retirement Wealth.* Philadelphia, PA: University of Pennsylvania Press, pp. 68–94.

Munnell, A. H., Webb, A., and Delorme, L. (2006). 'A New National Retirement Index', *Issue in Brief*, No. 48. Chestnut Hill, MA: Center for Retirement Research at Boston College. http://www.bc.edu/centers/crr/ib_48.shtml

Panis, C., and Lillard, L. (1999). 'Near Term Model Development', Final Report. SSA Contract No: 600-96-27335. Santa Monica, CA: RAND.

Sabelhaus, J. and Manchester, J. (1995). 'Baby Boomers and Their Parents: How Does Their Economic Well-Being Compare in Middle Age?', *Journal of Human Resources*, 30(4): 791–806.

Toder, E., Uccello, C., O'Hare, J., Favreault, M., Ratcliffe, C., Smith, K., Burtless, G., and Bosworth, B. (1999). 'Modeling Income in the Near Term-Projections of Retirement Income Through 2020 for the 1931–1960 Birth Cohorts', Report to the SSA. Washington, DC: The Urban Institute.

—— Thompson, L., Favreault, M., Johnson, R., Perese, K., Ratcliffe, C., Smith, K., Uccello, C., Waidmann, T. Berk, J., and Woldemariam, R. (2002). 'Modeling Income in the Near Term: Revised Projections of Retirement Income Through 2020 for the 1931–1960 Birth Cohorts', Final Report, SSA Contract No: 600-96-27332. Washington, DC: The Urban Institute.

Wolff, E. N. (2002). *Retirement Insecurity: The Income Shortfalls Awaiting the Soon-to-Retire.* Washington, DC: Economic Policy Institute.

Part II

**Changing Health Status and
Health Insurance**

Chapter 5

Are Baby Boomers Living Well Longer?

David R. Weir

How and when Baby Boomers choose to retire, and how prepared they are financially, are vital questions for this generation as well as for policymakers. An important factor in understanding the retirement prospects of Baby Boomers has to do with their health and how it may affect their capacity for continued work at older ages. The Health and Retirement Study (HRS) was conceived precisely to address key questions regarding the interplay of health, work, and economic status from middle age onward. The survey asks respondents relatively objective questions about major health conditions (e.g. heart problems, cancer, diabetes, stroke, lung disease, hypertension, and arthritis), and it also inquires about difficulty performing a range of physical and cognitive tasks (cf. Fonda and Herzog 2004; Fisher et al. 2005). In addition, the survey poses more subjective questions about how respondents rate their health, whether their health limits the kind or amount of work they can do, and what their expectations are of surviving to future target ages.[1] In addition to questions about hours, pay, and type of work, the HRS asks about work expectations past ages 62 and 65. These expectations questions appear to predict actual behavior and also respond to changes in factors predicting work (Chan and Stevens 2001).

The chapter begins with an overview of the relationship between physical function, disability, and work status by age, based on cross-sectional data from HRS 2004. This demonstrates that while poor health is an important factor in early labor force exit, most retirement occurs among people still fit enough to work. Further, there is a substantial reserve of physical capacity for work among the retired. We then turn to a cross-cohort comparison of 51–56-year olds in at three points in time, namely 1992, 1998, and 2004. We conclude that Baby Boomers in early middle age do not appear to be healthier than the cohorts born before them. We offer some thoughts about why this is so, and how it might still be consistent with improved functioning in old age.

Prior Evidence Linking Health and Retirement

Many prior studies have demonstrated that poor health is linked to labor force withdrawal (cf. Bound et al. 1999; Currie and Madrian 1999). In the

United States and to a greater degree in a number of European countries, this process is facilitated by disability insurance (DI) programs providing benefits to people deemed unable to work for medical reasons (Bound and Burkhauser 1999). Even with such programs, however, major health problems can still have a powerful depressing effect on work, income, and retirement saving (Smith 1999).

Important as such events are for the individuals and families experiencing them, they still represent a distinct minority of labor force exits for older Americans, as is clear from a review of the association between health and work at older ages. The HRS provides a perspective on the relationship between work and health at older ages in several different sections of the survey. For instance, it has direct questions about health conditions and difficulties performing simple tasks due to health problems. In a different part of the survey dealing with work disability, respondents are asked whether they are limited in any way in the kind or amount of work they can do, because of a health problem. We emphasize the more objective reports of health and functional status, over self-reported work limitations, due to the widely recognized problem of 'justification bias'. This is believed to arise when those not working seek to justify their status by alluding to health problems; obviously this renders self-reported work limitations endogenous (Bound 1991; Dwyer and Mitchell 1999; Kreider 1999). Thus some of the nonworking may misclassify themselves as unable to work when in fact they could work, and this is more likely for persons in age groups where most people work. At older ages where relatively few people work and many have been out of the labor force for a long time, the HRS question about health problems limiting work may seem irrelevant to many people (because their nonwork status is explained by other factors).

Our approach is to emphasize instead, persons' reported difficulty performing basic tasks. These are self-reported and therefore not immune to distortion, but they do not directly refer to work-related activities; further, they appear in a part of the survey about health, and not about work. These fall into two categories, namely the 'ADLs' or activities of daily living, and the IADLs or instrumental activities of daily living. Impairment in these activities (getting dressed, preparing a meal) generally signals a quite severe level of disability, often requiring assistance from other persons or special devices. Certainly many people with significant ADL or IADL impairments could be considered unable to work. Nevertheless, physical impairment short of the ADL/IADL threshold can also make paid work difficult or impossible. Accordingly, the HRS also asks twelve questions derived from research by Nagi (1991), regarding difficulty with other tasks ranging from jogging a mile to walking up a flight of stairs, and from pushing heavy objects to picking up a coin from a table. Having difficulty with six or more activities including these twelve Nagi items and the ADL and IADL

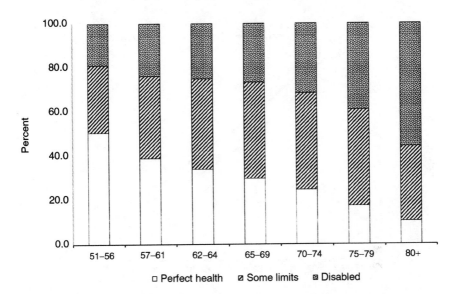

Figure 5-1. Health status by age in the cross section: HRS 2004. *Note*: Health categories are defined by the number of physical limitations based on Nagi items plus 6 ADLs plus 5 IADLs (see text). 'Perfect health' is zero or one limitation; 'Some limits' means 2–5 limitations; and 'Disabled' is 6+. Someone with two or more ADLs or two or more IADLs is also classified as disabled. (*Source*: Author's calculations.)

items is generally associated with a very high likelihood of inability to work. The six most common difficulties reported are (in descending order of frequency) jogging a mile, climbing several flights of stairs, stooping or crouching, walking several blocks, getting up from a chair after sitting for two hours, and pushing large objects. Six or more difficulties are an arbitrary cutoff, of course, but the descriptive results provided below will follow, given reasonable alternative measures.

Figure 5-1 shows how health changes with age.[2] The fraction of people with no functional limitations falls with age. Below age 60, some 20 percent of respondents have enough physical limitations that they probably cannot work, while about 40 percent have no limitations. The middle category with some functional limitations is relatively large but it does not grow terribly quickly with age. At older ages, more people move into the physically unable to work category, though even above age 80, nearly half the community-dwelling population is not impaired at that level.

The association between physical limitations and actual work is far from exact, as is evident from Figure 5-2 which links labor force attachment to age and functional status. Persons with six or more physical limitations are much less likely to work than the other two groups, but at ages 51–56,

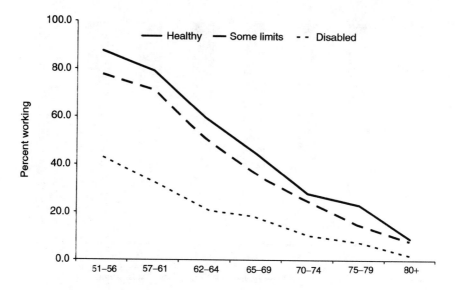

Figure 5-2. Percent working by age and health status: HRS 2004. *Notes*: Health status is as defined in Figure 5-1. Working is defined as reporting doing any work for pay. (*Source*: Author's calculations.)

almost 40 percent of that group does work. Slightly fewer people work in the intermediate health category than in the group with no limitations at all. The clear message from Figure 5-2 is that the decline in work with age is not primarily driven by age-related changes in health. Rather, work rates decline precipitously with age in all three categories. By age 70, fewer than 30 percent of the people with no physical limitations are working. These two observations—the 40 percent labor force participation rate of the most impaired below age 56, and the 30 percent participation rate of the least impaired at age 70—indicate the very great extent to which the decision to work at older ages is not completely tied to health status.

Next we combine the information from the first two figures to show the distribution across three states: working, able to work but not working (perfect health or some limits), and unable to work. Figure 5-3 shows that the middle category of 'able to work but not working' comprises nearly half the population between ages 65 and 79. At ages 70–74, almost three quarters of the population are able to work but less than one-quarter do. That many retired people are physically able to work is not an artifact of the cutoff we have used to define inability to work. Among persons aged 65–79 who are not working, 50 percent have three or fewer task difficulties. Among the 30 percent of that age group of nonworkers with six or more task difficulties is 10 percent of the population with six or seven difficulties.

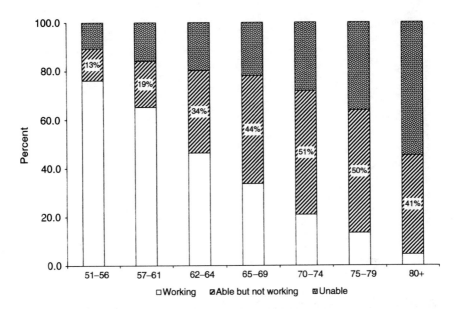

Figure 5-3. Work and health status by age: HRS 2004. *Notes*: Working is defined as doing any work for pay, regardless of health status. The not working population is divided between those unable to work (six or more physical limitations) and those able to work (five or fewer limitations). (*Source*: Author's calculations.)

One way to summarize the data in Figure 5-3 is to compute the expected years of life in each state. Demographers have similarly estimated 'active life expectancy', using slightly different and more severe definition of disability (a level severe enough to require assistance with basic daily activities). Here, we divide expected remaining years of life into work years, years of not working while in health that is good enough to permit work, and years of being physically unable to work, following Sullivan (1971). Using the 2002 life table for the general US population, people currently 51–56 years of age can expect to live an additional 27.3 years. This may be divided into 9.7 years of work, 9.9 years of reasonably good health while not working, and 7.7 years of physical limitations that would generally prevent work. While we lack adequate data to make similar calculations for earlier eras in American history, in all likelihood most of the increase in years of retirement over the last century has come through increases in years of 'healthy' retirement, that is, not working when physically able to do so. Those nearly ten years of expected healthy retirement represent a considerable reserve of potential work that prospective retirees could tap if necessary to maintain consumption levels in retirement.

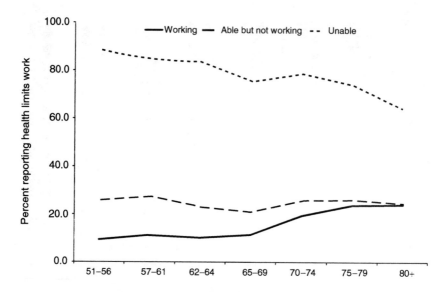

Figure 5-4. Percent reporting a health problem limits work by age and work/health status: HRS 2004. *Notes:* Work/health status defined in Figure 5-3. A health-related limitation on work is any limit on the kind or amount of work, not a complete inability to work. Due to a programming error in HRS 2004, everyone who reported a work limitation in 2002 was not asked in 2004. A fraction of this group was imputed to 'no' in 2004, based on conditional transition rates for 2000–02 by age, sex, work status, and health status. (*Source:* Author's calculations.)

Next, we introduce self-reports of work limitations due to health and compare them to the somewhat more objective health measures just reviewed. Figure 5-4 indicates the fraction of each group report it has a health problem that limits its ability to work in any way. At ages 51–56, some 90 percent of those in the group with multiple objective health problems also report that they are limited. Only 10 percent of those who are working say so (most of whom also have objective health problems as shown in Figure 5-2). With increasing age, the fraction of the objectively disabled who reports a work limitation declines. This is almost certainly a survey response problem, in that, as work becomes less and less relevant with age, people fail to link their nonwork with their poor health. With age, the fraction of workers reporting some limitations increases, as one would expect given the age-related changes in health.

We next show alternative ways of defining limited capacity to work (Figure 5-5). Generally speaking, the two measures agree: the largest group at each age is those who self-report having work limitations due to health problems and who also report objective health problems that would impair

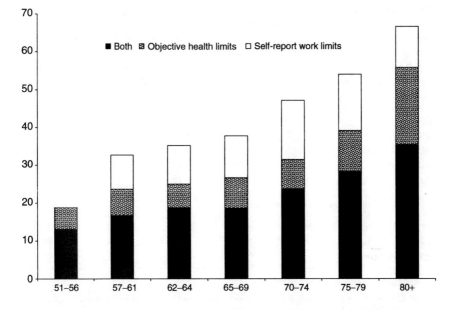

Figure 5-5. Ability to work: objective health and self-reported limits to work. *Notes:* 'Objective' health limits means six or more physical limitations. 'Self-report' is the work limitation question described in Figure 5-4. 'Both' means both are true. (*Source:* Author's calculations.)

most types of work. The sizes of the groups reporting their work capacity as limited but not reporting severe physical limitations, and those with severe limitations but who do not report any limit on ability to work, are about equal. Computing expected years of life by state, we find about 6.2 years in the state of disability by both definitions, and about three years in each of the discordant categories. Thus, by the most inclusive possible measure of disability—having *either* a self-reported limitation on work due to health *or* a number of physical limitations that should impair work—the total expectation of any kind of work constraint due to health is about twelve out of the twenty-seven years of life expectancy for a 51–56-year old. This leaves at least fifteen years of potential work.

Are Boomers Healthier?

Table 5-1 reveals what the Early Baby Boomer (EBB) group thinks of its own health, and compares these reports with those from previous birth cohorts at the same age. It is interesting that Boomers believe their health to be worse than their predecessors. For instance, to the general self-rated health

TABLE 5-1 Cross-Cohort Comparisons of Health Measures for Respondents
Aged 51–56 in Different HRS Cohorts

Birth Year	Self-rated Health (5 = poor, 1 = excellent)	Fair or Poor Health	Number of Limitations	Number of Health Conditions	Subjective Probability of Survival to Age 75	Health Limits Work
Men						
1936–41	2.39	16.7%	2.12	0.70	62.3	17.5%
1942–47	2.51	19.3%	2.12	0.68	61.8	17.8%
1948–53	2.59	22.1%	2.06	0.71	60.7	19.2%
t-statistic	4.82	3.83	−0.69	0.42	−1.42	1.22
Women						
1936–41	2.45	19.1%	3.01	0.67	67.0	18.4%
1942–47	2.60	22.4%	3.07	0.62	69.3	21.4%
1948–53	2.64	22.7%	3.04	0.71	66.2	19.8%
t-statistic	5.03	2.81	0.33	1.54	−0.86	1.05

Source: Author's calculations.

Notes: The t-statistic tests the hypothesis of no change between the birth cohort of 1936–41 (assessed in 1992) and the cohort of 1948–53 (assessed in 2004).

question (where 1 = excellent to 5 = poor), Boomers gave themselves a worse health rating of about two-tenths of a point. This was the same for both men and women and the differences are statistically significant. Such a change in mean self-rated health cannot be explained only by Boomers being less willing to report excellent health, since the fraction reporting fair or poor health also rose significantly from the original HRS cohort of 51–56-year olds to the Boomers a dozen years later. By contrast, most of the other summary health measures offers no clear time trend (if downwards, the trend is not statistically significant). For instance, Boomers report about the same number of physical limitations and very slightly more health conditions. They give themselves slightly lower chances of survival to age 75, and they are slightly more likely to report that their ability to work is limited by a health problem. The general pattern, then, is that objectively speaking, Boomer health is no better than that of the earlier cohort at the same age, yet subjectively Boomers feel themselves to be in slightly worse health.

Table 5-2 compares the cohorts on key health-related behaviors. It is evident that two opposing trends are at work: smoking is on the decline, but obesity is on the rise. Fewer Boomers ever smoked and fewer were still smoking at age 51–56 than in the HRS cohort. Obesity is detected using the body mass index (BMI), a measure of body weight relative to height. For a person of average height, one point of BMI is associated

TABLE 5-2 Health Behaviors for Respondents Aged 51–56:
Cross-Cohort Comparisons

	Ever Smoked	Smoke Now	Body Mass Index	Obese	No Church Attendance
Men					
1936–41	73.8%	30.2%	27.3	21.3%	32.3%
1942–47	69.1%	26.8%	28.2	28.9%	
1948–53	62.2%	26.2%	28.3	28.4%	36.3%
t-stat.	−6.81	−2.49	5.69	4.51	2.29
Women					
1936–41	54.7%	26.8%	26.8	24.6%	21.5%
1942–47	54.6%	24.4%	27.7	28.3%	
1948–53	47.3%	19.4%	28.3	34.1%	25.4%
t-stat.	−4.53	−4.53	7.26	6.30	2.74

Source: Author's calculations.

Notes: The *t*-statistic is for the hypothesis of no change between the birth cohort
of 1936–41 (assessed in 1992) and the cohort of 1948–53 (assessed in 2004).

with a gain of 5–7 pounds, and means BMI was up over a point in just a
dozen years. Obesity is commonly defined as a BMI of 30 or higher; in our
sample, the percentage of obese was up by 7 percentage points for men and
nearly 10 for women. While physical activity would be another important
health behavior to document, the HRS measures are not consistent across
waves. Regular church attendance is associated with lower mortality even
controlling for observable health, and Boomers are slightly more likely to
report not attending church in the past year than the HRS cohort (this
question was not asked in HRS from 1994 to 2002).

Turning to the prevalence of some specific health conditions, we see
from Table 5-3 that the patterns closely mirror other changes in health
behaviors. Lung disease, which is highly sensitive to smoking, declined from
1992 to 2004. Diabetes, which at older ages is highly related to obesity,
increased. Hypertension is affected by both and shows no clear trend. Obesity is also related to arthritis, mobility difficulty, and joint pain. Arthritis
rates are higher for the Boomers, and self-reported pain and pain-related
activity limitation are also up. These changes may help account for some of
the poorer self-ratings of health revealed in Table 5-1.

The Structure of Health Relationships

There are several interesting interrelationships among health variables.
For example, the expectation of survival to age 75 is potentially an

Table 5-3 Specific Health Conditions for Respondents Aged 51–56: Cross-Cohort Comparison

	Lung Disease	Diabetes	High Blood Pressure	Arthritis	Frequent Pain	Pain Limits Activities
Men						
1936–41	6.9%	8.5%	37.2%	24.4%	20.5%	12.7%
1942–47	4.2%	10.1%	34.9%	26.1%	24.5%	14.2%
1948–53	4.7%	12.5%	36.2%	27.4%	29.7%	16.9%
t-stat.	−2.53	3.65	−0.56	1.94	5.79	3.27
Women						
1936–41	7.3%	8.3%	33.8%	36.4%	26.9%	16.9%
1942–47	5.4%	8.3%	30.1%	37.7%	31.1%	21.6%
1948–53	6.2%	11.0%	35.4%	39.6%	33.2%	22.1%
t-stat.	−1.33	2.85	1.06	2.03	4.20	4.05

Source: Author's calculations.

Notes: The *t*-statistic is for the hypothesis of no change between the birth cohort of 1936–41 (assessed in 1992) and the cohort of 1948–53 (assessed in 2004).

important variable in models of retirement and saving. Earlier waves of HRS indicate that this question does have large measurement error variance and a pronounced heaping on focal values of 0, 50, and 100, it nonetheless does have validity both in its association with known risk factors and in its predictive power (Hurd and McGarry 2002; Hurd et al. 2004). One strategy for using this variable in empirical work is to use instrumental variables (IV) to mitigate the effects of measurement error, with self-rated health a potential candidate instrument (Gan et al. 2005). Figure 5-6 shows that the relationship between self-rated health and survival expectations is nearly identical in 1992 and 2004.[3]

Changes in self-rated health are explored more fully in Table 5-4 using multivariate linear regression models to assess how much of the change in self-rated health may be explained by observable health measures. The data used are pooled data on 51–56-year olds in 1992 (born 1936–41), 1998 (born 1942–47), and 2004 (born 1948–53). No individual appears more than once. The first model includes only year dummies (cohort).[4] As we saw in Table 5-1, the Early Boomers interviewed in 2004 rated their health about 0.2 worse (higher on the scale) than the 1992 group. The second model introduces the number of health conditions, number of physical limitations, and an indicator for experiencing frequent pain. These three variables explain a high fraction of the variance in self-rated health, but they reduce the Early Boomer differential only a little (and most of that is due to the increased report of pain). Our third model introduces

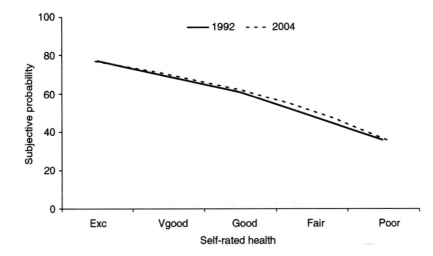

Figure 5-6. Subjective probability of survival to age 75 and self-rated health: comparing the original HRS (1992) to Early Boomers (2004). (*Source*: Author's calculations for the HRS 1992 final release and HRS 2004 early release.)

health behaviors. People who smoke or who are obese discount their health for these behaviors, even when controlling for their current health status. However, because those health behaviors are moving in opposite directions, they do not explain away the Boomer differential in self-rated health.

TABLE 5-4 Determinants of Self-Rated Health for Respondents Aged 51–56: Cross-Cohort Comparisons

Independent Variable	Coeff.	t-stat.	Coeff.	t-stat.	Coeff.	t-stat.
Constant	2.423	146.45	1.645	103.26	1.569	92.07
War Babies	0.137	4.75	0.130	5.99	0.130	6.00
Early Boomers	0.195	6.94	0.162	7.59	0.159	7.42
No. of conditions			0.373	29.65	0.363	28.81
No. of limitations			0.171	36.43	0.163	34.14
Frequent pain			0.337	12.06	0.335	12.03
Obese					0.130	5.73
Smoker					0.256	11.17
R^2		0.004		0.436		0.447

Source: Author's calculations.

Notes: The dependent variable is self-rated health, scored from 1 = excellent to 5 = poor. There are 11,906 observations pooling three cohorts of 51–56-year olds (5,578 for HRS in 1992, 3,083 for War Babies in 1998, and 3,257 for Early Boomers in 2004).

It seems, therefore, that the subjective decline is perceived in Baby Boomer health compared to earlier cohorts cannot be easily explained by observable changes. It is well to note, nevertheless, that the magnitude of the differential is not large; it is equivalent to having one additional physical limitation, and only about one-third of a condition like diabetes or heart disease. One likely place to look for explanation might be in mental health measures of stress or depression. Unfortunately, the depression measure used in HRS was changed after 1992 and it is not easy to render them comparable.

Links Between Health and Education

Finally, we turn to an examination of the relationship between health and education. Prior studies have found a so-called socioeconomic status (SES) 'gradient', in which health is better for those with more education, more income, and more wealth. Many economists have focused in particular on the relationship with education (Grossman and Kaestner 1997). A number of possible causal mechanisms have been hypothesized, such as a relationship between education and the ability to acquire information about health or to manage complex regimens (Goldman and Smith 2002). Models of reverse causality, from health to education, are more relevant to childhood health than to health of the elderly, but links from childhood health to health at older ages would qualify as an example of the third type of causal mechanism through unobserved third factors, which might also include factors such as rates of time preference, or unobserved, possibly genetic, correlates of health and educational attainment.

Mechanisms by which education could itself produce better health would suggest that cohort improvements in education should lead to cohort improvements in health. Freedman and Martin (1999) associated the trend improvement in physical functioning above age 65 from 1984 to 1993 with the time trend improvement in education. Based on the cross-sectional relationship of education and functioning, over half of the trend in function could be attributed to the trend in education (with an additional boost from a slightly stronger effect of education on function at the end of the period). Continued declines in disability at older ages would thus be predicted, as more recent cohorts with higher education entered their older years. What does this imply for Boomers? As noted above, Baby Boomers are significantly more educated than earlier cohorts: Early Boomers averaged 13.5 years of schooling versus 12.5 years for the original HRS cohort (t-statistic = 14). And yet, as we have seen, their health and functioning are no better (and possibly worse) at ages 51–56. Table 5-5 shows that, controlling for education, the health of the Early Boomers is

TABLE 5-5 Education and Health for Respondents Aged 51–56: Cross-Cohort Comparisons

	Self-Rated Health		No. of Conditions		No. of Limitations	
	Coeff.	t-stat.	Coeff.	t-stat.	Coeff.	t-stat
Constant	4.082	74.23	5.562	38.18	1.117	25.32
War Babies	0.210	7.69	0.156	2.35	−0.015	−0.72
Early Boomers	0.324	12.05	0.213	3.16	0.065	3.01
Years of educ.	−0.133	−31.70	−0.238	−21.47	−0.035	−10.32
R^2		0.114		0.014		0.059

Source: Author's calculations.

Note: See Table 5-4.

worse than that of the HRS cohort, and that is true for both the objective as well as self-rated health measures. Tests for change in the slope of the gradient show that the relationship between education and health itself has not changed—health is simply lower at every level of education in 2004 than in 1992. This is shown graphically for self-rated health in Figure 5-7.

Certainly these descriptive results are not conclusive proof that education does not have a causal role in improving health. They do, however, suggest

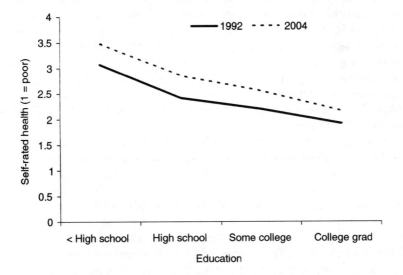

Figure 5-7. Comparing health and education for the original HRS (1992) to Early Boomers (2004). (*Source*: Author's calculations using HRS 1992 final release and HRS 2004 early release.)

that caution be used in projecting future improvements in health solely on the basis of improving education.

Looking Ahead

How might we reconcile the fact that the Early Boomers at age 51–56 seem to be in no better health objectively than the cohort twelve years before, and subjectively they feel in worse health? This is despite other evidence that disability has been declining and health improving for the last few decades (Cutler 2001; Freedman et al. 2002). Some have suggested that the rise in obesity may nullify the trend toward declining disability and longer life (Sturm et al. 2004; Olshansky et al. 2005). But crude extrapolation of trends based on cross-sectional correlations is no more reliable for obesity and health than for education and health. Already there is evidence that obesity's effect on health is weakening as it becomes more common (Flegal et al. 2005).

One point to note is that demonstrated health and functioning gains have come at older rather than younger ages (Freedman and Martin 1998), as to some extent they are the result of better medical treatments for established conditions. Thus treatments for cholesterol, hypertension, and diabetes have improved dramatically over the last 10–15 years, improving work and other outcomes (Kahn 1998). Offsetting the gain in obesity, reductions in cholesterol and blood pressure have been found in every category of body weight (Gregg et al. 2005). Medications for these are mainly given to people who have developed hypertension or diabetes or high cholesterol, and they can help prevent the worsening of those conditions and the progression to even worse problems, notably heart disease and stroke. Similarly, the treatment of survivors of heart attack and stroke has made great strides.

A key point to recall is that Early Boomers are still young, in their early 50s. To a large degree, then, most have not yet developed the more severe chronic diseases that will challenge their ability to work or to live independently. Nevertheless they are taking advantage of improved medications. For instance in 1992, 60 percent of 51–56-year olds with hypertension were on medication, a figure that rose to 78 percent by 2004. Similarly, in 1992 only 41 percent of people with diabetes were on oral medications; this rose to 69 percent by 2004. The numbers on insulin remained stable, indicating that the average severity of the disease was not increasing. Rather, the use and effectiveness of medications and other medical treatments will likely determine the future health of the Boomers, rather than mechanistic associations with education or obesity.

As Baby Boomers move into late middle age, there is no indication that their health is any better than for cohorts born a dozen years earlier but assessed at the same ages. Boomers have smoked less but suffer more from obesity and obesity-related conditions. Nonetheless, these health conditions should not deter Boomers from fulfilling their expectations of working longer (cf. Maestas, this volume). Most retirees in their 60s and 70s are physically able to work, so that even barring gains in health; most Boomers could defer retirement several years. In the meantime, the health trajectories of the leading Baby Boomers will be well worth watching.

Acknowledgments

The author acknowledges research support from the HRS and the National Institute on Aging (U01 AG009740).

Notes

[1] Beginning in 2006, the survey will add several direct health measures to the questionnaire, including blood pressure measurement, some limited blood tests, and measures of physical performance.

[2] The HRS sample design lends itself well to cross-cohort comparisons, though one must be aware of the distinction between HRS 'entry' cohorts, defined by the year they entered the sample, and 'true' birth cohorts, defined by their year of birth. The first HRS cohort introduced in 1992 consisted of persons aged 51–61 (born 1931–41), and their spouses. In 1998, a new cohort of persons aged 51–56 (born 1942–47) was introduced to refresh the sample due to the aging of the original HRS cohort (then aged 57–67). Some members had already joined the study in 1992 or later as younger spouses of original HRS cohort members. Thus the new sample added in 1998 consisted only of persons who were either single or married to someone born after 1941. A correct cross-cohort comparison of 51–56-year olds in 1992 and 1998 must include, in the 1998 group, both the new sample members inducted in 1998, and the other persons in the same birth cohort who entered the study before 1998. Similarly, in 2004, the sample was again refreshed with a new cohort of persons 51–56 years of age (born 1948–53), supplementing those already in the study as younger spouses with new sample members who were either single or married to someone born after 1947. Persons who entered the study in 1992 are referred to as the HRS entry or original cohort, persons who entered in 1998 as the War Baby (WB) entry cohort, and persons who entered in 2004 as the Early Boomer entry cohort. The same names can also be used for birth cohorts corresponding to the target birth years of each of those entry cohorts, with the understanding that not all members of the WB entry cohort were in the 1942–47 birth cohort, nor were all the members of the 1942–47 birth cohort brought in with the entry cohort of 1998 (and the same is true for the Early Boomers).

[3] More detailed statistical analysis also finds no significant structural change in the relationship between the two periods, although survival probabilities conditional on self-rated health are slightly higher (or, conversely, self-rated health is somewhat lower for the same survival probability; given the high variance of survival probabilities, the change is not statistically significant).

[4] As self-rated health is a categorical variable, ordered Probit may be a more appropriate statistical procedure. In fact, we find (in results not reported here in detail) that the ordering is not far from linear. That is, ordered Probit results do not differ in any meaningful way from those of OLS and are more difficult to summarize, so we present here the OLS results.

References

Bound, J. (1991). 'Self-Reported versus Objective Measures of Health in Retirement Models', *Journal of Human Resources*, 26: 106–38.

—— and Burkhauser, R. (1999). 'Economic Analysis of Transfer Programs Targeted on People With Disabilities', in O. Ashenfelter and D. Card (eds.), *Handbook of Labor Economics*, Vol. 3, Chapter 51, pp. 3418–528.

—— Schoenbaum, M., Stinebrickner, T., and Waidmann, T. (1999). 'The Dynamic Effects of Health on the Labor Force Transitions of Older Workers', *Labour Economics*, 6: 179–202.

Chan, S. and Stevens, A. H. (2001). 'Job Loss and Employment Patterns of Older Workers', *Journal of Labor Economics*, 19: 484–521.

Currie, J. and Madrian, B. (1999). 'Health, Health Insurance, and the Labor Market', in O. Ashenfelter and D. Card (eds.), *Handbook of Labor Economics*, Volume 3, Chapter 50, pp. 3309–416.

Cutler, D. M. (2001). 'Declining Disability among the Elderly', *Health Affairs*, Nov–Dec: 11–27.

Dwyer, D. S. and Mitchell, O. S. (1999). 'Health Problems as Determinants of Retirement: Are Self-Rated Measures Endogenous?', *Journal of Health Economics*, 18: 173–93.

Fisher, G. D., Faul, J. D., Weir, D. R., and Wallace, R. B. (February 2005). 'Documentation of Chronic Disease Measures in the Health and Retirement Study', (HRS/AHEAD), HRS Documentation Report DR-009.

Flegal, K. M., Graubard, B. I., Williamson, D. F., and Gail, M. H. (2005). 'Excess Deaths Associated With Underweight, Overweight, and Obesity', *Journal of the American Medical Association*, 293: 1861–7.

Fonda, S. and Herzog, A. R. (December 2004). 'Documentation of Physical Functioning Measures in the HRS', HRS Documentation Report DR-008.

Freedman, V. A. and Martin, L. G. (1998). 'Understanding Trends in Functional Limitations among Older Americans', *American Journal of Public Health*, 88(10): 1457–62.

—— —— (1999). 'The Role of Education in Explaining and Forecasting Trends in Functional Limitations among Older Americans', *Demography*, 36(4): 461–73.

—— —— and Schoeni, R. F. (2002). 'Recent Trends in Disability and Functioning among Older Adults in the United States: A Systematic Review', *Journal of the American Medical Association*, 288(24): 3137–46.

Gan, L., Hurd, M., and McFadden, D. (2005). 'Individual Subjective Survival Curves', in D. Wise (ed.), *Analyses in the Economics of Aging*. Chicago, IL: University of Chicago Press.

Goldman, D. and Smith, J. P. (2002). 'Can Patient Self-Management Help Explain the SES Health Gradient?', *Proceedings of the National Academy of Sciences*, 99: 10929–34.

Gregg, E. W., Cheng, Y. J., Cadwell, B. L., Imperatore, G., Williams, D. E., Flegal, K. M., Venkat Narayan, K. M., and Williamson, D. F. (2005). 'Secular Trends in Cardiovascular Disease Risk Factors According to Body Mass Index in US Adults', *Journal of the American Medical Association*, 293: 1868–74.

Grossman, M. and Kaestner, R. (1997). 'Effects of Education on Health', in J. R. Behrman and N. Stacey (eds.), *The Social Benefits of Education*. Ann Arbor, MI: University of Michigan Press, pp. 69–123.

Hurd, M. D. and McGarry, K. (2002). 'The Predictive Validity of Subjective Probabilities of Survival', *The Economic Journal*, 112: 966–85.

—— Smith, J. P., and Zissimopoulos, J. (2004). 'The Effects of Subjective Survival on Retirement and Social Security Claiming', *Journal of Applied Econometrics*, 19: 761–75.

Kahn, M. E. (1998). 'Health and Labor Market Performance: The Case of Diabetes', *Journal of Labor Economics*, 16: 878–99.

Kreider, B. (1999). 'Latent Work Disability and Reporting Bias', *Journal of Human Resources*, 34: 734–69.

Maestas, N. (Chapter 2). 'Cross-Cohort Differences in Retirement Expectations and Realizations'.

Nagi, S. (1991). *Disability Concepts Revisited: Implications for Prevention in Disability in America: Toward a National Agenda for Prevention*. Washington, DC: National Academy Press.

Olshansky, S. J., Passaro, D. J., Hershow, R. C., Layden, J., Carnes, B. A., Brody, J., Hayflick, L., Butler, R. N., Allison, D. B., and Ludwig, D. S. (2005). 'A Potential Decline in Life Expectancy in the United States in the 21st Century', *New England Journal of Medicine*, 352: 1138–45.

Smith, J. P. (1999). 'Healthy Bodies and Thick Wallets: The Dual Relation between Health and Economic Status', *Journal of Economic Perspectives*, 13: 145–66.

Sturm, R., Ringel, J. S., and Andreyeva, T. (2004). 'Increasing Obesity Rates and Disability Trends', *Health Affairs*, 23: 199–205.

Sullivan, D. F. (1971). 'A Single Index of Morbidity and Mortality', *Health Services Mental Health Administration Health Report*, 86: 347–54.

Chapter 6

Baby Boomers versus Their Parents: Economic Well-Being and Health Status

Joyce Manchester, David Weaver, and Kevin Whitman

As the leading edge of the Baby Boom turns age 60, many are interested in the anticipated well-being of this large cohort during their golden years. An active literature debates whether Boomers have saved enough to have adequate retirement income, defined various ways, while a separate literature makes projections of the health and disability status of retired Boomers. In this chapter, we merge the two questions by examining how Baby Boomers might compare with their parents' cohort, in terms of economic well-being and health status. We also explore interactions between two measures of well-being and note patterns in dispersion across income and wealth distributions. We define the parents' cohort in 1998 as persons aged 62–72, and we compare them to Baby Boomers in 2022, also at ages 62–72.

Our projections are derived from the MINT model developed by the Social Security Administration (SSA). The rich underlying data which feed the microsimulation model include longitudinal earnings records from SSA, which, in conjunction with other administrative and survey data, allow for the careful modeling of the major sources of income in retirement. In addition, wealth accumulation and spend down over the life cycle are modeled in MINT, providing an opportunity to assess whether Boomers will have saved enough for their retirement years. Also a number of health variables, both subjective and objective, are projected in MINT, offering another dimension along which we can compare Boomers' well-being with that of their parents' generation. To highlight the dispersion issues, we focus on results for the 10th and 25th percentiles, the median, and the 75th and 90th percentiles. In addition, we examine outcomes for special groups of interest including those in poor or fair health, those unable to work, the disabled, and those with less than average life expectancy.

In what follows, we first examine the literatures on economic well-being and health status, and then we describe the MINT model and variables used in the analysis. Particular attention is paid to descriptions of the health variables, as these have been used infrequently in MINT-based research.

Next, we analyze projected changes by cohort in economic outcomes, health conditions, and the interaction between these two measures of well-being.

Prior Research on Cross-Cohort Changes in Economic Well-Being and Health Status

Economic Well-being

Many studies have examined the economic well-being of Baby Boomers relative to that of earlier generations at the same ages. Those studies generally indicate that Baby Boomers seem to be a step ahead of their parents in accumulating resources for retirement. One study compared survey data on income, consumption, and wealth of Boomers in 1989 to that of their parents' generation in the early 1960s when they were the same age (Sabelhaus and Manchester 1995). Results showed that Boomers, on average, accumulated more wealth relative to income at ages 25–44 than their parents' generation at the same life stage thirty years before. But measured consumption had not increased as much as measured income for young adults. Other studies along the same lines were reviewed in a Congressional Budget Office report (2003). These studies did not compare the projected well-being of Boomers to their parents in retirement.

To assess Baby Boomers preparedness for retirement, some studies have asked whether Boomer households are likely to have enough income and assets to maintain their living standards in retirement. Research on the adequacy of saving concluded that significant under saving was likely (Bernheim 1993; Moore and Mitchell 2000). Using midpoint assumptions, Bernheim found that households were saving only 36–38 percent of the amount needed to maintain their standard of living in retirement, taking into account Social Security and pensions. Yet more recently, Gale (1997) argued that when housing equity is included in wealth, about two-thirds of Baby Boomer households appear to be accumulating adequate wealth. Butrica et al. (Chapter 4, this volume) report that some demographic subgroups of Baby Boomers are less likely than current retirees to maintain their preretirement living standards.

The methodology for measuring savings adequacy is undergoing change in recent analysis, mainly by introducing a stochastic life-cycle model in which families save both for retirement and as a precaution against uncertainty. Engen et al. (1999) define adequacy as wealth accumulation sufficient to permit consumption smoothing, or, more precisely, the marginal utility of consumption over the life cycle. Introducing a precautionary saving motive implies that, *ceteris paribus*, consumption rises with age. Their model calculates optimal saving rates for each household and then reports any shortfall relative to actual ratios of wealth to income found in the Health and Retirement Survey. The authors note that determining savings adequacy is difficult when preretirement earnings fluctuate. Thus households with the same age, education, and pension status will display a range of optimal savings levels if earnings shocks are experienced in the preretirement years. They conclude that more than 60 percent of the households exceeded the target ratio of wealth to earnings. Households in the bottom quartile of the distribution of actual wealth/earnings ratios were under saving.

Also using a stochastic life-cycle framework, Scholz et al. (2005) incorporate many behavioral features known to affect consumption, including precautionary savings, buffer stock behavior, asset-tested public transfers, end-of-life uncertainty, medical shocks, and a progressive income tax. Households are seen to form realistic expectations about earnings, Social Security benefits, and pension benefits. The authors use data from the Health and Retirement Study in 1992 as inputs in calculating optimal life-cycle consumption profiles and household-specific optimal wealth targets; Social Security earnings records provide forty-one years of information on actual earnings. As in Engen et al. (1999), earnings shocks cause optimal wealth to vary substantially, even for observationally identical households. Their results indicate that more than 80 percent of HRS households have accumulated more wealth than optimal. For those not meeting their targets, the magnitudes of the deficits are typically small.

Finally, several studies suggest poverty will decline and real income will rise among Boomer retirees because of real wage growth over time, which affects Social Security benefits, pensions, and other sources of retirement income. Butrica and Uccello (2004), using the DYNASIM model, project declining poverty and rising real income for Boomers. Wentworth and Pattison (2001–02) use data from the Current Population Survey (CPS) and simulate changes in aged poverty under different assumptions regarding real wage growth. They find sharp declines in poverty over the 1997–2020 periods under the assumption of real wage growth at 1 percent per year and noticeable declines occur even if real wage growth is half this level. Butrica et al. (Chapter 4, this volume) also project declining poverty and increasing real income for the Boomer generation.

Health Status

The future health status of Baby Boomers in retirement will influence their overall well-being as well as the quantity of resources needed to maintain their standards of living. Changes in the health and disability of older people during the last few decades may give us some insight into how Boomers may differ from their parents in terms of health. A recent review of the literature finds that most dimensions of health among the older population have improved during the last two decades (Crimmins 2004). Mortality has continued to decline, and disability and functioning loss are less common now than in the past. In addition, having a disease appears to be less disabling than in the past. However, the prevalence of most diseases has increased in the older population as people survive longer with disease.

Recent work on measuring disabilities points to three societal trends in areas other than health or functioning that might contribute to reported declines in disability levels (Wolf et al. 2005). Those societal trends include a reduced supply of informal care, changes in the technology of self-care, and changes in the definition and perception of both 'ability' and 'disability'. Such factors emphasize that reported disability may not be an objective measure of true health status, but certainly the interaction of true health status and one's ability to function under changing circumstances may be important in analyzing well-being from the perspective of health.

While the overall trends show improvements in health and disability, differences across demographic groups exist. Data from the National Long-Term Care Survey (NLTCS) show that Americans aged 65–69 in the 1980s and 1990s manifest a significant improvement in health over those decades, but the dynamics differ in gender and race groups (Arbeev et al. 2004). For example, the authors find a larger increase in the proportion of nondisabled blacks aged 65–69 compared with whites. In addition, they report a larger increase in the proportion of nondisabled males compared with females. It is interesting to speculate whether some of those differences may be traced to economic well-being.

A cloud on the horizon concerns the rising incidence of obesity. Sturm et al. (2004) investigate whether older Americans are becoming more or less disabled due to obesity. Unhealthy body weight has increased dramatically, but other data show that disability rates have declined. The authors use data from the Health and Retirement Study to estimate the association between obesity and disability and then combine those data with trend estimates of obesity rates from the Behavioral Risk Factor Surveillance Survey. They find that if current trends in obesity continue, disability rates will increase by 1 percent per year more in the 50–69 age groups than if there were no further weight gain.

Health status matters during the early years of retirement not only because it affects overall well-being but also because it has a bearing on financial resources needed for the retirement years. Research at the National Center for Health Statistics suggests that persons reporting better health at age 70 lived longer than persons in worse health (Lubitz 2004). Moreover, they spend most of their longer life span past age 70 in excellent or good health. Persons who report poor health at age 70 lived only two-thirds as long and spent most of that time in fair or poor health. An interesting finding is that the total, cumulative medical spending from age 70 until death was similar for persons in good health at 70 versus those in poor health at 70. That result holds even though the less healthy persons had fewer years to accumulate costs. Worse health, which produces higher yearly costs, offsets the effect of fewer years to accumulate costs.

Households with health insurance prior to retirement have a better chance of protecting their nest eggs than those with no health insurance (Levy, Chapter 8, this volume). In addition, the health status of persons in the early retirement years may reflect the level of health care they were able to access as working adults. Hence the measured wealth and health of households in their 60s is in part influenced by the presence of health insurance earlier in their working lives. One shortcoming of this study is that we have no data on which households had access to health insurance prior to becoming eligible for Medicare at age 65.

Methodology

In what follows, we use the SSA's MINT microsimulation model in which the starting population is based on samples from the Survey of Income and Program Participation (SIPP).[1] Survey data from the SIPP are augmented with matched administrative records on benefits and earnings from the SSA. The 1926 through 1972 birth cohorts are represented in MINT. The economic, demographic, and other experiences of these cohorts are projected through the year 2039.[2] In this analysis, persons from the 1926–1936 cohorts ('parents') are compared to individuals from the 1950–1960 cohorts whom here we loosely identify with Baby Boomers. While these comparison groups are not based on actual parent–child relationships, they are useful constructs in assessing generational changes. All members of the middle Boomers are represented in our Boomer sample, as are several cohorts from the Early Boomers and one cohort (the 1960 cohort) from the Late Boomers.[3] Economic and health conditions are examined for the year in which members of each group are aged 62–72 (1998 for the parents and 2022 for the Boomers). Thus, while the results do not address the circumstances of the 'oldest old' from each generation, the age range is wide enough to meaningfully discuss each generation's prospects in retirement.[4]

Projection methods in MINT vary with the type of factor being projected. Some variables are projected based on statistical relationships estimated from surveys such as the SIPP, the Panel Study of Income Dynamics (PSID), and the Health and Retirement Study (HRS). In other cases, a nearest-neighbor approach is used, which assigns the experiences of an older SIPP respondent to a younger respondent who is similar in observable ways. Finally, for the early birth cohorts, some variables for the 1990s are taken directly from the SIPP survey or the matched administrative records.

We consider four measures related to health, based on work by Toder et al. (2002). Two health measures are based on self-assessed health status and are projected using statistical equations estimated from HRS data. As in a number of surveys, respondents in the HRS are asked whether their general health status is 'excellent, very good, good, fair, or poor'. Researchers created a dichotomous variable (1 if in fair or poor health, 0 otherwise) and estimated its relationship to several socioeconomic variables; these estimates are used to predict health status at a starting age (age 51) for MINT respondents. Any changes in health status from age 51 forward are then assigned to MINT respondents based on additional empirical work, using the HRS, on transitions from one health status to another. A similar approach is taken with the other type of self-assessed health: whether an individual had an impairment that limited or prevented work.

Toder et al. (2002) found particularly strong relationships between self-assessed health status and education. For example, even after controlling for lifetime earnings, subsequent (observed) mortality, sex, and race/ethnic status, the coefficients on educational status were large and statistically significant. Education was also found to be an important variable in explaining transitions from one health status to another as one age. The estimated relationships between health status and education will drive many of the findings in this paper and, while suggestive, should also be viewed with caution. Baby Boomers were far less likely to drop out of high school than their parents (10.9% compared with 26.9% in the MINT samples) and because of this will be projected to exhibit improvements in health status. This study raises the possibility that education may not have a strictly causal relationship with health status and therefore projections across cohorts may produce inaccurate results. That work did not model an explicit time trend in the health equations for MINT. Rather, trends exhibited in the MINT model reflect changes in the underlying determinants of health (e.g. education). Toder et al. (2002) cite research suggesting a trend toward improved health status is occurring even after controlling for socioeconomic variables. Thus, projected improvements in health status for Baby Boomers in MINT may be somewhat understated.

The SIPP contains self-assessed measures of health status, but these are not used in MINT because the SIPP measures lack a necessary longitudinal component (Toder et al. 2002). In MINT, both Boomers and their parents have health status estimated from the HRS-based equations. However, because SIPP has health and economic measures at a point in time, it is possible to compare survey reports with MINT findings, at least for the parents of the Boomers. These comparisons reveal that MINT generates an appropriate incidence of health problems for the parents' generation, but that survey reports in SIPP indicate a stronger relationship between poor health and low income.[5] MINT estimates likely capture key relationships between health status and economic variables, but it is unknown whether the strength of those relationships is accurately measured and therefore an important topic for future research.

Projections of subjective measures (self-assessed health) have limitations. For this reason, we also rely on two more objective variables reflecting health status, namely mortality and receipt of disability insurance (DI) benefits from Social Security.[6] These variables have strengths (and some weaknesses) compared to self-assessed measures.[7] For example, at least for parents of the Boomers, DI receipt in MINT is taken directly from SSA's administrative records. For Boomers, many will also have DI receipt observed in administrative records, but receipt after middle age must be projected based on current law DI benefits; thus they do not take into account any future legislative changes. We note that DI receipt is not a pure measure of health status: workers must meet the insured status requirements for DI benefits, namely, that they have worked long enough and recently enough in Social Security covered employment. The insured status issue is important because many more Boomer women are likely to be insured for disability benefits compared to their parents' generation (we return to this point below).

Disability receipt, earnings, and mortality in MINT are projected forward using a 'nearest-neighbor' approach. For example, consider a Boomer in the SIPP who turns 44 in the year 2000 (the last year's matched administrative records are available). To project earnings from ages 45–49 for this 'target' respondent, a 'donor' in the SIPP population at least age 49 in the year 2000 will be found. The donor will be selected based on having characteristics, including pre-age 45 earnings (relative to the economy-wide average earnings), that are similar to the target. The age-44 Boomer will be assigned the relative earnings, disability status, and mortality experience of the donor for ages 45–49.[8] So, if the donor was observed to have become disabled between the ages of 45–49 (which would be known from matched SSA records), then the target respondent would be projected to become disabled between those ages. The procedure would be repeated, but using different donors, to complete a respondent's projected disability and mortality experience through age 65.[9] A final step involves benchmarking disability and mortality results to projections from SSA's Office of the Chief Actuary (OCACT). Mortality after age 65 is based on statistical equations relating mortality to socioeconomic and other variables.

In what follows, we use both income and wealth measures to characterize economic well-being. Two income measures are used: income relative to the poverty-level standard and income relative to average earnings in the economy. Income and poverty thresholds are used to form welfare ratios, which is defined as family income divided by the appropriate poverty threshold. Welfare ratios can then be used to define the population that is poor (with a welfare ratio < 1), but the distribution of welfare ratios can also be used to describe the well-being of the overall population. Income relative to average earnings in the economy provides another perspective, namely, indicating how retirees fare relative to workers and whether there are generational changes after adjusting for economy-wide wage growth. In MINT, family income equals the sum of individual and spouse (if married) income from Social Security, earnings, assets, defined benefit (DB) pensions, and Supplemental Security Income plus any income from a coresident family member.[10] For the parents, the matched earnings data are used to measure earnings in 1998 and used to calculate Social Security benefit amounts. For Boomers, future earnings must be projected and then used to determine earnings and Social Security benefit amounts in 2022. These projections assume no changes to Social Security benefits.[11] Poverty thresholds as per the US Bureau of the Census vary by family size and are updated each year to reflect price changes (the thresholds used for the Boomers in 2022 were derived by adjusting existing thresholds for expected inflation).

Pension income is captured in two ways in MINT. First, income from a DB plan is a direct source of income. For both Boomers and parents, some respondents have this source of income projected (although many of the parents have DB pension income in the SIPP).[12] Second, MINT projects account balances of defined contribution (DC) plans. The starting points for these projections are account balances reported in SIPP, adjusted to match levels in the Survey of Consumer Finances (SCF). Asset allocations within the account are based on age-specific profiles developed using data on 401(k) plans from the Employee Benefit Research Institute (EBRI) and the Investment Company Institute (ICI). Contributions to plans are based on SIPP responses and EBRI/ICI data. Rates of return on asset classes are based (approximately) on historical returns, but individual outcomes are modeled stochastically (based on draws from a normal distribution). The MINT projections attempt to account for future job changes and the possibility that retirement accounts will be cashed out and spent on a job change. Retirement account wealth is part of the wealth that is used to determine asset income in MINT. Thus, in principle, both types of pensions are captured in the income-related measures in MINT such as welfare ratios.[13]

The values of home equity and net financial wealth are also projected in MINT. The measure of net financial wealth we use for wealth comparisons is nonpension wealth, which excludes the value of retirement accounts such as 401(k) plans. By excluding retirement accounts, the wealth comparisons between Boomers and their parents will not be driven by changes in the types of pensions received by each generation (DB vs. DC). Financial wealth is net of credit card debt, doctors' bills, and other unsecured debt. Both the value of home equity and net financial wealth are expressed as per capita measures; for respondents who are married, the per capita measure is simply the household value divided by two.[14] Home equity projections in MINT compare closely to those reflected in the 1998 SCF, indicating that home equity values for the parents of the Boomers in 1998 (when they were age 62–72) are validated. Home equity values for Boomers as of 1998 also lined up with SCF values, but it is an open question as to whether MINT can accurately project the values forward to their retirement years. One concern is that the statistical equations used to project home equity were developed on data that do not reflect sharp trends associated with housing that occurred after 1998; both home values and debt secured by homes have increased sharply since 1998.[15]

Results

Demographic Overview

Table 6-1 summarizes key characteristics of the populations examined below. Here, 'parents' are defined as those born from 1926–36 (age 62–72 in 1998), while 'Boomers' are defined as those born from 1950–60 (age 62–72 in 2022). One finding is that parents have noticeably lower levels of educational attainment: nearly 27 percent did not finish high school and only 18 percent graduated from college. By contrast, only 11 percent of Boomers dropped out of high school and nearly 29 percent hold college degrees. Minority groups make up a larger percentage of the retiree population in 2022 than in 1998. Of particular note is the rapid growth of Asian/Native American and Hispanic retirees. The prevalence of marriage among members of the parents' generation is greater, but perhaps of equal interest, the relative sizes of the unmarried groups differ across generations. Specifically, Boomers will have decidedly higher percentages of never-married and divorced persons, making it a more heterogeneous group.

The Economic Status of Baby Boomers and Their Parents

In what follows, individuals are classified as being 'in poverty' if their family income is less than the appropriate household-size-adjusted poverty threshold in the year of analysis. MINT projects a significant decrease in

TABLE 6-1 Demographic Characteristics of Parents'
Generation in 1998 and Boomers'
Generation in 2022, Both at Age 62–72

	Parents (%)	Boomers (%)
Sex		
Female	54.0	53.7
Male	46.0	46.4
Ethnicity		
White	81.9	74.0
African-American	8.4	9.9
Asian/Native-American	3.5	6.5
Hispanic	6.2	9.6
Education Level		
High school dropout	26.9	10.9
High school graduate	55.3	60.4
College graduate	17.8	28.6
Marital Status		
Never married	4.2	6.5
Married	69.8	65.1
Widowed	16.2	11.9
Divorced	9.9	16.5

Source: Authors' calculations.

the poverty rate from 6.8 percent in the parents' generation to 4.4 percent among the Baby Boomers (see Table 6-2).[16] The projected decrease in poverty from earlier cohorts to Boomers is consistent with both historical trends in aged poverty and the findings of other studies (Butrica and Uccello 2004; Butrica et al., this volume). The projected decrease in poverty is largely the result of expected growth in real wages, since the poverty level is indexed to prices (wages are projected to grow faster than prices by an annual rate of 1.1%).

Next we report the welfare ratio, or the ratio of family income to the family poverty threshold.[17] Our results show that the welfare ratios at the 10th, 25th, 50th, 75th, and 90th percentiles will all rise, from the time the parents' generation is aged 62–72 to when the Boomers reach the same age (see Table 6-3). This again reflects, in large part, the effects of projected real wage growth. It is also possible to use the welfare ratio to measure *relatively* low income: one relative measure of low income is the percentage of persons with a welfare ratio less than half the median for the group. Using this measure, 19.4 percent of the parents have low income relative to their peers versus to 21.5 percent of Boomers (percentages not shown). This illustrates an important point regarding trends in the incidence of low

TABLE 6-2 Percentage in Poverty: Parents' Generation in 1998 and
Boomers' Generation in 2022, both at Age 62–72

Parents	6.8%
Boomers	4.4%
Percentage change	−35.2%

Source: Authors' calculations.

Notes: The official definition of poverty in the United States is based on a comparison of pretax cash income with poverty thresholds that vary by age, family size, and composition. The thresholds, which are adjusted each year for inflation, were initially developed in the 1960s based on a determination of the minimum amount of income needed to provide for an inexpensive but adequate food diet and other expenses (Fisher 1992). MINT analysis generally uses the official approach to measuring poverty in the United States. However, MINT projects only the major sources of cash income and uses only the thresholds that apply to the elderly population.

income: using an absolute standard (the poverty threshold), Boomers will be less likely to have low income than their parents, but the opposite is true using a relative standard.

Table 6-3 also shows that welfare ratios at each percentile are not projected to increase at the same rate: that is, the ratio between the 90th and the 10th percentiles is expected to increase from 7.98 to 11.17. Thus, there is an increase in absolute economic well-being throughout the income distribution, but also an increase in income inequality. Income inequality can be formally measured with a Gini coefficient, where the Gini of 0 represents complete income equality and a value of 1 represents complete inequality. For parents, the coefficient equals 0.513, and for Boomers, the coefficient rises to 0.596. Although this suggests rising inequality, it should be noted that the Gini coefficient is only one measure of inequality and that other inequality indices may rank distributions differently (Litchfield 1999).[18] Rising inequality of income across generations is consistent with recent

TABLE 6-3 Income as a Percentage of Poverty-Level Income: Welfare Ratios for
Parents' Generation in 1998 and Boomers' Generation in 2022, both
at Age 62–72

	10th Percentile	Lower Quartile	Median	Upper Quartile	90th Percentile
Parents	1.3	2.2	3.7	6.1	10.1
Boomers	1.6	2.9	5.3	9.5	18.0
Percentage change	27.8%	33.3%	40.3%	57.3%	78.8%

Source: Authors' calculations.

TABLE 6-4 Per Capita Income as a Percentage of the Average Wage: Parents'
Generation in 1998 and Boomers' Generation in 2022, both at Age
62–72

	10th Percentile (%)	Lower Quartile (%)	Median (%)	Upper Quartile (%)	90th Percentile (%)
Parents	23.2	40.6	69.5	115.2	193.6
Boomers	22.8	41.5	74.7	140.2	265.2
Percentage change	−1.6	2.3	7.4	21.7	37.0

Source: Authors' calculations.

Notes: For an unmarried person, per capita income equals his or her individual income. For a married couple, the total income of the couple is divided by two. The average wage equals historical or projected values of the Social Security Administration's Average Wage Index series, which measures average earnings in the economy.

research on increasing earnings inequality (Lee 2005). In addition, it may reflect the greater underlying heterogeneity in the Boomer population.

Another income-based measure of economic well-being is presented in Table 6-4: per capita income as a percentage of the average earnings in the economy. This measure provides two perspectives: how retirees fare relative to workers in the analysis year, and whether the income gains exhibited by Boomers persist after accounting for wage growth. Median per capita income of the parents' generation, at ages 62–72, is about 70 percent of average earnings in 1998. Per capita income rises sharply for Boomers at the upper part of the income distribution, but less so at the median. For Boomers, median per capita income at ages 62–72 is about 75 percent of the projected average earnings in the economy in 2022. At the 90th percentile, the figure is 265 percent of average earnings, which reflects a sizable increase relative to the parents' generation. The Gini coefficients for this income measure reflect the changes in the income distribution. For the parents' generation the Gini coefficient equals 0.517, but rises to 0.601 for Boomers.

Median per capita net wealth is also projected to increase relative to average earnings (Table 6-5). As a ratio of the average wage, it rises from 1.1 in the parents' generation to 1.3 for Boomers. In constant $2004 (not shown in Table 6-5), median wealth rises from $36,700 to $57,700. The projected increase in retirement wealth from the parents' generation to the Boomers is consistent with what would be expected given the results of previous studies examining recent trends in wealth. For example, Sabelhaus and Manchester (1995) determined that Boomers aged 25–44 were accumulating total wealth (housing and financial) more quickly than their parents at the same age. Poterba et al. (2001) found that the ratio of assets saved for

TABLE 6-5 Net Nonpension Financial Wealth for Parents' Generation in 1998
and Boomers' Generation in 2022, both at Age 62–72: Per Capita
Ratio of Wealth to Average Wage

	10th Percentile	Lower Quartile	Median	Upper Quartile	90th Percentile
Parents	0.0	0.2	1.1	4.2	11.3
Boomers	0.0	0.3	1.3	5.0	17.1
Percentage change	NA	113.3%	18.9%	18.4%	51.2%

Source: Authors' calculations.

Notes: For an unmarried person, per capita net wealth equals his or her net wealth. For a
married couple, the total wealth of the couple is divided by 2.

retirement to wage income increased from 0.39 to 2.02 during 1975–1999;
this result, however, was largely due to the increased prevalence and use of
DB pension plans.

As with the income distribution, the distribution of financial wealth is
more unequal for the Boomer generation. The Gini coefficient for the
wealth distribution of the parents' generation equals 0.816; the corresponding percentage for the Boomers is 0.861.[19] Again, however, wealth generally
increases at every part of the distribution for the Boomers.

There are also projected to be substantial cross-cohort differences in
housing wealth. The MINT model projects lower median home equity
relative to the average wage for Boomers (Table 6-6). This differs from
Coronado et al. (Chapter 14, this volume) but MINT uses data that do
not capture recent trends in the housing market so our results should be
viewed with caution. It is interesting to note that *mean* housing wealth is
projected to increase among Boomers both in constant dollar terms and
relative to the average wage. Tabulations from MINT (not shown in Table
6-6) indicate that, across generations, mean housing wealth increases from
$58,000 to $89,000 ($2004) and from 1.76 times the average wage to 2.04
times the average wage. In other words, MINT projects a more unequal

TABLE 6-6 Home Equity for Parents' Generation in 1998 and Boomers'
Generation in 2022, both at Age 62–72: Per capita Ratio of Home
Equity to Average Wage

	10th Percentile	Lower Quartile	Median	Upper Quartile	90th Percentile
Parents	0.0	0.1	1.2	2.5	4.2
Boomers	0.0	0.1	0.8	2.3	4.9
Percentage change	NA	0.00%	−33.1%	−8.0%	18.5%

Source: Authors' calculations.

distribution of housing wealth where the median declines but the mean rises. This can also be seen with Gini coefficients. The Gini coefficient for the home equity distribution of the parents' generation is 0.571, but rises substantially to 0.690 for the Boomers.[20]

Overall, the results presented in this section are consistent with the general conclusions offered by CBO (2003) following a review of studies on the Boomer population: namely, that economic well-being will improve for the typical Boomer. As the detailed distributions of outcomes presented in this section make clear, however, median outcomes do not present policymakers with a complete picture of relevant populations. Further, conclusions about the Boomers' prosperity relative to their parents depend crucially on the measure of economic well-being. By one measure of low income (poverty), Boomers will see sharp improvements in well-being. Using another measure (percentage with a welfare ratio less than half the group median), Boomers are characterized by a slightly higher proportion of low-income individuals. Finally, whether well-being for the typical Boomer improves sharply or only modestly depends on whether financial resources are adjusted across generations using price growth or wage growth. Relative to average wages in the economy, the typical Boomer will see only modest improvements in retirement income, while those at the upper end of the income distribution are expected to experience significantly larger improvements.

The Health Status of Baby Boomers and their Parents

Turning next to health status, our projections indicate sizable majorities of both parents and Boomers are in good or excellent health at ages 62–72 (Table 6-7). Almost three-quarters of Boomers are projected to assess their heath status as good or excellent at these ages. The percentage of persons in fair/poor health declines by over 4 percentage points across generations or at about a rate of 0.2 percentage points per year (twenty-four years separate the two groups under study).

TABLE 6-7 Self-Assessed Health Status: Parents'
Generation in 1998 and Boomers'
Generation in 2022, both at Age 62–72

	Fair/Poor (%)	Good/Excellent (%)
Parents	30.9	69.2
Boomers	26.6	73.4
Percentage change	−13.7	6.1

Source: Authors' calculations.

TABLE 6-8 Work Limitations for Parents' Generation in 1998 and Boomers' Generation in 2022, both at Age 62–67

	No Limitation (%)	Work Limited (%)	Unable to Work (%)
Parents	68.1	14.2	17.7
Boomers	72.2	12.6	15.3
Percentage change	5.9	−11.4	−13.7

Source: Authors' calculations.

Projections regarding work limitations also indicate health improvements for Boomers (Table 6-8). For 72 percent of Boomers in the 62–67 age range, health will not limit or prevent the kind or amount of work they can do, according to projections. The percentage without a work limitation is projected to increase by 4 percentage points across generations or about 0.2 percentage points per year. Note that only 15 percent of Boomers will be unable to work at these ages.

The projected decline from the parents' generation to the Baby Boomers in the incidence of health problems that either limit work or make work impossible is supported by recent historical data. Crimmins, Reynolds, and Saito (1997) find an overall decrease in the percentage of those aged 50–69 that report being unable to work, using National Health Interview Survey data from 1982 to 1993. The authors conclude that the most significant improvements in this measure of health occurred for those between the ages of 62 and 69 and were primarily correlated with increases in educational attainment.

As noted earlier, the MINT model does not include a time trend in its projections of health status. Toder et al. (2002) found that MINT captured improving health over time, but the magnitude of the improvements was smaller than historical data would suggest. Thus, the estimates of improved health among Boomers are likely conservative, meaning that Boomers may enjoy better health in retirement than these projections indicate. In addition, Weir (Chapter 5, this volume) suggests that improved medical treatments may lead to better health outcomes over the next few decades. A respondent is categorized as disabled in MINT if he or she ever received or is projected to receive disability benefits from Social Security. Upon initial inspection of the MINT data for those aged 62–72 in 1998 and 2022 (Table 6-9), an apparent paradox emerges: although Baby Boomers exhibit lower incidences of fair/poor health and work limitations than their parents, they simultaneously demonstrate an increase of 20.4 percent in receipt of disability benefits. This result requires explanation.

The receipt of DI benefits is not an entirely consistent measure of health across birth cohorts because numerous factors other than health

TABLE 6-9 Disability receipt

A. During Lifetime for Parents' Generation in 1998 and Boomers' Generation in 2022, both at Age 62–72

Parents	9.8%
Boomers	11.8%
Percentage change	20.4%

	Men (%)	Women (%)

B. By Generation and Gender for Parents' Generation in 1998 and Boomers' Generation in 2022, both at Age 62–72

	Men (%)	Women (%)
Parents	12.5	7.5
Boomers	12.8	10.9
Percentage change	2.7%	45.5%

Source: Authors' calculations.

can influence benefit receipt. Many of those factors are discussed in the Zayatz (1999) analysis of Social Security's DI program. These include legislative reforms, the state of the economy, demographic changes, shifts in work patterns, and changes in the medical requirements for enrollment. Some changes that are particularly relevant in the context of disability rates increasing from the parents' generation to the Boomers' are the programmatic expansion of DI eligibility and the involvement of more women in the workforce. MINT projects an increase in the percentage of persons who have ever received DI benefits by generation and by sex (panel 9A). The percentage of women aged 62–72 that are projected to ever receive DI benefits is projected to increase from 7.5 percent in the parents' generation to 10.9 percent in the Boomers' generation (a 45.5% increase). The increase for men is much smaller. Thus, while DI receipt has grown for both groups—for many of the reasons discussed by Zayatz—factors related specifically to women are of paramount importance. Baby Boomer women have more substantial work histories and are more likely to be insured for disability benefits. Thus, the trend in disability receipt across generations is driven by underlying work patterns and other factors and likely does not reflect declining health.

Life expectancy represents the mean projected age of death for those in the two analysis groups. Recall that the age range is 62–72 for each group; thus, all members in each group have lived or are projected to live to at least age 62. Although not as direct as self-reported health (SRH) status, life expectancy represents another important measure of physical well-being. MINT projects a modest increase in the average age of death for those living to at least age 62 from the 85.3 in the parents' generation to 86.7 for Baby

TABLE 6-10 Life Expectancy for Those Who Survive to at Least Age 62 for Parents' Generation in 1998 and Boomers' Generation in 2022, both at Age 62–72

Parents	85.3
Boomers	86.7
Percentage change	1.7%

Source: Authors' calculations.

Boomers (Table 6-10). This improvement in life expectancy is consistent with recent trends and projections from other sources. In the twentieth century life expectancy at age 65 rose by over nine years and although this trend is projected to slow somewhat, the positive change in mortality is expected to continue in the future (Wilmoth 2005).

The increase in life expectancy from the parents' generation to that of the Baby Boomers projected by MINT is another indicator of improvements in projected health status for the 1950–1960 birth cohort. In sum, MINT projections indicate Boomers can expect to live healthier lives, at least in the first ten years of retirement, as well as longer lives.

The Relationship between Health and Economic Well-Being

Thus far, we have concluded that the average Baby Boomer can expect to do better than his or her parents, according to almost all measures of economic well-being and health status. But good health will not be universal. The economic status of those who suffer from health problems is a significant concern, as past research indicates that this group is more likely to be financially disadvantaged. Although the correlation between economic and health status is well documented, the causal relationship is not fully known. For example, Sapolsky (2005) finds that relative poverty may actually decrease physical well-being. For our analysis of those aged 62–72, it is likely that the two factors are mutually reinforcing; the relatively poor become less healthy and are able to earn less during their lifetimes because of employment problems associated with physical problems.

Within each generation, the relationship between health status and economic well-being is clear: those with health problems have sharply lower economic status (Table 6-11). For example, the overall poverty rate in the parents' generation is 6.8 percent, but it rises to 10.3 percent for parents in poor/fair health. Similarly high poverty rates occur using other measures of health problems: 9.9 percent (limited in work), 10.1 percent (unable to work), 9.1 percent (DI receipt), and 8.2 percent (shorter than average

TABLE 6-11 Economic Well-Being and Health Status for Parents' Generation in 1998 and Boomers' Generation in 2022, both at Age 62–72

	Poverty	*Median Welfare Ratio*	*Median Wealth*
Overall			
Parents	6.8	3.7	1.1
Boomers	4.4	5.3	1.3
Percentage change	−35.2%	40.3%	18.9%
Poor/fair health			
Parents	10.3	3.0	0.6
Boomers	7.6	4.0	0.8
Percentage change	−26.8%	34.3%	32.2%
Work limited			
Parents	9.9	3.7	0.8
Boomers	6.2	5.2	1.2
Percentage change	−37.4%	39.8%	43.4%
Unable to work			
Parents	10.1	3.4	0.6
Boomers	6.5	4.3	0.9
Percentage change	−35.6%	28.2%	36.5%
Disabled			
Parents	9.1	2.5	0.3
Boomers	4.0	3.8	0.8
Percentage change	−56.2%	49.8%	203.9%
Less than average life expectancy			
Parents	8.2	3.4	0.9
Boomers	5.3	4.9	1.2
Percentage change	−35.6%	42.7%	30.7%

Source: Authors' calculations.

life expectancy). In addition, those in the parents' generation with health problems consistently have lower median welfare ratios and median net financial wealth. This same pattern appears for Boomers, though it is possible the MINT projections understate the relationship between poor health and low economic status. As noted earlier for the parents' generation, tabulations from survey data revealed a somewhat larger effect than did MINT estimates.

One concern for policymakers may be whether Boomers' improvements in economic well-being will be distributed equally with regard to health, or whether Boomers with health problems will miss out on the effects of economic growth. Table 6-11 suggests improvements in economic well-being even for persons with health problems. The overall poverty rate declines by 35.2 percent across generations. Declines of similar magnitude

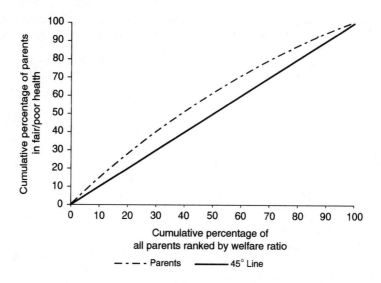

Figure 6-1. Concentration curve of fair/poor health by welfare ratio for parents. (*Source*: Authors' calculations using the Modeling Income in the Near Term (MINT) model. See text.)

are found across generations for persons with health problems. For example, Boomers unable to work are still 35.6 percent less likely to be in poverty than parents with the same health status. The results hold for other measures of health problems and other measures of economic well-being (median welfare ratios and net financial wealth). One intriguing result for Boomers relates to receipt of DI. The economic well-being of those who have survived to age 62 and received DI is projected to improve dramatically.

Another way to assess the relationship between health conditions and economic status is through a concentration curve or an associated concentration index. These tools are used in health economics to determine the extent to which health problems are concentrated among persons with limited resources (World Bank 2006). As an example, Figure 6-1 presents the concentration curve for the parents' generation using the poor/fair health measure. On the vertical axis is the cumulative percentage of persons in poor/fair health and on the horizontal is the cumulative percentage of all persons (ranked from low to high in economic status, using welfare ratios). The curve lies above the 45 degree line because poor/fair health is concentrated among persons with low welfare ratios. For example, the poorest 10 percent of the population contains 15 percent of the population that is in poor or fair health. A concentration index, which ranges from −1 to 1, can be calculated based on the area of the concentration curve

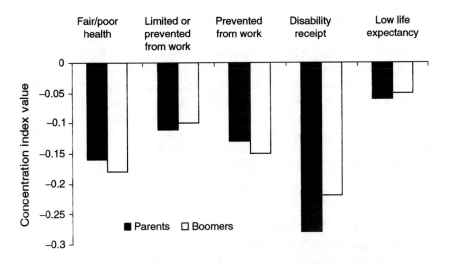

Figure 6-2. Concentration index by health measure. (*Source:* Authors' calculations using the Modeling Income in the Near Term (MINT) model. See text.)

(World Bank 2006). Negative values are associated with curves above the 45 degree line. The concentration index value associated with Figure 6-1 is −0.16 which indicates that, in the parents' generation, poor or fair health is moderately concentrated among persons with low income. For ease of exposition, concentration index values, rather than graphical displays of concentration curves, are presented for each generation and each health measure (see Figure 6-2).

The concentration index values presented in Figure 6-2 can be used to assess three issues: whether health problems are associated with low income, the degree to which such problems are concentrated among those with low economic status, and whether the relationship between health and income is changing across generations. First, all values of the index, regardless of health measure or generation, are negative. Thus, health problems are consistently found to be concentrated among persons with low income. Second, the degree of concentration appears to be limited. None of the index values are close to the negative bound for a concentration index (−1). In addition, except for DI receipt, the index values are not far from 0 (ranging from about −0.05 to −0.15). An index value of 0 would indicate that health problems are spread evenly among the population without regard to income. Finally, there is no pattern to suggest Boomers will exhibit greater health inequality (concentration index values for the Boomers are lower for three of the five health measures).

Disability receipt stands out from the other measures because of the high value of its concentration index. It is important to keep in mind, however, that the estimation methods for the self-assessed health measures may not fully capture the relationship between economic status and health outcomes. As noted earlier, actual survey data revealed a stronger relationship than MINT estimates. In contrast, DI receipt may be measured more accurately (it is based wholly or in part on SSA administrative data). This suggests some caution in interpreting the absolute size of the index values for the self-assessed health variables. Finally, note that the value of the concentration index for DI receipt falls sharply across generations. This is consistent with results from Table 6-11: Boomers will witness a weaker relationship between low income and disability receipt.

Conclusions and Discussion

The well-being of the Baby Boomers in retirement is a topic of increasing importance to researchers and policymakers. Our study examines economic well-being in the context of projected health and disability status, an approach we believe offers a more complete picture of how Boomers will fare in their retirement years. Our projections indicate that Boomers will enjoy higher levels of real income and lower levels of poverty in retirement than their parents. Income among Boomers is projected to be more unequal, but it is important to note that real income rises across generations at all parts of the income distribution. Income relative to average earnings in the economy is also projected to increase among Boomers. As the average wage is one measure of a society's standard of living, these results suggest that Boomers' economic progress is not limited to inflation-adjusted gains. It should be noted, however, that increases in income relative to average earnings occur mainly at the upper portions of the income distribution and are only of modest size at median values. Further, these results address income relative to earnings in a given analysis year but do not consider income relative to career earnings. Butrica et al. (Chapter 4, this volume) suggest that replacement rates for many Boomers will be lower than for current retirees.

Results regarding net nonpension financial wealth exhibit a similar pattern to the income results. Boomers are projected to have higher levels of this measure of wealth, both in real terms and relative to the average wage. Gini coefficients indicate wealth is more unequal among the Boomers than their parents, but all parts of the net nonpension wealth distribution exhibit improvements. Mean home equity is projected to increase for the Boomers, but not median home equity, a result that may indicate problems in projecting home equity.

Boomers are projected to have relatively fewer health problems in retirement than their parents. This is true regardless of the health measure employed. These results bode well for policy efforts to encourage additional work at later ages. Only 15 percent of Boomers is projected to be unable to work at ages 62–67 because of health problems. Another encouraging result is that improvements in economic well-being for the Boomer generation occur even for those with health limitations. For example, among persons in poor or fair health, the poverty rate falls by nearly 27 percent when comparing Boomers to their parents. Unlike the results regarding income and wealth, projections do not indicate increasing inequality in health status. Poor health is not increasingly concentrated across generations among persons with limited resources. Nevertheless, we find a consistent correlation between low economic status and health problems. Policymakers concerned with low-income individuals should realize such individuals also fare poorly when health status is used to assess well-being.

Our analysis suggests several directions for future research. Additional research on methods to project health conditions is warranted, perhaps focusing on direct measurement of health trends as well as changes due to underlying population characteristics. In addition, direct measures of disabling conditions would be invaluable, including functional limitations or an inability to engage in activities related to independent living. Finally, one of the important economic variables used in the study—home equity—does not appear to move in tandem across generations with other variables measuring economic resources. Projections on home equity in MINT could be examined in light of more recent data on housing wealth.

Acknowledgments

The authors thank Andrew Biggs, Sharmila Choudhury, Lionel Deang, Edward DeMarco, Lynn Fisher, Howard Iams, Olivia S. Mitchell, Mark Sarney, and Dave Shoffner for their help and comments.

Notes

[1] The MINT model used for this paper is the combined MINT 3.0/4.0 version, which is based on SIPP panels from 1990–93 and 1996. Earlier versions of MINT such as MINT 3.0 do not include the 1996 panel.

[2] A MINT extended or 'MINTEX' model has also been developed, which projects outcomes for birth cohorts through 2017. Results from MINTEX are not needed for this paper because the latest birth cohort examined here is from 1960.

[3] Regarding the parents' sample, our birth cohorts generally predate the 'original HRS' cohorts.

[4] By restricting the age range to 10 years, data on the parents' generation is often drawn directly from survey or administrative data and not subject to the uncertainties associated with projections.

[5] Both the 1998 MINT results and the 1996 SIPP survey reports indicate that about 30 percent of persons aged 62–72 are in poor or fair health. Both sources indicate persons in poor or fair health have a higher poverty rate, but the MINT results indicate a weaker relationship. In MINT, the poverty rate of those in poor or fair health is 1.5 times higher than the rate for persons of all health statuses. The corresponding figure in the SIPP is 1.9.

[6] The DI beneficiaries are converted to retired worker beneficiaries at the full retirement age (FRA) under Social Security. The measure in this paper is based on whether the respondent received DI benefits at some point, which includes persons who converted at the FRA.

[7] Note, however, that Rupp and Davies (2004) found that self-assessed health was predictive of subsequent mortality.

[8] MINT is benchmarked to several projections in the 2004 report of the Social Security Trustees, including projections of real wage growth at a level of 1.1 percent per year.

[9] Note that earnings after age 50 are projected using a specific retirement model rather than a nearest-neighbor approach.

[10] Coresident income is estimated as an aggregate in MINT and is not broken down by source of income.

[11] Social Security is projected to be able to pay current law scheduled benefits until 2040 (Board of Trustees, *Federal Old-Age and Survivors Insurance and Disability Insurance Trust Fund* 2006). The FRA under Social Security is scheduled to increase under current law and the Boomers will face a larger early retirement penalty than did their parents.

[12] Projections of DB pension income for private sector jobs utilize plan formulas maintained in the Pension Insurance Modeling System (PIMS). The PIMS information is statistically matched to each job of the respondent covered by a pension. Different methods are used for public-sector pensions.

[13] Additional information on DB and DC pension projections is available in Toder et al. (2002).

[14] The techniques used in MINT to project home equity and financial wealth are complicated. A good discussion can be found at Toder et al. (2002) and Smith et al. (2005). Initial values of home equity and financial wealth are available for SIPP respondents. The initial values for financial wealth (but not home equity) are adjusted to match outcomes in the SCF. A series of statistical equations based on the PSID, HRS, and SIPP are used to 'age' a respondent's home equity and wealth values.

[15] The SCF data indicate median house values, relative to the average wage, increased by about 30 percent between 1998 and 2004. The increase in the median debt secured by homes also rose sharply (24%).

[16] All figures in this paper include data reported to the 10th place, however the percentage change figures are computed using the same data with the 100th place included. Thus, if attempting to compute percentage change based on the included data, results will differ.

[17] For more on poverty line concepts see Fisher (1992).

[18] Litchfield (1999) contains a discussion of this issue and methods to resolve ambiguous rankings by different measures.

[19] Relative to income, wealth typically has a more unequal distribution. For United States, Rodríguez et al. (2002) report a Gini of 0.803 for household net worth and a Gini of 0.553 for income.

[20] Although the results on home equity should be viewed with caution, Toder et al. (2002) offer possible rationales for the declining median values projected by MINT including the larger percentage of the population that is African-American or Hispanic, significant growth in housing values compared to wage growth during the 1960s and 1970s that benefited the parents' generation, longer mortgage terms, and increased use of home equity loans.

References

Arbeev, K. G., Butov, A. A., Manton, K. G., Sannikov I. A., and Yashin, A. I. (2004). 'Disability Trends in Gender and Race Groups of Early Retirement Ages in the USA', *Sozial-Und Praventivmedizin*, 49(2): 142–51.

Bernheim, B. D. (1993). 'Is the Baby Boom Generation Preparing Adequately for Retirement?', Summary Report, Princeton, NJ: Merrill Lynch.

Board of Trustees, Federal Old-Age and Survivors Insurance, and Disability Insurance Trust Funds (2006). *The 2006 Annual Report of the Board of Trustees of the Federal Old-Age and Survivors Insurance and Disability Insurance Trust Funds.* Washington, DC: Social Security Administration. Available at http://www.ssa.gov/OACT/TR/TR06/tr06.pdf

Butrica, B., Iams, H., and Smith, K. (this volume). 'It's All Relative: Understanding the Retirement Prospects of Baby Boomers'.

—— and Uccello, C. (2004). 'How Will Boomers Fare at Retirement?' AARP Public Policy Institute Paper 2004–05, American Association of Retired Persons, Washington, DC.

Congressional Budget Office (2003). *Baby Boomers' Retirement Prospects: An Overview,* Congressional Budget Office, Washington, DC.

Coronado, J., Maki, D., and Weitzer, B. (this volume). 'Retiring on the House? Cross-Cohort Differences in Housing Wealth'.

Crimmins, E. M. (2004). 'Trends in the Health of the Elderly', *Annual Review of Public Health,* 25: 79–98.

—— Reynolds, S. L., and Saito, Y. (1997). 'Trends and Differences in Health and Ability to Work—Older Working and Early Retirement Ages', *Social Security Bulletin,* 60(3): 50–2.

Engen, E. M., Gale, W. G., and Uccello, C. R. (1999). 'The Adequacy of Retirement Saving', *Brookings Papers on Economic Activity,* 2: 65–165.

Gale, W. G. (1997). 'The Aging of America: Will the Baby Boom Be Ready for Retirement?', *Brookings Review,* 15(3): 4–9.

Fisher, G. M. (1992). 'The Development and History of the Poverty Thresholds', *Social Security Bulletin,* 55(4): 3–14.

Lee, C. (2005). 'Rising Family Income Inequality in the United States, 1968–2000: Impacts of Changing Labor Supply, Wages, and Family Structure', National Bureau of Economic Research Working Paper No. 11836, Cambridge, MA.

Levy, H. (this volume). 'Health Insurance Coverage of the Baby Boomers Approaching Retirement'.

Litchfield, J. A. (1999). 'Inequality: Methods and Tools', World Bank, Washington, DC.

Lubitz, J. (2004). 'Getting Older, Staying Healthier: The Demographics of Health Care', Testimony before the Joint Economic Committee, US Senate, Washington, DC.

Moore, J. F. and Mitchell, O. S. (2000). 'Projected Retirement Wealth and Saving Adequacy', in O. S. Mitchell, P. B. Hammond, and A. M. Rappaport (eds.), *Forecasting Retirement Needs and Retirement Wealth.* Philadelphia, PA: University of Pennsylvania Press, pp. 68–94.

Poterba, J., Venti, S., and Wise, D. (2001). 'The Transition to Personal Accounts and Increasing Retirement Wealth: Macro and Micro Evidence', National Bureau of Economic Research Working Paper No. 8610, Cambridge, MA.

Rodríguez, S. B., Díaz-Giménez, J., Quadrini, V., and Ríos-Rull, J-V. (2002). 'Updated Facts on the U.S. Distributions of Earnings, Income, and Wealth', *Federal Reserve Bank of Minneapolis Quarterly Review,* 26(3): 2–35.

Rupp, K. and Davies, P. S. (2004). 'A Long-Term View of Health Status, Disabilities, Mortality, and Participation in the DI and SSI Disability Programs', in S. W. Polachek (ed.), *Research in Labor Economics 23, Accounting for Worker Well-being.* Amsterdam: Elsevier, JAI Press, pp. 119–83.

Sabelhaus, J. and Manchester, J. (1995). 'Baby Boomers and Their Parents: How Does Their Economic Well-being Compare in Middle Age?', *The Journal of Human Resources,* 30(4): 791–806.

Sapolsky, R. (2005). 'Sick of Poverty', *Scientific American,* (December): 93–9.

Scholz, J. K., Seshadri, A., and Khitatrakun, S. (2005). 'Are Americans Saving "Optimally" for Retirement?', Faculty Research Paper, University of Wisconsin-Madison.

Smith, K. E., Cashin, D., and Favreault, M. (2005). *Modeling Income in the Near Term 4: Revised Projections of Retirement Income Through 2020 for the 1931–1960 Birth Cohorts.* Washington, DC: Urban Institute.

Sturm, R., Ringel, J. S., and Andreyeva, T. (2004). 'Increasing Obesity Rates and Disability Trends', *Health Affairs,* 23(2): 199–205.

Toder, E., Thompson, L., Favreault, M., Johnson, R., Perese, K., Ratcliffe, C., Smith, K., Uccello, C., Waidmann, T., Berk, J., and Woldemariam, R. (2002). *Modeling Income in the Near Term: Revised Projections of Retirement Income Through 2020 for the 1931–1960 Birth Cohorts.* Washington, DC: Urban Institute.

Weir, D. (this volume). 'Living Well Longer? Generational Trends in Health at Middle Age, 1992–2004'.

Wentworth, S. G. and Pattison, D. (2001–02). 'Income Growth and Future Poverty Rates of the Aged', *Social Security Bulletin,* 64(3): 23–37.

Wilmoth, J. (2005). 'Overview and Discussion of the Social Security Mortality Projections', Working Paper for the 2003 Technical Panel on Assumptions and Methods, Social Security Advisory Board, Washington, DC.

Wolf, D., Hunt, K., and Knickman, J. (2005). 'Perspectives on the Recent Decline in Disability at Older Ages', *Milbank Quarterly*, 83(3): 365–95.

World Bank (2006). 'The Concentration Index. Quantitative Techniques for Health Equity Analysis', World Bank Technical Note No. 7, Washington, DC: World Bank.

Zayatz, T. (1999). 'Social Security Disability Insurance Program Worker Experience', Actuarial Study No. 114, Office of the Chief Actuary, Social Security Administration, Washington, DC.

Chapter 7

Cross-Cohort Differences in Health on the Verge of Retirement

Beth J. Soldo, Olivia S. Mitchell, Rania Tfaily, and John F. McCabe

The demographic cohort known as the Baby Boom has always had profound impacts on society, first with a tsunami of young children washing through the educational system, and later with a wave of young people inundating job and marriage markets. Now the oldest Boomers are poised to flood into retirement with important implications for public and private pension systems, health care programs, and cross-generational transfers. Yet because this cohort has not yet fully retired, it is difficult to project how well Boomers will fare in retirement. This chapter compares the health of the Early Boomer cohort to that of previous generations, as they were poised on the verge of retirement. Our work will help evaluate whether evidence from past cohorts can be used for projecting Boomers' future health and retirement security.

Our analysis relies on responses to the Health and Retirement Study (HRS) to examine individual determinants of health for respondents born in 1948–53, the so-called Early Baby Boomer (EBB) cohort, with two older cohorts born 1936–41 and 1942–47. Our goal is to determine whether and why stocks of health capital differ across cohorts on the verge of retirement. We estimate fixed-effect models with life-cycle and lifestyle factors, both past and present, as 'inputs' into a model of health capital accumulated by age 51–56, that is, the age of entry into the HRS. We conclude that Boomers do not appear to be entering retirement better positioned than their recent predecessors.

In what follows, we first discuss the motivation for cohort models of preretirement health. Next, we summarize our analysis sample and statistical framework including an Item Response Theory (IRT) model of health. Empirical findings regarding the stock of health are then provided using first a fixed-effect model with no interactions, and then allowing for sex and cohort interactions with a number of background predictors. The last section offers conclusions and draws out policy implications.

Cohort Models and Methods

Demographers consider each birth cohort unique because it represents the singular intersection of historical time and chronological age. People born just before World War II, for example, enjoyed the benefits of penicillin and antibiotics throughout most of their adult lives, as well as economic growth during their 20s, the decade of labor market entry and family formation, and also during their 40s, their peak earnings period. This cohort also is smaller than subsequent ones, giving it the benefit of little competition from peers. By contrast, the Baby Boom generation was substantially larger than all precursor cohorts, which Easterlin and colleagues (1987) have argued exposed it to extraordinary competition over its life cycle.

Our motivation for examining differences in the stock of health of sequential birth cohorts on the verge of retirement is to dissect the 'influences of the past' (Hobcraft 1982) that shaped their life histories to date and will imprint on the remainder of their lives. Norman Ryder (1965) was among the first to recognize the inherent potential of a birth cohort as 'an agent of social change.' More recently, a number of demographers and sociologists have broadened the cohort concept by embedding it in a life cycle based on the principle:

... that the influence of historic events var(ies) depending on the stage of life at which they are experienced. Tracing cohorts through time is one way to examine the influence of [such] historic events on aggregates of individuals' different ages.

(O'Brien 2000: 124)

Analytic leverage can also be gained by comparing birth cohorts at the same age or life-stage at different points in time. This strategy also may suggest the factors differentiating cohort experiences and the outcome of interest. A cross-sectional array of cohorts by period and by age defies easy analysis, however, because the three temporal dimensions are linearly dependent on the value of the other two (Mason et al. 1973). To achieve identification, various mathematical transformations have been proposed, such as imposing an equivalency assumption on any two adjacent age groups, periods, or cohorts. Others have estimated models in which only two of the three dimensions are assumed to affect the outcome or that the effect of one of the temporal domains is assumed to be proportional to a substantive variable.

These approaches and others (Tarone and Chu 1996; Brewster and Padavic 2000) require strong theoretical assumptions that cannot be easily verified empirically. Moreover, mathematical adjustments for the sake of identification fail to specify the mechanisms by which adjacent age groups or cohorts are differentiated. Because age-a is nested within cohort-c at time-t, we estimate fixed-effect models that account for variance between, but not within, cohorts.

Data and Sample

The Health and Retirement Study (HRS) is a nationally representative longitudinal survey of Americans over the age of 50. Supported primarily by the National Institute on Aging (NIA), the study tracks health, assets and liabilities, and patterns of well-being in older households over time.[1] Beginning in 1992, a 90-minute core questionnaire has been administered every two years to age-eligible respondents and their spouses or partners. The initial or 'original' HRS cohort was aged 51–61 when first interviewed in 1992 (along with their spouses of any age). Subsequently, two new cohorts have 'aged-into' the survey. For this research, we focus on the three birth cohorts for whom we have comparable HRS data obtained at the same ages (51–56). We define three 6-year birth cohorts and designate them following the conventions of the HRS as follows. The original HRS (born 1926–41) was first interviewed in 1992, the War Babies (WBS) (born 1942–47) was inducted in 1998, and the EBBS (born 1948–53) was first introduced to the survey in 2004. These three cohorts span eighteen years of accelerated change in nearly all economic and demographic aspects of life.

The HRS ages-in new cohorts every six years. This design feature has the advantage of making the survey a representative sample of the noninstitutionalized[2] population aged 50 and over in waves where a new cohort ages-in. Furthermore, the 1998 and 2004 waves of the HRS also are representative cross-sections of the new cohort. Thus, the new age-eligible respondents, in combination with extant respondents born in the same years, are representative of their respective birth cohorts.[3] In what follows, therefore, we define birth cohorts in terms of year of birth rather than year of first interview.

We also note that the HRS poses one statistical issue common to analyses based on data collected using a multistage cluster design. Specifically, error terms in the HRS are correlated at the household level when two spouses or partners coreside and each participates in the HRS.[4] Such is the case in the following analysis where we pool male and female respondents, some of whom are spouses/partners. We adjust for clustering at the household level by deriving robust standard errors.

Determinants of Health on the Verge of Retirement

Previous studies have suggested that the notion of health is fruitfully conceptualized as a multidimensional state defined by physical (Fonda and

Herzog 2004), affective (Steffick 2000), functional, and cognitive (Ofstedal et al. 2005) domains associated with pathology (Fisher et al. 2005). In the HRS, all health indicators derive from self-reports rather than performance or clinical assessments, with the exception of cognitive measures. Chronic disease reports are predicated on a health care professional ever having told the respondent that he or she had a specific condition, namely, diabetes, hypertension, cancer, heart disease, cerebrovascular disease (e.g. stroke or transient ischemic attacks, TIAs), arthritis, or respiratory diseases (e.g. asthma or emphysema).[5] Self-reports of chronic diseases usually yield lower prevalence rates than clinical assessments, although differentials by age, sex, and race are typically of the same order of magnitude for the same chronic conditions collected by the National Health and Nutrition Examination Study (NHANES).[6] Furthermore, self-reports are less reliable than clinical assessments and are affected by recall bias, length of the recall period, and saliency. On the other hand, only respondents can gauge the overall level of their own health, the degree of difficulty they experience in performing common physical tasks, and the severity of their pain. Both survey and clinical interviews also depend on respondents to communicate their accumulated or episodic health risks, such as smoking or drinking.

The full range of health variables included in our empirical analyses is shown in Table 7-1, arrayed by cohort and sex. With several exceptions, we include only variables that were identical in question wording and response set across the three 'intake' interviews.[7] A two-tailed ANOVA tests whether the sex-specific means of the two more recent cohorts, WB and EBB, are statistically different from the estimated means of the original HRS cohort.

The first panel of Table 7-1 shows the health index computed for each respondent. This scoring index is usually centered on 0, ranges from −4 to +4, and corresponds to a Z score. We discuss the derivation of this index in the next section. In terms of the descriptive data in Table 7-1, the index behaves as one would anticipate: that is, the score for men exceeds that for women in all three cohorts.[8] Members of the two more recent cohorts have statistically lower scores indicating worse health than those in the original HRS cohort. Most of this decline occurred by the time the WB cohort entered the HRS.

The next panel shows the components used to craft the summary index of health. In spite of advances in diagnosis and surgical and pharmacological treatments, members of both the WB and the EBB cohorts are less likely than the cohort born prior to World War II to evaluate their overall health as 'excellent or very good'. The younger cohorts report more difficulty, on average, than the original HRS respondents in performing most of the ten physical tasks listed, especially the more physically demanding ones such as climbing several flights of stairs without resting, lifting or carrying more

TABLE 7-1 Weighted Descriptive Statistics[a] for HRS Sampled Birth Cohorts[b]: Health-Related Variables, HRS, 1992, 1998, and 2004

HRS Cohort Birth Years Yr. aged 51–56	Original HRS born 1936–41 1992 (5,354)		War Babies born 1942–47 1998 (5,078)[c]		Early Baby Boomers born 1948–53 2004 (5,030)[c]	
	Male	Female	Male	Female	Male	Female
Health Status[d]						
Health index mean	0.1706	−0.007	0.01***	−0.222***	−0.04***	−0.262***
Health index components						
SRH: excel./very good	57.41	56.92	53.62**	52.19**	49.92***	50.21***
Problem[e] with						
walk 1 blk	3.21	4.6	4.28[†]	6.86***	5.95***	7.27***
several blks	9.14	13.1	11.98**	18.58***	11.72**	18.84***
1 flight of stairs	5.07	8.68	6.28	10.8*	7.17**	14.18***
several flights	16.63	26.74	19.1[†]	36.63***	19.96**	38.43***
sit for 2 hrs	14.45	15.37	12.65	18.68**	14.62	19.5***
up from chair	10.62	13.74	21.45***	31.91***	22.15***	33.12***
lift 10 lbs.	5.56	15.78	8.5***	18.92**	8.88***	18.11*
kneel or crouch	13.71	21.82	25.95***	33.75***	26.24***	35.11***
push large object	6.81	14.46	12.19***	22.08***	10.9***	21.65***
arms over head	3.27	4.87	10.74***	12.21***	10.15***	11.68***
Pain	16.76	23.86	22.94***	29.88***	29.09***	32.9***
Demographics						
Sex	47.99	52.01	47.01	52.99	47.8	52.2
Race: white	87.04	85.85	87.74	84.88	81.59***	79.96***
Married/partnered	82.12	73.74	78.26**	69.42***	76.61***	67.83***
HS grad	78.8	77.32	86.19***	83.99***	88.63***	89.08***
Mother is HS grad	37.4	30.18	56.27***	49.36***	66.62***	60.09***
Father is HS grad	27.83	24.59	45.82***	46.35***	55.38***	53.87***
Born in US	88.32	88.34	93.94***	91.7***	88.85	88.72
Mother is alive	52.63	51.73	54.15	51.03	52.98	53.69
Father is alive	22.67	22.05	27.87***	27.48***	28.93***	28.52***
SRH as a child: ex./vg	77.87	75.58	82.03**	79.31**	82.67***	79.14**
SES as a child: ex./vg	70.26	72.17	72.37	74.66[†]	76.4***	76.24**
Health indicators						
CAGE[f] score > 1	21.41	7.18	23.07	10.67***	28.08***	11.63***
More than 2 drinks day[g]	9.74	2.03	9.08	1.12*	9.55	2.08
Ever smoked	73.51	54.43	68.69**	55.07	65.41***	55.39

TABLE 7-1 (*continued*)

HRS Cohort Birth Years Yr. aged 51–56	Original HRS born 1936–41 1992 (5,354)		War Babies born 1942–47 1998 (5,078)ᶜ		Early Baby Boomers born 1948–53 2004 (5,030)ᶜ	
	Male	*Female*	*Male*	*Female*	*Male*	*Female*
Psychiatric problems	7.87	12.03	17.23***	26.88***	21.26***	27.87***
No chronic conditions	46.73	41.85	46.45	41.21	40.07***	35.35***
Chronic disease count (mean if condition counts > 0)	1.51	1.56	1.57*	1.57	1.68***	1.71***

† $p < 0.10$; * $p < 0.05$; ** $p < 0.01$; *** $p < 0.001$.

ᵃ Differences of means are *t*-tests for equivalent means, with the sex-specific means for the original HRS cohort as the contrast for comparison to the means for both the WB and EBB cohorts.

ᵇ Sample cohorts based on birth year only.

ᶜ War Babies and Early Boomer cohorts contain fewer respondents than the HRS cohort so are weighted to make the cohort sizes equivalent.

ᵈ Item Response Theory was used to compute the components of the health index, shown in the first panel of the table. In this sample, the health index ranges from −2.62 to 1.03.

ᵉ Because of changes in the response set across waves for the Nagi items, we use the RAND recoded variables that allow for comparison across waves. In 1998 and 2004, responses were for matted as simple 'yes' or 'no' questions, but in 1992, three yes affirmative responses were offered: 'yes—a little difficult', 'yes—somewhat difficult', and 'yes—very difficult'. In the RAND files, those responding 'yes—a little difficult' are combined with the 'no problem' response.

ᶠ Respondents coded as having a potential drinking problem if they responded positively to more than one of the four standard CAGE items: ever felt should cut down on drinking, ever criticized for drinking, felt bad or guilty about drinking, or ever taken a drink first thing in the morning. A score greater than 1 is used clinically to screen for alcoholism (Mayfield et al. 1974).

ᵍ In 1992, alcohol use was assessed using one question that asked respondents to report the number of drinks they had per day, without a time frame. In 1998 and 2004, respondents were first asked how many days per week did they drink alcohol, on average, over the last three months. For respondents who reported that they had anything to drink in the past ninety days, a follow-up question asked about how many drinks they had on these days. For 1998 and 2004, we used the two items to calculate a weekly drink total, divided by seven, to obtain a daily average.

Source: Authors' calculations.

than ten pounds, or kneeling/crouching. This downwards drift is evident for both men and women, with the exception of one activity in which the reported level of difficulty for men in the EBB cohort is statistically indistinct from that reported by their counterparts in the HRS cohort.

Relatively more men and women also report having more frequent and severe pain than those born prior to 1942. The last panel of Table 7-1 describes health indicators, and it offers a nuanced picture. More recent cohorts are just as likely to have chronic health problems, and in about the same number, as those in the original HRS cohort (cf. Weir, Chapter 5, this volume).

The second panel of Table 7-1 confirms several demographic trends documented in a variety of statistical publications. The EBB cohort, the most recent of the three cohorts we consider, is proportionately less white but better educated as are the mothers and fathers of the most recent cohort. Changes in marital status also are noteworthy. While a clear majority of both men and women were married at the time of the original HRS interview in 1992, the proportions married or partnered dropped in subsequent cohorts. Men are more likely to be married/partnered than are women in all three cohorts. The persistent male mortality disadvantage, as well as higher probability of men remarrying if divorced, accounts for the lower proportion of married/partnered women at the baseline interview in all cohorts. Both men and women in all 3 cohorts have at least a 50:50 chance of having a living mother while they themselves are in their 50s. In contrast the unadjusted probability of having a living father is only about 0.27 but increasing across cohorts. This change reflects both improvements in male survivorship and delayed age at fathering a child but these trends do not offset the persistent differences in life expectancy that favor women and the normative pattern of women marrying men about three years older than themselves.

Regardless of cohort, most respondents have rosy memories of their childhood health and family status. Nonetheless, more recent cohorts are more likely than those in the original HRS cohort to recall their childhood health as excellent or very good. Only respondents in the EBB cohort recall the socioeconomic status of their families as being very good or better when they were aged 10 or under.

In the last panel of Table 7-1, we document differences in health behaviors across the cohorts, by sex. The first variable is a standard indicator of drinking problem, the CAGE index. Respondents are coded as having a problem with drinking if they reported any three out of four CAGE items: ever felt should cut down on drinking, ever criticized for drinking, felt bad or guilty about drinking, or ever taken a drink first thing in the morning. A score greater than 1 is used clinically to screen for alcoholism (Mayfield et al. 1974; Ewing 1984; Bush et al. 1987; Ewing et al. 1998) The proportion of women considered as having a drinking problem is consistently lower by half of the relative proportion of men who are potential alcoholics, but significantly higher than that of women born in the 1930s. The proportion of men in the WB cohort with a drinking problem is indistinguishable from a comparable proportion of men in the original HRS. By the EBB cohort, the proportion of both men and women screen for drinking problem was statically distinct from the proportion of their counterparts in the original HRS cohort. Cohort differences in drinking, however, are not reflected in the proportion of men and women who acknowledge having more than two drinks per day. This inconsistency may be associated with a change in question wording after 1992.

Smoking is a leading, but preventable cause of death. The proportion of the three cohorts stating that they have ever smoked trends down for both men and women. The lifetime prevalence of smoking has declined substantially over the three cohorts and at about the same rate. In spite of this, EBB women have a one-third lower risk of having ever smoked compared to men in the same cohort.

Whether because of increasing social acceptance or availability of psychotropic medications, the self-reporting of prior psychiatric problems is higher for women in both of the recent cohorts. Only men in the EBB cohort acknowledge psychiatric problems at a higher rate than the original HRS counterparts.

Creating a Summary Health Index

For the most part, Americans on the verge of retirement present a bimodal health picture. A large group of the respondents aged 51–56 reports few chronic conditions, little pain, no restrictions in activity, or cognitive problems. But a small fraction is in very poor health, with multiple chronic conditions, regular and severe pain, or moderate cognitive impairment. The remaining group indicates some problem on one or more health domains that are neither severe nor negligible.

To summarize all these health indicators succinctly into a single index, we use IRT to construct a score for each individual in the analysis sample (McHorney and Cohen 2000; Dor et al. 2003). This method is used to evaluate the measurement of survey questions and to estimate individuals' scores on a derived index. It postulates that an individual's response to a health question is a function of the individual's unobservable, or latent, 'true' health status, and the characteristics of the health items in question. The item characteristics include the slope (or discrimination) and threshold (or difficulty). The slope is a measure of the steepness of the item curve such that a steeper curve indicates a more reliable item, while the threshold describes the location of the item on the trait scale. The threshold of a binary item corresponds to the item inflection point, the trait value at which the respondents have an equal probability of reporting that they have/do not have the health condition in question. The item parameters are independent of each other (Andrich 1988; Embretson and Reise 2000; Baker 2001).

The IRT computes an overall score for each individual based on his or her responses to the four different health components discussed above and shown in Table 7-2. The scoring of individuals is done in two steps. Item characteristics (slope and thresholds) for each health component are estimated, and these estimates are then used in computing an overall score for each individual. The scale of measurement generally has an arbitrary midpoint of 0, a unit measurement of 1, and values that range from −4 to +4, corresponding to that of Z scores (Camilli and Shepard 1994). The mathematical relationship between trait level and the characteristics of the item in a two-parameter IRT model is expressed by the following equation:

$$P(X_{is}) = 1|\theta_s, \beta_i) = \exp(a_i(\theta_s - \beta_i))/[1 + \exp(a_i(\theta_s - \beta_i))]$$

where X_i is the response of respondent s to item i; θ_s is the trait level of respondent s; β_i is the difficulty value/threshold of item i; and a_i is the discrimination value/slope of item i.

In the analysis below, we use the graded-response model (Ostini and Nering 2006), a generalization of the two-parameter IRT model because the health components are categorical rather than binary. Multiple dichotomizations are used to estimate the item parameters, that is, category one versus categories two and above; categories one and two versus categories three and above; categories one, two, and three versus category/categories four and above, and so on. Each health component has one slope and $k − 1$ between category thresholds, where k corresponds to the number of categories of a health component (Embretson and Reise 2000). Figure 7-1 shows the response pattern for the five-level self-reported health (SRH) to illustrate IRT results. Note first of all that each of the category curves has the same slope. Only the extreme categories of an ordered polytomous variable, such as SRH, are monotonically decreasing or increasing, as shown in Figure 7-1. The interim categories, 'fair', 'good', and 'very good', are also shown in Figure 7-1. Consider the curve for category one, 'poor health'. The threshold value for the contrast of 'poor' versus 'fair' or better SRH is −2.22. This is the point as which the curves for the two categories indicating 'poor' and 'fair' health intercept. It is also the point on the trait scale at which the probability of choosing 'fair' or higher categories is equiprobable, 0.5 and over; threshold$_2$ is the point at which the probability of choosing 'good' or higher is 0.5 and over, while threshold$_3$ and threshold$_4$ correspond to the probability of choosing 'very good' or higher and the probability of choosing 'excellent', respectively (du Toit 2003). In this sense, the graded-response model is an exercise in curvefitting (Ostini and Nering 2006) across multiple domains.

The components of the health index we use are similar to those in the Short Form Health Survey SF-36 and 18 (Ware et al. 1995). Specific

TABLE 7-2 Slope and Threshold IRT[a] Parameters for the Four Components of Health Index

IRT Parameters	Self-Reported Health (SRH)	Mobility	Agility	Pain
Slope[b]	1.67	2.98	3.17	2.03
	−0.03	−0.06	−0.06	−0.05
Threshold[c]$_1$[d]	−2.2	−2.08	−2.28	−2.36
	−0.04	−0.03	−0.03	−0.05
Threshold[e]$_2$	−1.12	−1.68	−1.83	−1.23
	−0.03	−0.02	−0.02	−0.02
Threshold$_3$	0.01	−1.19	−1.48	−0.84
	−0.02	−0.02	−0.02	−0.02
Threshold$_4$	1.14	−0.58	−1.13	
	−0.03	−0.01	−0.02	
Threshold$_5$			−0.75	
			−0.01	
Threshold$_6$			−0.23	
			−0.01	

[a] The graded-response model, a generalization of the two-parameter IRT model and which allows for ordered categorical items, is used in estimating the slope and threshold parameters (Embretson and Reise 2000).

[b] The slope is a measure of item discrimination and steepness of the curve. The slope indicates how rapidly the probability of choosing a particular response category changes as the trait level increases. Items with larger slopes are more discriminating and more reliable. In the graded-response model, different categories of the same item are assumed to have the same slope (Embretson and Reise 2000).

[c] Threshold describes the location of items (in cases of binary items) or the item categories (for categorical items) on the trait scale. Larger (and more positive) thresholds indicate more difficult items/item categories that are further located on the trait scale (Embretson and Reise 2000).

[d] Threshold$_1$ corresponds to the trait level at which the respondents have a probability of 0.5 and higher of choosing any but the lowest response category. This is: fair, good, very good, or excellent (rather than poor) in the case of SRH; three, two, one, or no difficulties (rather than four difficulties) in the case physical mobility; five, four, three, two, one, or no difficulties (rather than six difficulties) in the case of agility; moderate, mild, or no pain (rather than severe pain) in the case of pain rating.

[e] Threshold$_2$ corresponds to the trait level at which the respondents have a probability of 0.5 and higher of choosing any but the lowest two response categories. This is: good, very good, or excellent (rather than poor or fair) in the case of SRH; two, one, or no difficulties (rather than three or four difficulties) in the case of physical mobility; four, three, two, one, or no difficulties (rather than five or six difficulties) in the case of agility; mild or no pain (rather than moderate or severe pain) in the case of pain rating.

Source: Authors' calculations.

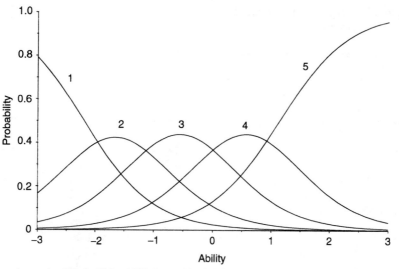

1 = poor (n = 739); 2 = fair (n = 1,548); 3 = good (n = 3,063); 4 = verygood (n = 3,220); 5 = excellent (n = 2,361)

Figure 7-1. Item characteristic curve for self-reported health: HRS respondents Aged 51–56 in 1992, 1998, and 2004. (*Source*: Authors' calculations.)

components considered are: self-rated health (poor, fair, good, very good, and excellent), perception of physical pain (severe, moderate, mild, and no pain), and difficulty in physical mobility (can't do/has difficulty doing; does not do, and has no difficulty), and difficulty in agility (can't do/has difficulty doing; does not do, and has no difficulty). The physical mobility items include standard items (Nagi 1976) measuring lower body function, including degree of difficulty experienced in: walking several blocks, walking one block, climbing several flights of stairs, climbing one flight of stairs, sitting for about two hours, getting up from a chair after sitting for long periods, stooping, kneeling, or crouching. Upper body agility items include reaching or extending arms above shoulder level, pulling or pushing large objects, and lifting or carrying weights over ten pounds.

Table 7-2 shows the slope and thresholds estimates for all four components of the Summary Health Status index. Each of the components has a relatively large slope parameter, indicating that they are reliable health items. Physical mobility and agility, which have the largest slope estimates of 2.98 and 3.17, respectively, are more related to the unobservable health trait continuum than either SRH or pain. The threshold parameters correspond to the location of various response categories on the health trait scale. The SRH, and to a lesser extent the agility component, however, tap a wider range of trait levels than the other two components. The item parameters, shown in Table 7-2, are then used to compute an overall health score for each individual. In our pooled sample the health status index ranges from −2.618 to 1.034, with a median of 0.665.

Fixed-Effect Models of Health

We model health, measured with the Health Status Index described above, using a fixed-effect OLS specification in which we pool male and female respondents and use all the variables listed in Table 7-1 as right-hand side variables. At ages older than those of respondents included in our analysis, gender differences typically emerge with increasing proportions of men reporting potentially fatal chronic conditions while women report higher levels of disability. The decision to use a pooled sample, rather than separate models for males and females, was based on testing two-way interactions with sex for each of the demographic variables, including the binary variables for WB and EBB, and all of the health indicators. Most of these interaction terms were not statically significant. We retain only those that were significant at $p < 0.10$. These are shown in Table 7-3 in the second set of columns. A positive coefficient for a main effect in Column 1 indicates a direct association with the health index outcome.

Of overall importance is the effect of the WB and EBB cohorts on health, relative to the original HRS cohort. The effects of the binary cohort variables are significant at $p < 0.001$ in both the main effects and the interaction models. In the interaction model, the cohort coefficients are approximately equal in size and negative. Although we use different health outcomes, these findings are consistent with those reported by Weir (Chapter 5, this volume). Adjusting for demographic factors, childhood conditions, and individual health behaviors, the more recent cohorts, on average, have poorer health than the original HRS cohort.

Based on our preliminary analysis, the main effect of sex on the health index is significant and consistently negative, that is, women in the younger cohorts have worse health than men in the same cohort. Compared to white respondents, the predicted health index score is lower for both black and 'other race' respondents, although only the effect of this latter category is significant. Most of these respondents describe themselves as Hispanic, whether US-born or foreign-born.

Either as a main effect or as an interaction with sex, education has a positive effect on health. In both equations contained in Table 7-3, the main effect of education indicates that the rate of return to the Summary Health Index in the gender interaction model is about 0.03. In the model excluding interactions, each additional year of education only modestly shifts the intercept, but in the interaction model, a high school education,

TABLE 7-3 Fixed Effect Models of Select Demographic and Socioeconomic Variables on IRT-Derived Health Index: HRS Birth Cohorts Interviewed in 1992, 1998, and 2004

Predictors	No Interactions		With Interactions	
	Coeff.	S.E.	Coeff.	S.E.
Cohort (ref. = HRS)				
WB	−0.137***	0.018	−0.211***	0.046
EBB	−0.153***	0.018	−0.214***	0.051
Sex (ref. = Male)				
Female	−0.137***	0.015	−0.396***	0.068
Race (ref. = White)				
Black	−0.016	0.023	−0.011	0.023
Other	−0.105***	0.033	−0.1**	0.033
Marital status (ref. = currently married)				
Union ended	−0.012	0.020	−0.012	0.020
Never married	−0.032	0.039	−0.03	0.039
Education years	0.033***	0.003	0.032***	0.003
Mother's education (ref. = <HS)				
High school	0.03	0.019	0.033†	0.019
> High school	0.045†	0.026	0.045†	0.026
Missing	−0.028	0.035	−0.029	0.034
Father's education (ref. = <HS)				
High school	0.038†	0.020	0.038*	0.020
> High school	0.053*	0.024	0.052*	0.024
Missing	−0.009	0.028	−0.007	0.028
No. of chronic conditions	−0.324***	0.008	−0.298***	0.010
Chronic*WB			−0.063***	0.018
Chronic*EBB			−0.014	0.016
Smoking status (ref. = never smoked)				
Former	−0.022	0.017	−0.05*	0.024
Current	−0.125***	0.020	−0.172***	0.028
Missing	0.037	0.048	0.098	0.095
Former*Female			0.039	0.034
Current*Female			0.075*	0.038
Missing*Female			−0.068	0.108
Drinking problems^a (ref. = 0)				
1	−0.081***	0.022	−0.08***	0.022
>1	−0.104***	0.023	−0.105***	0.023
Missing	−0.019	0.033	−0.006	0.033
# Alcoholic drinks (ref. = 0)				
0 < # drinks < 1	0.123***	0.017	0.076***	0.023
1 to 2	0.178***	0.025	0.112***	0.031
> 2	0.167***	0.035	0.136***	0.039

TABLE 7-3 (*continued*)

Predictors	No Interactions		With Interactions	
	Coeff.	*S.E.*	*Coeff.*	*S.E.*
<1*Female			0.084**	0.031
1 to 2*Female			0.159***	0.048
> 2*Female			0.116	0.086
Mental health problems? (ref. = none)				
Mental health prob(yes)	−0.344***	0.022	−0.484***	0.043
Mental*Female			0.084*	0.041
Mental*WB			0.134**	0.050
Mental*EBB			0.103*	0.049
Health in childhood (ref. = fair/poor)				
Good	0.155***	0.037	0.102†	0.055
V. good	0.21***	0.035	0.13*	0.052
Excellent	0.335***	0.034	0.221***	0.050
Missing	0.132†	0.076	−0.047	0.088
Good*Female			0.084	0.074
V. good*Female			0.124†	0.070
Excellent*Female			0.193**	0.067
Missing*Female			0.355***	0.083
SES in childhood (ref. = fair/poor)				
Average	0.037*	0.018	0.037*	0.018
Well off	0.04	0.033	0.037	0.033
Missing	0.154*	0.065	0.144*	0.065
Region of residence (ref. = rural south)				
Urban south	0.037	0.028	−0.013	0.033
Rural north	0.04	0.025	−0.024	0.030
Urban north	0.06*	0.024	−0.017	0.029
Not in US	0.118***	0.030	0.051	0.036
Missing	0.055†	0.032	−0.009	0.038
Urban south*WB			0.146*	0.059
Rural north*WB			0.1†	0.054
Urban north*WB			0.135**	0.052
Not in US*WB			0.167*	0.068
Missing*WB			0.297*	0.120
Urban south*EBB			0.008	0.068
Rural north*EBB			0.089	0.059
Urban north*EBB			0.086	0.055
Not in US*EBB			0.047	0.067
Missing*EBB			0.055	0.071
Mother (ref. = deceased)				
Alive	0.06***	0.015	0.058***	0.015
Missing	0.058	0.077	0.059	0.078

(*cont.*)

TABLE 7-3 (*continued*)

Predictors	No Interactions		With Interactions	
	Coeff.	S.E.	Coeff.	S.E.
Father (ref. = deceased)				
Alive	0.009	0.017	0.009	0.017
Missing	−0.058	0.056	−0.056	0.057
Constant	−0.352		−0.147	
R^2	0.4		0.41	

Source: Authors' calculations.

[a] Respondents coded as having a potential drinking problem if they reported positively to at least two of the four standard CAGE items: ever felt should cut down on drinking, ever criticized for drinking, felt bad or guilty about drinking, or ever taken a drink first thing in the morning. A score greater than 1 is used clinically to screen for alcoholism (Mayfield et al. 1974).

[†] $p < 0.10$; [*] $p < 0.05$; [**] $p < 0.01$; [***] $p < 0.001$

ceteris paribus, shifts the Summary Health Index by 0.237, and a college education by 0.512, the equivalent of scoring in the 40th and 75th percentile on the health index. Similarly, higher levels of parental education, particularly father's education, are significantly and positively associated with better health in midlife. The consistent positive effect of education on health is consistent with the pioneering work by Marmot (2001, 2006) on the SES gradient in all dimensions of health, including mortality.

We now turn to examine how lifestyle and life-cycle factors affect the health index score. Each additional chronic disease reduces the health index by 0.298, one of the strongest effects in Table 7-3.[9] Relative to the original HRS cohort, those in subsequent cohorts not only have more chronic conditions, but the effect of these is amplified for persons born between 1942 and 1947.

Smoking is recognized as having an enduring negative effect on health. Relative to having never smoked, being a current smoker reduces the health index score by 0.172. Compared to persons with no drinking problems, persons who acknowledge that they had a drinking problem sufficient to elicit a positive response to even one of the four CAGE drinking behaviors reduces the Summary Health Index by 0.08, while those reporting two or more problem behaviors reduce their score by 0.105. Controlling for all other factors in the interaction model, the number of drinks per day has a positive effect on overall health with the greatest gain accruing to those who have two or more drinks per day. Interacting drinks-per-day with being female increase the improvement relative to that for men.[10] Having psychiatric problems has an inverse effect on health relative to those who do not report such problems. With the advent of new treatment modalities, the health implications for those born after 1942 are attenuated. Because psychiatric problems are often associated with women, the consequences of reporting such problems are attenuated for women but remain negative for men.

Variables that capture early life conditions are included in order to capture what has been described as the 'long reach of childhood' on adult health (Case et al. 2002; Hayward and Gorman 2004). Relative to having poor health as a child, those reporting better early life health also have better health in midlife. There also is a distinct gradient in the childhood effect such that those who consider their health as excellent have a greater return on the health index than those who report even 'very good' health before age 10. There is an added benefit of being a woman in excellent health rather than a comparable man. Note that the coefficient for 'missing' on childhood health is positive and highly significant. Here, as in other variables where we code the effect of having incomplete data, we interpret as an adjustment for statistical noise. Finally note that the effect of childhood socioeconomic status at the same period has minor effects on adult health. It is reasonable to assume that economic status of the family of origin has a positive effect on childhood health, and that the latter variable captures some of the SES effect from childhood.

The last life-cycle variable we include is the region in which the respondent attended elementary school. We do so because at the time when the members of the three cohorts of interest began their elementary education, schools in the Rural South, the reference category, were deemed inferior to those in urban areas in the North. Growing up outside the United States is positively associated with midlife health. The interaction terms included in the second equation provide additional insight. Members of the WBs cohort whose early schooling was in the Urban North have a midlife health advantage compared to members in the original HRS cohort who were first schooled in the Rural South. No effect is discernable for the EBBs regardless where they attended elementary school.

Finally note that having a living, rather than a deceased, mother has a positive effect on midlife health in the two equations shown in Table 7-3. This may indicate a hereditary advantage that accrues to those with long-lived mothers, but more likely it signifies the psychological benefit to have the parent with whom most adult children have the strongest attachment. Most adult children lose their father first and a surviving mother protects adult children from transitioning to 'orphan hood'.

We also analyze the data using multilevel analyses with individual respondents nested within birth years. Table 7-4 provides a summary of the fit of three multilevel models. The first column shows results from a model that includes only the constant. This equation yields the baseline for the

TABLE 7-4 Determinants of Health and Intraclass Correlation Coefficient (Standard Errors in Parentheses)

	Model 1 Constant Only[a]	Model 2 Micro Variables No Interactions[b]	Model 3 Micro Variables With Interactions[c]
Variance			
Birth year level	0.012	0.004	0.004
	−0.004	−0.001	−0.002
Individual level	0.665	0.409	0.407
	−0.009	−0.006	−0.006
Intraclass correlation coefficient (%)	1.77	0.97	0.97
−2 log-likelihood	26,608.85	21,285.59	21,229.54
Number of observations	10,931	10,931	10,931

[a] The model includes a random intercept only.

[b] The model includes a random intercept in addition to the microlevel variables shown in Table 7-3.

[c] The model includes all the variables in the previous model in addition to interaction terms between sex and each of the following: smoking status, alcoholic drinks, mental problems, and health status during childhood.

Source: Authors' calculations.

variance decomposition. The constant only model attributes almost all of the variance in our data to within birth year differences rather than between birth year differences. In the second column, we summarize the decomposition of variance in the main effects model shown in the first column of Table 7-3. The ICC shown in the third row of Table 7-4 is a measure of the total variance associated with a given model. The ratio of the variance in the main effect model to the baseline variance (0.97/1.77) indicates a 54.8 percent reduction in the initial variance. While the model that includes the interaction terms, column 3 in Table 7-4, does not contribute any additional explained variance, this decomposition is not a test of the significance of specific variables.

To summarize these findings, we derived a health index measure for respondents on the verge of retirement based on four domains: SRH, mobility, agility, and pain. An IRT measurement model is used to predict a Summary Health Status score for each respondent. We find that the health of both recent cohorts, the WBs and the Early Boomers, has deteriorated relative to their HRS counterparts. In addition to own education, the main predictors of good health are years of education, parental schooling, and childhood health. Smoking, heavy drinking, a large number of chronic health problems, a history of psychiatric problems, and attending elementary schooling in the Rural South have negative consequences for health on the threshold of retirement.

Conclusions and Discussion

Baby Boomers have left a unique imprint on US culture and society in the last sixty years, and it might be anticipated that they will also put their own stamp on retirement, the last phase of the life cycle. Yet because Boomers have not all fully retired, we cannot yet judge how they will fare as retirees. Instead, we focus on how this group compares with prior groups on the verge of retirement, that is, at ages 51–56. Accordingly, this chapter evaluates the stock of health which Early Boomers bring to retirement and compare these to the circumstances of two prior cohorts at the same point in their life cycles.

Using three sets of responses from the Health and Retirement Study, we find some interesting patterns. Overall, the raw evidence indicates that Boomers on the verge of retirement are in poorer health than their counterparts 12 years ago. Using a Summary Health Index designed for this study, we find that those born 1948–53 share health risks with the WB cohort. This suggests that most of the health decline instead began before the late 1940s. A more complex set of health conclusions emerges from the specific SRH measures. Boomers indicate they have relatively more difficulty with a range of everyday physical tasks, but they also report having more pain, more chronic conditions, more drinking and psychiatric problems than their HRS earlier counterparts. This trend portends poorly for the future health of Boomers as they age and incur increasing costs associated with health care and medications. Using our health index, only those at the 75th percentile or higher are likely to be characterized as having good or better health.

We are not the first to signal the eroding health of middle-aged persons in the United States. Using comparative data from sources including the HRS, Banks et al. (2006) obtain similar findings even after controlling for health insurance coverage and other health inputs such as weight, exercise patterns, and other covariates omitted from our models. Moreover, they conclude that adult health in Britain is superior to Americans at ages 50 and older. What should we make of our conclusions in the context of increased public and private health care spending? There are several hypotheses that warrant consideration. Promising ones included: the very act of seeking care for even minor health problems increases awareness of other, seemingly unrelated health problems; the barrage of advertisements for prescription medication increases disease or symptom awareness as much as it encourages care seeking; and changing notions of health in aging increase intolerance of minor pain, slight loss of stamina, or even minute loss of muscle strength to the extent that younger cohorts are less accepting of physiological changes that are not pathologic. Future research will need to consider unobserved factors that correlate with health, such as cognition, obesity, and use of health care services.

Acknowledgments

The authors are grateful for research support from the Pension Research Council and the Boettner Center for Pensions and Retirement Research at The Wharton School, the Population Aging Research Center (PARC) at the University of Pennsylvania, and NIH/NIA grant no. 1R13AG028231-01.

Notes

[1] For more on the Health and Retirement Study, see http://hrsonline.isr.umich.edu/

[2] At baseline, all members of the entering cohort are community residents. As they age, sampled persons continue to be followed even if they enter a nursing home or other type of facility categorized as an institution. It is unlikely that the entry restriction comprised the representativeness of the sample at baseline because very few of those aged 51–56 are institutionalized in any type of facility.

[3] Neither the age-in supplement nor the 'younger spouse' component are independently representative of a given birth cohort. The WB and EBB cohorts, however, contain individuals who were previously interviewed as the younger spouses of age-eligible respondents. So, for example, a woman born in 1948 may have been first interviewed in 1998 as the younger spouse of a WB entrant born in 1945. In 1998 her record would have had a zero case weight. Her first cohort interview would have been conducted in 2004 as other members of her birth cohort, the EBB, entered the study. At this time her record would carry its own nonzero person weight.

[4] That is, the probability of observing one spouse is conditional on the probability of observing the other spouse/partner. This issue does not arise in households where we observe only one respondent at baseline.

[5] To maintain comparability across cohorts we use the initial or screener question for each disease: 'Has a doctor ever told you that you had _____?'

[6] These data cover 1997–2003; see http://www.cdc.gov/nchs/health_data_for_all_ages.htm

[7] The exceptions are the Nagi (1976) items and questions eliciting number of drinks per days on occasions when respondent drinks. These differences especially are described at the end of Table 7-1.

[8] Although women have lower mortality risks, women regularly report higher rates of disease and disability.

[9] The HRS asks if a physician ever told respondents that they ever had hypertension, diabetes, arthritis, lung disease, cancer (other than skin cancer), heart attack, and stroke. The count variable ranges from 0 to 7.

[10] These results are somewhat surprising, although Hurd and McGarry (1995) report similar results using the 1992 wave of HRS.

References

Andrich, D. (1988). *Rasch Models for Measurement*. Beverly Hills, CA: Sage.

Baker, F. B. (2001). *The Basics of Item Response Theory*. College Park, MD: ERIC Clearinghouse on Assessment and Evaluation.

Banks, J., Marmot, M., Oldfield, Z., and Smith, P. (2006). 'Disease and Disadvantage in the United States and in England', *Journal of the American Medical Association*, 295(17): 2037–45.

Brewster, K. L. and Padavic, I. (2000). 'Change in Gender-Ideology, 1977–1996: The Contributions of Intracohort Change and Population Turnover', *Journal of Marriage and Family*, 62(2): 477–87.

Bush, B., Shaw, S., Cleary, P., Delbanco, T. L., and Aronson, M. D. (1987). 'Screening for Alcohol Abuse Using the Cage Questionnaire', *American Journal of Medicine*, 82(2): 231–5.

Camilli, G. and Shepard L. A. (1994). '*Methods for Identifying Biased Test Items.*' Thousand Oaks, CA: Sage.

Case, A., Lubotsky, D., and Paxson, C. (2002). 'Economic Status and Health in Childhood: The Origins of the Gradient', *American Economic Review*, 92(5): 1308–34.

Dor, A., Sudano, J. J., and Baker, D. W. (2003). 'The Effect of Private Insurance on Measures of Health: Evidence from the Health and Retirement Study', NBER Working Paper 9774.

du Toit, M. (2003). *IRT from SSI: BILOG-MG, MULTILOG, PARSCALE, TESTIFACT*. Lincolnwood, IL: Scientific Software International.

Easterlin, R. A. (1987). *Birth and Fortune: The Impact of Numbers on Personal Welfare*, 2nd edn. Chicago, IL: University of Chicago Press.

Embretson, S. E. and Reise, S. P. (2000). *Item Response Theory for Psychologists*. Mahwah, NJ: Lawrence Erlbaum Associates, Publishers.

Ewing, J. A. (1984). 'Detecting Alcoholism. The CAGE Questionnaire', *Journal of the American Medical Association*, 252(14): 1905–7.

—— Bradley, K. A., and Burman, M. L. (1998). 'Screening for Alcoholism Using CAGE', *Journal of the American Medical Association*, 280(22): 1904–5.

Fisher, G. G., Faul, J. D., Weir, D. R., and Wallace, R. B. (2005). 'Documentation of Chronic Disease Measures in the Health and Retirement Study (HRS/AHEAD)', HRS Documentation Report DR-009.

Fonda, S. and Herzog, A. R. (2004). 'Documentation of Physical Functioning Measures in the Health and Retirement Study and the Asset and Health Dynamics among the Oldest Old Study', HRS Documentation Report DR-008.

Hayward, M. D. and Gorman, B. K. (2004). 'The Long Arm of Childhood: The Influence of Early-Life Social Conditions on Men's Mortality', *Demography*, 41(1): 87–107.

Hobcraft, J., Menken, J., and Preston, S. H. (1982). 'Age, Period, and Cohort Effects in Demography: a Review', *Population Index*, 48(1): 4–43.

Hurd, M. and McGarry, K. (1995). 'Evaluation of the Subjective Probabilities of Survival in the Health and Retirement Study', *Journal of Human Resources*, 30(Special Issue on the Health and Retirement Study Supplement): S268–92.

McHorney, C. A. and Cohen, A. S. (2000). 'Equating Health Status Measures with Item Response Theory: Illustrations with Functional Status Items', *Medical Care*, 38(9): II: 43–59.

Marmot, M. (2001). 'Economic and Social Determinants of Disease', *Bulletin of the World Health Organization*, 79(10): 988–9.

—— (2006). 'Status Syndrome: A Challenge to Medicine', *Journal of the American Medical Association*, 295(11): 1304–7.

Mason, K. O., Mason, W. M., Winsborough, H. H., and Poole, W. K. (1973). 'Some Methodological Issues in Cohort Analysis of Archival Data', *American Sociological Review*, 38(2): 242–58.

Mayfield, D., McLeod, G., and Hall, P. (1974). 'The CAGE Questionnaire: Validation of a New Alcoholism Screening Instrument', *American Journal of Psychiatry*, 131(10): 1121–3.

Nagi, S. Z. (1976). 'An Epidemiology of Disability among Adults in the United States', *Milbank Memorial Fund Quarterly Health and Society*, 54(4): 439–67.

O'Brien, R. M. (2000). 'Age Period Cohort Characteristic Models', *Social Science Research*, 29(1): 123–39.

Ofstedal, M. B., Fisher, G. G., and Regula Herzog, A. (2005). 'Documentation of Cognitive Functioning Measures in the Health and Retirement Study', HRS Documentation Report DR-006.

Ostini, R. and Nering, M. L. (2006). *Polytomous Item Response Theory Models*, Thousand Oaks, CA: Sage.

Ryder, N. B. (1965). 'The Cohort as a Concept in the Study of Social Change', *American Sociological Review*, 30(6): 843–61.

Steffick, D. E. (2000). '*Documentation of Affective Functioning Measures in the Health and Retirement Study*'.

Tarone, R. E. and Chu, K. C. (1996). 'Evaluation of Birth Cohort Patterns in Population Disease Rates', *American Journal of Epidemiology*, 143(1): 85–91.

Ware, J. E. J., Kosinski, M., Bayliss, M. S., McHorney, C. A., Rogers, W. H., and Raczek, A. E. (1995). 'Comparison of Methods for the Scoring and Statistical Analysis of SF-36 Health Profile and Summary Measures: Summary of Results from the Medical Outcomes Study', *Medical Care*, 33(4): AS264–79.

Chapter 8

Health Insurance Patterns Nearing Retirement

Helen G. Levy

Almost one in seven of Early Baby Boomers (EBBs)—those born in 1948 through 1953—had no health insurance in 1998 when this group attained age 50.[1] Gaps in health insurance coverage among the near-elderly should be of particular policy concern because uninsured household may significantly deplete its retirement savings in the event of a serious illness. And since the probability of poor health increases with age, these older individuals are at higher risk of health shocks. Also unlike younger households who may have very little in the way of assets to lose, households in their 50s often have a retirement nest egg at stake.[2] Whether Baby Boomers will be able to maintain desired levels of consumption in retirement depends, in part, on how well they are protected against these later-life health shocks. The erosion of employer-sponsored health insurance coverage over the 1980s and 1990s implies that at least some Boomers may arrive on the threshold of retirement less well-prepared to deal with these shocks than were earlier cohorts.[3]

This chapter compares health insurance coverage for a cohort of Baby Boomers with health insurance coverage for earlier cohorts, using data from the Current Population Survey (CPS) and the Health and Retirement Study (HRS). Early Boomers (which here we identify as those born 1948–53) first appear in the HRS in 2004, when they were aged 51–56. We compare their health insurance coverage to that of two earlier cohorts at the same ages: the so-called War Babies (born 1942–47) who first appear in the HRS in 1998 at age 51–56, and the younger half of the first HRS cohort (born 1936–41) who were aged 51–56 in the initial wave of the HRS in 1992. In addition to comparing age-specific rates of current health insurance coverage across cohorts, we calculate what we call the 'long-term' risk of uninsurance, which we define as the probability that an HRS respondent reports being uninsured in one or more of the three survey waves just prior to Medicare eligibility (i.e. at ages 59, 61, and 63, or else 60, 62, and 64).

Analyzing patterns of health insurance coverage informs us about whether exposure to health risk has changed across cohorts. The risk itself has two dimensions: the magnitude of the potential loss if one occurs—that is, how much wealth is at stake?—and the probability of experiencing a loss. In order to determine how much is at stake, we calculate mean and median total net nonpension wealth and mean and median total net nonpension, nonhousing wealth for insured and uninsured households in each cohort. Finally, for a subset of the original HRS cohort, we calculate the probability of being hospitalized at least once in the three waves just prior to Medicare eligibility. We use information on whether insurance paid for any part of the hospital bills to calculate the probability of experiencing an 'uninsured' hospitalization. If the younger cohorts are similar to the 1936–41 birth cohorts on these dimensions as well, then the experience of the HRS respondents provides some indication of how much of a threat uninsured health shocks pose to the financial security of the Boomers as they approach retirement.

Our main finding is that while exposure to risk is relatively high, the realization of risk is unlikely and relatively little wealth is at stake. Almost one-quarter (23%) of the original HRS cohort was uninsured at some point in the six-year window before Medicare eligibility, but only 2 percent of the HRS cohort had an uninsured hospitalization in this window. This number is equal to 12 percent of those uninsured when they were first interviewed. Moreover, the amount at stake for the median uninsured person is relatively low: median total net nonhousing non-pension wealth among the uninsured HRS cohort members hovers between $10,000 and $20,000 (in $2004) as these households approach age 65—less than the average charge for a hospital stay. While households might lose their nest egg as a result of a hospital stay, even without catastrophic medical bills, these households do not seem to be approaching old age in good financial shape. In other words, lack of assets may be a larger problem for these households than lack of health insurance. Policies aimed at preventing poverty among the elderly may be more important for the well-being of these households than policies to expand insurance coverage among the near-elderly.

Empirical Approach

Our analysis of differences across cohorts in health insurance coverage relies in part on data taken from the CPS, a monthly household survey of labor force participation and demographic information conducted by the US Census Bureau. The March Supplement collects information on households' health insurance, including sources of public and private health insurance coverage during the prior calendar year. The CPS has approximately 6,000–9,000 individuals from the 1936–41 birth cohort, 8,000–12,000 individuals from the 1942–47 birth cohort, and 11,000–16,000 from

TABLE 8-1 HRS Respondents for Which Health Insurance Data are Available

| Cohort | Birth Years | Age Range of Cohort at Each Wave | | | | | | |
		1992	1994	1996	1998	2000	2002	2004
Original HRS	1936–41	51–56	53–58	55–60	57–62	59–64	61–66	63–68
War Babies	1942–47				51–56	53–58	55–60	57–62
Early Boomers	1948–53							51–56

Source: Author's calculations.

the 1948–53 birth cohort. The CPS is not a longitudinal cohort study; it is a repeated cross section.[4] In presenting these CPS results, we label the different birth cohorts consistently with HRS terminology (namely original HRS, War Babies, and Early Boomers), even if two different CPS waves contain different members of those birth cohorts. All CPS estimates use sampling weights for the March supplement.

In what follows, we also rely on data from the Health and Retirement Study, a longitudinal data collection effort on the health, wealth, income, and labor force participation of older Americans since 1992. The study began with a nationally representative sample of individuals who were then between the ages of 51 and 61 in 1992. Subsequent cohorts have been added to the study as they age. The HRS analysis draws on three different cohorts. Table 8-1 shows the availability of data by sample wave and the ages of cohort members at each wave. The Early Boomers, defined as the cohort born 1948–53, first appear in HRS 2004 when they are aged 51–56; the sample size in this cohort was 3,372. The War Babies (born 1942–47) are first surveyed in 1998 at age 51–56, with about 3,000 observations each time they are observed. The younger half of the first HRS cohort (born 1936–41) was aged 51–56 in the initial wave of the study in 1992; for this group there are 4,300–5,500 observations per wave. Following the convention adopted in this volume, we refer to this younger half of the first HRS cohort as 'original HRS' in the remainder of this chapter. All estimates using the HRS are calculated using the weight for the first appearance an individual makes in the sample.

Health Insurance Patterns Among Near-Retirees

For some of the analyses, we focus on the six-year window just prior to age 65 when most respondents become eligible for Medicare, the national health insurance plan for the elderly in the United States. Early Boomers and War Babies have not yet made this transition in our data, so this analysis necessarily relies on the HRS cohort alone for whom we use three

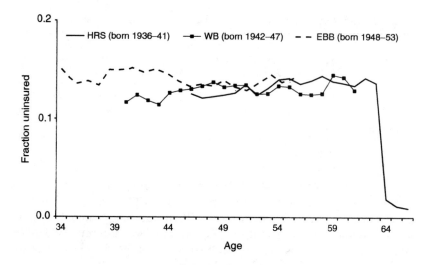

Figure 8-1. Fraction with no health insurance by age and birth cohort: current population survey (1989–2004). (*Source*: Author's calculations.)

consecutive observations when respondents were aged 59, 61, and 63 (or 60, 62, and 64). Depending on how old a sample member was in 1992, then, the first observation for these purposes occurs between 1996 and 2000 (see Table 8-1). By 2004, all members of the original HRS will have passed through this window or left the sample due to death, nonresponse, or sample attrition. The sample size for our longitudinal analyses is 3,992, as we exclude sample members who die before age 65. This has important implications for the interpretation of some results, a point we return to below.

Differences in Insurance Coverage by Cohort

Figure 8-1 presents the fraction of the uninsured by age and cohort in the CPS data. Throughout the prime working years, the fraction uninsured is about 13 percent in all cohorts. The Early Boomers have slightly higher age-specific rates of being uninsured than either of the other cohorts, although only some of these differences are statistically significant.[5] The higher rate of uninsurance among the Early Boomers is driven by their lower rates of private coverage at each age (see Figure 8-2), that are offset only partly by slightly higher rates of public coverage (Figure 8-3).

The fact that earlier cohorts have slightly better health insurance coverage than the Early Boomers (higher rates of private coverage, lower overall uninsurance) is somewhat surprising, in light of the fact that other

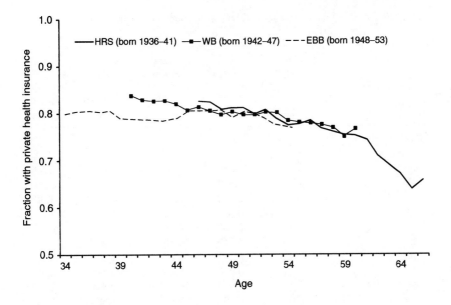

Figure 8-2. Fraction with private health insurance by age and birth cohort: current population survey (1989–2004). (*Source*: Author's calculations.)

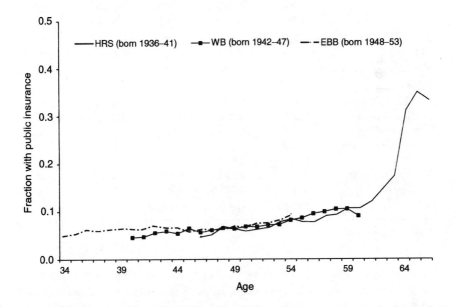

Figure 8-3. Fraction with public health insurance by age and birth cohort: current population survey (1989–2004). (*Source*: Author's calculations.)

TABLE 8-2 Cohort Characteristics: Current Population Surveys, March
1989–2004

	Original HRS	War Babies	Early Boomers	t-Stat. on H_0: Boomers Differ from...	
				Original HRS	War Babies
Fraction working at age					
40	—	0.863	0.858	—	0.52
41	—	0.864	0.862	—	0.29
42	—	0.864	0.854	—	1.90
43	—	0.864	0.856	—	1.51
44	—	0.853	0.853	—	0.07
45	—	0.845	0.865	—	4.16
46	0.830	0.849	0.854	2.38	0.93
47	0.833	0.840	0.850	2.31	2.08
48	0.827	0.833	0.845	2.81	2.43
49	0.812	0.831	0.838	4.32	1.42
50	0.816	0.824	0.837	3.61	2.47
51	0.800	0.814	0.813	2.16	0.14
52	0.796	0.807	0.807	1.65	0.13
53	0.764	0.792	0.783	2.45	1.22
54	0.757	0.776	0.767	0.98	0.92
Female	0.714	0.714	0.690	14.65	16.35
Married	0.521	0.512	0.510	6.29	1.45
Female and married	0.344	0.346	0.344	0.27	1.50
Education					
< High School	0.197	0.138	0.110	70.49	24.99
High School	0.377	0.339	0.322	32.07	10.88
Some college	0.206	0.245	0.273	43.42	19.70
College or more	0.220	0.278	0.295	47.23	12.03
Black	0.103	0.099	0.114	9.87	14.78
Other nonwhite	0.041	0.042	0.045	6.38	4.50
Hispanic	0.072	0.073	0.081	8.99	8.91
N	123,343	168,004	211,893		

Source: Author's calculations.

characteristics suggest that Early Boomers should have higher rates of
private coverage than earlier cohorts. In particular, the Early Boomers have
much more education: only 11 percent of them have less than a high school
education, compared to 14 percent of War Babies and 20 percent of the
original HRS cohort (Table 8-2). Early Boomers are also much more likely

to have a college degree or more (30% compared to 28 for War Babies and 22% of the original HRS). In fact, adjusting for the characteristics listed in Table 8-2 using a linear regression yields slightly larger gaps for the Early Boomers versus the original HRS, and slightly smaller gaps for the Early Boomers versus the War Babies.[6]

The main points from this comparison are, first, that there is a small but significant decline in the probability of the Early Boomers having private coverage compared to earlier cohorts. This is in part because Early Boomers are approaching retirement during an era when employer-sponsored health insurance has been eroding (Farber and Levy 2000). Second, rates of public coverage are slightly higher for Early Boomers than for earlier cohorts at the same ages, but not by as much as private coverage rates are lower. Therefore, overall, the Early Boomers are slightly more likely than earlier cohorts to be uninsured (though these differences are not always statistically significant; see Appendix 8-1).

Long-run Risks of Having an Uninsured Spell

While some 13 percent of individuals in their 50s are uninsured at a point in time, there is a longer-run risk of having an uninsured spell at some point before Medicare coverage begins. Individuals can move in and out of insurance coverage, so the point-in-time estimate of the uninsured provides a lower bound on the longer-term probability of having an uninsured spell. To calculate this long-run risk of being uninsured, we turn to the HRS data and follow individuals through time. In particular, we evaluate the three observations before respondents turn age 65 (respectively, age 59, 61, and 63 or 60, 62, and 64). Table 8-3 shows the 'insurance histories' of individuals in this sample, and it indicates that some 20 percent of the sample reports being uninsured at one or more interviews. That is, an individual with the insurance history '111' was insured at all three interviews; one with the history '101' was insured at the first and third interviews but not at the second one; one with the history '000' was not insured at any of the interviews, and so on. Four-fifths of this sample (82%) was covered by insurance at all three interviews. Most of these (94% or 77% of the total sample) reported that they were continuously insured between the interview waves as well. Thus 23 percent of this sample spent at least some time uninsured in the six-year window just before Medicare eligibility.

Being uninsured at some point during one's 50s is thus not an uncommon event and it is much more likely than the point-in-time estimate of 13 percent uninsured suggests: nearly a quarter of the sample has a spell without insurance in the six years before Medicare coverage begins. Four

TABLE 8-3 Insurance Histories in the Three Interviews just
Prior to Age 65: Original HRS Cohort

'Insurance History' (Any Coverage at Wave 1-2-3)	Unweighted Sample Size	Weighted Fraction of Sample
000 (never insured)	200	0.043
001	97	0.024
010	21	0.005
011	183	0.043
100	49	0.011
101	93	0.022
110	151	0.034
111 (always insured)	3,198	0.818
Total	3,992	1.000

Source: Author's calculations.

Note: See text.

percent were uninsured at all three interviews.[7] Table 8-4 shows that the risk
of a spell of uninsurance is much higher for individuals with less education,
and slightly higher for women than for men.

The fact that the long-run probability of a spell of uninsurance is so
much higher than the point-in-time probability of being uninsured suggests
considerable movement into and out of insurance among this population.
This raises the question of what events cause near-elderly individuals to
lose insurance. Since the main sources of health insurance are one's own
or a spouse's employment, the most likely candidates would seem to be
employment transitions (job loss or retirement) and marital status transitions (divorce or death of a spouse).

TABLE 8-4 Probability of Being Uninsured in at Least One
Wave in the Three Interviews just Prior to Age 65
by Sex and Education: Original HRS cohort

	Men	Women	Total
< High School	0.347	0.389	0.370
High School	0.210	0.223	0.218
Some college	0.204	0.245	0.227
College or more	0.135	0.143	0.138
Total	0.217	0.250	0.235

Source: Author's calculations.

Note: See text.

TABLE 8-5 Who Loses Insurance and Why?

	Unweighted Sample Size	Weighted Fraction of Sample
1. Single man, lost private coverage and stopped work	33	0.034
2. Single woman, lost private coverage and stopped work	79	0.051
3. Single man or woman, lost coverage but not (1) or (2)	306	0.237
4. Married woman, lost spousal coverage and spouse stopped work	45	0.025
5. Married woman, lost spousal coverage and spouse died	7	0.003
6. Married woman, lost spousal coverage and got divorced	7	0.007
7. Married woman, lost spousal health insurance but not (4), (5), or (6)	163	0.105
8. Married woman, lost own coverage and stopped work	56	0.039
9. Married woman, lost coverage but not (4)—(8)	263	0.166
10. Married man, lost own coverage and stopped work	83	0.053
11. Married man, lost own coverage but did not stop work	159	0.108
12. Married man, lost coverage but not (10) or (11)	255	0.173
Total	1,456	1.000

Source: Author's calculations.

Note: Data are for the Original HRS and War Babies cohorts. See text.

In order to determine how much of insurance loss can be explained by employment and marital status transitions, we use data on the 31,802 wave-to-wave transitions observed for members of the original HRS and War Babies cohorts before they reach the age of 65. That is, an individual observed for two consecutive waves contributes one transition to this analysis; an individual observed for three consecutive waves contributes two transitions, and so on. The Early Boomers, having been observed only once so far in the HRS, are necessarily excluded from this part of the analysis; observations from individuals age 65 and older are dropped since all of these individuals will have Medicare. About 5 percent of the 31,802 transitions in this sample, or 1,456 of them involve insurance loss, where an individual has either private or public insurance coverage in one wave and is uninsured in the subsequent wave. These 1,456 instances of health insurance loss are the basis for the analysis in Table 8-5, which categorizes health insurance losers by their sex, marital status, employment status, and insurance type, prior to the insurance loss occurs, to see whether the commonsense stories about job loss, retirement, death, or divorce accounts for most health insurance loss. Results show that, in fact, these explanations are far from sufficient. For example, individuals who lose their own employer-sponsored insurance and stop work (categories one, two, eight, and ten in Table 8-5) make up only 18 percent of the sample. Married women with employer-sponsored insurance coverage through their husbands who lose health insurance and whose husbands stop working, die, or divorce them (categories four, five, and six in Table 8-5) make up only about 3.5 percent of all incidents of health insurance loss.[8] Thus we cannot account for the majority of health insurance events, in the sense that they do not occur at the same time as these employment or marital status transitions. Further exploration of the reasons for health insurance loss in this population is a subject for future research.

Wealth at Stake For Uninsured Households

Figure 8-4 shows the median total net nonpension household wealth by cohort, age, and insurance status in the HRS (in $2004). Evidently, wealth for the uninsured is much lower than for the insured, with a median that ranges between $20,000–$90,000 for the uninsured (depending on age

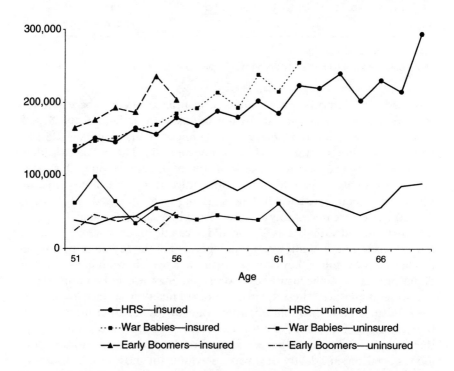

Figure 8-4. Median total net nonpension wealth by cohort, age, and insurance status: health and retirement study (1992–2004). (*Source*: Author's calculations.)

and cohort) versus $130,000–$250,000 for the insured. Some might also want to exclude housing wealth from the measure of how much is at stake for the uninsured, which might make sense if one believes that hospitals and physicians would not pursue outstanding debt owed by uninsured individuals to the point where they had to sell their homes to pay that debt.[9] Most of the wealth held by the uninsured turns out to be housing wealth; when we subtract housing wealth from the amount above, the median uninsured household in the original HRS cohort has about $10,000 in real nonhousing assets; the median War Babies household has $8,000 and the median Early Boomer household has only $4,000 (Figure 8-5). Compared to the average hospital charge of $17,300 (in 2002; Merrill and Elixhauser, 2005), the uninsured do not have much money on hand.[10] In fact, this nest egg would probably be wiped out by a single hospitalization. But it is a very small sum to begin with. In other words, households facing old age with less than $10,000 in the bank probably have bigger problems than being uninsured.

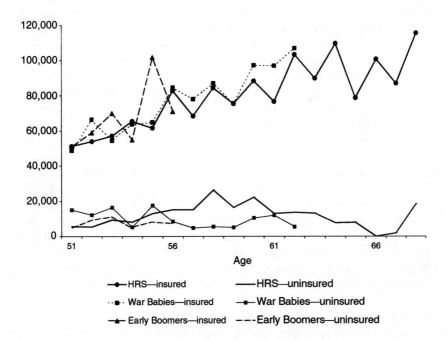

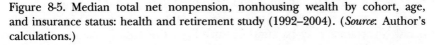

Figure 8-5. Median total net nonpension, nonhousing wealth by cohort, age, and insurance status: health and retirement study (1992–2004). (*Source*: Author's calculations.)

TABLE 8-6 Probability of any Hospital Stay in the Six
Years Prior to Age 65: Original HRS Cohort

Probability of hospital stay	
Individual	0.399
Individual or spouse, if any	0.574
Probability of *uninsured* hospital stay	
Individual	0.023
Individual or spouse, if any	0.031

Source: Author's calculations.
Note: See text.

Health Shocks During Uninsured Spells

Not surprisingly, hospitalization is a relatively common event for older households. Some 40 percent of the original HRS cohort has a hospitalization at some point in the three waves prior to age 65 (Table 8-6).[11] Among married couples, of course, the relevant question is whether the individual or his/her spouse will be hospitalized, since a spouse's hospitalization also poses a threat to the household's financial well-being. Including shocks to spouses, then, 60 percent of the HRS households had either a head or spouse hospitalized in the six years before age 65. In other words, the median individual in the HRS cohort was subject to a potentially very serious threat to household finances in the six years before retirement.

Nevertheless, most of these hospitalizations were covered by insurance, mitigating the threat. The HRS asks respondents whether a hospitalization was fully covered, partly covered, or not covered at all by insurance; here we consider a hospitalization to be uninsured if the respondent reports that it was not covered at all by insurance. Only 2 percent of this subset of the original HRS cohort had an *uninsured* hospitalization in the six years before age 65; only 3 percent had an uninsured hospitalization for themselves or their spouse. This number seems very low, but several important points are worth making when interpreting this number. First, one must recall that this sample included only individuals observed for three waves just prior to Medicare eligibility. In particular, anyone who died during this window was excluded from the analysis, as noted above. Such an exclusion could bias the measure of uninsured hospitalizations toward zero even more seriously than it does the estimate of all hospitalizations, if uninsured hospitalizations are disproportionately likely to result in death. A second point is that the definition of an 'insured' hospitalization used here probably includes many hospital stays for which health insurance paid very little. Individuals with health insurance may be 'underinsured' in the sense that their out-of-pocket costs associated with a hospitalization are large enough to threaten their financial security. Indeed, this is consistent with the fact that households citing health problems as a proximate cause of their bankruptcy filing are as likely to be insured as to be uninsured (Warren et al. 2000). There is not a one-to-one mapping between an uninsured hospitalization, as defined here, and a health shock that poses a financial threat.

Another consideration is that health insurance coverage, health, and use of medical care are simultaneously determined. Having health insurance coverage certainly affects the use of medical care (Newhouse et al. 1993; Card et al. 2004). Further, health status likely also affects the availability of insurance coverage; this effect could go either direction, but it is worth noting that some public insurance programs are explicitly intended to cover the disabled and individuals with high medical expenses. Uninsured hospitalizations may be unlikely either because individuals avoid the hospital when they are uninsured, or because hospitalization triggers coverage by public insurance. Either of these two scenarios would reduce the number of hospitalizations that are uninsured, but they have very different implications for the well-being of the uninsured elderly. Distinguishing between them—and, more generally, identifying more precisely the nature of the financial threat that health shocks pose to insured and uninsured near-elderly households—is a high priority for future research.

Discussion and Conclusion

The fraction of Baby Boomers who lack health insurance is slightly higher than the fraction uninsured in earlier cohorts. The probability of a health shock requiring is hospitalization is high (60% when considering both an individual and his or her spouse), but the probability of an *uninsured* health shock is quite low, with only 3 percent of original HRS respondents who are observed in all three waves before age 65 reporting a hospitalization for self or spouse for which insurance paid nothing. Moreover, the amount of personal wealth at stake turns out to be quite low: the median uninsured near-elderly household has less than $10,000 in net nonpension, nonhousing wealth.

These results raise the question of whether lack of health insurance is really the key problem facing uninsured older households: the fact that the median near-elderly uninsured household is facing retirement with so little in assets is striking. Consequently, policies aimed at alleviating poverty among the elderly may be far more important for the well-being of this population than policies to expand health insurance coverage prior to Medicare eligibility. This is not to suggest that lack of insurance is not a problem in this population; being poor and uninsured surely reduces access to medical care even for serious conditions (Asplin et al. 2005). But health insurance might do relatively little to change the *financial* situation of poor uninsured households as they approach retirement.

Acknowledgments

The author thanks Debra Sabatini Dwyer, Michael Hurd, and David Weir for helpful comments.

Notes

[1] Calculated by the author using the March 1999 CPS.

[2] For instance Hurst et al. (1998) show that in 1994, median wealth for households in their 50s was about 18 times larger than median wealth for households in their 20s and more than twice as large as median wealth for households in their 40s. The actual values of median wealth reported were, in $1996: $6,873 (20s); $63,446 (40s) and $129,007 (50s).

[3] The long slow decline in employer-sponsored coverage has been well documented (cf. Farber and Levy 2000). Also Swartz and Stevenson (2001) find a rising risk of not having insurance among the 55–64-year olds in 1999 versus 15 years previously (15% vs. 13%); see also Baker and Sudano (2005).

[4] In fact, the CPS has some features of a longitudinal survey since residents of a given dwelling unit are interviewed eight times over the course of sixteen months; nevertheless, here we do not exploit this and instead treat the CPS as repeated cross sections.

[5] Appendix Table 8A-1 presents a complete set of *t*-tests of the null hypothesis that the Early Boomers' health insurance coverage differs from that of the HRS cohort or War Babies at each age.

[6] A complete set of multivariate results is reported in Appendix Table 8A-1.

[7] This is not the same as saying that 4 percent of the sample was continuously uninsured for six years; individuals with no insurance at the time of the interview were not asked whether they had ever had insurance since the previous interview.

[8] In fact, Weir and Willis (2002) find that being widowed *increases* women's probability of having health insurance coverage.

[9] On the other hand, medical providers may pursue uninsured households energetically if debts are sold off to collection agencies. Of course even in that case, bankruptcy may afford some protection for housing assets (but homestead exemptions vary by state). Warren et al. (2000) report that a third of bankruptcy filers have significant medical debts and that one quarter of filers cite medical problems as a key factor contributing to their bankruptcy. Interestingly, this is true for filers with health insurance as well as those who are uninsured. Clearly additional research is required on the role of medical debt and health insurance in bankruptcy.

[10] Inflating this amount to $2004 gives $18,165. See also Goldman and Zissimopoulos (2003).

[11] This estimate presumably understates the risk of hospitalization since the sample, as described above, excludes individuals who died before they were observed for three waves; many of them are likely to have been hospitalized.

TABLE 8A-1 Raw and Regression-adjusted Differences in Health Insurance Coverage: Early Boomers versus War Babies and Original HRS and Current Population Survey, March 1989–2004

	Early Boomers versus War Babies				Early Boomers versus Original HRS			
	P(uninsured), WB—EBB Regression Adjusted?		t-Statistic for H_0: Gap is 0 Regression Adjusted?		P(uninsured), HRS—EBB Regression Adjusted?		t-Statistic for H_0: Gap is 0 Regression Adjusted?	
	No	Yes	No	Yes	No	Yes	No	Yes
Panel A: Difference in fraction uninsured								
Age								
40	**−0.029**	**−0.025**	3.64	3.26	—	—	—	—
41	**−0.023**	**−0.018**	3.79	3.02	—	—	—	—
42	**−0.025**	**−0.022**	4.61	4.30	—	—	—	—
43	**−0.033**	**−0.031**	6.47	6.39	—	—	—	—
44	**−0.016**	**−0.014**	3.44	3.16	—	—	—	—
45	−0.006	−0.007	1.34	1.67	—	—	—	—
46	0.000	0.000	0.06	0.11	−0.005	−0.009	0.49	1.02
47	0.001	0.001	0.23	0.16	−0.011	**−0.018**	1.56	2.62
48	0.006	0.008	1.47	1.92	−0.008	**−0.019**	1.39	3.24
49	−0.003	−0.003	0.71	0.70	**−0.011**	−0.022	2.10	4.26
50	0.005	0.003	1.16	0.74	−0.002	**−0.011**	0.47	2.21
51	0.008	0.008	1.64	1.61	0.009	0.000	1.64	0.05
52	−0.008	−0.008	1.52	1.57	−0.009	**−0.017**	1.68	3.14
53	**−0.016**	**−0.015**	2.60	2.47	−0.011	**−0.016**	1.66	2.61
54	−0.001	0.000	0.12	0.04	0.006	−0.001	0.65	0.10
Panel B: Difference in fraction with private health insurance								
40	**0.050**	**0.045**	5.40	5.45				
41	**0.042**	**0.033**	5.89	5.23				
42	**0.041**	**0.035**	6.45	6.29				
43	**0.042**	**0.038**	7.09	7.25				
44	**0.030**	**0.026**	5.43	5.38				
45	0.000	0.006	0.05	1.37				
46	0.008	**0.010**	1.50	2.05	0.021	**0.032**	1.93	3.34
47	0.001	0.004	0.16	0.81	**0.020**	**0.033**	2.40	4.46
48	−0.009	**−0.009**	1.76	2.03	0.002	**0.020**	0.32	3.18
49	**0.010**	**0.011**	1.97	2.37	**0.018**	**0.039**	2.91	6.97
50	−0.006	0.000	1.03	0.08	0.009	**0.027**	1.45	4.94
51	−0.001	0.000	0.09	0.03	0.001	**0.015**	0.11	2.63
52	**0.014**	**0.013**	2.20	2.33	**0.018**	**0.031**	2.71	5.13
53	**0.027**	**0.023**	3.58	3.50	0.014	**0.028**	1.84	4.06
54	0.013	0.010	1.33	1.17	0.004	**0.018**	0.34	1.98

TABLE 8A-1 (*continued*)

	Early Boomers versus War Babies				Early Boomers versus Original HRS			
	P(uninsured), WB—EBB Regression Adjusted?		t-Statistic for H_0: Gap is 0 Regression Adjusted?		P(uninsured), HRS—EBB Regression Adjusted?		t-Statistic for H_0: Gap is 0 Regression Adjusted?	
	No	Yes	No	Yes	No	Yes	No	Yes

Panel C: Difference in fraction with public health insurance

Age

Age	No	Yes	No	Yes	No	Yes	No	Yes
40	**−0.021**	**−0.020**	3.73	3.86				
41	**−0.018**	**−0.015**	4.37	3.92				
42	**−0.016**	**−0.013**	4.05	3.60				
43	**−0.009**	**−0.007**	2.51	2.12				
44	**−0.014**	**−0.012**	4.09	3.93				
45	0.006	0.001	1.80	0.28				
46	**−0.008**	**−0.009**	2.55	3.13	**−0.016**	**−0.023**	2.49	3.85
47	−0.002	−0.004	0.59	1.54	−0.009	**−0.015**	1.75	3.27
48	0.003	0.001	0.83	0.39	0.006	−0.001	1.40	0.28
49	**−0.007**	**−0.008**	2.19	2.72	−0.007	**−0.017**	1.81	4.78
50	0.000	−0.004	0.09	1.20	−0.006	**−0.016**	1.68	4.61
51	**−0.008**	**−0.008**	2.04	2.27	**−0.009**	**−0.015**	2.35	4.17
52	−0.006	−0.005	1.44	1.37	**−0.009**	**−0.014**	2.01	3.46
53	**−0.011**	−0.008	2.16	1.87	−0.004	**−0.012**	0.69	2.52
54	−0.012	−0.010	1.84	1.68	−0.009	**−0.017**	1.32	2.82

Notes: Differences significantly different from 0 with $p < 0.05$ indicated in bold.

References

Asplin, B. R., Rhodes, K. V., Levy, H., Lurie, N., Crain, A. L., Carlin, B. P., and Kellermann, A. L. (2005). 'Insurance Status and Access to Urgent Ambulatory Care Follow-up Appointments', *JAMA*, 294: 1248–54.

Baker, D. and Sudano, J. (2005). 'Health Insurance Coverage During the Years Preceding Medicare Eligibility', *Archives of Internal Medicine*, 165: 770–6.

Card, D., Dobkin, C., and Maestas, N. (2004). 'The Impact of Nearly Universal Insurance Coverage on Health Care Utilization and Health: Evidence from Medicare', NBER Working Paper No. 10365, March.

Farber, H. and Levy, H. (2000). 'Recent Trends in Employer-Sponsored Health Insurance: Are Bad Jobs Getting Worse?', *Journal of Health Economics*, 19: 93–119.

Goldman, D. and Zissimopoulos, J. (2003). 'High Out-of-Pocket Health Care Spending By The Elderly', *Health Affairs*, 22(3): May/June; 194–202.

Hurst, E., Luoh, M. C., and Stafford, F. (1998). 'Wealth Dynamics of American Families: 1984–1994', *Brookings Papers on Economic Activity*, 1: 1998.

Merrill, C. T. and Elixhauser, A. (2005). *Hospitalization in the United States, 2002.* Publication Number 05-0056, June, Washington, DC: Agency for Health Care Research and Quality.

Newhouse, J. P. and the RAND Insurance Experiment Group (1993). *Free for All? Lessons from the RAND Health Insurance Experiment.* Santa Monica, CA: The RAND Corporation.

Swartz, K. and Stevenson, B. (2001). 'Health Insurance Coverage of People in the Ten Years before Medicare Eligibility', in P. P. Budetti, R. V. Burkhauser, J. M. Gregory, and H. A. Hunt (eds.), *Ensuring Health and Income Security for an Aging Workforce.* Washington, DC: National Academy of Social Insurance.

Warren, E., Sullivan, T., and Jacoby, M. (2000). 'Medical Problems and Bankruptcy Filings', *Norton's Bankruptcy Adviser*, May.

Weir, D. and Willis, R. J. (2002). 'Widowhood, Divorce, and Loss of Health Insurance Among Near-Elderly Women: Evidence from the Health and Retirement Study', Working Paper, Economic Research Initiative, July.

Part III

New Roles for Retirement Assets

Chapter 9

The Impact of Pensions on Nonpension Investment Choices

Leora Friedberg and Anthony Webb

Workers have experienced a major shift in pension coverage over the last two decades, with US employer-provided defined contribution (DC) pensions displacing traditional defined benefit (DB) pensions. At the time, the rate of stock market participation among US households escalated. The DB and the DC plans differ in how risks are allocated to workers and firms and in the degree to which workers are exposed to financial decision-making. This chapter documents the investment choices of workers outside their company pensions, focusing on a sample of respondents to the Health and Retirement Study (HRS). In what follows, we first discuss the long-term trends in pension structure and stock market participation by households. Next, we discuss the risks involved in DB and DC pensions and theoretical predictions about their impact on behavior; following this, we review related literature. Subsequently, we present our estimation strategy, data, and estimation results, and conclude with a discussion of directions for future research.

Motivation

Employer-provided DC pensions including 401(k) plans have displaced traditional DB pensions for many US workers over the last two decades. Among full-time employees with a pension, DC coverage rose over 1983–98 from 40 to 79 percent, while DB coverage dropped from 87 to 44 percent (Friedberg and Webb 2005). During the same period, the rate of stock market participation among US households escalated, jumping from 32 percent in 1989 to 49 percent in 1998 (Bertaut and Starr-McCluer 2000). While the proliferation of DC plans explains part of the overall increase in stock market participation, it also rose for other households.[1] Hence, of special interest is how investment choices *outside of worker pension plans* changed over time.

This shift in pension structure has transformed the environment in which workers make most of their life-cycle saving decisions. In times gone by, employers offering DB plans made all investment choices and bore risks associated with those choices. Today, employees generally make investment choices and bear the associated risks in DC plans. For instance, an unexpectedly high rate of return helps employers with DB plans and workers with DC pensions. Conventional theory suggests that workers with DC plans, bearing more investment risk, should invest more conservatively outside of their pensions than workers with risk-free DB plans. Yet DB plans have traditionally imposed substantial risks as well. The promised benefit is often not fully guaranteed until the worker nears or reaches retirement, so the DB pension risk should also influence workers' willingness to bear nonpension investment risk, especially since it is likely to be correlated with salary risk they bear.

The allocation of household nonpension portfolio risk may also be influenced by other pension risks. One possibility is that the proliferation of DC pensions *raised* stock market participation outside of pensions, perhaps by helping households overcome barriers to stock market participation (Poterba 2001; Weisbenner 2002). Another factor to consider is taxes. Rational investors are believed to do best when they put taxable assets in DC plans where they are taxed less heavily (Bergstresser and Poterba 2004). Especially for those in higher tax brackets, the same pretax rate of return earned on bonds will be taxed more heavily than that earned on equity. On the other hand, equity historically has a higher average pretax return, so predictions about the optimal location of assets may be ambiguous. We will consider what the evidence reveals about these effects.

Our research provides a key ingredient for understanding the impact of pension structure on overall wealth accumulation. Many researchers have analyzed how people make investment choices in DC plans. However, data from pension plan managers and employers does not allow one to analyze the resulting impact on nonpension wealth. Another branch of research has used data like ours from the HRS or the Survey of Consumer Finances (SCF) to study how the presence or amount of wealth in pension plans relates to the *amount* of nonpension wealth. Little attention has been given, though, to understanding the effect of pensions on the *allocation* of nonpension wealth. By influencing rates of return and the subsequent need to save, the allocation of wealth determines total wealth at retirement. Poterba et al. (2005) laid out the impact of allocation choices in DC plans on retirement wealth and expected utility while treating the allocation of nonpension wealth as exogenous. Their work demonstrates the importance of understanding responses to risk that alter other wealth holdings. The question of whether the structure of pensions lead people to make offsetting choices in the allocation of their nonpension portfolio will drastically affect conclusions about the impact of pensions on overall wealth at retirement.

It is also important to understand these effects for several additional reasons. First, our results shed light on the overall impact of major changes in the pension environment, since DB pension coverage continues to plummet for young workers and in newer jobs. Second, there is increasing attention to how the shift in pension risk may alter other behavior such as retirement patterns. The extent to which real actions are taken to offset such risk is governed by the opportunities to make other portfolio adjustments. Third, the shift in pension structure may provide new insights about the importance of constraints on portfolio allocation. Finally, some reform proposals recommend replacing at least a portion of traditional Social Security benefits with personal accounts. The latter may raise wealth if they earn a higher return than the 2–3 percent real return by which social Security benefits would be reduced (President's Commission to Strengthen Social Security 2001). Yet if participants responded to this change by reallocating their nonpension portfolios away from equities, much of the anticipated risk diversification benefit might disappear. At the other extreme, events like the collapse of Enron have led to calls to reduce the amount of risk to which workers are exposed in their pensions.

Predictions from Economic Theory

From a theoretical perspective, DB and DC pensions differ in crucial ways. Figure 9-1 shows the path of pension wealth accrual in two such plans drawn from the HRS.[2] Pension wealth here is defined as the real discounted present value of the worker's expected future pension benefits, if the job ends at the age shown on the horizontal axis. In this section, we first describe differences in the risks associated with the accrual of pension wealth in both types of plan shown in Figure 9-1, and then we offer predictions about the impact of those risks on optimal portfolio choices. We also discuss theoretical considerations about voluntary contributions, which are often difficult to identify in practice.

Risk Characteristics of Pension Plans

The DC pensions are relatively simple to explain: contributions go into an account which earns a market return. The account is portable after vesting (usually immediate or within two years), so workers can 'roll over' or take their funds with them as a lump-sum, when they leave their job. Some DC plans are invested entirely in company stock or another risky asset, while many allow some choice in how to invest their funds. While the nature of the investment risk varies to some extent across plans, workers bear the investment risk in all DC plans. Thus, the path of DC pension wealth

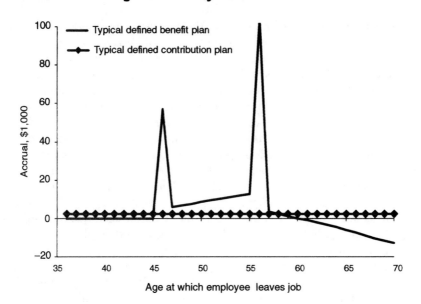

Figure 9-1. Pension wealth accruals in typical pension plans, 1992 HRS. *Notes:* Employer-provided pension wealth is defined as the real present value of expected future employer-provided pension benefits, if the employee leaves the job at the age shown on the horizontal axis. Pension wealth accrual, shown on the vertical axis in thousands of dollars, is the change in pension wealth if the employee works one additional year and then leaves the job. (*Source:* Adapted from Friedberg and Webb (2005).)

accrual shown in Figure 9-1 is not actually known in advance, but is in fact uncertain.

The DB pensions offer a defined payout to workers at retirement. The benefit is typically an annuity that is a proportion of either the worker's average or final salary, with the proportion often increasing with tenure. In the United States, corporate employers are obligated to prefinance promised benefits in a manner that is financially sound, so they bear the resulting investment risk.[3] The DB plans are not actually riskless, of course; the path of DB pension wealth shown in Figure 9-1 is 'spiky', which makes DB pension wealth highly vulnerable to the risk of early departure, in contrast with portable DC pensions. Losses from early exit arise because benefits depend on nominal, not real, earnings; because of nonlinear effects of job tenure on the nominal benefit; and because of vesting provisions. The risk of losing one's pension because of early departure from a job shrinks as tenure increases, both because expected pension wealth is realized and because uncertainty over future contingencies may diminish. Accordingly, the pension risk in DB plans diminishes over time, while the investment risk in DC pensions remains.[4]

How Pensions Affect Optimal Portfolio Choice

In a standard model of portfolio choice without frictions, risk-averse individuals choose an optimal combination of expected return and undiversifiable capital market risk that depends on their degree of risk aversion. All other risk that arises from investing in capital markets can be diversified away by making investments that have negatively correlated risks. What if people face risk in their income streams as well as their investments? This 'background' income risk is generally viewed as being undiversifiable, and it will generally reduce the amount of risk that people are willing to absorb in their financial assets. Labor income is considered a major source of background risk.

The full impact of risky pensions will depend on the nature of those risks. As noted, DB and DC pensions are both subject to background risk from uncertain future earnings highly correlated with labor income risk, and DB pensions are subject to additional background risk due to possible early departure from the job. Given that, paying workers with a risky flow in either the form of a pension or its equivalent in cash would, at the outset, induce similar effects on portfolio choices. However, since these sources of background risk diminish over time, this could boost the risk people are willing to adopt outside their pension. This prediction is stronger for DB pensions because of the diminishing risk of early departure and the accruals of DB wealth that workers experience as tenure increases. Besides that, DC pensions carry investment risk. Giving a worker a risky DC plan instead of a safe DB plan should lead to offsetting behaviors elsewhere.

To sum up, if workers make optimal portfolio choices, then we expect that workers holding risky assets in their DC plans should adopt more conservative investment strategies outside their pensions, and workers with DB plans should adopt accordingly less conservative strategies.

The Effect of Pensions on Optimal Portfolio Choice with Frictions

Recent behavioral economics studies have suggested that many US households do not invest in equity markets at all, even if equity is recommended theoretically as a key element of any optimal portfolio in the absence of a risk-free asset. Explanations for barriers to stock market participation include costs of participation, whether financial, informational, or psychological. A related piece of evidence is that stock market participation jumped in the 1990s, perhaps because the proliferation of DC plans played a role in surmounting some barriers to participation. If households face an up-front cost of learning how to invest or acquiring information, then DC plan participants with investment choices can overcome that barrier. In point of fact, DC participants are usually offered information about investment choices such as risk characteristics and past performance of different types of mutual funds, and they can learn from observing performance over time. Even being given an investment such as company stock without choice may raise awareness about the operation of financial markets. Moreover, some employers seek to boost DC participation in order to comply with tax law by offering financial education, which has been shown to lift contributions to retirement accounts (Bernheim and Garrett 2003; Duflo and Saez 2003).[5] Weisbenner (2002) found some evidence of this, where he concluded that households with DC plans permitting investment choices were more likely to hold equities and held a higher share of equities outside of their plans, than otherwise similar households in DC plans that did not permit such choices.

Taxes

The portfolio allocation problem gains an additional dimension when considering DC plans, since assets held in such accounts are taxed lightly.[6] Investors should therefore locate assets that are taxable at the highest rates in DC plans, subject to liquidity constraints. The same pretax rate of return earned on bonds tends to be taxed more heavily than that earned on equity, especially at higher tax rates, though the tax differential was much greater in 2004 than in 1992.[7] On the other hand, equity historically has a higher average pretax return than bonds. Thus, we might observe different nonpension portfolio allocations for people with DB versus DC plans for tax-related reasons. The differential in tax rates should encourage the concentration of bonds in DC plans and equity outside, while differential rates of return would lead to offsetting effects. However, research by Bergstresser and Poterba (2004) indicates that tax minimization is not a major driver of DC versus non-DC allocations.

Voluntary Contributions

A final consideration is that some DC plans allow voluntary contributions, and in some cases these are matched by an employer. In a frictionless world, if we observed voluntary contributions, we would predict that workers would continue to offset the riskiness of their pension wealth elsewhere in their portfolio. In a world with barriers to stock market participation, on the other hand, observing voluntary contributions to a risky asset reveals important information. If such contributions were not otherwise encouraged by matching employer contributions or tax preferences, it provides additional support for the notion we discussed earlier—that DC pensions offer a less costly way to invest in risky assets. Additional motivations from taxes or employer match rates that subsidize such investments mitigate this argument, but not fully. Unfortunately, it is difficult to observe voluntary and matched contributions in the HRS. Below, we highlight what we can infer in our estimation approach.

Related Literature

One important set of papers relevant to our topic analyzes the theoretical effect of various risks on portfolio choices and real behaviors in a life-cycle setting. Many recent papers have analyzed the impact of adding undiversifiable 'background' income risk to the household problem, including Kimball (1991) who shows that an increase in income risk in a static framework reduces an agent's willingness to bear investment risk, even when the risks are independent. The implication is that, when a risky DC plan replaces a safe DB plan, individuals who also face background risk should seek safer assets outside of their pension. Background risk also can induce agents to take other actions. For instance these features reduce both consumption and investment in the risky asset (cf. Koo 1998, 1999) in simulations of dynamic models with income risk and borrowing constraints. Viceira (2001) incorporated exogenous retirement, while Chan and Viceira (2000) allowed labor supply to vary endogenously, which mitigates but does not eliminate the demand for hedging when stock and labor income shocks are positively correlated.[8]

It should be noted that much of the theoretical literature on optimal allocation in the face of background risk focuses only on financial assets. We extend the focus to pension wealth, which is facilitated by our recognition that pension risks closely resemble risks in either labor income or financial wealth. We will follow the lead of others and ignore housing and self-owned businesses, but some features of our analysis reduce concerns along those lines. Flavin and Yamashita (2002) showed that introducing housing can cause substantial differences in optimal stock holdings over the life cycle, but age-related heterogeneity is not a major problem in our sample of older workers. Also, households with closely held businesses are less likely than others to have pensions at all because they are disproportionately self-employed.

Limitations of Empirical Research

Empirical researchers have avoided estimating a full life-cycle problem like those laid out in the theoretical literature, focusing instead on testing limited implications. One reason is that actual behavior departs from theoretical predictions in important ways. Many papers have assessed the magnitude of departures from theoretical predictions, but the explanations for them remain highly unclear. A common finding is that stock market participation is far too low (King and Leape 1987) and that individuals actively rebalance their portfolio far too infrequently (Ameriks and Zeldes 2004), relative to theoretical predictions. Explanations have focused on barriers to stock market participation, which we alluded to earlier. For example, Vissing-Jørgenson (2002) found that stock market participation is persistent and that the frequency of trades increases with income, which may indicate the importance of fixed per-period participation costs.

Another problem is the nature of available data, which limits the scope of empirical analysis. Some studies use data from financial companies, occasionally longitudinal, but they lack information on nonpension behavior or on many household characteristics that affect financial behavior. Other studies use the SCF, which collects detailed wealth data for repeated cross-sections. The first panel to collect detailed asset data was the HRS. We use data from the HRS, but we use it cross-sectionally because of measurement error. Measuring changes in asset values magnifies the difficulties involved in measuring asset levels, which are already subject to substantial misresponse and nonresponse in survey data.[9]

Empirical Research on Portfolio Behavior

To study portfolio allocation, we are particularly interested in studies that focus on DC pension plans and other assets together, and those that focus on the impact of risk. In the former category, Uccello (2000) noted that 401(k) participants with a DB plan were more likely to invest their 401(k) assets in equities, as compared to those without a DB plan. While the allocation of pension and nonpension investments is endogenous, she controlled for the allocation of nonpension investments to stocks. In what follows, we extend the focus to the determinants of non-DC investments. Poterba and Samwick (2003) carefully estimated the impact of marginal tax rates on the allocation of assets to tax-deferred accounts [including 401(k) plans] and other accounts, though not on allocations within tax-deferred accounts. Below, we follow many of the details of their empirical specifications. In addition, Bergstresser and Poterba (2004) studied whether tax considerations appear to drive allocations in and out of DC plans. While people with DC plans in our data hold more equity outside of their pensions than people with DB plans, Bergstresser and Poterba showed that people with DC plans in the SCF also hold more equity in their DC accounts, and that DC and non-DC allocations are typically quite similar. Since relatively small reallocations would be required for many households to achieve tax-efficient portfolios, their work suggests that tax minimization does not drive DC versus non-DC allocations.

A separate group of papers found that measures of *ex ante* risk or *ex post* outcomes of risky processes influence portfolio choices. Guiso et al. (1996) showed that higher self-reported labor income risk is associated with smaller holdings of equity in Italian data. Vissing-Jørgenson (2002) found that higher volatility in nonfinancial income is associated with a reduced share of assets in the stock market, and Souleles (1999) reported similar effects of consumption volatility. Vissing-Jørgenson did not find, however, that the correlation of income and stock market returns influenced allocations. Below, we directly extend this literature by analyzing the impact of exposure to pension risk on portfolio choices.

A few recent papers have analyzed risk-taking in the HRS. Goldman and Maestas (2005) found that households that are more likely to have Medigap policies to supplement Medicare, and thus face reduced risk of out-of-pocket medical expenditures, are more likely to invest in risky assets. Benítez-Silva (2004) estimated that work flexibility, as measured by the ease with which one can alter one's work hours, raised holdings of equity in the HRS. He interpreted the results as showing that those who can self-insure their labor income by adjusting hours of work are more willing to take on other risks. Our analysis on pension risks, which are substantial, extends these results.

Empirical Research on Other Effects of Risk

Several studies have analyzed the impact of recent stock market fluctuations on retirement, with very mixed results. Gustman and Steinmeier (2002) estimated a structural model of retirement and saving in the HRS with stochastic rates of return, but they did not model portfolio choices. Coronado and Perozek (2003) found that the stock market run-up led to earlier-than-planned retirement in the HRS. Other papers specifically exploited variation in exposure to stock market risk through DC pensions. Hurd and Reti (2001) and Coile and Levine (2004) did not find evidence of an effect on retirement, while Sevak (2005) did.

Methodology and Estimation Strategy

As we have noted, DB and DC pensions carry different risks and opportunities. DB pensions grow relatively less risky over time, so we expect to see a gradual increase in exposure to risk outside of DB pensions. On the other hand, the proliferation of DC plans may have helped to boost stock market participation in the 1990s. Next, we describe our approach to studying these effects.

Econometric Specifications

Using cross-sectional data from the first wave of the HRS, we will investigate the impact of pension type on the riskiness of nonpension investments.[10] Specifically we examine the probability of holding equities in nonpension financial assets and the share of nonpension financial assets allocated to equities.[11] The estimation is based on an underlying latent variable model in which s^* indicates the desired share of assets allocated to equity but is subject to censoring at the endpoints of 0 and 1, as follows:

$$s_i^* = X_i\beta + \varepsilon_i$$

$$s_i = 0 \quad \text{if } s_i^* < 0, \quad s_i = s_i^* = X_i\beta + \varepsilon_i \quad \text{if } s_i^* \in [0, 1], \quad s_i = 1 \quad \text{if } s_i^* > 1$$

Here, X consists of pension characteristics and other explanatory variables that may affect portfolio choices, as we discuss later. A Tobit specification assumes that the probability density function $f(\varepsilon_i) \sim N(0, \sigma^2)$. A Probit specification assumes the same thing and estimates the likelihood of $s_i > 0$ versus $s_i = 0$, in which case σ^2 is not identified.

Identifying the Effect of Pension Risk

In order to distinguish the effects of pension risk, we control for both the type of pension and years in that type of plan, and whether DC plans offer investment choices. We remain concerned, though, about unobserved factors that may be correlated with pension characteristics and undermine inference about the effect of pension risk on portfolio allocations. For example, workers who are relatively risk-tolerant may sort into jobs with risky DC plans, or workers who are more likely to leave a job early may prefer a job that offers a portable DC plan and may also be more risk-tolerant. Unfortunately, we lack instruments for pension characteristics, so we will take other steps to address concerns about unobserved heterogeneity. We will focus on a relatively homogeneous sample of workers with a pension (as in Weisbenner 2002). People without a pension differ in many dimensions—they have lower income and wealth and are less likely to be working full-time. Many are retired, and retirement may cause portfolio changes that confound the analysis. We therefore also control for answers to HRS questions about tolerance for risk.

We remain hesitant to ascribe a causal interpretation to the estimated effect of pension type on stock market investment, however. Concerns about endogenous selection into pension type are exacerbated by the recognition that participation in some DC plans is voluntary. Ideally, we would either omit DC plans that were purely voluntary, or focus on DC eligibility rather than DC participation, or else use information on voluntary contributions to gain insight about preferences for risky investments. Unfortunately, we cannot readily identify voluntary contributions to DC plans in our data, and we are not confident that we observe all those who are eligible but do not participate—that is, we can verify nonparticipating eligibles whose employers report another pension, but we must rely on individual reports for nonparticipating eligibles who report having no other pension. This issue will compound the problem of unobserved heterogeneity in risk preferences.

On the other hand, the possibility of endogenous selection of workers into pension plans works in our favor in identifying years-in-plan effects. Our hypothesis is that workers will take on more nonpension risk the longer they stay in a DB plan. Endogenous mobility would confound inference of such an effect if workers with a greater tolerance for risk stay longer in jobs with DB plans. However, this is the opposite of what follows from our arguments above—we expect workers with less tolerance for risk to choose DB plans and to stay in them longer. Therefore, concerns about endogenous mobility would bias against finding evidence supporting our hypothesis, and any effect that we observe would underestimate the true effect.

Empirical Evidence

Our empirical analysis sheds light on these issues by investigating the investment allocations of workers with DB or DC pensions. The Health and Retirement Study reports detailed data for a large sample of older Americans on wealth holdings and on pension plans. We use data from 1992 and 2004 to compare workers with different types of pension plans, and we incorporate information on the number of years workers have been in their pensions. This allows us to distinguish effects on stock market investment that are present immediately from effects that emerge as time in the plan increases. If DB pension wealth were riskless, then workers with DB plans would be expected to take on more risk elsewhere in their portfolios. Viewing DB pensions more accurately as risky, but declining in risk as tenure increases and DB pension wealth becomes more certain, then workers with DB plans should take on more risk over time. In our empirical results, we observe this effect—stock market participation is significantly higher as years in a DB plan rise, relative to years in a DC plan. We confirm in our 1992 data that DB pension wealth at risk diminishes rapidly as workers age through their 50s. We also find that years spent in either type of plan reduce stock market investment in 2004 when compared to 1992. This suggests a jump in the perceived risk of both types of pensions. This is not surprising given both increasingly common reports of underfunding of DB plans, and also recent experience with stock market volatility among DC plan holders in 2004.

The HRS surveyed households with at least one spouse aged 50–60 in 1991. Analyzing a large sample in this age range is useful, since they are in their peak saving years and most likely to be making active decisions about the allocation of wealth. We focus on the original HRS cohort in 1992, when it was aged 51–61, and we replicate some of the analysis for the War Babies (WBs) and Early Baby Boomers (EBBs) cohorts using 2004 data, when those cohorts were aged 51–62. The key advantage of data from 1992 is that the HRS also obtained information from employers about pension coverage at the time, as we describe below. Similar data is lacking for the later cohorts in 2004.[12]

Investment Data

The HRS collected data on specific assets through questions of the following type, which asked in 1992 about equity holdings:

For the next few questions, please exclude any assets held in the form of IRA and Keogh accounts. Do you have any shares of stock in publicly held corporations, mutual funds, or investment trusts?

Respondents were then asked the total amount invested in assets of this kind. Similar data were collected on other types of financial assets including holdings of any kind of bonds (comprising 'corporate, municipal, government, or foreign bonds, or any bond funds') and liquid assets (comprising 'checking or savings accounts, or money market funds', and, 'certificates of deposit, government savings bonds, or Treasury bills'). Data were also collected about the balances of IRAs and Keoghs, but not about their asset allocation until 1998, so we have excluded them.

An important feature that distinguishes the HRS from many other datasets is the degree to which it sought to obtain at least some information from people who refused to answer these questions in full. When respondents said they had an asset but refused to provide its value, they were prompted to reveal the range in which the value lay. The HRS used the range data to impute dollar amounts for both partially and completely missing responses. We use the imputed values when actual values were not obtained.

Pension Data

The HRS offers two sources of data about pensions. People were asked in detail about their pensions, and in 1992 they were also asked to give permission for the HRS to contact their employer to get plan information. The HRS obtained plan descriptions from employers of 65 percent of workers who said they had a pension.[13]

It turns out that many people are surprisingly unfamiliar with details of their pensions. Gustman and Steinmeier (1999) underscore that people confuse even the type of pension they have: among the 48 percent of their employers reporting that they offered only a DB plan, 56 percent of the workers in such a plan described it as DB, while 15 percent described it as DC, and 27 percent said they had both types. Mistakes were similarly high among employers reporting that they offered only DC plans or reporting both types. This raises the question of how to use these two sources of information: much more accurate employer-reported (ER) data for a smaller, and possibly selected, sample; and much less accurate individual-reported data for the full sample. Complicating the situation, only workers report key variables for our analysis—how long they have been in their plans and whether they have investment choices in DC plans. For our 1992 sample, we try various combinations of self- and employer-reported data on pension type and pension wealth, motivated by the recognition that even incorrect beliefs can affect behavior.[14] Chan and Stevens (2004) found that inaccurate information about pensions affects retirement decisions, as does accurate information among those who are well-informed. For the 2004 sample, of course, we can only use self-reported data.

Other Data

We include other explanatory variables that are expected to influence portfolio choices. The HRS asked questions about preferences for risk-taking. Individuals were first asked,

Suppose that you are the only income earner in the family, and you have a good job guaranteed to give you your current family income every year for life. You are given the opportunity to take a new and equally good job, with a 50-50 chance it will double your family income and a 50-50 chance that it will cut your family income by a third. Would you take the new job?

After answering yes or no, they were asked a similar question proposing either a more or less risky gamble. We explored different parameterizations of this information, but the controls for risk aversion are statistically significant in only some of our empirical specifications. People may have difficulty processing this somewhat complicated hypothetical.[15] Therefore, the responses may not capture the full range of heterogeneity in risk preferences.

Our other control variables are relatively standard. As in other studies, we control for noncapital income and wealth. Because labor income and pensions both comprise a part of compensation, we control separately for labor income and for other noncapital income and separately for employer-provided pension wealth and for other components of net nonpension wealth. While net nonpension wealth may be endogenously determined by past portfolio choices, it is commonly included and has strong explanatory power. It is justified by, among other things, the possibility of fixed costs of participation, since higher wealth makes it easier to surmount such costs. Employer-provided pension wealth is defined here, differently from Figure 9-1, as the expected present value of benefits if a worker stays in a job until age 65.

We can control for information about current health status and about life expectancy until ages 75 and 85, with the latter capturing information about the value to individuals of annuitized DB pension income versus unannuitized DC lump-sum payouts. Finally, we will include demographic variables (age, marital status, gender, and educational attainment) that influence life-cycle behavior.

Sample Selection

We concentrate on the effect of men's pensions, and we treat the household as the decision unit. On the whole, men are much more likely to have a pension in the original HRS cohort—about 40 percent of our 1992 sample has a wife with a pension, and wives' pension wealth is relatively low. Studying wives' pensions, as well as household decision-making more generally, is complicated by evidence from our other research; for instance, Friedberg and Webb (2006) show that the spouse with higher earnings has more influence over major household decisions, and moreover that women with more influence invest significantly less in the stock market.

Of the 7,607 households interviewed in the HRS cohort in 1992, we focus on those in which a male is working (4,138 households); and among those, men who are not self-employed and who report having a pension (2,271); and among those, households that report the data discussed above (1989); and among those, households with positive net nonpension wealth (1950).[16] Of the 6,034 households interviewed in the WB and EBB cohorts in 2004, we employ the same criteria, focusing on those in which a male is working (2,010), the male is not self-employed (1,550), the household has positive net nonpension wealth (1,461), and the male reports having a pension (1,019). For our main sample of 1,950 in 1992, 1,343 were matched to ER data. As we noted earlier, we will make use of pension data reported both by workers and, when available, their employers. Of those 1,343, some 706 of the workers (or 51%) knew their pension type (categorized as DB-only, DC-only, and DB and DC)). Mistakes can be of several types. Fully 11 percent of the matched sample are completely confused, reporting DB-only when the plan is DC-only or vice versa; 19 percent are somewhat confused, reporting both types when they only have one; and 18 percent are absentminded, reporting one type when they have both.

Characteristics of the Sample

Tables 9-1 and 9-2 reports summary statistics for our full sample and relevant subsamples. Table 9-1 shows summary statistics for the full sample, divided by self-reported (SR) pension type; and for the subsample that has matched employer data, divided by ER pension type. Table 9-2 reports key financial statistics (excluding IRAs and Keoghs, as mentioned earlier) for additional subsamples.

There are two notable patterns that emerge among the pension and financial variables of interest in the 1992 sample. First, people with DC plans (with or without a DB plan as well) had a greater likelihood of investing in equities than did people with only a DB plan. Among those in the SR data with a DB-only plan, 28.9 percent owned stock outside their pension, compared to 38.1 percent of those with a DC-only plan and 47.7 percent with DB and DC plans. For the matched subsample using ER data, the overall differences were less stark (34.3% for DB-only, 40.4% for DC-only, and 39.3% for DB and DC); while for those in the matched sample who knew their pension type (as shown in Table 9-2), the differences were a little more stark (26.6, 42.9, and 52.6). Conditional on investing, though, there was little difference in the share of financial assets allocated to equities.

The second key pattern is that, among those with DB plans in 1992, the likelihood of investing in equities rose with years in the plan. Table 9-2 distinguishes among those in DB plans for 0–10 versus 11+ years for self-reported samples (since, importantly, only SR data reports years in a plan). For workers in DB-only plans, 23.4 percent in their plan for 0–10 years invested in equities versus 30.7 percent in their plan for 11+ years. For workers in DB and DC plans, the differences (by years in the DB plan) were 41.8 and 49.9 percent.

As our results in the next section confirm, the two key patterns described above persist when we control for covariates in the estimation. This is important because of disparities in some sample characteristics shown in

TABLE 9-1 Key Characteristics of HRS Sample

	1992						2004		
	Self-Reported Pension Type			Employer-Reported Pension Type			Self-Reported Pension Type		
	DB-Only	DC-Only	DB and DC	DB-Only	DC-Only	DB and DC	DB-Only	DC-Only	DB and DC
Wealth and income in thousands of $2004									
Labor income	49.1	54.3	66.5	54.5	56.2	59.8	55.7	64.4	78.7
Other noncapital income	20.5	22.3	22.9	22.1	24.0	20.5	24.4	31.3	32.2
Net nonpension wealth	212.8	235.4	272.3	216.5	267.3	242.7	341.2	374.2	564.2
Employer pension wealth	165.9	91.2	288.7	291.4	181.9	336.1	80.9	140.0	237.9
Stock ownership outside of employer-provided pension									
% Owning stock	28.9	38.1	47.7	34.3	40.4	39.3	37.3	37.7	45.3
Stock/nonpension financial wealth	15.4	19.8	25.5	17.9	22.4	21.6	22.1	23.7	27.6
"", if own stock	53.2	52.0	53.6	52.3	55.5	55.0	59.2	62.8	60.9
Employer-provided pension characteristics									
Years in DB plan	19.4	—	19.1	—	—	—	19.7	—	14.5
Years in DC plan	—	9.8	8.4	—	—	—	—	10.0	10.9
DC plan has choice	—	51.1	63.5	—	—	—	—	81.9	76.2
Demographic and other characteristics									
Most risk averse	70.9	63.0	66.7	70.0	57.9	72.6	60.6	58.0	55.0
Married	87.9	89.1	88.3	85.7	91.4	86.7	86.3	89.4	88.5
Age	56	55	55	55	56	55	55	54	54
No high school	25.4	28.3	12.5	20.6	21.9	19.3	12.7	11.7	5.5
Attended college	39.3	44.3	59.2	49.8	48.6	49.3	63.0	63.2	70.9
Black	16.6	10.9	8.7	14.3	11.6	12.8	15.8	8.8	10.2
Hispanic	6.2	7.4	4.5	6.9	5.1	3.7	9.5	10.6	8.4
Bad health	1.8	1.3	1.0	0.6	0.7	2.6	0.4	0.9	0.8
Sample size	820	530	600	621	292	430	284	443	382

Source: Authors' calculations from the 1992 HRS.

Notes: The sample includes all households in which a male works, is not self-employed, and reports having a pension, and which have positive net worth and answer all questions about the information reported above. Variable definitions: pension type is defined benefit (DB)-only, defined contribution (DC)-only, or defined benefit and defined contribution; distinct information on pension type is reported by both individuals and by their employers. Labor income, employer-provided pension wealth, and demographic characteristics are reported for the male in the household. See text for more details.

TABLE 9-2 Financial Characteristics of Various Subsamples

	% Owning Stock	Stock/Financial Wealth		Most Risk Averse
		All	If Own Stock	
1992 Full sample, by self-reported (SR) pension type (N = 1,950)				
DB-only (820)	28.9	15.4	53.2	70.9
0–10 yrs	23.4	12.4	53.1	68.5
11+ yrs	30.7	16.3	53.2	71.6
DC-only (530)	38.1	19.8	52.0	63.0
0–10 yrs	35.3	17.8	50.6	60.6
11+ yrs	44.1	24.0	54.3	68.2
DB and DC (600)	47.7	25.5	53.6	66.7
DB 0–10 yrs	41.8	23.1	55.3	66.1
11+ yrs	49.9	26.4	53.0	66.9
Employer reports a pension, by SR pension type (N = 1,343)				
DB-only	34.3	17.9	52.3	70.0
DC-only	40.4	22.4	55.5	57.9
DB and DC	39.3	21.6	55.0	72.6
SR/ER pension type agrees (N = 706)				
DB-only	26.6	12.8	48.2	72.2
0–10 yrs	16.4	7.6	46.4	65.6
11+ yrs	28.8	13.9	48.4	73.6
DC-only	42.9	24.3	56.8	52.2
DB and DC	52.6	29.9	56.9	68.2
DB 0–10 yrs	48.7	28.2	57.9	66.7
DB 11+ yrs	53.6	30.4	56.7	68.6
SR/ER pension type disagrees a little, by SR pension type (N = 505)				
DB-only	27.4	15.1	55.1	76.0
DC-only	39.3	19.9	50.7	75.4
DB and DC	46.0	25.2	54.7	63.4
SR/ER pension type disagrees a lot, by SR pension type (N = 143)				
DB-only	34.3	19.0	55.3	68.6
DC-only	35.6	19.8	55.5	76.7
2004 Full sample, by self-reported (SR) pension type (N = 1,109)				
DB-only (284)	37.3	22.1	59.2	60.6
0–10 yrs	29.9	22.0	73.8	59.7
11+ yrs	40.1	22.1	55.2	60.9
DC-only (443)	37.7	23.7	62.8	58.0
0–10 yrs	35.3	21.5	60.8	58.4
11+ yrs	42.0	27.7	66.0	57.3
DB and DC (382)	45.3	27.6	60.9	55.0
DB 0–10 yrs	43.9	26.1	59.4	52.0
11+ yrs	46.4	28.9	62.2	57.4

Notes: See Table 9-1. Definitions: SR—self-reported pension data. ER—employer-reported pension data. Disagree a little—person misreports DB-only or DC-only as DB and DC, or misreports DB and DC as DB-only or DC-only. Disagree a lot—person misreports DB-only as DC-only or vice versa.

Table 9-1. People who had both types of pensions were richer—with higher earnings, pension wealth, and net worth—than people with one type, and people with DC-only plans were richer than people with DB-only plans. It is crucial to ascertain that it was not higher wealth that drove greater stock market investment.

In addition, the highest degree of risk aversion is observed for those in DB-only plans and the lowest for those in DC-only plans—so this is partly, but not completely, correlated with the pattern in stock market investment, raising concerns that workers who were more tolerant of risk selected into riskier pensions. On the other hand, risk aversion was a little higher among those who have been in their DB pensions the longest. This supports the argument we made earlier that there may be endogenous mobility of the less risk averse out of DB and into DC plans—which would bias downwards the estimated effect of years in a DB plan. Still, the range of variation in risk aversion across pension types was only moderate, with 63–71 percent of each type reporting the highest degree of risk aversion.

Some additional features are noteworthy. The share of the 1992 sample in Table 9-1 who has a wife with a pension is generally similar, at 40–46 percent for each pension type, and it is highest for the DC-only group. This reduces concerns that about our choice to focus mostly on men's pensions. In addition, people in DC plans with choice invested substantially more in the stock market, as did people who had been in their DC plans for longer. These differences related to choice and to years-in-plan for those with DC plans are not sustained when we include other covariates in the estimation, though.

Finally, note that DC pension coverage rose considerably for the 2004 cohort, compared to the 1992 cohort. In 2004, 74 percent of our sample had a DC plan, compared to 58 percent in 1992. In parallel, DB coverage dropped to 51 percent in 2004, down from 73 percent in 1992. While stock market investment at the ages that we focus on did not change much between 1992 and 2004, the differential across pension types narrowed, with a substantial increase among those with only a DB plan and slight decline among those with DC plans. The similarity of conditional stock market investment across types of plans persists, as does the differential by years in a plan.

Taxes

Before proceeding to discuss estimation, we will briefly mention evidence about the potential impact of tax minimization on our analysis. As we noted earlier, nonpension portfolio allocations might differ for people with DB versus DC plans simply for tax-related reasons. On the other hand, results from Bergstresser and Poterba (2004) suggested that tax efficiency does not seem to play a major role in affecting DC versus non-DC allocations. We find corroborating evidence in the HRS by considering sample selection criteria that parallels that of Bergstresser and Poterba. Beginning with our sample of 1950 in 1992, we select households with nonpension financial wealth of at least $25,000, pension wealth of at least $25,000, and access to a DC plan that allows them to choose the allocation of their assets. The resulting sample of households who are likely to have much to gain from tax minimization consists of only eighty-three observations. Such a small number will have little effect on our overall analysis.

Estimation

The multivariate estimation models described next test whether pension type and years in a plan influence the riskiness of nonpension investments. First, we discuss our simple Probit and Tobit estimates for the main 1992 sample; next, we turn to estimates for additional 1992 and 2004 subsamples; and finally, we discuss robustness checks for the variables used in the basic specification. For Probits we report estimated marginal effects, showing the impact of a marginal change in a covariate on the likelihood of investing in the stock market; for the Tobits, we report estimated coefficients, showing the impact of a marginal change on the 'desired' percentage s_i^* of nonpension financial wealth invested in the stock market.

Main 1992 Sample

Table 9-3 shows estimation results for all covariates, for the main 1992 sample that uses self-reported pension data. The evidence indicates that 37 percent of the SR sample invested in the stock market, and the average of the unconditional share of nonpension financial wealth invested was 19 percent. The control variables in Table 9-3 generally have the expected signs in the Probit and Tobit specifications. Stock market investment rises with wealth and income. While the effect of employer-provided pension wealth was relatively small, the effect of net nonpension wealth was substantial—being in the top quartile of the wealth distribution significantly raises the likelihood of investing in the stock market by 50 percentage points, relative to the bottom quartile. Meanwhile, being in the top 5 percent of the labor income distribution significantly raises the likelihood by 35 percentage points. Being in the most risk-averse category (consisting of about two-thirds of the sample) significantly reduces the likelihood of investing in the stock market by 5.5 percentage points. Households with older men are less likely to invest in the stock market, with the probability falling by a little

TABLE 9-3 Estimation Results, Basic Specification

Independent Variables	Holds any Stock Outside Pension (Probit)		Share of Nonpension Financial Wealth Held in Stock (Tobit)	
	Marginal Effect	Standard Error	Coefficient	Standard Error
Pension type (omitted: DB-only)				
DC-only	0.1332**	0.0569	0.1507*	0.0825
DB & DC	0.1001***	0.0341	0.1328***	0.0497
DC plan offers choice	0.0040	0.0623	0.0451	0.0914
Years in pension plan				
DB	0.0039***	0.0015	0.0047**	0.0022
DC	0.0010	0.0021	0.0011	0.0031
DC plan offers choice	0.0005	0.0045	0.0001	0.0063
Employer pension wealth, second quartile	0.0710*	0.0376	0.1174**	0.0554
Third quartile	0.0827*	0.0402	0.1462**	0.0584
Top quartile	−0.0401	0.0433	−0.0290	0.0661
Net nonpension wealth, second quartile	0.2033***	0.0295	0.3175***	0.0456
Third quartile	0.3321***	0.0349	0.4747***	0.0531
Top quartile	0.5028***	0.0399	0.6362***	0.0727
Labor income, second quartile	0.0006	0.0288	0.0102	0.0436
Third quartile	0.0483	0.0399	0.1162**	0.0568
Top 75–95%	0.1405*	0.0756	0.2420**	0.0956
Top 95–100%	0.3523***	0.1114	0.3165**	0.1251
Other noncapital income, second quartile	−0.0295	0.0333	−0.0174	0.0500
Third quartile	0.0354	0.0373	0.0768	0.0542
Top 75–95%	0.1138**	0.0569	0.1904**	0.0756
Top 95–100%	0.2103**	0.0939	0.1755	0.1155
Occupation is unskilled	0.0154	0.0331	0.0115	0.0500
Skilled	0.0326	0.0328	0.0249	0.0489
Married	−0.1750	0.1462	−0.2950	0.2036
Age, husband	−0.0073**	0.0033	−0.0110**	0.0049
Age, wife	0.0034	0.0025	0.0058*	0.0037
Risk averse	−0.0547**	0.0257	−0.0326	0.0374
Education < high school	−0.0599*	0.0338	−0.0645	0.0546
Attended college	0.0545*	0.0305	0.0956**	0.0456
Black	−0.1354***	0.0349	−0.2124***	0.0638
Hispanic	−0.1314***	0.0456	−0.1533*	0.0853
Constant	—	—	−0.1306	0.2775
σ	—	—	0.6278	0.0192
Log-likelihood/N	−0.5432		−0.6628	

Source: Authors' calculations from the 1992 HRS.

Notes: Pension type and other information is self-reported (SR), 1992 data. The sample includes households in which a male works, is not self-employed, and reports having a pension, and which have positive net nonpension wealth and answer all questions about the information reported above. Sample size is 1950. See Table 9-1 notes and text for more information.

*$p < 0.05$; **$p < 0.01$; ***$p < 0.001$.

under a percentage point for each year of age. Households with older wives are more likely to invest, with a smaller effect in absolute value. Hispanics and blacks are significantly and substantially less likely to invest in the stock market.

Next, we turn to a discussion of key pension variables. People with DC plans (whether DC-only or DB and DC) are significantly more likely— 10–13 percentage points—to invest in the stock market, relative to having a DB-only plan. These effects become a little smaller if years-in-plan variables are excluded, in results that are not shown. Meanwhile, in the Tobit specification these variables lose a little significance but have a slightly greater effect on the desired share of wealth invested in stocks. The other main finding is that years in a DB plan (whether DB-only or DB and DC) also has a statistically significant and positive effect on stock market investment. Each year in a DB plan raises the likelihood of investing in stocks by 0.39 percentage points (standard error of 0.15), or 3.9 percentage points for each 10 years—this amounts to a little over 10 percent of the sample mean rate of stock market investment. In the Tobit specification, each year in a DB plan raises the desired share of wealth in the stock market by 0.48 percentage points.[17] By contrast, the effect of years in a DC plan (whether DC-only or DB and DC) is virtually 0; notably, if we control for years on a job, it does not affect the results. Finally, it is interesting that we do not observe any statistically significant or substantive effect on stock market investment of having investment choices in a DC plan. This occurs whether we assume a constant effect or allow it to vary by years in a plan with choice.

To sum up, we find that workers with DC pensions invested more in the stock market, but independently of how long they have been in their plans. This suggests the presence of either endogenous sorting or an immediate learning effect from DC plans—unfortunately, we are not able to distinguish which. Moreover, the effect of having a DC plan will be overstated, relative to having a DB plan, if people with a greater taste for investing in stocks are more likely to contribute and hence be classified in the first place as having a DC plan. Finally, we find that workers with DB pensions invested more in the stock market over time. As we argued earlier, the presence of endogenous mobility would lead us to underestimate the true effect of years in a DB plan.

Additional 1992 Subsamples

Table 9-4 shows the estimated marginal effects for the key pension variables for various subsamples of the 1992 data that distinguish between self- and employer-reported pension information; this distinction is not possible

TABLE 9-4 Additional Estimation Results

| | 1992 Data | | | |
| | Pension Type is Employer-Reported (ER) | | SR/ER Pension Type Agrees | |
	Probit	Tobit	Probit	Tobit
Pension type				
DC-only	0.0635 (0.0687)	0.1442 (0.1010)	0.2107* (0.1166)	0.3106* (0.1653)
DB and DC	0.1304* (0.0708)	0.1968* (0.1052)	0.3213*** (0.1161)	0.4970*** (0.1704)
DC plan offers choice	—	—	-0.0858 (0.0790)	0.0054 (0.1217)
Years in a pension plan				
DB-only	0.0048** (0.0022)	0.0072** (0.0033)	0.0083*** (0.0032)	0.0140*** (0.0049)
DC-only	0.0045 (0.0030)	0.0054 (0.0045)	0.0068 (0.0051)	0.0090 (0.0070)
DB and DC	0.0009 (0.0024)	0.0021 (0.0037)	0.0022 (0.0038)	0.0045 (0.0054)
N	1,382		706	
Log-likelihood/N	-0.5601	-0.6778	-0.5426	-0.6576
	SR/ER disagrees—Pension Type is SR		SR/ER disagrees—Pension Type is ER	
DC-only	0.2256** (0.1096)	0.3000** (0.1520)	-0.0129 (0.0995)	-0.0066 (0.1481)
DB and DC	0.0591 (0.0556)	0.0795 (0.0800)	0.0373 (0.0910)	0.0445 (0.1347)
DC plan offers choice	0.0768 (0.1474)	0.1185 (0.1941)	—	—
Years in pension plan (see notes)				
DB	0.0048** (0.0024)	0.0060* (0.0035)	0.0045 (0.0032)	0.0049 (0.0045)
DC	-0.0005 (0.0039)	-0.0013 (0.0055)	0.0043 (0.0041)	0.0050 (0.0061)
DB and DC	—	—	-0.0016 (0.0034)	-0.0022 (0.0051)
N	648		676	
Log-likelihood/N	-0.5409	-0.6598	-0.5448	-0.6638

2004 Data

	Pension Type is Self-Reported (SR)	
	Probit Marginal Effects (Standard Errors)	Tobit Coefficients (Standard Errors)
Pension type		
DC-only	0.0193 (0.0664)	0.0428 (0.1024)
DB and DC	0.1125** (0.0486)	0.1544** (0.0741)
DC plan offers choice	0.0068 (0.0716)	0.0024 (0.1099)
Years in a pension plan		
DB	0.0008 (0.0022)	0.0005 (0.0034)
DC	−0.0049* (0.0027)	−0.0043 (0.0042)
DC plan offers choice	0.0067 (0.0047)	0.0081 (0.0071)
N	1,019	1,019
Log-likelihood/N	−0.5516	−0.7162

Notes: Estimation of same specification for subsamples of full sample reported in Table 9-3; see Table 9-3 notes for details. SR—self-reported pension data, ER—employer-reported pension data. SR/ER agrees—sample for which the SR and ER pension type agrees. SR/ER disagrees—sample for which the SR and ER pension type disagrees. When SR and ER pension type disagrees and we use ER data on pension type, we interact ER pension type with maximum years in a plan that individual reports. Selected samples, subset of covariates reported. See also Table 9-3.

using 2004 data. We include the years-in-plan variables, although these effects are more difficult to interpret when we use ER data. Employers do not report years in a plan, so we have interacted the ER plan type with the maximum years in a plan reported by the individual.

The 1992 ER sample, which has pension data provided by employers, consists of about two-thirds of the full SR sample. The effects of pensions, shown in the top panel of Table 9-4 on the left, are similar in magnitude and significance to the SR results discussed above. Having a DC pension raises the likelihood of stock market investment by 6–14 percentage points, and each year in a DB plan significantly raises the likelihood by 0.48 percentage points, a bigger effect than before.

Notably, the effects of pensions are much stronger in the 1992 subsample in which the same pension type is reported by the worker and employer. In this 'agree' subsample, shown in the top panel of Table 9-4 on the right, the effect of having a DC plan is particularly large. People in DC-only plans are 21.1 percentage points (standard error of 11.7) more likely to invest in the stock market than people in DB-only plans, while people in DB and DC plans are 32.1 percentage points (11.6) more likely. The effect of years in a DB plan (again, DB-only or DB and DC) is also larger, with each year raising the likelihood by 0.83 (0.32) percentage points. The length of time in a DC plan is positive and not that much smaller but insignificant, at 0.68 (0.51) percentage points, and this is considerably larger than for the full SR sample.

The estimated effects of pensions may be greater in the 'agree' group for two reasons. People who know their pension type reveal themselves to be more financially savvy and, perhaps, more responsive to pension incentives. However, they may also be more interested in the stock market. Thus, the very large estimated effects of pension type raise extra concern about endogenous selection.

Interestingly, people who are misinformed about their pension type respond to their self-reported pension information sometimes significantly, but less strongly, in results shown in the middle panel of Table 9-4 on the left. In contrast, the estimated effects for the same confused sample when we instead use ER information, in the middle panel on the right, are always statistically insignificant and small.

2004 Sample

The bottom panel of Table 9-4 shows the estimated marginal effects using self-reported pension data for the WB and EBB cohorts in 2004. The estimation results are similar in a key respect to the 1992 results but are different in other interesting ways. The differential between the estimated effects of tenure in DB versus DC plans remains similar—in both samples, stock market participation is significantly higher as years in a DB plan rise, relative to years in a DC plan. Once again, this suggests that DB plans grow relatively less risky, compared to DC plans, as workers approach retirement and thus gain DB pension wealth accruals.

In addition, the absolute magnitudes of the year-in-plan estimates for 2004 have changed in important, revealing ways. Both estimated years-in-plan effects are substantially smaller than they were in 1992, now indicating a 0.08 percentage point increase (standard error of 2.2) in the likelihood of investing in the stock market for each year in a DB plan and a 0.49 (2.7) percentage point decrease for each year in a DC plan.

The substantial reductions in these estimated effects suggest there was a jump in the risk that people perceive as accumulating over time in both types of pensions. This is not surprising given recent developments. Reports of employers underfunding, freezing, or terminating DB plans have grown common in the last few years, and many plans in some key sectors of the economy have been turned over to the Pension Benefit Guaranty Corporation (PBGC). The PBGC pays off obligations based only on years of service accumulated to date, so many workers lose out on substantial future accruals that they expect; also the maximum payout is capped so that highly compensated employees are only partially insured. Meanwhile, DC plan holders today have had considerable recent experience with stock market volatility. The last finding of note is that people in DC plans with choice invest increasingly in the stock market over time, though the estimated effect falls a little short of statistical significance. This gives stronger support than the 1992 data did to the idea that DC plans may help reduce barriers to stock market participation.

Understanding DB Pension Risks

We complete the analysis by quantifying the risks associated with early exit from DB pensions. The expected loss from early exit depends on two factors—how much pension wealth is at risk (which we compute in the 1992 HRS), and the incidence of unexpected job loss. The latter is difficult to quantify, since we do not observe individual expectations. Instead, we simply used information about reasons for leaving one's job for the original HRS cohort observed in subsequent years. Table 9-5 shows some illustrative results. For people in a DB pension at the outset of the HRS, it shows DB pension wealth at risk by age in 1992 and subsequent reasons for job exits by age. The median pension wealth at risk is very substantial for workers in their early 50s and declines sharply with age. The median loss in pension wealth if someone leaves his job at age 51 is 61.4 percent of total pension

TABLE 9-5 Pension Wealth at Risk in Defined Benefit Plans, 1992 HRS

Age	% of Job Exits Due to		Loss in Pension Wealth if Job Ends Now		Actual Loss Due to Involuntary Dismissals
	Involuntary Dismissal	Poor Health	Median ($)	% of Total Pension Wealth	Median ($)
51	2.1	1.3	57,163	61.4	65,594
52	0.8	1.5	54,590	56.8	41,172
53	1.4	2.0	46,312	52.6	36,214
54	0.8	0.6	40,949	47.3	55,910
55	1.0	1.0	31,783	39.4	53,670
56	1.4	1.0	27,616	34.6	11,546
57	0.9	0.7	23,398	29.4	63,820
58	1.7	1.6	19,496	23.0	15,592
59	0.6	1.4	14,705	10.9	14,898
60	1.7	1.5	9,366	11.7	10,071
61	1.4	1.4	7,914	9.1	5,354
62	1.0	2.0	5,854	6.9	3,616
63	1.0	1.0	5,175	6.3	3,413
64	2.0	1.0	4,024	5.4	2,126
65	1.9	1.9	1,829	2.8	2,075
66	0.0	0.8	3,585	4.4	0

Source: Authors' calculations from the HRS, 1992–2002.

Notes: Sample: all men in jobs with a defined benefit pension in 1992. Sample size is 1,852. Definitions: pension wealth equals the real present value of an employee's expected future pension benefits, if the employee leaves the job at the age shown on the horizontal axis. Involuntary dismissals are those in which the individual said that he or she quit, had been laid off, or would have been laid off had he not quit.

wealth ($57,163). The median falls to $31,783 at age 55 and $9,336 at age 60.[18] On the other hand, the rate of involuntary job loss is low, at around 1–2 percent per year among people who started the year in the job, and does not show a clear age-related pattern.[19] Another 1–2 percent per year left their job at each age because of poor health or disability, which might also be considered by voluntary. While the rate of involuntary job loss might be low, the consequences are severe, as shown in the final column. The median pension loss suffered due to involuntary exits is $65,594 at age 51, and it declines rapidly, falling to $10,071 at age 60.

Conclusions and Discussion

The shift from DB to DC plans over the last two decades has led to important changes in risks borne by workers in their pensions. Employers make investment choices and bear capital market risks associated with those choices in DB plans, while workers bear capital market risks in DC plans. Of course, many DB pensions also carry the risk of a substantial loss in pension wealth resulting from an unexpectedly early exit from one's job or from termination and bankruptcy. When we consider the impact of these changes in pension structure on the risks workers are willing to absorb in their investment choices outside of their pensions, the main results show significant and substantial differences in stock market investment among workers, depending on their pension characteristics. The longer workers are in their DB plans, the riskier the investments they make outside of their pensions. In comparison, workers with DC plans invest more in the stock market overall—yet this effect is independent of how long they have been in their plans.[20] This pattern suggests that workers with a greater preference for risk (who would invest more in the stock market anyway) sort themselves into jobs with DC pensions. Importantly, this type of sorting would bias against estimating a positive effect on stock market investment of years in a DB plan, since if anything workers staying longer in jobs with DB plans should be more risk averse, according to the sorting hypothesis.

In the more recent data, we find a similar differential in the estimated effects of tenure in DB versus DC plans, so once again it appears that DB plans grow relatively less risky, compared to DC plans, as workers approach retirement and thus gain DB pension wealth accruals. In addition, the absolute magnitudes of the year-in-plan estimates in 2004 have shrunk, suggesting that there was a jump in the risk that people perceive as accumulating over time in both types of pensions.

This research illustrates another of the myriad consequences of the shift in pension structure, which may also alter patterns of job mobility at young and older ages and consumption after retirement. We identify some effects of the shift in investment risk from employers to workers, as well as recent changes in those risks. Moreover, our conclusions shed light on important policy concerns. Some reform proposals would replace at least a portion of traditional Social Security benefits, which have characteristics of DB plans, with personal accounts, which have characteristics of DC plans, thereby shifting investment risk onto workers. Our results indicate that individuals might respond to the jump in risk by reallocating their nonpension portfolios, reducing the boost in retirement wealth which is expected from personal account.

Acknowledgments

The authors thank Irena Dushi, Brigitte Madrian, Olivia S. Mitchell, and James Poterba for helpful comments.

Notes

[1] Statistics on both pension and stock market trends are computed from the SCF. Also using the SCF, Poterba (2001) reported that the share of the adult population owning stock outside of employer-provided pensions in taxable accounts rose from 31.8 to 48.5 percent between 1989 and 1998, and the share owning stock in Individual Retirement Accounts rose from 10.3 to 20.9 percent.

[2] The pension plans in Figure 9-1 were slightly altered to protect confidentiality (see Friedberg and Webb 2005).

[3] Cash balance plans are hybrids. Workers accrue a notional contribution and rate of return which may be fixed or tied to economic indicators or company performance, in which case they share the investment risk. Funds are portable after vesting, but the account does not actually exist, and employers follow DB funding rules and bear some or all of the investment risk. They were not common during the 1992 HRS (US General Accounting Office 2000).

[4] Pensions involve other risks as well, but they are less important for our analysis. Both DB and DC plans generally compound risk which workers face in their future earnings. DB pension wealth generally depends on one's last or highest years of earnings, while the whole path of earnings may determine DC contributions. This source of risk in both types of plans also diminishes over time as the uncertain path of earnings is realized, while in DC pensions it is converted into investment risk. The risk of uncertain life spans is usually borne by employers in DB plans since most DB benefits are annuitized, and by workers in DC plans since most DC benefits are not (Brown et al. 1999). We can control for this risk in our estimation and simulations because the HRS reports data on subjective life expectancy. Finally, workers face a risk that their employer's DB pension fund may become insolvent, but their benefits are partially insured by the PBGC. The PBGC guarantees the pension earned at the time of insolvency up to a maximum amount, so it does not shield workers from the early departure risk that we already discussed. The guaranteed amount depends on age and survivorship; for a pension with no survivor benefit payable at age 65, the monthly limit in 2005 was $3,801.

[5] Another explanation is that the stock market boom of the late 1990s altered perceptions, rightly or wrongly, about the riskiness of the stock market, relative to expected returns. Since our estimation uses data from 1992, concerns about a bubble driving up participation are absent.

[6] Income earned on assets in DC plans is taxed on withdrawal rather than when it is earned. This deferral reduces the effective tax rate and also gives some leeway to time withdrawals to coincide with years when the marginal tax rate is low.

[7] Taxing capital gains only on realization reduces the effective tax rate on long-held equity. In addition to that, long-term gains (usually defined as a year or more) have been further favored since 1991. The maximum marginal tax rates in 1992 were 31 percent on other income and 28 percent on capital gains, so the differential was small; maximum rates in 2004 were 35 and 15 percent, with the latter applying to dividend income as well.

[8] We do not extend our focus here to real responses, because DB and DC pensions differ in other important ways that directly affect saving and retirement behavior and may only affect portfolio allocations indirectly, while the differences

in risk should affect portfolio allocations directly and other real behavior only indirectly.

[9] For example, Rohwedder et al. (2004) argued that asset levels in many categories were substantially understated when the initial AHEAD cohort of the HRS was surveyed in 1993, leading to overestimates of saving in subsequent years.

[10] Many of the econometric issues we confront are noted in Miniaci and Weber (2002) and Poterba and Samwick (2003).

[11] Alternately, we could study the allocation of the entire portfolio including pensions. This would be more difficult because the HRS reports only whether DC plans are invested 'mostly in stock, mostly in bonds, or both'.

[12] Except in the case of variables related to number of years in a pension plan and to total pension wealth, we use data from the RAND HRS data files in the interests of comparability with other studies. We obtained very similar estimates for our 1992 sample when using either source of data, obtained from the HRS directly or from RAND.

[13] Some respondents refused to give permission, and some employers failed to reply. We do not know whether workers who report not having a pension (and whom we omit from our data) actually have one, since employers were not contacted in that case. Gustman and Steinmeier (1999) estimated that the likelihood that the HRS obtained employer data rose significantly with education, firm size, self-reported pension wealth, and working in a nonmanufacturing firm, and fell with wealth and earnings. However, the overall explanatory power of these variables was low, so we treat the availability of employer data as exogenous.

[14] Data on pension wealth computed from both self-reported and ER data has been provided by researchers through the HRS/AHEAD website (Anonymous 1998; Peticolas and Steinmeier 1999).

[15] They may have difficulty separating preferences for risk and for other characteristics of their current job in answering the question. The SCF question that Poterba and Samwick (2003) and Weisbenner (2002) used asked whether respondents were willing to take more or less risk to get a greater or smaller expected return.

[16] Among those with a pension, the most common missing data was pension type, other information needed to determine pension wealth, and risk preferences.

[17] As an alternative to assuming a normal distribution and estimating a Tobit, we tried censored quantile regression (CQR; Guiso et al. 1996). Unlike censored least absolute deviations (Powell 1984), CQR is possible when the median itself is censored, as it is in this case. Stata code to estimate CQR was written by Moreira for Chay and Powell (2001). However, the estimation did not converge, suggesting that the model does not explain portfolio allocations in the upper quantiles very well.

[18] The level of pension wealth at any age is sensitive to the assumed interest rate, and we assume a 1.9 percent real rate. The pattern of decline through the 50s is not sensitive to this assumption.

[19] We classify a quit as involuntary if someone said that he or she quit, had been laid off, or would have been laid off had he not quit. Other possible reasons for job exit include family care, better job, or retired.

[20] For a related study in the Swedish context, see Karlsson et al. (this volume).

References

Ameriks, J. and Zeldes, S. (2004). 'How Do Household Portfolio Shares Vary With Age?', Columbia University Working Paper.

Anonymous (1998). 'Researcher Contribution: 1992 HRS Self-Reported Pension Wealth (v.1.0)', Available at https://ssl.isr.umich.edu/hrs/files.php?versid=21

Benítez-Silva, H. (2004). 'Labor Supply Flexibility and Portfolio Choice: An Empirical Analysis', SUNY-Stony Brook Working Paper.

Bergstresser, D. and Poterba, J. (2004). 'Asset Allocation and Asset Location: Household Evidence from the Survey of Consumer Finances', *Journal of Public Economics*, 88(9–10 August): 1893–915.

Bernheim, B. D. and Garrett, D. (2003). 'The Effects of Financial Education in the Workplace: Evidence from a Survey of Households', *Journal of Public Economics*, 87: 1487–519.

Bertaut, C. and Starr-McCluer, M. (2000). 'Household Portfolios in the United States', Federal Reserve Board of Governors Working Paper, Finance and Economics Discussion Series No. 2000-27.

Brown, J., Mitchell, O., Poterba, J., and Warshawsky, M. (1999). 'Taxing Retirement Income: Nonqualified Annuities and Distributions from Qualified Accounts', *The National Tax Journal*, 52: 563–91.

Chan, S. and Stevens, A. H. (2004). 'What You Don't Know Can't Help You: Pension Knowledge and Retirement Decision-Making', Working Paper, University of California, Davis.

Chan, Y. L. and Viceira, L. (2000). 'Asset Allocation with Endogenous Labor Income: The Case of Incomplete Markets', Harvard University Working Paper.

Chay, K. and Powell, J. (2001). 'Semiparametric Censored Regression Models', *Journal of Economic Perspectives*, 15: 29–42.

Coile, C. and Levine, P. (2004). 'Bulls, Bears, and Retirement Behavior', National Bureau of Economic Research Working Paper No. 10779.

Coronado, J. and Perozek, M. (2003). 'Wealth Effects and the Consumption of Leisure: Retirement Decisions during the Stock Market Boom of the 1990s', Federal Reserve Board of Governors Working Paper, Finance and Economic Discussion Series 2003–20.

Duflo, E. and Saez, E. (2003). 'The Role of Information and Social Interactions in Retirement Plan Decisions: Evidence from a Randomized Experiment', *The Quarterly Journal of Economics*, 118: 815–42.

Flavin, M. and Yamashita, T. (2002). 'Owner-Occupied Housing and the Composition of the Household Portfolio', *American Economic Review*, 92: 345–62.

Friedberg, L. and Webb, A. (2005). 'Retirement and the Evolution of Pension Structure', *Journal of Human Resources*, 40: 281–308.

—— —— (2006). 'Determinants and Consequences of Bargaining Power in Households', University of Virginia Working Paper.

Goldman, D. and Maestas, N. (2005). 'Medical Expenditure Risk and Household Portfolio Choice', National Bureau of Economic Research Working Paper No. 11818.

Guiso, L., Jappelli, T. and Terlizzese, D. (1996). 'Income Risk, Borrowing Constraints, and Portfolio Choice', *American Economic Review*, 86: 158–72.

Gustman, A. and Steinmeier, T. (1999). 'What People Don't Know about Their Pensions and Social Security: An Analysis Using Linked Data from the Health and Retirement Study', National Bureau of Economic Research Working Paper No. 7368.

—— —— (2002). 'Retirement and the Stock Market Bubble', National Bureau of Economic Research Working Paper No. 9404.

Hurd, M. and Reti M. (2001). 'The Effects of Large Capital Gains on Work and Consumption: Evidence from Four Waves of the HRS', RAND Corporation Labor and Population Program Working Paper No. 03-14.

Karlsson, A., Massa, M., and Simonov, A. (this volume). 'Pension Portfolio Choice and Menu Exposure'.

Kimball, M. (1991). 'Standard Risk Aversion', *Econometrica*, 61: 589–611.

King, M. and Leape, J. (1987). 'Asset Accumulation, Information, and the Life Cycle', National Bureau of Economic Research Working Paper No. 2392.

Koo, H. K. (1998). 'Consumption and Portfolio Selection with Labor Income: A Continuous-Time Approach', *Mathematical Finance*, 8: 49–65.

—— (1999). 'Consumption and Portfolio Selection with Labor Income: A Discrete-Time Approach', *Mathematical Methods of Operations Research*, 50: 219–43.

Miniaci, R. and Weber, G. (2002). 'Econometric Issues in the Estimation of Household Portfolio Models', in L. Guiso, M. Haliassos, and T. Jappelli (eds.), *Household Portfolios*. Cambridge, MA.: MIT Press: pp. 143–78.

Peticolas, B. and Steinmeier, T. (1999). 'Researcher Contribution: 1992 HRS Pension (Level 1) Present Value Database (v.1.0)'. HRS Working Paper, University of Michigan.

Poterba, J. (2001). 'The Rise of the 'Equity Culture': U.S. Stockownership Patterns, 1989–98', Working Paper, Massachusetts Institute of Technology.

—— and Samwick, A. (2003). 'Taxation and Household Portfolio Composition: US Evidence from the 1980s and 1990s', *Journal of Public Economics*, 87: 5–38.

—— Rauh, J., Venti, S., and Wise, D. (2005). 'Utility Evaluation of Risk in Retirement Saving Accounts', in D. Wise (ed.), *Analyses in the Economics of Aging*. Chicago, IL: The University of Chicago Press, pp. 3–52.

Powell, J. (1984). 'Least Absolute Deviations Estimation for the Censored Regression Model', *Journal of Econometrics*, 25: 303–25.

President's Commission to Strengthen Social Security (2001). *Strengthening Social Security and Creating Private Wealth for All Americans: Report of the President's Commission.* Washington, DC: http://csss.gov/reports/Final_report.pdf

Rohwedder, S., Haider, S., and Hurd, M. (2004). 'Increases in Wealth among the Elderly in the Early 1990s: How Much Is Due to Survey Design?', National Bureau of Economic Research Working Paper No. 10862.

Sevak, P. (2005). 'Wealth Shocks and Retirement Timing: Evidence from the Nineties', Hunter College.

Souleles, N. (1999). 'Household Securities Purchases, Transactions Costs, and Hedging Motives'. Rodney L. White Center for Financial Research Working Paper No. 024-99, University of Pennsylvania, The Wharton School.

Uccello, C. (2000). '401(k) Investment Decisions and Social Security Reform', Center for Retirement Research at Boston College Working Paper No. 2000–04.

US General Accounting Office (2000). 'Cash Balance Plans: Implications for Retirement Income', GAO/HEHS-00-207 (Washington, DC: US General Accounting Office).

Viceira, L. (2001). 'Optimal Portfolio Choice for Long-Horizon Investors with Non-Tradable Labor Income', *Journal of Finance*, 56: 433–70.

Vissing-Jørgenson, A. (2002). 'Towards an Explanation of Household Portfolio Choice Heterogeneity: Nonfinancial Income and Participation Cost Structures', Northwestern University Working Paper.

Weisbenner, S. (2002). 'Do Pension Plans with Participant Investment Choice Teach Households to Hold More Equity', *Journal of Pension Economics and Finance*, 1: 223–48.

Chapter 10

Measuring Pension Wealth

Chris Cunningham, Gary V. Engelhardt, and Anil Kumar

Pension wealth plays a critical role in older individuals' retirement behavior and financial security. Accordingly, the magnitude and distribution of pension wealth is important in the ongoing debate about whether households, especially Baby Boomers, have saved adequately for retirement.[1] For this reason, researchers and policymakers need accurate measures of pension wealth if they are to assess the impact of pensions, prompting substantial effort devoted to gathering information on pension characteristics and wealth from households nearing retirement.[2] Unfortunately, there is growing awareness of the fact that many respondents are unaware of and unable to articulate many key attributes of their pension plans.[3] This has led to concern that respondent-reported pension information may give an inaccurate picture of older persons' financial security, and it may also impart bias to empirical studies of the role of pensions on retirement.[4] For this reason, researchers and policymakers need accurate measures of pension wealth if they are to assess the impact of pensions, prompting substantial effort devoted to gathering information on pension characteristics and wealth from households nearing retirement.[5]

To supplement respondent-reported pension information, some analysts have turned to pension plan reports and administrative data, seeking to generate more accurate measures of pension wealth. For example, the Health and Retirement Study (HRS) linked lifetime earnings records from the Social Security Administration (SSA) and pension plan rules collected from employer-provided pension Summary Plan Descriptions (SPDs) for many respondents. These can then be used in concert with the Pension Estimation Program (PEP), a computer software program which calculates pension entitlements at alternative retirement dates. This approach is gaining favor for measuring retirement wealth for policy analysis.

Our research, summarized in this chapter, describes a long-term effort to develop an improved methodology for measuring defined contribution (DC) pension wealth of older Americans. Specifically, we have devised a new pension benefit calculator that can be used with the HRS, which we call the HRS DC/401(k) Calculator. This new software extends researchers' ability to model DC plans, building in detailed plan characteristics and time-varying rates of return, annual earnings, and pre-tax deferrals. We are able to show that prior estimates of pension wealth have probably overstated DC plan wealth by as much as 20 percent, and 401(k) plan balances by as much as 40 percent. The findings imply that accurate measurement of pension wealth hinges on a set of complex assumptions, and even small changes in assumptions can generate large differences in pension wealth and substantively change policy prescriptions. We also believe that administrative pension data is invaluable in supplementing respondent-reported information from household surveys. Accordingly, those engaged in or starting surveys of older households should devote substantial effort to incorporate such data into their research designs.

In what follows, we begin with a brief description of pension information found in the Health and Retirement Study, which is the basis for most research on Baby Boomers and their retirement preparedness. Next, we present new estimates of DC pension wealth for the first 'original' HRS cohort interviewed in 1992, based on the employer-provided plan descriptions and administrative data, and we compare our results with those generated from previous methodology. Then we extend the analysis for the cohort of so-called War Babies (WBs), first interviewed by the HRS in 1998. Finally, we offer a summary and implications for research.

Methodology for Generating Pension Wealth for DC Pension Participants

Several sources of data have been gathered that are useful in producing estimates of pension wealth for DC plan participants. Here we discuss various approaches to combining these.

Respondent Reports

In surveys designed to elicit retirement wealth including the HRS, respondents and spouses are routinely asked to describe their pensions on their current and past jobs. Specifically, in the HRS, respondents are asked first if they are included in a pension, retirement, or tax-deferred savings plan. If the individual answers 'yes', then he is asked additional detailed questions about as many as three plans on that job. This respondent-reported information includes the type of plan (e.g. formula-based (DB), account-based (DC), or combination). In addition, questions are asked about the number of years the worker has been included in the plan, the amount of the employer contribution, the amount of the employee contribution, and the plan balance. If the individual has more than three plans on the current job, then the sum of the balances on the fourth and higher plans is requested. Those with a DC plan are asked to identify the type: thrift or savings, 401(k)/403(b)/SRA, profit-sharing, stock purchase/employee stock ownership (ESOP), and other. Answers to these pension questions have been used to calculate respondent-reported pension assets including 401(k) assets.

The primary advantage of respondent-reported DC wealth is that it can be thought of as reflecting what a household believes its pension plan balance to be at the time of the survey. Yet substantial measurement error can plague these data. One reason is that respondents may report their pension plan type incorrectly; for instance, a worker who really has a DB may report having a DC plan (or vice versa); a respondent with a non-401(k) DC plan could report having a 401(k); someone with a DB and a 401(k) plan could report just one plan, and so on. Another problem is that even if individuals correctly identify their plan type, they may report plan values inaccurately. This may be particularly true for DB participants, as these plans embody complicated formulas based on salary, age, years of service, early and normal retirement dates, about which the respondent may not be aware; even small errors in reporting early and normal retirement ages for such plans can dramatically alter the implied accrual profiles and present value calculations. In addition, measurement error in reported plan type is almost surely correlated with error in reported plan value. Finally, research on HRS respondents' plan reports indicates that there are many missing values which must be imputed by the researcher in order to arrive at pension wealth numbers. Thus Venti and Wise (2000) report that records for almost 40 percent of HRS households require that at least one piece of pension information be imputed to construct measures of self-reported pension wealth. Such imputations can result in additional measurement error.[6]

Employer-Based Plan Information

To complement this respondent-reported pension information, the HRS also attempted to collect pension SPDs from employers of HRS respondents for all current and previous jobs in which the respondent reported being covered by a pension. Researchers at the University of Michigan then coded these SPDs and linked them to a software program called the PEP. Taking this as inputs, estimates of DC pension wealth can be generated along with assumptions about earnings and saving trajectories, rates of return and inflation. Nevertheless, the PEP makes some simplifying assumptions in its modeling strategy for calculating DC wealth, including the assumption of a single time-invariant rate of return common to all participants, a time-invariant inflation rate, a time-invariant voluntary contribution rate to 401(k)-type plans, a simple earnings forecasting equation for career earnings, and the presumption of plan eligibility since the date of hire (cf. Rohwedder 2003; Engelhardt et al. 2005).

By contrast, our pension Calculator software includes a more flexible set of economic assumptions for estimating DC wealth. We also include an additional source of data, namely lifetime earnings histories provided under restricted data conditions by the SSA.[7] The great advantage of these records is that they provide an accurate source of earnings from 1980 and also reports of pre-tax employee contributions to pension plans since 1984. Unlike respondent-reported information, these reports are not subjected to measurement error as they represent employer official reports on earnings and deferrals (Cunningham and Engelhardt 2002). This information, combined with respondent-reported earnings, permits us to construct a complete earnings history from 1951 to the survey entry year, for those who entered the HRS in 1992 and 1998. We believe that the improved earnings data, combined with the enhanced pension wealth Calculator, generate substantially better calculations of DC pension wealth.

The Calculator is designed so that it can replicate the PEP, but it also incorporates several important innovations not found in the earlier program. Specifically, it (*a*) invokes plan adoption and amendment dates indicated in the SPD to determine eligibility for plan features, (*b*) allows time-varying, individual-specific rates of return, (*c*) allows time-varying inflation rates, (*d*) allows time-varying, individual-specific voluntary contribution rates, and (*e*) allows easier, more direct use of administrative earnings data. It does not attempt to estimate DB wealth, which is handled quite well by the PEP.[8]

Pension Wealth Computations: Replicating the Baseline

To show how the Calculator works, we first seek to replicate the results generated by the PEP; subsequently, we will demonstrate how changing assumptions and data alter results. Accordingly, we first compare the total DC plan balances evaluated at the time of job severance, known as the quit date, generated by both approaches.[9]

For replication purposes, each plan can be characterized as belonging to one of three types. First, for the majority of plans, the Calculator and PEP produce identical output. Second, there is a small group of plans for which the Calculator and Program fail to produce the same output, because of identifiable programming anomalies in the PEP.[10] The Calculator contains two sets of code for these plans: the first is the correct code and the second overrides the correct code and hard-codes the plans to match the Program's coding.[11] Finally, there is a very small set of plans, covering around 5 percent of the DC plan participants in 1992, for which the Calculator and Program fail to produce the same output because of unidentifiable programming anomalies.[12] As a result, when comparing output from the Calculator and the PEP, there may be a small number of participants and plans for which there is potentially large disagreement.

Table 10-1 summarizes some key outcomes across the two programs. Here, we report the DC plan balance at the quit date for some 2,352 respondents in the HRS Participant Data.[13] The Calculator is parameterized to replicate the PEP, and we assume a time-invariant real rate of return of 2.3 percent, inflation of 4 percent, self-reported earnings from the HRS interview and wage equation parameters from the default Participant file, and time-invariant voluntary contributions equal to what respondents self-report in the initial interview (the default in the Participant file). We also assume that participants were eligible for both employer and employee contributions to the plan since their hire date.[14]

The first row of the table reflects the absolute value of the percentage difference between the plan balances computed under the Calculator and the PEP; the mean difference is 5.7 percent. Of course, the mean includes outliers, as is evident from the 75th percentile of the distribution; the fact that this is 0 indicates that at least 75 percent of the participants have exact matches. At the 90th percentile, the percentage difference between the two programs is just under 4 percent. Therefore, the disagreement between the two programs is less than 4 percent for 90 percent of the participants. What drives the mean difference of 5.7 percent is a relatively small number of plans and participants for which the programs do not agree which show up in the 95th and higher percentiles (these are the programming anomalies mentioned above). We note that differences of around 15 percent, as seen for the 95th percentile, are not that surprising given that even tiny differences are compounded over time in DC plans. In contrast, the observed difference of 116 percent at the 99th percentile is almost surely more systemic in nature.

Table 10-2 shows the Calculator's results for separate runs that illustrate the impact of the hard-coding of plans to match the PEP. Specifically, the first row in panel A shows selected statistics on plan balances at quit date, when the Calculator invokes hard-coding to match the Program. In the second row, we show the same statistics when plans are coded in a manner more consistent with others. In general, hard-coding results in lower plan balances as of the quit date: the mean difference of 6.6 percent (or $14,392) and the median is 5.4 percent (or $1,648). In other words, the differences are larger at higher percentiles in the distribution, so that at the 95th percentile, the balances differ by 9.5 percent.

TABLE 10-1 Comparing DC Plan Balances at Quit Date for HRS Participants: Results for the Calculator and the Program ($2004; N = 2,352)

Measure	Mean	Standard Deviation	10th Percentile	25th Percentile	Median	75th Percentile	90th Percentile	95th Percentile	99th Percentile
Percentage difference between *Calculator's* and *Program's* plan balance	5.70	59.81	0	0	0	0	3.96	15.80	116.90
Calculator's plan balance ($)	206,978	450,608	0	0	30,413	218,626	598,620	967,365	2,006,049
Program's plan balance ($)	215,023	506,684	0	0	29,237	220,310	607,167	990,897	2,228,760

Source: Authors' calculations.

Notes: *N* refers to sample size. Here the *Calculator* is parameterized to replicate PEP outcomes; see text.

TABLE 10-2 Comparing DC Plan Balances for HRS Participants at Quit Date and the Expected Present Value of DC Wealth in 1992: Plans 'Hard-Coded' to Replicate the Pension Estimation Program ($2004; N = 2,383)

Parameterization	Mean	Standard Deviation	10th Percentile	25th Percentile	Median	75th Percentile	90th Percentile	95th Percentile	99th Percentile
A. DC plan balance at quit date									
Invoke hard-coding to replicate the *Program*	204,579	448,198	0	0	29,152	214,647	593,923	947,834	2,006,049
Do not invoke hard-coding	218,971	514,750	0	0	30,800	224,901	629,199	997,485	2,112,629
B. Expected PV of DC wealth in 1992									
Invoke hard-coding to replicate the *Program*	64,178	131,978	0	0	15,927	75,416	182,693	270,578	575,831
Do not invoke hard-coding	69,562	155,670	0	0	16,883	80,154	190,700	286,630	673,056

Source: Authors' calculations.

Notes: For this comparison, the Calculator was parameterized as follows: the default participant file was used; years of pension eligibility for both voluntary and employer contributions were measured since the date of hire; the voluntary contribution rate was taken from the default participant file; the real rate of return was set equal to 2.3%; the inflation rate was set to 4%; and annual earnings were calculated using the self-reported earnings in the participant file and the earnings equation from the PEP.

One difficulty with the analysis of plan balances at the retirement date is that individuals in the analysis sample are of different ages and have different retirement dates. This means that the balances in Panel A are not measured in the same calendar year's dollars. Panel B of the table addresses this and shows the same statistics, but for the expected present value of DC wealth in 1992, which takes into account the probability of survival to the retirement date. At the mean, DC pension wealth is 8.4 percent higher when hard-coding is not invoked. At the median, this difference is 6 percent, and it remains at this level even up to the 95th percentile.

Sensitivity of Pension Wealth Computations to Economic Assumptions

The Calculator is designed to allow the researcher to explore the impact of moving away from default economic and plan assumptions, should the researcher seek this flexibility. In what follows, we briefly outline how varying these influences estimates of DC wealth (see also Rohwedder 2003; Engelhardt et al. 2005).

Time-Varying Rates of Return

When calculating DC wealth with the PEP, the researcher chooses the rate of return to use, but the Program assumes for the pension calculations that the real rate of return is common across individuals and time-invariant. For example, in a commonly used parameterization for 1992, the real rate of return is assumed to be 2.3 percent, which was the SSA's intermediate forecast in that year. This means that the PEP assumes that real returns are always 2.3 percent, commonly experienced by all participants. The potential impact of this assumption depends on the application.

In fact, of course, real rates of return have varied substantially over time (see Appendix, Table 10A-1). For the 20 years prior to the 1992 HRS, the mean 1972–91 real return for the portfolio of bonds was 2.6 percent with substantial variation ranging from −16.8 percent in 1979 to 31.6 percent in 1982. In principle, for any given across-period mean return, the DC balance at the end of that period will be path-dependent; that is, the temporal pattern of deviations from that mean return matters for DC balances because of the role of compounding. In addition, because contributions to DC plans are defined frequently as a percentage of pay, the temporal pattern of real returns will interact with the shape of the age-earnings profile to generate differences in plan balances that would not be captured under the assumption of a time-invariant mean rate of return.

It is also worth noting that DC plans differ, in terms of the financial instruments in which participants can invest their contributions, and of course, they will experience different patterns of returns over time.[15] Accordingly, in our approach, the Calculator permits both future and past time-varying rates of return to be used in the calculations. Table 10-3 compares selected statistics on the distribution of plan balances in 1991 using the historical returns on a portfolio of 100 percent long-term bonds from Ibbotson (2003), extended back to the earliest start year in the sample; the mean real return for this period was 1.8 percent.[16] Table 10-3 indicates little difference in plan balances using time-invariant or time-varying returns. Yet there is an important caveat, in that for any given mean return, the timing of the annual returns matters. In this particular application, there is little difference in balances but if the order of the returns were reversed (e.g. assuming the 1991 return occurred in 1952 etc.), then balances would be lower with time-varying returns than with time-invariant returns.

Altering Assumptions about Pre-Tax Voluntary Contributions and Eligibility

Also of interest is how sensitive results are to the PEP assumptions that (*a*) pre-tax voluntary contributions to DC plans vary across individuals, but are time-invariant, and (*b*) that eligibility for such contributions begins at the date of hire. While the source of the SPD, the effective date of the plan, and the effective date of the last amendment of the plan were collected, the PEP does not incorporate those dates when calculating DC pension wealth; rather, the software assumes that respondents were eligible for their plans since they were hired. The potential impact of changing this assumption depends on the application, but for many research questions involving DC plans, the timing of when the plan was first available to the participant is likely to be of great importance for calculating pension measures. For example, 401(k) plans were not permitted until 1978 and few were adopted until after 1981 when the IRS issued clarifying regulations for these plans; for this reason, 1982 can be taken as the de facto earliest year of 401(k) introduction after which plan adoption rates increased rapidly (see Figure 10-1). We seek to assess what difference it makes to incorporate the plan's inception date, as well as assuming that participants were likely ineligible for 401(k) saving before 1982.[17] Furthermore, some of the voluntary pre-tax saving options in the SPDs matched to HRS respondents were also adopted in the mid- to late-1980s.

Table 10-4 illustrates the impact of these assumptions for DC quit-date balances and expected present values for a variety of Calculator parameterizations. Panel A shows the quit-date balance, and the first row replicates

TABLE 10-3 DC Plan Balances for HRS Participants in 1991, Computed Using Calculator and Time-Varying Rates of Return ($2004; $N = 2,306$)

Parameterization	Mean	Standard Deviation	10th Percentile	25th Percentile	Median	75th Percentile	90th Percentile	95th Percentile	99th Percentile
Time-invariant rate of return	46,075	123,632	0	0	5,197	44,490	128,880	219,319	495,001
Time-varying rate of return	49,148	134,072	0	0	5,283	47,401	137,629	236,187	520,199

Source: Authors' calculations.

Notes: The Calculator was parameterized as follows: the default participant file was used; years of pension eligibility for both voluntary and employer contributions were measured since the date of hire; the voluntary contribution rate was taken from the default participant file; in the first row, the real rate of return was set equal to 1.8%; the inflation rate was set to 4%; and annual earnings were calculated using the self-reported earnings in the participant file and the earnings equation from the PEP.

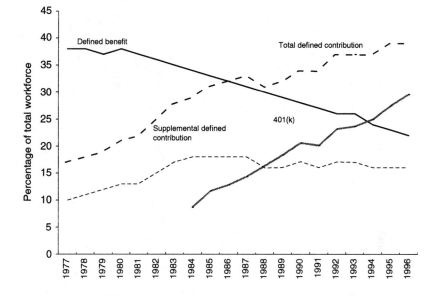

Figure 10-1. Private sector pension plan participation by plan type: 1977–96. (*Source:* US Department of Labor (2001).)

the baseline results from Table 10-2. The mean and median plan balances at the quit date are $218,971 and $30,802, respectively. The second row provides lower results for both figures of $105,297 and 0, respectively, assuming that participants did not contribute voluntarily in any of the years since hire. In other words, these statistics indicate balances associated only with employer and mandatory employee contributions over the course of employment. This highlights the important role that voluntary saving plays in DC plan balances, even for HRS workers not exposed to 401(k)-type pension arrangements for much of their careers. In particular, the mean amounts to only 48 percent of the baseline computation, which indicates that voluntary saving (and accrued earnings thereon) comprise about half of DC balances at retirement; further the typical HRS individual had only a voluntary-saving provision.[18]

The third row in Panel A indicates the quit-date balance had all participants voluntarily contributed 5 percent of pay each year of employment. At every percentile, participants now would be predicted to have positive balances at the quit date: mean and median balances would be $254,778 and $130,356, respectively. The fourth row of Panel A illustrates the impact of limiting the number of years of eligibility for pre-tax voluntary contributions. This limit is derived from three pieces of information, namely the plan adoption date, the date of last amendment in the SPD, and the first

TABLE 10-4 DC Plan Balances for HRS Participants at the Quit Date and the Expected Present Value of DC Wealth in 1992, Computed Using Calculator and Taking into Account Voluntary Contributions ($2004)

Parameterization	N	Mean	Standard Deviation	10th Percentile	25th Percentile	Median	75th Percentile	90th Percentile	95th Percentile	99th Percentile
A. DC plan balance at quit date										
Contribution rate from participant file	2,383	218,971	514,750	0	0	30,802	224,901	629,199	997,486	2,112,629
Zero contribution rate	2,383	105,297	333,753	0	0	0	95,129	308,518	512,165	1,110,494
Five-percent contribution rate	2,383	254,778	451,853	9,922	43,381	130,356	315,015	612,495	875,112	1,715,939
Contribution rate from participant file; restricted eligibility	2,383	184,736	449,148	0	0	30,023	196,331	527,525	809,779	1,741,739
W-2 contribution rate; eligibility since the date of hire	2,383	179,992	416,388	0	0	38,662	197,850	495,454	780,603	1,741,373
W-2 contribution rate; restricted eligibility	2,383	163,339	386,793	0	0	34,545	186,476	456,638	705,285	1,603,888
B. Expected present value of DC wealth in 1992										
Contribution rate from participant file	2,383	69,562	155,669	0	0	16,884	80,155	190,700	286,603	673,056
Zero contribution rate	2,383	37,869	115,268	0	0	0	38,937	105,153	160,285	346,014
Five-percent contribution rate	2,383	94,008	152,007	11,673	25,133	59,068	114,238	202,278	278,671	536,131
Contribution rate from participant file; restricted eligibility	2,383	59,203	139,254	0	0	16,159	69,981	153,743	233,794	503,408

W-2 contribution rate; eligibility since the date of hire	2,383	64,343	155,906	0	0	20,483	74,686	159,411	268,066	556,579
W-2 contribution rate; restricted eligibility	2,383	55,822	127,295	0	0	19,083	69,046	141,189	204,987	481,944
C. DC plan balance in 1991										
Contribution rate from participant file	2,306	49,148	134,072	0	0	5,283	47,401	137,629	236,188	520,199
Zero contribution rate	2,306	27,798	97,831	0	0	0	20,900	79,238	126,672	286,890
Five-percent contribution rate	2,306	70,767	136,265	2,651	10,950	34,174	87,927	171,379	231,966	476,262
Contribution rate from participant file; restricted eligibility	2,306	59,203	139,254	0	0	16,159	69,981	153,743	233,794	503,408
W-2 contribution rate; eligibility since the date of hire	2,306	44,931	136,551	0	0	7,526	40,824	116,352	217,056	479,863
W-2 contribution rate; restricted eligibility	2,306	35,638	104,711	0	0	13,277	35,121	91,013	148,210	324,942

Source: Authors' calculations.

Note: The Calculator was parameterized as follows: the default participant file was used; years of pension eligibility for both voluntary and employer contributions were measured since the date of hire in the first, second, third, and fifth rows, and as described in the text in the fourth and last rows; the voluntary contribution rate was taken from the default participant file for the first and fourth rows, and as described in the text for the second, third, fifth, and last rows; the real rate of return was set equal to 2.3%; the inflation rate was set to 4%; and annual earnings were calculated using the self-reported earnings in the participant file and the earnings equation from the PEP.

date in which a pre-tax deferral was made from the W-2 data.[19] The fourth
row indicates that restricting the years of eligibility has an important impact
on mean quit date DC plan balances; in particular, the mean based on
restricted eligibility for voluntary contributions is $184,736, or 15.6 percent
lower than the first row. Not surprisingly, the impact is largest in the upper
portion of the distribution.

The Impact of Voluntary Contribution Rates from W-2 Data

The final two rows of Panel A in Table 10-4 illuminate how using administrative records (W-2 data) on pre-tax deferrals changes outcomes, by inte-
grating actual workers' time-varying, individual-specific voluntary contributions to their DC plans over time. As Cunningham and Engelhardt (2002)
have previously found, this has the effect of reducing plan balances at the
mean by 17.8 percent compared to the baseline. It is interesting that the
median balance rises by 25 percent, because some participants made actual
contributions in 1984–91 at rates that exceeded what they indicated in their
initial 1992 interviews. In other words, capturing actual contribution rates
in the W-2 data does a much better job of capturing voluntary contribution
patterns.

The final row in Panel A shows the combined impact of using both the W-
2 contribution rates and the restrictions on years of eligibility for voluntary
contributions. The results for quit date balances are striking: means plan
balances are 25.4 percent lower under this parameterization than under
the baseline assumptions, and median plan balances are 12 percent higher.
In other words, the differences compared to the PEP assumptions are not
linear, as the PEP attributes less to the middle group and more to the top
end of the distribution.

Panels B and C of Table 10-4 show similar statistics for expected present
values of DC wealth (in 1992) and plan balances (in 1991), respectively. Our
message is the same: the mean present value of DC wealth is lower by about
20 percent and means plan balances are about 28 percent lower when we
use the W-2 contribution rates and tighter eligibility restrictions.[20] It would
appear that the baseline assumptions understate DC wealth in the middle
of the distribution but overstate it at the upper end of the distribution. And
clearly the bottom line is that DC wealth estimates are sensitive to modeling
assumptions.

DC Pension Wealth Estimates Based on Administrative Earnings Data

Thus far, the analysis has examined the sensitivity of DC wealth estimates
assuming respondent-reported pay at the time of the survey and a very

simple earnings projection equation built into the PEP. Next, we turn to examine how pension wealth numbers differ if we estimate an earnings model using as input the administrative SSA covered-earnings data from 1951 to 1979 and W-2 data from 1980 to the year prior to the survey year (1991 for the Original HRS cohort and 1997 for the WBs).[21] For those respondents who gave consent to match administrative earnings data, parameter estimates from this model and administrative data were used to construct complete earnings histories for each HRS respondent who entered in 1992 or 1998.[22]

The first row of Panel A in Table 10-5 estimates quit-date DC plan balances for members of the original HRS cohort using these new earnings trajectories and imposing the eligibility restrictions discussed above.[23] The mean and median DC balances are $321,846 and $68,089, respectively, substantially higher than the first row of Table 10-4. The second row provides the plan balances for just the subset of 1,857 individuals who had their Social Security earnings histories and W-2s linked to the surveys; the results show that removing individuals for whom earnings had to be imputed raises the mean to almost $363,528 and is monotonic across the pension-value distribution.

In the third row of Panel A, we repeat the analysis but instead use the WBs cohort; the sample is smaller so there are only 551 observations (the match rate for employer SPDs was also lower and the consent rate for matched administrative earnings was lower as well). The mean and median DC plan balances at the quit date were $399,363 and $27,875, respectively. But these balance figures obscure what appears to be a dramatic increase in pension wealth inequality. For the original HRS cohort in 1992, the pension balance at the 75th percentile was about four times larger than the median pension value. In 1998, for the WBs, the 75th percentile was more than 16 times the median. Whether this reflects the longer exposure to DC plans by the WBs or is simply due to differences in those for whom the administrative data could be obtained is unclear. The fourth row of Panel A shows the balances at the quit date for the subsample of 311 individuals from the War Baby cohort who gave permission to link their Social Security earnings; Panels B and C show the present value of DC wealth and the plan balance in the survey entry year, respectively.

Some final results appear in Table 10-6, which shows the DC plan balances due to employee pretax voluntary contributions and associated employer matching contributions, for the subset of participants from Table 10-6 who had a pretax saving option. Panel A shows that for participants with matched W-2s, the mean balance from pretax saving excluding the employer match was $16,850, but the median came to 0; this indicates that most of the original HRS respondents who were eligible for pretax saving did not participate in their plans. Indeed, even at the 75th percentile,

TABLE 10-5 DC Plan Balances for HRS Original Cohort and War Babies Cohort: Using Administrative Earnings Records to Measure Earnings, Voluntary Contributions, and Eligibility ($2004)

Cohort and Sample	N	Mean	Standard Deviation	10th Percentile	25th Percentile	Median	75th Percentile	90th Percentile	95th Percentile	99th Percentile
A. DC plan balance at quit date										
Original cohort full sample	2,383	321,846	750,202	0	0	68,089	324,116	874,137	1,422,381	3,483,233
Original cohort Subsample with matched earnings	1,857	363,527	820,932	0	0	78,883	353,360	1,002,432	1,659,664	3,613,718
War Babies cohort full sample	551	399,363	1,030,290	0		27,911	437,485	1,169,626	1,825,488	4,137,835
War Babies cohort subsample with matched earnings	311	674,051	1,298,836	0	44,457	259,609	814,325	1,743,379	2,404,895	4,607,698
B. Expected present value of DC wealth in entry year										
Original cohort full sample	2,383	133,112	301,055	0	0	34,737	129,819	335,621	597,988	1,485,251
Original cohort subsample with matched earnings	1,857	152,123	331,163	0	0	40,490	151,245	391,372	705,339	1,559,285
War Babies cohort full sample	551	120,278	239,276	0	0	23,606	157,546	321,382	533,764	940,049
War Babies cohort subsample with matched earnings	311	200,028	289,615	0	36,714	126,154	263,355	484,804	651,546	1,089,068
C. Plan balance in year prior to entry into the survey										
Original cohort full sample	2,306	119,680	307,226	0	0	13,057	95,553	328,235	610,695	1,475,872
Original cohort subsample with matched earnings	1,793	138,835	338,476	0	0	18,067	116,670	380,545	735,481	1,538,111
War Babies cohort full sample	544	83,749	175,157	0	0	2,520	100,709	269,727	397,432	799,645
War Babies cohort subsample with matched earnings	305	134,802	212,758	0	6,428	57,145	175,563	336,049	529,928	898,201

Source: Authors' calculations.

Notes: The Calculator was parameterized as follows: the default participant file was used; years of pension eligibility for both voluntary and employer contributions were measured using a combination of the plan adoption date, date of last amendment, and year of first pre-tax deferral from the W-2s; voluntary contribution rates from the W-2s for those who gave consent and self-reported from the participant file for those who did not give consent; earnings from covered-earnings and W-2 data for those who gave consent and imputed based on the earnings regression described in the text for those who did not give consent; and the real rate of return and inflation rate were time-varying and taken from Ibbotson (2003), where the return data were based on a portfolio of 100% corporate bonds.

TABLE 10-6 DC Plan Balances Due to Employee Pre-Tax Voluntary and Employer Matching Contributions: HRS Original Cohort and War Babies Cohort, for Year Prior to Survey Entry ($2004)

Cohort and Sample	N	Mean	Standard Deviation	10th Percentile	25th Percentile	Median	75th Percentile	90th Percentile	95th Percentile	99th Percentile
A. Voluntary contribution balances for eligible participants										
Original cohort full sample	1,840	14,073	32,925	0	0	0	12,956	42,650	79,805	163,637
Original cohort subsample with matched earnings	1,437	16,850	36,019	0	0	0	16,839	52,963	93,893	170,030
War Babies cohort full sample	524	53,113	133,193	0	0	0	51,256	182,733	256,641	529,928
War Babies cohort subsample with matched earnings	294	94,183	166,559	0	2,038	33,944	144,804	239,989	329,979	679,709
B. Employer matching contribution balances for the subsample offered matching										
Original cohort full sample	903	5,974	13,417	0	0	0	5,549	19,317	34,468	62,042
Original cohort subsample with matched earnings	711	7,320	14,781	0	0	347	7,718	23,453	39,782	66,788
War Babies cohort full sample	263	12,325	25,863	0	0	0	13,426	40,340	66,741	109,119
War Babies cohort subsample with matched earnings	145	22,356	31,483	0	534	10,709	29,619	64,921	79,885	148,997
C. Sum of voluntary and matching contribution balances for eligible participants										
Original cohort full sample	2,477	17,004	38,903	0	0	0	15,298	51,787	99,413	190,098
Original cohort subsample with matched earnings	1,934	20,472	42,680	0	0	0	20,049	64,192	115,982	205,648
War Babies cohort full sample	706	59,300	144,096	0	0	0	65,431	198,085	284,433	529,928
War Babies cohort subsample with matched earnings	396	105,209	179,377	0	2,506	41,798	157,435	280,808	376,378	679,709

Source: Authors' calculations.

balances are quite modest ($16,839), in sharp contrast with the fourth row WBs who had longer exposure to 401(k)-type plans; mean and median balances for them were $94,183 and $33,944, respectively. Panel B shows the distribution of balances due to employer matching contributions for the subset of plans that offered matching (about half the plans). Median balances due to matching are $347 and $10,709 for the original HRS and WBs cohorts, respectively. Panel C shows balances for the sum of the employee voluntary and employer matching contributions. Even with matching, the average balance for the original HRS cohort was only $20,472, substantially less than the WBs, again reflecting their longer exposure to these DC plans.

Conclusions and Discussion

Inasmuch as pensions represent a substantial component of older households' retirement saving, it is critical to measure the level and distribution of pension wealth properly. Yet asking respondents about their pension wealth may run the risk of measurement error. In this chapter, we show how our newly developed Calculator software can be used to construct alternative estimates of DC plan balances for HRS participants. We have emphasized the crucial role of economic assumptions, and we demonstrate several conclusions. First, pension wealth resulting from voluntary saving (and accrued earnings thereon) comprises half of DC pension wealth calculated for HRS respondents with matched SPDs. Second, our Calculator yields substantially lower mean estimates of DC pension wealth for HRS participants than the PEP that has been used to date. In particular, we calculate DC pension wealth to be 20 percent lower when we use reasonable modeling assumptions and arguably better input data; wealth in 401(k)-type pension plans alone is estimated at 40 percent less. Third, most of the reduction in estimated DC wealth occurs for the right tail of the pension–wealth distribution. Fourth, the PEP understates DC wealth in the middle of the pension–wealth distribution. Overall, we find that the mean 401(k) balance, including employer matching contributions, was about $20,472 for the original HRS cohort in 1992, but the median was 0; this suggests that the majority of those eligible did not participate in such plans back then. By contrast, the later generation known as the WBs had greater and earlier exposure to such plans; their mean and median balances were $105,209 and $41,798, respectively, indicating the growing importance of 401(k)s in retirement saving for younger cohorts.

These results suggest that research which has used pension wealth figures created from HRS sources to date may have mismeasured DC pension and retirement wealth adequacy for a sizable fraction of HRS participants. Accordingly, this analysis implies that researchers must think more carefully about the economic assumptions underlying pension measures. We have shown that the default assumptions in the PEP overstates DC pension wealth, with the extent of mismeasurement dependent on what the researcher assumes about eligibility and employer (nonmatching) contributions. In other words, the SPDs alone offer an incomplete picture of employer pension provisions, which are needed to accurately estimate pension entitlements to DC plans. Future work will need to recognize that pension plans are dynamic as well so that SPDs must be collected repeatedly for covered workers. In addition, it is important to frequently update administrative records on earnings; fortunately, the HRS has received respondent consent to update administrative earnings files through 2003. This will permit substantially more accurate modeling of the dynamics of retirement and saving behavior of older Americans and cohort trends in retirement wealth.

Acknowledgments

All research with the restricted-access data from the HRS was performed under agreement in the Center for Policy Research at Syracuse University, Federal Reserve Bank of Dallas, and Federal Reserve Bank of Atlanta. The authors are especially grateful to Bob Petticolas and Helena Stolyarova for their efforts in helping them understand the HRS employer-provided pension plan data. This research is part of a long-term effort to better measure pension wealth in the HRS and has received generous support from Syracuse University, TIAA-CREF, and SSA through the Center for Retirement Research at Boston College, the US Department of Labor, the National Science Foundation, and the National Institute on Aging.

Notes

[1] See, e.g. Mitchell and Moore (1998, 2000) and Mitchell et al. (2000).

[2] See, for instance, the US Health and Retirement Study (HRS); the English Longitudinal Survey of Ageing (ELSA); the Survey of Health, Ageing and Retirement in Europe (SHARE), which covers Denmark, Sweden, Austria, France, Germany, Switzerland, Belgium, the Netherlands, Spain, Italy, and Greece; and similar ongoing or new surveys in Mexico, New Zealand, Israel, South Korea, and Japan.

[3] e.g. Mitchell (1988).

[4] See, e.g. Mitchell and Moore (1998, 2000) and Mitchell et al. (2000).

[5] See, for instance, the US Health and Retirement Study; the ELSA; the SHARE, which covers Denmark, Sweden, Austria, France, Germany, Switzerland, Belgium, The Netherlands, Spain, Italy, and Greece; and similar ongoing or new surveys in Mexico, New Zealand, Israel, South Korea, and Japan.

[6] Gustman and Steinmeier (1999), Johnson et al. (2000), and Engelhardt (2001) have analyzed pension measurement issues in the HRS.

[7] For those who entered the survey in 1992, these data include Social Security covered-earnings histories from 1951 to 1991 and W-2 earnings records for jobs held

from 1980 to 1991; for those who entered in 1998, these include covered-earnings from 1951 to 1997 and W-2s from 1980 to 1997. Unfortunately, these data are not yet available for the EBB.

[8] We refer interested readers to Rohwedder (2003) for an extensive discussion of the conceptual issues in measuring DC pension wealth from the SPDs and how those relate to the PEP and to Engelhardt et al. (2005) for detailed descriptions and comparisons of the two programs. Research that uses the Calculator to model the impact of DC pension incentives on economic behavior include Cunningham and Engelhardt (2002) and Engelhardt and Kumar (2005).

[9] Our replication is based on the original Pascal version of the Program, which since has been rewritten in Visual Basic. The (unreported) comparison based on the Visual Basic version is the same as the VB version matches the Pascal version.

[10] These anomalies were brought to the attention to and confirmed by the HRS, which addressed them in the VB version of the PEP.

[11] When parameterizing the Calculator, the user must choose which code to invoke.

[12] Specifically, we and the HRS staff compared output from the Calculator and Program and concluded that the Program's output appeared to be incorrect for these plans, but neither we nor the HRS staff could determine the root cause of the differences. Without knowledge of the underlying problem, there is no way to specify alternative calculations for these plans to override the Calculator's code.

[13] The sample size of 2,352 individuals is the set of individuals for which both the Program and Calculator produced output. In the Tables 10-3–10-5, we use a slightly larger sample of 2,383 individuals based solely on the Calculator's output.

[14] The assumed interest and inflation rates are 1992 SSA intermediate forecasts; other parameters (aggregate wage growth, etc.) are taken from the default Parameter file for the PEP. In other words, this parameterization represents the default used for Scenario 1 in the HRS-supplied Pension Values Database.

[15] These options are coded in the Pension Plan Data file but only for plans that allow for participant-directed investment of plan balances. The Pension Estimation Program does not use this information to help define rates of return; the Calculator does not either, although it does allow the user to output dummy variables indicating these investment options to the output data set.

[16] Calendar year 1991 is chosen for this comparison because it was the last year prior to the initial 1992 HRS interview, which allows solely for the use of past returns in the calculations and, from a practical perspective for the purpose of this illustration, avoids the need to forecast returns beyond 1991. In addition, 1991 is a useful year because the plan balance is recorded just prior to the initial interview, and the individual was asked to self-report the plan balance during the interview. This allows for a comparison of self-reported balances versus those implied by the Calculator.

[17] The effective and amendment dates from the SPDs were not used in the PEP because its designers implicitly assumed that a plan effective as of a particular calendar year replaced another plan of equal generosity. There is dispute in the literature about whether 401(k) plans were actually good substitutes for previously existing pension plans.

[18] It is also important to note that the zero balances in the lower percentiles in the baseline in the first row of Panel A in Table 10-4 occur because participants self-reported in the initial HRS interview that they made no voluntary contributions in 1992. Under the baseline parameterization, the Calculator assumes that the rate in

1992 was time-invariant so that if this rate is zero, then that individual was always and forever will be a noncontributor, and, thus, a zero contribution rate always held throughout the duration of employment so that the individual ends up with zero plan balance at retirement. This is what the Program would assume and calculate as well.

[19] Engelhardt et al. (2005) describe the algorithm for determining eligibility in this fashion in detail.

[20] The sample for the plan balance in 1991 is 2,306 individuals, slightly smaller than in panels A and B, because there were a small number of participants who started their jobs in 1992 and did not have coverage in 1991.

[21] We follow Cunningham and Engelhardt (2002) and Engelhardt and Kumar (2005) in using administrative earnings to construct career earnings, based on the parameter estimates from an annual earnings equation using all HRS individuals with matched Social Security earnings histories. The following model is estimated using a two-limit Tobit model to account for the censoring imposed from below by zero earnings from labor force nonparticipation and from above by the FICA cap on all person-year observations in the Social Security earnings database:

$$\ln(y_{it}) = \kappa_{1t} + \sum_{g=1}^{G} \kappa_{2gt} D_i^{\text{OwnEduc}\,g} + \kappa_{3t}\text{Age}_{it} + \kappa_{4t}\text{Age}_{it}^2 + \kappa_{5t}\text{Age}_{it}^3 + \kappa_{6t}Age_{it}^4$$

$$+ \kappa_{7t} D_i^{\text{White}} + \kappa_{8t} D_{it}^{\text{GovtJob}} + \theta \mathbf{Z}_i + \eta_{it} \tag{1}$$

The dependent variable, $\ln(y)$, is the natural log of real covered-earnings (nominal covered-earnings from the database deflated into 1992 dollars by the all-items Consumer Price Index, or CPI). The earnings equation is estimated separately by sex and HRS cohort and employs a flexible functional form that allows for (reading the terms on the right-hand side of the equation from right to left in order) calendar-year effects; time-varying returns to the respondent's education, measured by educational attainment group, g (high school graduate, some college, college graduate, graduate degree); time-varying quartic age-earnings profiles; time-varying white-non-white earnings gaps; and time-varying returns to government jobs. In addition, the specification includes a vector of explanatory variables, $\mathbf{Z}$, which include a large set of time-invariant differences in earnings that are interpreted as part of the individual's human capital endowment: an indicator for whether US born; sets of indicators for mother's and father's education, respectively, measured by educational attainment group (high school graduate, some college, college graduate, and education not reported); own Census region of birth; and interactions of race, education, and region of birth.

[22] Actual earnings were used from the calendar year the respondent turned 20 through 1979, for those person-year observations with actual earnings below the FICA cap; for those observations with earnings above the FICA cap, the larger of the predicted value from the earnings equation and the cap was used. For 1980 through the year prior to the entry year, the actual uncapped earnings were taken from the W-2 database for all observations. Finally, earnings were forecast for years beginning with the entry year and future years up until the quit date, producing a real earnings history from age 20 until the quit date. For respondents who did not give consent, the predicted values from the estimation based on their

socio-demographic characteristics were used to calculate an earnings growth rate from each single year of age, starting at 20, to the age in the survey entry year. Then using the respondent-reported annual earnings in the survey entry year, annual earnings were backdated using these growth rates. Finally, earnings were forecasted from the survey entry year to the quit date.

[23] For those individuals having matched earnings records, the voluntary contributions were taken from the W-2 data; for those lacking a match, voluntary contributions were those self-reported in the in-person interview.

Appendix

TABLE 10A-1 Annual Real Returns and Inflation, 1972–91, in %

Year	Annual Real Return on a Portfolio of			
	(1)	*(2)*	*(3)*	*(4)*
	Inflation	*100% Stocks*	*100% Bonds*	*50% Stocks, 50% Bonds*
1972	3.2	14.0	3.6	8.8
1973	6.0	−24.3	−7.3	−15.8
1974	10.5	−42.3	−14.7	−28.5
1975	8.7	24.9	6.9	15.9
1976	5.6	16.7	12.4	14.5
1977	6.3	−14.0	−4.8	−9.4
1978	7.3	−2.3	−8.7	−5.5
1979	10.8	4.4	−16.8	−6.2
1980	12.7	16.4	−14.4	1.0
1981	9.8	−13.6	−9.8	−11.7
1982	6.0	15.6	31.6	23.6
1983	3.2	16.6	2.4	9.5
1984	4.2	2.2	11.7	6.9
1985	3.5	24.2	22.6	23.4
1986	1.8	15.8	17.0	16.4
1987	3.6	0.8	−4.6	−1.9
1988	4.1	11.2	5.8	8.5
1989	4.7	22.8	10.5	16.7
1990	5.3	−9.2	0.7	−4.2
1991	4.1	23.6	15.1	19.4
1972–91 mean	6.1	5.2	2.6	4.1
1984–91 mean	3.9	11.4	9.8	10.6

Notes: This table shows the real asset returns for three representative portfolios and inflation for the twenty years prior to the 1992 HRS. Real returns calculated by Ibbotson (2003). Bonds are defined as Aaa corporate bonds. Stock returns are based on the S&P 500. Inflation was calculated by the authors from government sources for the CPI-U.

References

Cunningham, C. R. and Engelhardt, G. V. (2002). 'Federal Tax Policy, Employer Matching, and 401(k) Saving: Evidence from HRS W-2 Records', *National Tax Journal*, 55(3): 617–45.

Engelhardt, G. V. (2001). 'Have 401(k) s Raised Household Saving? Evidence from the Health and Retirement Study', Working Paper, Syracuse University.

—— and Kumar, A. N. (2005). 'Employer Matching and 401(k) Saving: Evidence from the Health and Retirement Study', Working Paper, Syracuse University.

—— Cunningham, C. R., and Kumar, A. (2005). ' "Users" Guide for the DC/401(k) Pension Calculator Designed for the 1992 Health and Retirement Study', Working Paper, Syracuse University.

Gustman, A. L. and Steinmeier, T. L. (1999). 'Changing Pensions in Cross-Section and Panel Data: Analysis with Employer-provided Plan Descriptions', *Proceedings of the National Tax Association*: 371–77.

Ibbotson Associates (2003). *Stocks, Bonds, Bills, and Inflation 2003 Yearbook*. Chicago, IL: Ibbotson Associates.

Johnson, R. W., Sambamoorthi, U., and Crystal, S. (2000). 'Pension Wealth at Midlife: Comparing Self-Reports with Provider Data', *Review of Income and Wealth*, 46(1): 59–83.

Mitchell, O. S. (1988). 'Worker Knowledge of Pension Provisions', *Journal of Labor Economics*, 6: 21–39.

—— and Moore, J. F. (1998). 'Retirement Wealth Accumulation and Decumulation: New Developments and Outstanding Opportunities', *Journal of Risk and Insurance*, 65(3): 371–400.

—— —— (2000). 'Projected Retirement Wealth and Savings Adequacy in the Health and Retirement Study', in O. S. Mitchell, B. Hammond, and A. Rappaport (eds.), *Forecasting Retirement Needs and Retirement Wealth*. Philadelphia, PA: University of Pennsylvania Press, pp. 68–94.

—— —— and Phillips, J. W. (2000). 'Explaining Retirement Saving Shortfalls', in O. S. Mitchell, B. Hammond, and A. Rappaport (eds.), *Forecasting Retirement Needs and Retirement Wealth*. Philadelphia, PA: University of Pennsylvania Press, pp. 139–66.

Rohwedder, S. (2003). 'Measuring Pension Wealth in the HRS: Employer and Self-Reports', Working Paper, Rand Corporation.

Venti, S. F. and Wise, D. A. (2000). 'Choice, Chance, and Wealth Dispersion at Retirement', NBER Working Paper.

US Department of Labor, Pension and Welfare Benefits Administration (2001). *Private Pension Plan Bulletin: Abstract of 1996 Form 5500 Annual Reports*. Washington, DC.

Chapter 11

Trends in Pension Values Around Retirement

Michael D. Hurd and Susann Rohwedder

Retirees in the United States generally rely on a mix of financial resources to support old-age consumption including Social Security retirement benefits, Medicare benefits (and sometimes Medicaid), personal wealth, and often, company pensions. Previous research has explored ways to measure Social Security and private saving,[1] but it has been more difficult to assess the value of pension resources partly because many workers have difficulty recollecting and reporting their pension entitlements, and also because dual-earner couples may be individually (and often jointly) entitled to claims on company pension benefits. This chapter develops and applies a new method of valuing pension wealth, to determine the importance of pension benefits in retiree well-being. Specifically, we use workers' self-reports of pension characteristics and pension benefits at the time of separation from a job, to determine their pension values on the verge of retirement.

Drawing on the Health and Retirement Study (HRS), we apply this method to estimate pension values for workers on the threshold of retirement at three different points in time, 1992, 1998, and 2004. We create these pension valuations for three cohorts of workers observed at age 51–56; here we term these groups the HRS cohort, the War Baby (WB) cohort, and the Early Baby Boomers (EBBs).[2] Using workers' self-reports at the time of job separation is more robust to reporting error than alternative techniques, particularly in the context of the HRS. Results indicate a decline in the number of workers with defined benefit (DB) plans near retirement, though their average pension value grew conditional on having a plan. Turning to defined contribution (DC) plans, coverage and the average real value of the pension grew noticeably, producing an overall increase in average pension wealth over the period examined. There is no support for the view that pensions are becoming less important for near-retirees, on average.

Trends in Pension Coverage and Pension Plan Type

Respondents to HRS are asked to self-report whether they have a pension on their current jobs if they are working; Table 11-1 reports responses

TABLE 11-1 Percentage of Workers with Pension Coverage on their Current Job (%)

	HRS Cohort 51–56 in 1992 N = 4,045	War Babies 51–56 in 1998 N = 2,308	Early Boomers 51–56 in 2004 N = 2,522
Men	61.5	62.3	61.4
Women	55.1	58.0	59.5
All	58.5	60.2	60.4

Source: Authors' calculations based on HRS Waves 1–7, collected every two years between 1992 and 2004.

to this question by different cohorts, with the questions posed at the time each group was 51–56 years of age. It is interesting that some 59 percent of all workers had an employer-based pension in 1992, and the rate did not change much by 2004 (60 percent); in fact, the difference between the point estimates is not statistically significant.[3] Yet there is an upward trend for women workers, with 55 percent of the females in 1992 having coverage; by 2004, women's coverage stood at 60 percent, only 2 percentage points below men's, and the difference between the coverage rates of men and women is no longer statistically significant. This pattern mirrors the overall national stability in plan coverage over time (Copeland 2005).

There has also been an economy-wide trend away from DB plans and toward DC plans, a pattern also discerned in HRS self-reports. Table 11-2 shows that, among workers with a pension, the rate of DB plan coverage fell by 18 percentage points for both men and women. Of course self-reports are subject to reporting error at the individual level, about which we say more below; nevertheless, the similarity with national trends suggests that the HRS respondents get the plan type questions about right, on average.

Valuing Pension Entitlements

One approach to valuing pensions would use HRS questions asking each worker whether he has a pension (or more than one pension) on his current job; if so, he is asked a follow-on series of questions seeking to reveal the value of these pension entitlements. The value of a pension is defined and measured differently for DB than for DC pensions, so the questions used to assess their value have differed in the survey, according to whether the respondent indicated his plan type was of one kind or the other. Specifically, it was believed that many covered workers might not know the terms 'defined benefit' or 'defined contribution;' instead, the HRS

TABLE 11-2 Distribution of Pension Plans by Type on Current Job, Conditional on Having a Pension (%)

	Men			Women		
	HRS	*War Babies*	*Early Boomers*	*HRS*	*War Babies*	*Early Boomers*
DB	38.8	28.1	22.2	44.7	30.7	27.2
DC	29.3	36.4	48.3	33.5	43.2	50.9
Both/other	31.9	35.6	29.6	21.8	26.1	21.9
All	100.0	100.0	100.0	100.0	100.0	100.0

Source: Authors' calculations based on HRS Waves 1–7, collected every two years between 1992 and 2004.

Note: DB—Defined Benefit Plan; DC—Defined Contribution Plan; columns do not exactly add up to 100.0 due to rounding.

survey questions ask whether the respondent has a pension of 'Type A', where benefits are based on a formula involving age, years of service, and salary, or of 'Type B', where money is accumulated in an account. When a respondent reports his plan is Type A (which we interpret as a DB plan), he is asked about his expectations of future benefits as an income flow or possible lump sum distribution. On the other hand if he reports his plan is of Type B (which we interpret as a DC plan), the respondent is asked about the value of the account.

Routing respondents into different pension question sequences based on what plan type they think they have can create a problem, as many workers either cannot, or do not, answer the first question about plan type accurately. This may be because they do not know what type of pension they have, or because of the way the question is asked. In any event it creates confusion, as indicated in Table 11-3 which includes only workers who said that their plan type *had not changed* over time. Nevertheless, many such workers report a different plan type in one wave of the survey, compared to

TABLE 11-3 Transition Rates of Plan Types Between Waves Among Those Reporting no Change in Plan Type (%)

Plan Type Reported in Previous Wave	*Plan Type Reported in Current Wave*			
	DB	*DC*	*Both*	*All*
DB	79.0	17.6	3.5	100.0
DC	22.4	74.2	3.3	100.0
Both	53.5	32.1	14.4	100.0

Source: Adapted from Hurd and Panis (2003).

the reported plan type in the previous wave.[4] In principle, there should be complete concordance of such reports, with all the observations lying along the diagonal. Yet as the table shows, there is considerable discordance: for example, 17.6 percent of those who reported having a DB plan in the previous wave report having a DC plan in the subsequent wave of the survey, even though they had previously said their plan had not changed. Conversely, 22.4 percent of those initially stating their plan was of the DC variety said it was a DB plan when next questioned (and yet they affirmed their plan had not changed).

The problem this poses for pension valuation is that the follow-up questions are inappropriate when the worker gets the initial plan type question wrong. For instance, a respondent saying his plan was of the DB variety then is asked what benefit flows he expects as income in retirement. However, if the plan were actually a DC pension which typically pays out as a lump sum, the respondent may not be able to respond to the follow-ups. Conversely, a respondent saying he has a DC plan is then asked his balance amount, which cannot be answered if in fact the plan were really a DB pension.

As an alternative strategy, some prior studies have relied on Summary Plan Descriptions (SPDs) gathered by the HRS project for a subset of workers reporting they have a pension in the HRS and for whom these SPDs could be collected. These SPDs are generally used as inputs to a pension estimation software program to value estimated flows from the various plans (Mitchell et al. 2000; Gustman and Steinmeier 2001; Cunningham et al. this volume). There are pros and cons of using the SPDs.[5] For one thing, SPD match rates are far from perfect, particularly for the later waves of the HRS. This leaves open the possibility of reporting error in plan type and plan values as well as possible bias from missing data. For another thing, relying on the SPDs and software also requires the researcher to make educated guesses about many key pieces of information (e.g. contribution histories, rates of return earned on the accounts, whether benefits are inflation indexed after retirement, and so on).

A novel approach, adopted for the first time here, is to take yet a different path. This relies on information about the respondent's report of his pension benefits and attributes at the time he separates from a pension covered job, rather than asking about the pension before he leaves. Our argument is that, at job separation, the employee is more likely to receive information about his pension and make decisions about the disposition of the benefits. Thus when a worker leaves his job, the HRS asks about characteristics of the pension plan, his pension value, and how he disposed of the pension. Thanks to the longitudinal nature of the survey, we can then follow workers over time and observe this information about pension 'extractions' which

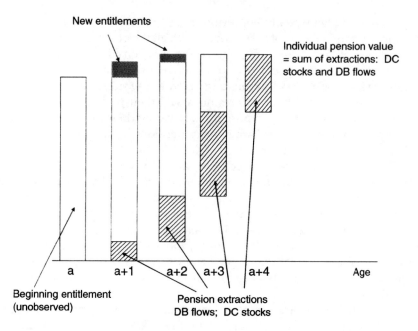

Figure 11-1. Conceptual approach to valuing pension entitlements: an illustration. (*Source*. Authors' computations.)

we use to estimate the value of the plan benefit amounts. To our knowledge, no prior study has made this use of the panel nature of the data for pension valuation purposes.

Our conceptual approach is illustrated in Figure 11-1. Consider a worker first observed at age *a*, who is then resurveyed at subsequent dates (called 'waves' in the HRS). The initial entitlement is unobserved, but as the worker ages, he can, at some point, extract some of his pension wealth. This can be a periodic benefit, as in the form of a DB annuity, or as a lump sum. Each period there is some probability that the worker will separate from his job and extract resources from his pension, and there is also some chance of remaining on the job and acquiring additional pension entitlements. By age *a* + 4 in this example, the worker has left the firm with probability 1 and extracted his entire pension value. In such a case, the total pension value is obtained by adding up the present discounted value of all the extractions. In the case of a DB plan, the summation would be over the present value of future income flows or annuity streams weighted by the probability of survival; for a DC plan, the sum would be a stock of pension wealth discounted to the relevant period. Combination plans would presumably have both.

TABLE 11-4 Distribution of Separations from
Employer: Workers 51–56 in 1992

HRS Wave	N	Percent
2	871	24.7
3	544	15.4
4	429	12.2
5	416	11.8
6	424	12.0
7	271	7.7
Still working	568	16.1
Total	3,523	100.0

Source: Authors' calculations based on HRS Waves 1–7,
collected every two years between 1992 and 2004.

Note: 1992 was the first HRS Wave, with subsequent
waves following every two years, so that Wave 2 refers
to the year 1994, Wave 3 to 1996 and so on.

Pension Entitlements in 1992

To arrive at the desired extraction measures for members of the HRS
cohort, we follow all people working in 1992 until they retire or separate
from that 1992 job. The oldest individual in the HRS original cohort was 56
in 1992; by the latest available survey date, that individual would be aged
68. Accordingly, most of the pension extractions would be accounted for
by that point. To illustrate the point, the pattern of job separations for this
cohort (age 51–56 in 1992) appears in Table 11-4.[6] The evidence shows
when separations are observed from the job held in Wave 1 of the survey.
It is interesting that the majority had left by 2004, yet some 16 percent was
still working for the same employer (the youngest was age 63). For this
group there is a (limited) right-censoring problem; below we explain how
we correct for this.

When the worker leaves his job, the survey inventories pensions from
that job. The DC holders are asked about the amount in the account and
what happened to the balance; disposition categories include 'rolled into
IRA', cash out, annuitize, and leave to accumulate. Partial amounts in each
category are also permitted. For those with DB pensions, respondents are
asked about immediate receipt of benefit and amounts, expectation of
benefits in future, and amounts and lump sum cash-outs.

To highlight the degree of worker uncertainty about their pensions
while working, Table 11-5 summarizes pension extraction at job separation,
cross-classified by whether people said they had a pension previously. It is
interesting that 17 percent of those who said they had no pension on their

TABLE 11-5 Concordance of 1992 Pension Reports
            about Current Job with Job Separation
            Pension Reports (%)

Reported Pension on Job in 1992	Reported Pension at Job Separation		
	No	Yes	All
No	82.9	17.1	100.0
Yes	6.4	93.7	100.0

Source: Authors' calculations based on HRS Waves 1–7, collected
every two years between 1992 and 2004.

job in 1992 eventually received some pension at job separation.[7] And for
those who reported a pension on the job earlier, some 94 percent reported
an extraction. In other words, if we merely rely on reports of pension
coverage from the 1992 wave, we might substantially underestimate pension
prevalence for older workers.

In Table 11-6 we classify workers according to their reported plan type
in 1992, and we include those who did not report having a pension then.
Table 11-6 then shows the distribution of actual plan type at separation.
Results are qualitatively similar to those seen earlier in Table 11-3: there are
substantial discrepancies between the 1992 reports and reports on pensions
at job separation. For example, among those stating in 1992 that they had
only a DC plan, 25 percent reported only having a DB plan at separation
(conversely, 15 percent of those saying they had only a DB plan end up with
only a DC plan). Of course, some plans may have changed between 1992
and separation, but in view of the broad shift toward DC plans it seems
unlikely that as many as 25 percent would actually transit from DC only to
DB only.

TABLE 11-6 Relationship Between Type of Pension Extracted and
            Report in 1992 (%)

Pension Type Reported on Job in 1992	Pension Type Reported on Job Separation				
	None	DB Only	DC Only	Both	All
None	83.4	5.3	10.6	0.7	100.0
DB only	5.9	68.4	14.6	11.1	100.0
DC only	10.6	24.6	52.4	12.4	100.0
Both	1.0	55.3	15.6	28.1	100.0

Source: Authors' calculations based on HRS Waves 1–7, collected every two
years between 1992 and 2004.

TABLE 11-7 Present Value of Pension Wealth Extractions: Derived from Lump Sum Amounts (DC and DB) and Annuities (DB), Conditional on Having an Extraction: Workers 51–56 in 1992 (Thousands of $2004)

	N	Mean	Median
Present value of PW derived from lump sums (DC and DB)	1,960	75.4	28.3
Present value of PW derived from annuities (DB)	1,921	201.7	111.5

Source: Authors' calculations based on HRS Waves 1–7, collected every two years between 1992 and 2004.

The plan valuation numbers we have estimated appear in Table 11-7, which provides numbers of persons and dollars extracted on average and for the median, conditional on there being an extraction. There are several types of extractions, which fall in two broad categories: lump sum extractions from DC plans or from DB plans and extractions in form of annuities derived from DB plans. We convert future income flows from DB plans into the corresponding present value to make the magnitudes comparable across the two types of extractions.[8] In total, we find 1,960 workers received lump sum extractions amounting to $75,400 on average, and to $28,300 at the median ($2004). About the same number of workers (1,921) received annuity income from their DB pension plans with an average present value of $201,700 and $111, 500 at the median.

Predicting Future Pension Extractions

Having valued pension values for HRS workers in 1992, most of whom had completed their extractions, we next seek to estimate what pension wealth might be for the entire HRS cohort, and also for subsequent cohorts who turned age 51–56 in 1998 and in 2004. As these cohorts are more recent, their pension extractions are not yet complete: some of the original HRS respondents have not yet retired; many of the WB cohorts have not; and hardly any of the EBB cohorts have completed their extractions. Accordingly, our approach uses all the respondent information available from pension self-reports in 1992, to predict the present values of observed pension extractions in later survey waves. For instance, information collected in 1992 includes the current account balance and the earliest age when the worker can draw benefits, for workers saying they had a DC plan. For those having a DB pension, the information includes the expected claiming age and the expected pension benefit amount, the early retirement age, and the normal retirement age. Other covariates in the prediction models include 1992 labor income, job tenure, the worker's industry, education, sex, and other variables related to pension entitlements.

We estimate the probability of each type of extraction at each future age using a multivariate logistic regression model.[9] Conditional on extraction, we also estimate models to describe the amount of each type of extraction expressed in present value terms (and constant dollars). From these estimates, we predict the expected present value of pensions using each worker's observed characteristics. Besides predicting pension extractions for those who have completed their extractions, we also predict extractions for the 16 percent of HRS workers observed in 1992 who had not completed them by the end of the 2004 survey. This method accounts for future separations and retirement as well as future pension growth and the trend toward DC plans; as long as these relationships are similar to what is observed in the data, the technique produces good estimates of population pension wealth at retirement. Its weakness is that that some accumulations remain to be earned through future work and extracted; however, as long as the relationship between those future accruals and the 1992 covariates remains the same, extractions based on those accumulations should be well predicted.[10]

Our next objective then is to estimate pension wealth in cohorts where the extraction is incomplete (for the right-censored HRS workers) and for the new cohorts added to the survey in 1998 and also in 2004. We estimate the present discounted value of expected individual pension entitlements *ex ante*, based on our estimated probability of an extraction and on the expected value of an extraction conditional on an extraction. The total present discounted value of expected extractions is just the sum of these expected extractions. This approach is appealing for several reasons: it relies on plan type information collected at or near job separation; accordingly it reproduces nonlinearities in DB pension entitlements around the time of job separation; it can be augmented with information from SPDs from employers if available; and it can integrate worker reported information about early and normal retirement ages.[11]

Estimated expected pension wealth refers to the present value of benefits, expressed in $2004, that workers take out of their pensions, either in the form of a lump sum (DC and some DB plans) or as an annuity (DB plans). We show summary statistics for respondents age 51–56 in 1992, 1998, and 2004 in Table 11-8. The first panel shows the average present values of extractions received as lump sums, the second those received as annuities, and the third panel shows the sum of all extractions by sex. As one would expect, pension entitlements of men are substantially higher than those of female workers. However, the present values of expected entitlements have increased substantially for female workers, much faster than for male workers, as can be seen from comparing cohorts: lump sum entitlements increased by 69 percent from the HRS cohort to the WBs cohort, and by another 27 percent from the WBs cohort to the cohort of

TABLE 11-8 Average Estimated Present Value of Pension Wealth:
Workers 51–56 (Thousands of $2004)

	HRS 1992	WB 1998	EBB 2004
PW (lump sums)			
Males	53.6	62.1	71.1
Females	17.7	29.9	37.9
All	37.0	46.5	54.8
PW (annuities)			
Males	131.0	122.1	125.3
Females	56.3	65.4	71.8
All	96.5	94.7	99.0
PW (lump sums + annuities)			
Males	184.6	184.2	196.4
Females	73.9	95.2	109.7
All	133.5	141.3	153.9

Source: Authors' calculations based on HRS Waves 1–7, collected every two years between 1992 and 2004.

the EBBs, reaching a level of $38,000. Increases in lump sum entitlements among male workers were much more modest (16 percent and 15 percent). Pension resources paid in form of annuities come from DB plans. While DB plans have been on the decline as some employers close these pension plans to new workers or discontinue them altogether, annuities still make up for a large fraction of retirement resources among the cohorts under study. Among men in their 50s we only see a modest decline in entitlements from annuities and the levels are in excess of $120,000. For women, we see again substantial increases across cohorts (16.2% between HRS and WBs; 9.8% between WBs and EBBs). The observed patterns for female workers are a result of women's stronger attachment to the labor market among younger cohorts. Aggregating over men and women, one finds that pension entitlements derived from annuities have not changed much in real terms over time, despite the decline in DB plan coverage.

The statistics in the third panel of Table 11-8 show the present value of total pension wealth, or the sum of entitlements to lump sums and annuities. Total pension wealth is higher in real terms for younger cohorts, by about 15 percent for the EBB cohort compared to the HRS cohort. Yet by 2004, women's extracted pension wealth is still only about half of men's. It is worth noting that measuring pension wealth of individual workers is not necessarily informative for assessing household retirement resources, since a worker can share retirement resources with a spouse who may or may not have pension entitlements from a job. Table 11-9 shows the cohort

TABLE 11-9 Average Predicted Pension Extractions:
Workers 51–56 (Thousands of $2004)

	HRS 1992	WB 1998	EBB 2004
Singles	92.8	81.2	82.2
Couples	178.0	217.3	243.1

Source: Authors' calculations based on HRS Waves 1–7, collected
every two years between 1992 and 2004.

comparison of pension entitlements from current jobs for singles and couples; where for the latter we have taken the sum of the entitlement of the
husband and the wife.[12] Results show that couples' pension wealth derived
from current employment is substantially larger than that of singles, and
the gap is largest for younger cohorts. Thus, in the original HRS cohort,
couples have about twice as much pension wealth as singles; in the Early
Boomer cohort, couples' pension wealth is about three times that of singles.

Conclusion and Discussion

The objective of this chapter is to estimate trends in the value of pensions
among workers approaching retirement. Previous efforts to value pension
wealth have relied on workers' self-reports about their pension balances
for DC plans, or anticipated pension benefits for DB plans. But these
self-reports are subject to considerable reporting error. Furthermore, self-
reports have considerable item nonresponse because respondents may not
know the requested values. By contrast, we value pensions using pension
outcomes when the worker leaves his employer and therefore needs to
decide on how to dispose of his pension rights. Our findings suggest that
pension entitlements of the Early Boomers are higher in real terms than
for the same age group a dozen years previously. Despite the decline in DB
plan coverage, entitlements have only fallen moderately among men, but
increased among women. We also note that most workers now approaching
retirement are married, so results for individuals do not take into account
household pension entitlement changes. That is, married individuals can
share their retirement resources, so an assessment of elderly well-being
should include household entitlements.

In evaluating the importance of this household pension wealth concept
for married couples by summing respondent and spouse entitlements, we
find high values of couples' pension wealth, which also rise strongly for
the youngest cohorts. This is likely due to women's increased attachment
to the labor market, leading to increased dual-career lifestyles for more
recent couples. For example, between 1992 and 2002, couples' pension

wealth values rose by about 37 percent in real terms, while they fell by 12 percent for nonmarried persons. Consequently, by 2004, couples averaged $243,000 in predicted pension wealth extractions, compared to $82,000 for singles.

It may be instructive to compare our estimated pension values to bequeathable wealth numbers, which refer to total wealth excluding entitlements to pensions and Social Security. For instance, Early Boomer couples averaged bequeathable wealth of $457,000 (in 2004) including housing; excluding housing, the sum came to $308,000. Since average couples' pension wealth totaled $243,000, it seems that pension values amount to about 79 percent of nonhousing bequeathable wealth. Boomer singles had substantially less bequeathable wealth, at $173,000 (total) or $104,000 without housing; their pension wealth of $82,000 is also lower and amounts to a similar fraction of bequeathable wealth (79%).

In sum, for the three cohorts studied in this analysis, pension wealth has risen over time rather than fallen, and this is true over all workers, not just those with a pension. Consequently, the results should reassure those who express concern that Boomers might enter retirement with fewer financial resources than previous cohorts. Our study could be extended, of course, to focus in more detail on those in the lower part of the wealth distribution. Such an analysis would need to include Social Security entitlements as well, because of their relatively greater importance for low-wealth retirees. Another positive note is the temporal rise in women's pension resources over time, inasmuch as many of them were relatively more exposed to old-age poverty in the past.

Acknowledgments

The authors are grateful for financial support from the Pension Research Council, the National Institute on Aging, The Social Security Administration, and The Department of Labor.

Notes

[1] For earlier research on the Health and Retirement Study, see Mitchell et al. (2000).
[2] This is in keeping with the standard nomenclature of this volume, see Mitchell (Chapter 1, this volume).
[3] Tests of statistical significance are conducted at the conventional 5 percent level.
[4] This table is adapted from Hurd and Panis (2003) and is based on data from Waves 1, 2, 3, 4, and 5 of HRS.
[5] See Rohwedder (2003) and Engelhardt and Kumar (2004) for further discussion of these points. Gustman and Steinmeier (2001) and Chan and Huff Stevens (2004)

provide pension wealth estimates based on HRS self-reports; while Mitchell et al. (2000) and Gustman et al. (1999, 2000) derive pension wealth using the HRS pension estimation program in combination with information from Summary Plan Descriptions. Engelhardt and Kumar (2004) offer refined estimates of DC pension wealth using their own pension calculator that combines the information from the Summary Plan Descriptions with information from respondents' administrative earnings history files and W2 information.

[6] We limit the HRS cohort in this way for comparability with data for 1998 and 2004 when we have fresh cohorts of those ages.

[7] Of course, workers could have become vested after 1992, but the number is likely to be small given the short vesting period and the age of the workers.

[8] The conversion of income flows into present values occurs in two steps. First, we compute the present value for the year the worker starts receiving the benefit by summing over future income flows weighted by the probabilities of survival and discounted by the rate of inflation assumed at 2.5 percent. In the second step we compute the wealth equivalent of that present value in 1992 by discounting by the nominal interest rate assumed at 5.5 percent (2.5% inflation and 3% real rate of return).

[9] We distinguish a total of five types of extractions for the purpose of estimation: DC extractions, DB lump sum extractions at the time of leaving the current job, DB lump sum extractions expected at a future date, DB annuity income first received at time of leaving the current job, and DB annuity income expected at a future date.

[10] It is important to note that these estimates reflect the amount of pension resources workers realize from the 1992 job at separation, and not the amount of pension wealth as of 1992.

[11] In future work, we will also draw on Social Security earnings records to link with the estimates.

[12] For couples, the total is the sum of the pension entitlements of each working spouse. If the spouse is not working that entitlement would be zero.

References

Chan, S. and Huff Stevens, A. (2004). 'Do Changes in Pension Incentives Affect Retirement? A Longitudinal Study of Subjective Retirement Expectations', *Journal of Public Economics*, 88(7–8) July: 1307–33.

Copeland, C. (2005). *Employment-Based Retirement Plan Participation: Geographic Differences and Trends*. EBRI Issue Brief No. 286. Washington, DC: EBRI. Measuring Pension Wealth.

Cunningham, C., Engelhardt, G. V., and Kumar, A. (this volume). 'Measuring Pension Wealth'.

Engelhardt, G. V. and Kumar, A. (2004). 'Defined Contribution Pension Plans and the Measurement of Retirement Wealth: Implications for Studies of Pension Knowledge, Saving, and the Timing of Retirement', Report to TIAA-CREF. http://www.tiaa-crefinstitute.org/research/grants/comp2_Englehardt2.html

Gustman, A. L. and Steinmeier, T. L. (2001). 'What People Don't Know About Their Pensions and Social Security', in W. G. Gale, J. B. Shoven, and M. J. Warshawsky (eds.), *Private Pensions and Public Policies*. Washington, DC: Brookings Institution, pp. 57–125.

—— Mitchell, O. S., Samwick, A. A., and Steinmeier, T. L. (1999). 'Pension and Social Security Wealth in the HRS', in J. Smith and R. Willis (eds.), *Wealth, Work and Health, Innovations in Measurement in the Social Sciences*. Ann Arbor, MI: University of Michigan Press, pp. 150–208.

—— —— —— —— (2000). 'Evaluating Pension Entitlements', in O. S. Mitchell, P. B. Hammond, and A. M. Rappaport (eds.), *Forecasting Retirement Needs and Retirement Wealth*. Philadelphia, PA: University of Pennsylvania Press, pp. 309–26.

Hurd, M. D. and Panis, C. (2003). 'The Choice to Cash Out Pension Rights at Job Change or Retirement', Unpublished manuscript, RAND.

Mitchell, O. S. (this volume). 'Will Boomers Redefine Retirement?'

—— Hammond, B., and Rappaport, A. (eds.) (2000). *Forecasting Retirement Needs and Retirement Wealth*. Philadelphia, PA: University of Pennsylvania Press.

Rohwedder, S. (2003). 'Measuring Pension Wealth in the HRS: Employer and Self-Reports', Unpublished Manuscript, RAND.

Chapter 12

Pension Portfolio Choice and Menu Exposure

Anders Karlsson, Massimo Massa, and Andrei Simonov

This chapter examines how the introduction of a funded defined contribution (DC) retirement system affects participants' propensity to participate in the stock market. This is an interesting topic in view of the transition to funded individual account plans in many nations around the world. Here we focus on what we call the 'Swedish experiment;' in the year 2000, the traditional Swedish pay-as-you-go retirement system was partially replaced by a national DC plan commonly referred to as the premium pension (PPM) system (Sunden 2000). Our main question is whether individuals perceive their investments in the pension scheme as a substitute for direct investments, and whether allocating more equities in their pension accounts induces participants to reduce or increase their directly held equity investments.

Standard portfolio choice theory suggests that investors would choose an optimal overall market exposure taking into account both direct and indirect (e.g. through a pension scheme) investment in equity. That is, pension and nonpension equity holdings would be seen as substitutes, at least to a first order. By contrast, behavioral finance theorists instead hypothesize that investors tend to categorize their investments, along with associated gains and losses, according to narrow categories. This approach, labeled 'mental accounting' or 'narrow framing', predicts that investors apply such mental accounting to stock holdings and react separately to gains and losses for different stocks (Barberis and Huang 2001).

The implications of the two theories are starkly different. Standard portfolio theory would posit that inducing investors to hold their retirement accounts in pension funds would crowd out direct equity investment. Behavioral theory, instead, suggests that if investors perceive their investment in pension funds and equity to be different sorts of accounts, one investment would not necessarily crowd out the other. The best way to examine this issue is to see whether introducing a DC individual account system changes investor incentives to directly participate in the stock market. To do a proper analysis, we would require information on investors' portfolio choices before the change, and to explore what happened after the introduction of the new pension system. Until now, this sort of information has been unavailable.

Our contribution is to exploit data on a large and representative sample of Swedish individuals tracked over time. Not only do we have information on their wealth, income, tax position, and demographic characteristics, but also we have semiannual information on the value of each investor's stock positions as well as the daily value of his transactions in the PPM system. In particular, the data-set on the individual retirement accounts includes all individual choices made from the introduction of the system until October 2004. We use the evidence provided on investors' patterns in the PPM system to test whether having a pension account containing mutual fund investments changes investor incentives to participate directly in the stock market.

The results show that investors do not perceive direct investment in the equity market as a close substitute for their retirement accounts, suggesting that an individual account system does not crowd out direct equity market investment. The new Swedish system may actually help educate investors of the benefits of stock market participation, increasing participation and therefore, indirectly, boosting saving. In what follows, we first describe the Swedish experiment and provide institutional details. Next, we describe the data and our main evidence. A short conclusion offers policy implications.

The Swedish 'Experiment'

The Swedish government made changes to its old pay-as-you-go national retirement program in the fall of 2000. The 'basic' portion of the system is a guaranteed benefit designed to ensure that no retiree will be completely without benefits in retirement, regardless of her or his previous income. There are two earnings-related elements of the new pension system, one being the Notional Defined Contribution (NDC) plan, financed by a tax of 16 percent of annual pay; revenue from this system is used to finance current retirees, and the amount paid in also serves as a base in calculating future pension payments. The second earnings-related component, of most interest here, is the premium pension (PPM) portion. This is financed by a mandated contribution 2.5 percent of annual pay, which is invested according to each individual's discretion. At inception, each participant was mailed a prospectus describing the investment menu of 464 funds, from which the participant had to elect from 1 to 5 of these choices.

Table 12-1 represents the information provided to investors in the PPM system. In addition to the fund identification number, name, and fund family, information is provided on fees, past return, and risk. Risk is

TABLE 12-1 Extract from the PPM Investor Information Folder, for a Specific Fund Example

Fund Number	Fund Name and Management Company	Information Regarding Fund	Fund Fee (%/yr)	Percentage Return 99-12-31 (After Fees)						Total Risk
				In the Year					Last 5 yrs	Last 3 yrs
				1995	1996	1997	1998	1999		
191080	Baring Global Emerging Markets; Baring International Fund Managers (Ireland) Ltd	Emerging market equity and equity related assets	1.59	−32	10	25	−25	77	25.3	32 (Red)

Source: Premiepensionsmyndigheten (2000).

Notes: The percentage return for the last five years equals the compounded annual growth rate of return for the years 1995 through 1999. The total risk corresponds to an annualized percentage standard deviation of three-year monthly historical fund returns. The total risk is also categorized into five different classes, and colors, with respect to standard deviation; Class 1: very low risk, dark green, and percentage standard deviation in the range 0–2; Class 2: low risk, light green, and 3–7; Class 3: average risk, yellow, and 8–17; Class 4: high risk, orange, and 18–24; Class 5: very high risk, red, and 25+.

represented by a simplified graph displaying a jagged red line for very risky or a flat green line for very low risk. There are five risk categories of this kind. In addition, each fund has a number representing the fund's annualized standard deviation over the past thirty-six months. If, for some reason, no menu choice is actively elected, the participant's money is invested in the default which is the Seventh Swedish Pension Fund; this is an equity fund run by the government. The accrued amount from the PPM part will be paid out on a monthly basis to the individual at the time of retirement.

In total, 18.5 percent of the annual pension-based income for each individual is invested to finance this system, and all annual income from the age of 16 is included. Yet there is a contribution crediting limit: individuals who earn more than 7.5 income 'base amounts'[1] per year are only credited with 18.5 percent of 7.5 income base amounts, even though they still pay the contribution on their entire pension-based income.[2] The first pension investments in the PPM system, in October 2000, involved 4.4 million individuals. At that time, workers' initial contribution was set at 2 percent of pay for 1997–8 and 2.5 percent for 1999 and 2000. The average amount invested was 12,651 SEK for the entire population and 13,506 SEK for those who made an active investment election;[3] the maximum invested was 26,202 SEK.

When the PPM system was introduced, the government and the mutual fund industry launched a massive advertising campaign (Cronqvist and Thaler 2004; Cronqvist 2006). Though low on information content (level of fees, risks, etc.), the ads did help create a positive image of investing in financial markets. More than 86 percent of all investors were exposed to TV ads, 75 percent were exposed to some advertising in print media, 59 percent saw some kind of outdoor ads, and 36 percent listened to radio ads (Cronqvist 2006). Accordingly, virtually the entire population was exposed to information about investing in financial markets at the time of the PPM launch.

Figure 12-1 shows how the Swedish stock market peaked in March 2000 showing a 15-month gain of 141 percent (January 1999–March 2000). In the second half of 2000 (when the PPM was introduced), the market fell 20 percent, and it then continued to fall for the first 6 months of 2001, dropping about 15 percent further.

About 6 percent of our sample population was invested directly in the stock market in June 30, 1999. This figure increased to 8.5 percent by June 2000 and further to 9 percent by the end of 2000 and 9.35 percent by June 2001. Thus, our three dates after this extreme bull market show an increase in stock market participation. This increased interest for the stock market could be a delayed reaction of the 1999 bull market. But it is also possible that rising interest in the stock market despite the bear market of 2000–1 can be attributed to the substantial marketing

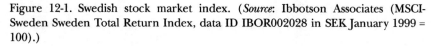

Figure 12-1. Swedish stock market index. (*Source*: Ibbotson Associates (MSCI-Sweden Sweden Total Return Index, data ID IBOR002028 in SEK January 1999 = 100).)

campaigns in 2000 encouraging individuals to make an active choice in PPM.

The Data

To analyze investment choices under the PPM model, we have collected data from three different sources: investment allocations in the PPM system, investor stock market holdings' and investor demographics. Our sample is a representative cross section of the Swedish workforce, whose PPM investment choices have been linked to individual demographic data collected by Statistics Sweden for the year 2000. This linked data-set makes it possible to study investment behavior in great detail.

Asset Allocation Information

Data on individual retirement accounts are collected from PPM, and they indicate all individual choices made from the introduction of the system until October 2004. Both the transaction date and clearing date are known. We also know the universe of funds that was available to investors at each point in time. Thus, for each individual, there is information on the amount invested in each fund, and in which funds the individual invested. Approximately two-thirds of the 4.4 million participants in PPM made an active investment decision. For these individuals, we can investigate the exact allocation of assets in their portfolios. The remaining third did not make an active investment decision, so their money was defaulted into the government-run equity fund.

Portfolio Data

For each investor, we have detailed information about individual stockholdings, mutual funds, bank accounts, real estate, and other types of wealth for the period 1995–2000. The Security Register Center (VPC or Vardepapperscentralen) have data on both stocks held directly and in a street name, including holdings of US-listed ADRs. In addition, SIS Ägarservice AB collects information on the ultimate owners of shares held via trusts, foreign holding companies, and the like (cf. Sundin and Sundquist 2002). Overall, the records provide information about the owners of 98 percent of the market capitalization of publicly traded Swedish companies. For the median company, we have information about 97.9 percent of the equity, and in the worst case, 81.6 percent of market capitalization of the company. The data provided by SIS Ägarservice AB are linked by Statistics Sweden to the demographic data described below.

Additional Data

We also use data on demographic statistics reported by Statistics Sweden, the Swedish version of the US Census Bureau. Data sources include HEK 2000 (a report on household economics), IoF 2000 (a report on individual and household measures of income), and SUN 2000 (a report on educational status). These three reports represent a cross section of the Swedish population and contain detailed information including the amount of foreign assets held per person by asset class. The data also describe individuals' demographic status in 2000, at the time the initial PPM choice was made. We also have information on the investor's age as of December 31, 2000, whether the investor is an immigrant, his income, and net wealth,[4] if the investor lives in an urban or rural area or small town, the investor's education level and major, his occupation, sex, and marital status. Excluding individuals too young or too old to make a selection in the PPM system in 2000, the sample includes 15,651 individuals, of whom 10,373 made an active choice.

Preliminary descriptive statistics appear in Table 12-2, where we note that the average investor holds 2.60 funds (conditional on making an active choice, 3.47 funds). Men hold slightly fewer funds than women; though the difference is statistically significant, the economic magnitude is only

TABLE 12-2 Descriptive Statistics for PPM Investors

	Mean	Std. Dev.
ENTERSIM	0.010	0.010
ENTERAFTER	0.012	0.012
EXITSIM	0.053	0.057
EXITAFTER	0.086	0.079
Choice	0.669	0.221
Equity	0.901	0.170
Number of funds	2.602	1.409
Age	43.028	11.111
Swede	0.887	0.316
Income	202,269	188,121
Net wealth	444,108	3,174,320
Urban	0.354	0.478
Town	0.356	0.479
Rural	0.289	0.454
Education: less then high school	0.181	0.385
Education: high school	0.513	0.500
Education: college	0.306	0.461
Major: social science	0.262	0.440
Major: engineering	0.239	0.426
Major: medical	0.134	0.341
Major: other	0.365	0.482
Occ: public sector	0.287	0.452
Occ: private sector	0.558	0.500
Occ: self-employed	0.048	0.213
Occ: other	0.108	0.310
Male	0.509	0.500
Married	0.778	0.415

Source: Authors' calculations.

Notes: $N = 15,497$. Key outcomes are ENTERSIM if between July 2000 and December 2000; ENTERAFTER takes the value of 1 if a person entered the stock market between January 2001 and June 2001; both are set to 0 otherwise. EXITSIM (EXITAFTER) equals 1 if person exited the stock market between July 2000 and December 2000 (January 2001 and June 2001) and 0 otherwise. CHOICE is set to 1 if investor made an active choice in the PPM system, 0 otherwise; Equity represents the amount invested in equity divided by the total amount held in the PPM. Number of funds represents the number of funds included in the participant's PPM portfolio. Age refers to the participant's age as of December 31, 2000; Sweden is set to 1 if the individual was born in Sweden, 0 else; INCOME is the individual's net income in 2000; NET WEALTH is the individual's net wealth, which is the market value of financial wealth + real estate − debt; Urban, Town, and Rural are set to 1 respectively if the individual lived in one of the three major cities in Sweden, any smaller town, or on the countyside, correspondingly; education level is split into three dummies set to 1 if the person's schooling was less than, equal to, or more than high school, correspondingly; Education major is split into four dummies set to 1 if person's higher education major was social science, engineering, medical, or other; occupation is split into four dummies set to 1 if the person was employed in the public sector, private sector, self employed, or unknown employment/unemployed; Male is set to 1 if the person was male; and Married is set to 1 if the person was married.

about 0.02. Younger investors (under age 40) hold more funds than older persons (3.27 and 3.71 respectively). Note that while portfolios of older investors are less exposed to equity and less risky. Older investors hold 80 percent of their portfolios in equity versus 86 percent for young investors. Turning to transactions, investors on average rebalance their portfolios 1.64 times over our time period (with the median of 1, a 99th percentile of 8 and a maximum of 155). This frequency is lower for men (women rebalance 1.59 times per year, while the men did so 1.70 times per year).[5]

Investment Patterns in the PPM System

In what follows, we first analyze how investors choose the funds in their retirement account. Some investors choose specific combinations of equity and bond funds. We call them active investors. Others do not make a deliberate choice but instead opt for the default government-run equity fund. Next, we focus on stock market participation to test the link between the choice in the PPM system and stock market participation. We show that for the case of the active investors being active in their retirement choice increases the probability of stock market participation. That is, an individual who did not participate in the stock market is more likely to enter it once he has been presented with the new pension scheme. This effect is not only statistically significant but also economically relevant.

Choice of Funds

The key question of interest is whether PPM participation affects stock market participation. We first approach this by providing descriptive statistics about how investors select their funds in the PPM system. Some investors make a deliberate choice and choose specific combinations of equity and bond funds, while others just opt for the default. This allows us to define active and passive investors.

Table 12-3 describes entry and exit rates, defined as ratio of people who entered or exited the stock market between two different periods. Our focus is on two periods: simultaneous with the rollout of the PPM system (January 7, 2000–December 31, 2000) and after the PPM system was in place (January 1, 2001–June 30, 2001). Panel A compares people who actively choose funds in the PPM system to those who did not, whereas more than 66 percent of the households made a deliberate decision. These households were younger, in general. If we concentrate on ENTERSIM, one can see that entry rate is almost two times larger (1.25% vs. 0.65%) among the people who made active choice. This difference is also statistically significant (p-value of both t-test and Wilcoxon test is 0.0009). Similar

TABLE 12-3 Entry and Exit Rates as Function of PPM Investment Choice

	ENTERSIM		ENTERAFTER		EXITSIM		EXITAFTER	
	N	Mean	N	Mean	N	Mean	N	Mean
Panel A: Entry and Exit Rates as Function of Active Choice								
Choice								
0 (No choice)	4,792	0.0065	4,783	0.0084	332	0.0663	341	0.1114
1 (Active choice)	9,378	0.0125	9,314	0.0135	995	0.0533	1,059	0.0784
Test of the difference								
t-statistic		−3.3285		−2.6921		0.8877		1.8907
p-value		0.0009		0.0071		0.3748		0.0589
Wilcoxon' Z		−3.3266		−2.6919		0.8881		1.8890
p-value		0.0009		0.0071		0.3747		0.0589
Panel B: Entry and Exit Rates as Function of Number of Funds Chosen								
Number of funds								
1	6,140	0.0085	6,119	0.0083	490	0.0633	511	0.0978
2	1,272	0.0071	1,266	0.0150	120	0.0250	126	0.0556
3	1,997	0.0080	1,993	0.0085	212	0.0566	216	0.1157
4	1,872	0.0107	1,865	0.0123	173	0.0751	180	0.0611
5	2,889	0.0177	2,854	0.0196	332	0.0482	367	0.0763
Test of the difference between groups 1 and 5								
t-statistic		−3.8360		−4.5921		0.9126		1.1067
p-value		0.0001		0.0000		0.3617		0.2687
Wilcoxon' Z		−3.8330		−4.5870		0.9130		1.1070
p-value		0.0001		0.0000		0.3614		0.2685
Test of the difference between groups 1 and combined 2, 3, 4, and 5								
t-statistic		−2.0229		−3.3178		−0.8139		−1.1525
p-value		0.0431		0.0009		0.4158		0.2493
Wilcoxon' Z		−2.0229		−3.3170		−0.8140		−1.1530
p-value		0.0431		0.0009		0.4156		0.2492

This table reports entry and exit rates for subgroups of people who actively selected funds in the PPM system, and the ones who did not (Panel A); and subgroups of people who choose different number of funds (Panel B).

Source: Authors' calculations.

Note: For variable definitions, see Table 12-2.

results were obtained for period after introduction of PPM system (January 2001–June 2001). People who made active choice 61 percent more likely to enter stock market during this period (1.35% vs. 0.84%, *p*-value of mean and median test is 0.0071). At the same time, active participation in PPM system does not affect exit rate strongly. Panel B divides the sample into subgroups of investors who choose different numbers of funds. As in Panel A, people who choose multiple funds are more likely than people who choose only one fund to enter the stock market and same chances to exit.

Pension Choice and Stock Market Participation

We next focus on the link between PPM system choice and stock market participation. We focus both on investors who did participate in the stock market and look at their exit rates, and also those who did not participate initially and evaluate their later entry rates. These we model as a function of investors' demographic characteristics and choices made in the PPM system. The sample is affected by selection bias inasmuch as people with certain demographic characteristics are more likely to invest in the stock market. To deal with this issue, we estimate a two-stage Heckman-type probit selection model for the decision to enter the stock market (cf. van de Ven and van Praag 1981). That is, we first estimate the probability that the investor holds equity already at time $t-1$, and then, conditional on that behavior, we relate it to the decision to enter the stock market. For example, for investor j with characteristics x_j, z_j we estimate the following equation:

$$\text{Entry}_j = (x_j\beta + u_{1j} > 0).$$

The selection equation is $z_j\gamma + u_{2j} > 0$, where $u_1 \sim N(0, 1)$, $u_2 \sim N(0, 1)$ and $\text{corr}(u_1, u_2) = \rho$. Choice in the pension scheme is posited to depend on a number of investor demographic characteristics, income, wealth, residential location, and education.[6]

The dependent variables of most interest are indicators of individuals exiting or entering the stock market during this period, and a continuous variable for how much the individual investor has increased or decreased her investments. In particular, ENTERSIM takes the value of 1 if the investor entered the stock market simultaneous with the PPM launch (July 1, 2000–December 31, 2000), while ENTERAFTER takes the value of 1 if the person entered the stock market after the launch (January 1, 2000–June 30, 2001). Similarly, EXITSIM (EXITAFTER) takes the value of 1 if the person exited the stock market between July 1, 2000 and December 31, 2000 (or January 1, 2001–June 30, 2001).

The behavioral variables on which we focus most are choice, equity, and number of funds. We refer to these as proxies for activity in the PPM system. Choice takes on a value of 1 if the investor made an active choice in the PPM system, and equals 0 otherwise. Equity represents the fraction invested in equity out of the total amount invested in PPM. Number of funds refers to the number of funds included in the investor's PPM portfolio. Also included are other demographic factors defined as above.

Table 12-4 illustrates one specification for the period during the intro-duction of PPM system (July 2000–December 2000) and a second after the introduction of the PPM system (January 2001–June 2001). We start by considering the decision to enter the stock market, and we provide results for models with and without a Past Stock Market Participation Dummy (set equal to one if investor held equity in December 1998, June 1999, or December 1999). The results confirm that those who made a deliberate choice under the PPM system have a higher probability of stock market participation. In particular, there is always a positive relationship between our three proxies for activity in the PPM system, namely Choice, Equity, and Number of funds, and the ensuing decision to enter the stock market. This result is robust, holding for all specifications and cases presented. Not only is it statistically significant but also economically relevant; thus making a deliberate choice under the PPM increases the probability of stock market participation by 0.28 percent (see bold value in row one, column five). This is equivalent to a 24 percent increase with respect to the unconditional mean. Analogously, a one standard deviation rise in the number of funds that the investor selects for his retirement portfolio raises the probability of stock market entry by 0.12 percent (bold value in row two, column 11). This represents a 10 percent increase with respect to the unconditional mean. Finally, an increase in the fraction invested in equity funds by one standard deviation increases the probability of stock market entry by 0.4 percent. This represents a 34 percent increase with respect to the unconditional mean. These results hold for both after the introduction of PPM system (January 2001–June 2001) and also during the PPM introduction (July 2000–December 2000; and point estimates in this earlier period are somewhat larger).

We now consider the decision to exit the market with estimates appearing in Table 12-5. Here, results indicate that making a deliberate choice under the PPM system is either irrelevant to the investor's exit decision, or it reduces the probability of leaving the stock market (after the introduction of PPM system). The results for the period of July 2000–December 2000 (Panel A) show that our three proxies for activity in the PPM system do not affect the exit decision at this point. In Panel B, after the introduction of PPM (January 2001–June 2001), there is always a negative relationship between our three proxies for activity in the PPM system and the probability of leaving the stock market. This result holds across all the different specifi-cations. The results are strongly statistically significant, but the economic significance is modest. In particular, making a deliberate choice in the retirement account reduces the probability of leaving the stock market by 0.22 percent, or 2.8 percent of unconditional mean. Analogously, an increase in the number of funds that the investor selects for his retirement portfolio by one standard deviation decreases the probability of leaving the

TABLE 12-4 Effect of PPM Choice on Entry Decision

	Est.	t-stat	ME	Est.	t-stat	ME	Est.	t-stat	ME	Est.	t-stat	ME
Panel A: Decision to Enter the Stock Market: July 2000–December 2000												
Decision to participate in the stock market (ENTERSIM)												
Choice	0.212	(4.25)	0.0038	0.201	(3.84)	**0.0039**						
Number of funds							0.056	(5.60)	0.0011	0.053	(4.80)	0.0011
Equity							0.286	(4.98)	0.0054	0.279	(4.67)	0.0055
Past Participation Dummy	1.083	(10.08)	0.0763				1.100	(9.96)	0.0773	1.094	(10.16)	0.0755
Pseudo R^2	0.094			0.072			0.097			0.076		
Panel B: Decision to Enter the Stock Market: January 2001–July 2001												
Decision to participate in the stock market (ENTERAFTER)												
Choice	0.127	(2.51)	**0.0028**	0.1253	(2.79)	**0.0028**						
Number of funds							0.0570	(3.81)	**0.0012**	0.0533	(3.99)	0.0012
Equity							0.1810	(2.39)	**0.0039**	0.1732	(2.55)	0.0040
Past Participation Dummy	0.604	(4.36)	0.0327				0.6786	(4.63)	0.0339	0.6494	(4.70)	0.0332
Pseudo R^2	0.103			0.096			0.107			0.104		

This table reports the results of two-stage Heckman-type Probit selection models for the decision to enter the stock market during the introduction of PPM system (July 2000–December 2000, reported in Panel A) versus after the introduction of PPM system (January 2001–June 2001, reported in Panel B). We report the result for two specifications with and without Past Participation Dummy (which is equal to 1 if the person held equity in our sample in December 1998, June 1999, or December 1999. Other control variables are described in Table 12-2. Marginal effects (ME) are given for the second stage; t-statistics are reported in parentheses.

Source: Authors' calculations.

Notes: All controls from Table 12-2 and an intercept are also included in the model.

TABLE 12-5 Effect of PPM Choice on Exit Decision

	Est.	t-stat	ME	Est.	t-stat	ME	Est.	t-stat	ME	Est.	t-stat	ME	Est.	t-stat	ME	Est.	t-stat	ME
Panel A: Decision to Exit the Stock Market; July–December 2000																		
Decision to participate in the stock market (EXITSIM)																		
Choice	−0.030	(−0.40)	−0.0002	−0.052	(−0.55)	−0.0005												
Number of funds							−0.009	(−0.23)	0.0000	−0.004	(−0.09)	0.0000						
Equity	0.427	(6.24)	0.0033				0.427	(5.97)	0.0033				0.113	(1.21)	0.0007911	0.104	(1.43)	0.0011
Past Participation Dummy													0.400	(5.48)	0.0039884			
Pseudo R^2	0.086			0.053			0.085			0.052			0.086			0.053		
Panel B: Decision to Exit the Stock Market; January–July 2001																		
Decision to participate in the stock market (EXITAFTER)																		
Choice	−0.215	(−3.19)	−0.0022	−0.215	(−3.18)	**−0.0021**	−0.068	(−2.05)	−0.0007	**−0.069**	(−2.09)	−0.0006						
Number of funds																		
Equity													−0.315	(−3.74)	**−0.0031**	−0.315	(−3.79)	**−0.0030**
Past Participation Dummy	−0.075	(−0.85)	−0.0007				−0.064	(−0.69)	−0.0006				−0.075	(−0.84)	−0.0007			
Pseudo R^2	0.047			0.046			0.052			0.048			0.051			0.047		

This table reports the results of two-stage Heckman-type Probit selection models for the decision to exit the stock market during the introduction of PPM system (July 2000–December 2000, reported in Panel A) and after the introduction of PPM system (January 2001–June 2001, reported in Panel B). We report the results for two specifications with and without Past Participation Dummy which is equal to 1 if the person held equity in sample in December 1998, June 1999, and December 1999. Other control variables are our described in Table 12-2. We report marginal effects (ME); *t*-statistics are reported in parentheses.

Source: Authors' calculations.

Notes: All controls from Table 12-2 and an intercept are also included in the model.

stock market by 0.07 percent (about 0.8% of unconditional mean). Finally, an increase in the fraction invested in equity funds by one standard deviation reduces the probability of leaving the stock market by 0.31 percent. This represents a 3.9 percent decrease with respect to the unconditional mean.[7]

Overall, then, the findings suggest a sort of 'learning effect'. That is investors afforded the choice to invest their retirement money in equity funds and then make a deliberate choice to do so, are more likely to enter the stock market.

Pension Choice and Stock Market Participation: Controlling for Endogeneity.

Next we consider the issue of endogeneity which arises because the investor determines the value for his Choice, Equity, and Number of Funds variables jointly with the decision to participate in the stock market. To correct for this, we adopt an Instrumental Variables (IV) methodology. Specifically, we estimate both a two-Stage Least Squares (2SLS) linear probability model and an IV-Probit model of the decision to enter the stock market, as a function of our three proxies for activity in the PPM system as well as the other controls. We use as instruments Age and Age squared.

Our estimates appear in Tables 12-6 and 12-7, where the explanatory variable in Panel A is the active choice decision under the PPM system; in Panel B, it is the number of funds chosen; and in Panel C, it is the fraction of equity in the chosen portfolio. As in the previous case, we estimate a specification for the period during the introduction of PPM system (July 2000–December 2000) and after the introduction of the PPM system (January 2001–June 2001).

As before, there is a positive relationship between the three proxies for PPM activity and the ensuing decision to enter the stock market. Furthermore, this result holds across all specifications and is economically significant. For example, an increase in the probability of making a deliberate choice in the retirement account triples the unconditional probability of stock market entry. Marginal effect related to making active choice is about 3 percent, which is three times unconditional probability of entry. Similar numbers for the effect of choosing multiple funds and choosing larger fraction of equity are 35 percent and 170 percent increase with respect to unconditional probability of entry, correspondingly. These results hold for both the period during the introduction of PPM system (July 2000–December 2000) and afterward as well (January 2001–June 2001).[8]

TABLE 12-6 Effect of PPM Choice on Entry Decision: IV Estimates

	Entry June–Dec 2001 (ENTERSIM)							Entry Jan–June 2001 (ENTERAFTER)						
	First Stage		2SLS		Probit			First Stage		2SLS		Probit		
	Est.	t-stat	Est.	t-stat	Est.	t-stat	ME	Est.	t-stat	Est.	t-stat	Est.	t-stat	ME
Panel A: Decision to Enter Stock Market and Make Active Choice in PPM System														
Choice			0.0337	(1.91)	1.1501	(4.09)	0.0316			0.0576	(1.96)	1.6570	(7.24)	0.1149
Past Participation Dummy	0.0333	(0.71)	0.1256	(11.66)	0.9555	(4.89)	0.0878	0.0413	(0.58)	0.0669	(5.32)	0.4576	(2.41)	0.0577
	F-test of instruments		*Hansen OIR Test*		*Wald Exogeneity Test*			*F-test of instruments*		*Hansen OIR Test*		*Wald Exogeneity Test*		
	F-stat.	p-val	Hansen J	p-val	χ^2	p-val		F-stat.	p-val	Hansen J	p-val	χ^2	p-val	
	31.52	0.000	1.528	0.2164	8.300	0.004		29.78	0.000	0.161	0.688	22.020	0.000	
Panel B: Decision to Enter the Stock Market and Number of Funds Chosen in PPM System														
Number of funds			0.0048	(1.77)	0.1806	(3.49)	0.0038			0.0066	(1.94)	0.2590	(3.49)	0.0062
Past Participation Dummy	0.0363	(0.31)	0.1265	(11.89)	1.0777	(7.76)	0.0795	0.0893	(0.59)	0.0687	(5.62)	0.6906	(2.27)	0.0373
	F-test of instruments		*Hansen OIR Test*		*Wald Exogeneity Test*			*F-test of instruments*		*Hansen OIR Test*		*Wald Exogeneity Test*		
	F-stat.	p-val	Hansen J	p-val	χ^2	p-val		F-stat.	p-val	Hansen J	p-val	χ^2	p-val	
	213.78	0.000	0.711	0.399	6.410	0.011		211.75	0.000	0.015	0.9033	6.470	0.011	

Panel C: Decision to Enter the Stock Market and Fraction of Equity Chosen in PPM System

Equity	0.0393 (0.88)	0.0211 (1.79)	0.8268 (4.11)	0.0179	0.0429 (0.64)	0.0270 (1.99)	1.0972 (4.35)	0.0317
Past Participation Dummy		0.1259 (11.80)	1.0442 (7.09)	0.0765		0.0680 (2.10)	0.6407 (2.32)	0.0382

F-test of instruments		Hansen OIR Test		Wald Exogeneity Test		F-test of instruments		Hansen OIR Test		Wald Exogeneity Test	
F-stat.	p-val	Hansen J	p-val	χ^2	p-val	F-stat.	p-val	Hansen J	p-val	χ^2	p-val
155.78	0.000	0.503	0.478	8.230	0.004	152.56	0.000	0.122	0.7253	13.270	0.000

This table reports the result of 2SLS linear probability model and IV-Probit estimates of a decision to enter the stock market as a function of active choice decision (Panel A), number of funds chosen (Panel B), and fraction of equity in the chosen portfolio (Panel C). We used as instruments Age and squared Age of the investor. We report the results of first stage estimate and joint F-test of significance of the instruments. For 2SLS linear probability model, we report Hansen over identifying restrictions test. For IV-probit estimates, we report Wald test of exogeneity. We report marginal effects (ME) for probit estimates; t-statistics are reported in parentheses.

Source: Authors' calculations.

Notes: All controls from Table 12-2 and an intercept are also included in the model.

TABLE 12-7 Effect of PPM Choice on Exit Decision: IV Estimates

	Exit June–Dec 2000 (EXITSIM)							Exit Jan–June 2001 (EXITAFTER)						
	First Stage		2SLS		Probit			First Stage		2SLS		Probit		
	Est.	t-stat	Est.	t-stat	Est.	t-stat	ME	Est.	t-stat	Est.	t-stat	Est.	t-stat	ME
Panel A: Decision to Exit the Stock Market and Active Choice in PPM System														
Choice			0.4046	(1.31)	2.2024	(2.88)	0.4726			−0.0835	(−0.29)	−0.7281	(−0.59)	−0.1334
Past Participation Dummy	−0.0061	(−0.91)	0.0525	(3.15)	0.1701	(2.76)	0.0578	−0.0082	(−1.22)	−0.0114	(−0.73)	−0.0719	(−0.83)	−0.0101
Panel B: Decision to Exit the Stock Market and Number of Funds Chosen in PPM System														
Number of funds			0.0396	(1.96)	0.3858	(3.02)	0.0607			−0.0243	(−1.05)	−0.1462	(−1.98)	−0.0199
Past Participation Dummy	0.0542	(1.47)	0.0465	(3.30)	0.3368	(3.56)	0.0564	0.0590	(1.74)	−0.0062	(−0.39)	−0.0463	(−0.51)	−0.0063

Tests — Exit June–Dec 2000 (EXITSIM)

Panel A:

F-test of instruments		Hansen OIR Test		Wald Exogeneity Test	
F-stat.	p-val	Hansen J	p-val	χ^2	p-val
2.28	0.103	0.981	0.322	36.72	0.000

Panel B:

F-test of instruments		Hansen OIR Test		Wald Exogeneity Test	
F-stat.	p-val	Hansen J	p-val	χ^2	p-val
26.660	0.000	0.154	0.695	7.800	0.005

Tests — Exit Jan–June 2001 (EXITAFTER)

Panel A:

F-test of instruments		Hansen OIR Test		Wald Exogeneity Test	
F-stat.	p-val	Hansen J	p-val	χ^2	p-val
2.33	0.0977	2.96	0.085	0.170	0.169

Panel B:

F-test of instruments		Hansen OIR Test		Wald Exogeneity Test	
F-stat.	p-val	Hansen J	p-val	χ^2	p-val
25.480	0.000	1.911	1.669	5.320	0.021

Panel C: Decision to Exit the Stock Market and Fraction of Equity Chosen in PPM System

Equity	0.2415 (1.77)	1.9007 (5.46)	0.4385		−0.1114 (−0.76)	−0.6713 (−1.74)	−0.0915
Past	−0.0107 (−1.29)	0.0517 (3.57)	0.2976 (3.57)	0.0715 (−1.90) −0.0131	−0.0109 (−0.70)	−0.0687 (−0.76)	−0.0093
Participation Dummy							

F-test of instruments		Hansen OIR Test		Wald Exogeneity Test		F-test of instruments		Hansen OIR Test		Wald Exogeneity Test	
F-stat.	p-val	Hansen J	p-val	χ^2	p-val	F-stat.	p-val	Hansen J	p-val	χ^2	p-val
9.350	0.000	0.431	0.511	18.350	0.000	9.380	0.000	1.900	0.168	1.100	0.294

This table reports the result of 2SLS linear probability model and IV-probit estimates of a decision to exit the stock market as a function of active choice decision (Panel A), number of funds chosen (Panel B), and fraction of equity in the chosen portfolio (Panel C). We used as instruments Age and squared Age of the investor. We report the results of first stage estimate and joint *F*-test of significance of the instruments. For 2SLS linear probability model, we report Hansen over identifying restrictions test. For IV-probit estimates, we report Wald test of exogeneity. We report marginal effects (ME) for Probit estimates, and *t*-statistics are reported in parentheses.

Source: Authors' calculations.

Notes: All controls from Table 12-2 and an intercept are also included in the model.

We now consider the decision to exit the market. When endogeneity is properly controlled, it is interesting that the results for the period July 2000–December 2000 now show a strong positive impact of our proxies for activity in PPM on the decision to exit the stock market. It is consistent with some participants in the stock market (probably bubble era entries) being induced by the PPM publicity campaigns to review stock market risks (or perhaps they simply looked at their holdings which dropped 20% in value during that period) and decided to leave. The decision to leave the stock market after the introduction of the PPM system proves to be unrelated to the PPM behavior. Results in Table 12-7 are weaker than those reported in Table 12-5; further the 2SLS estimates lose significance, as do the estimates based on the Choice variable (Panel A). The estimates based on the Number of Funds and the Fraction of Equity are, however, still negative and significant.

Overall, these findings again support a 'learning effect'. In other words, exposure to decision-making about risky choices educates people. Those who otherwise would not have made risky decisions are thereby induced to participate in the stock market.

A Counterfactual Test

Next we perform a counterfactual experiment to test whether our main explanatory variables—Choice, Number of Funds, and Equity—might proxy for some individual-specific characteristics that are not necessarily related to the introduction of the PPM system. That is, it might be that people who make a deliberate selection of pension assets, or people that invest most of their contributions in equity are also the ones who would in any case participate more in the stock market, regardless of whether PPM is in force.

To address this issue, we re-estimate the same model as before, but now over a different period. Specifically, we select a time prior to the introduction of the PPM, so entry and exit decisions now refer to December 1999–June 2000. The goal is to use the same model as before. We hypothesize that if the decision to participate in the stock market is related to the introduction of the new pension scheme, as opposed to individual-specific characteristics, we would anticipate that the very same variables which explain stock market participation later on would also explain it beforehand. Results in Table 12-8 support our hypothesis. That is, we find no relationship between our main explanatory variables and the decision to enter or exit the stock market. For the control variables, instead, the same relationship holds. This suggests that it was the introduction of the new Swedish retirement scheme that affected stock market behavior as opposed

TABLE 12-8 Placebo Test: Effect of PPM Choice on Entry Decision before PPM System Introduction: IV Estimates

	First Stage		2SLS		Probit		First Stage		2SLS		Probit		First Stage		2SLS		Probit	
	Est.	t-stat	Est.	t-stat	Est.	t-stat	Est.	t-stat	Est.	t-stat	Est.	t-stat	Est.	t-stat	Est.	t-stat	Est.	t-stat
Panel A: Decision to Enter Stock Market from December 1999 to June 2000																		
Choice			0.0091	(0.20)	0.1060	(0.12)			0.0028	(0.56)	0.0448	(0.65)			0.0139	(0.65)	0.2591	(0.86)
Number of funds	0.0509	(0.88)					0.0916	(0.36)					0.0485	(0.87)				
Equity			0.3610	(7.78)	1.4901	(16.40)			0.3612	(7.74)	1.4903	(18.30)			0.3608	(7.73)	1.4835	(18.94)
Past Participation Dummy																		
	F-test of instruments		*Hansen OIR Test*		*Wald Exogeneity Test*		*F-test of instruments*		*Hansen OIR Test*		*Wald Exogeneity Test*		*F-test of instruments*		*Hansen OIR Test*		*Wald Exogeneity Test*	
	F-stat.	p-val	Hansen J	p-val	χ²	p-val	F-stat.	p-val	Hansen J	p-val	χ²	p-val	F-stat.	p-val	Hansen J	p-val	χ²	p-val
	30.310	0.000	1.506	0.220	0.000	0.988	219.110	0.000	1.311	0.252	0.090	0.762	153.720	0.000	1.246	0.264	0.140	0.711
Panel B: Decision to Exit the Stock Market from December 1999 to June 2000																		
Choice			0.0949	(1.29)	0.0983	(1.28)			0.0201	(1.07)	0.3612	(1.87)			0.1166	(1.10)	1.6020	(1.14)
Number of funds	0.0193	(0.49)					0.2074	(1.20)										
Equity			0.0298	(2.56)	0.3442	(4.73)			−0.5894	(−27.96)	−2.1812	(−9.51)			−0.5868	(−27.02)	0.3687	(1.27)
Past Participation Dummy													−0.0016	(−0.03)				
	F-test of instruments		*Hansen OIR Test*		*Wald Exogeneity Test*		*F-test of instruments*		*Hansen OIR Test*		*Wald Exogeneity Test*		*F-test of instruments*		*Hansen OIR Test*		*Wald Exogeneity Test*	
	F-stat.	p-val	Hansen J	p-val	χ²	p-val	F-stat.	p-val	Hansen J	p-val	χ²	p-val	F-stat.	p-val	Hansen J	p-val	χ²	p-val
	4.750	0.009	0.553	0.457	2.470	0.116	19.040	0.009	0.626	0.429	2.250	0.134	9.150	0.000	0.478	0.489	5.940	0.015

This table reports the result of 2SLS linear probability model and IV-Probit estimates of a decision to enter (Panel A) and exit the stock market as a function of PPM choice. The entry and exit referred to the period from December 1999 to June 2000 (prior to PPM introduction). We used as instruments Age and squared Age of the investor. We report the results of first stage estimate and joint F-test of significance of the instruments. For 2SLS linear probability model, we report Hansen over identifying restrictions test. For IV-probit estimates, we report Wald test of exogeneity. Past Participation Dummy is defined as equal to 1 if the person held equity in our sample in December 1998 or June 1999; t statistics are reported in parentheses.

Source: Authors' calculations.

Notes: All controls from Table 12-2 and an intercept are also included in the model.

to participants' characteristics. The findings also provide strong evidence of causality from PPM choice to subsequent investment behaviors.

Discussion and Conclusion

This chapter has focused on how the introduction of a DC retirement system affects investors' propensity to participate directly in the stock market. Our unique evidence on investor patterns before and after the Swedish PPM was introduced permits us to focus on the decision to invest in stocks. Results show how this pattern changes, once investors were permitted to participate in the new pension system. Specifically, we showed that introducing the chance to invest in retirement funds increased peoples' tendency to enter the stock market. We also show that investors who made a deliberate choice of their pension asset allocation also boosted stock market participation once the plan was in place. Investors who previously did not participate in the stock market turn out to have a higher likelihood of entering once they are presented with the new pension scheme.

What this means, we argue, is that requiring workers to invest in mutual funds can act as a triggering device which induces them to enter the stock market as well; being induced to choose among different pension funds appears to 'educate' participants about the stock market. The fact that investors do not treat their retirement account investments as close substitutes for direct equity investment also implies that the adoption of a capitalization-based system does not necessarily crowd out direct investment. This may be of interest to policymakers in the current debate about moving from a pay-as-you-go to a fully funded DC system.

Acknowledgments

Financial support from Jan Wallander and Tom Hedelius Stiftelse is acknowledged by Andrei Simonov and Anders Karlsson.

Notes

[1] For the year 2006, one income base amount equals 44,500 SEK.

[2] For example, for a person with 360,000 SEK as her pension-based income in the year 2006, only 18.5% of 333,750 SEK (7.5 × 44,500) will count toward her pension. In other words, her defined contribution to PPM in 2006 is 8,344 SEK (0.025 × 333,750), which is the maximum contribution per individual for that year. The typical exchange rate in 2000 was 10 SEK for US$1 and for 2006 around 7 SEK/USD.

[3] The slightly higher average for active investors is consistent with Engström and Westerberg (2003) who show that active investors tend to have slightly higher income than the 'default' investors.

[4] Net wealth is made up of the market value of domestic and international financial assets such as bank account, fixed income, mutual funds, stocks and options, and an estimated market value of real estate, minus debt.

[5] The table also shows that the average age of our sample is 43; 89% were born in Sweden; average gross income in 2000 was 202,269 SEK, and average net wealth was 444,108 SEK. Some 29% lived in the countryside, with the remaining 71% living in either one of the three major cities in Sweden (35%) or in a town (36%). Few, 18%, had not completed high school; 51% had completed high school; and 31% went to college. Around one-quarter majored in social science (including economics, law, sociology and so on); another quarter had an engineering major; 13% majored in medicine; and 36% had unspecified majors. Public sector employees made up 29% of the sample, while 56% were in the private sector and only 5% were self-employed. Most (78%) were married and 51% were male. After matching all the different sources, 154 observations were deleted due to missing demographic information.

[6] Specifically, we control on investors' Age in 2000; Swedish nationality; Net Income (in 2000 measured as the logarithm of income in SEK plus 1); Net Wealth defined as the market value of financial wealth and real estate less the value of debt (measured as the logarithm of Net Wealth plus 1); Urban, which takes the value of 1 if the investor lived in one of the three major cities in Sweden; Town takes the value of 1 if the investor lived in a smaller town; and Rural equals 1 if the investor lived in the countryside. We also include three variables which measure educational levels, respectively set to 1 if the person's schooling was less than, equal to, or exceeded high school. We control for participants' education major by using four variables which take on a value of 1 if the investor's higher education major was social science, engineering, medical school, or other respectively. Analogously, we control for occupational differences using four variables set to 1, respectively, if the person was employed in the public sector, private sector, self employed, or had unknown employment or was unemployed. Finally, we include Male and Married controls, respectively set to 1 if the investor were a male and 1 if the investor was married. To achieve identification, in Tables 12-3 and 12-4, we used Age, Age Squared, and set of dummies related to education major in selection equation and not in the second stage.

[7] It is interesting that, for most of our estimates, the correlation coefficients of the Probit and selection equation error terms are not statistically significant (i.e. in our case, selection does not affect the Probit results). This allows us to ignore the issues of selectivity and to concentrate on the issues related to the endogeneity of the choice.

[8] It is worth noticing that the tests of the goodness of instruments show indeed that our instruments do a good job. We report the first-stage estimates and a joint F-test of significance of the instruments; they are jointly significant at the first stage. For the 2SLS linear probability model, we report Hansen over identifying restrictions test. For IV-probit estimates we report Wald test of exogeneity. For 2SLS estimates, the test of over identified restrictions fails to reject the model.

References

Barberis, N. and Huang, M. (2001). 'Mental Accounting, Loss Aversion, and Individual Stock Returns', *Journal of Finance*, 56: 1247–92.

Cronqvist, H. (2006). 'Advertising and Portfolio Choice', Ohio State University, Fisher College of Business Working Paper.

—— and Thaler, R. H. (2004). 'Design Choices in Privatized Social Security Systems: Learning from the Swedish Experience', *American Economic Review*, 94(2): 424–8.

Engström, S. and Westerberg, A. (2003). 'Which Individuals Make Active Investment Decisions in the New Swedish Pension System?', *Journal of Pension Economics and Finance*, 2(3): 225–45.

Premiepensionsmyndigheten (2000). Fondkatalog för din premiepension.

Sunden, A. (2000). 'How Will Sweden's New Pension System Work?', *Issue Brief* No. 3, March. Chestnut Hill, MA: Boston College, Center for Retirement Research.

Sundin, A. and Sundqvist, S.-I. (2002). 'Owners and Power in Sweden's Listed Companies', *SIS Ägarservice AB*.

Van de ven, W. P. M. M. and van Praag, B. M. S. (1981). 'The Demand for Deductibles in Private Health Insurance: A Probit Model with Sample Selection', *Journal of Econometrics*, 17: 229–52.

Chapter 13

Saving between Cohorts: The Role of Planning

Annamaria Lusardi and Jason Beeler

Employers have increasingly shifted from defined benefit (DB) to defined contribution (DC) pensions in many nations, and particularly in the United States. In DC plans, workers must select not only their contribution levels, but also the allocation of their retirement portfolios. To facilitate these decisions, employers and the government have worked to foster retirement savings and improve financial literacy via retirement seminars and other financial preparedness efforts. At the same time, the financial industry has worked to produce products and tools aimed at improving workers' capacity to undertake retirement planning. Whether these have had any impact on saving is the subject of this chapter.

We address the issue by comparing the saving behavior of two generations: the Early Baby Boomers (EBBs), who were aged 51–56-year old in 2004, and an earlier cohort (hereafter, the original HRS cohort), who were aged 51–56-year old a dozen years before, in 1992. By examining individuals of the same age but born in different years, we can assess how being exposed to different economic circumstances affects saving patterns.[1] We find that most EBBs have accumulated more wealth than the previous generation, but most of this is attributable to appreciation in housing equity. By contrast, measures of nonhousing wealth show little or no change between cohorts. There is also a sizable group of Early Boomers who have less wealth than the HRS cohort; these families are disproportionately those with low educational attainment or minorities. For both cohorts, low wealth may be traced to lack of retirement planning, which translates into low saving rates. At the median, nonplanners hold 20 percent less wealth than planners, but figures are much higher (closer to 45%) for households at lower levels of the wealth distribution.

This chapter proceeds by comparing personal and income characteristics between the earlier and later cohorts. Next, we examine levels and composition of household wealth. We show that wealth is higher for those who plan, but many Boomers have not planned for retirement.

Empirical Approach

This chapter relies on data from the Health and Retirement Study (HRS), comparing the 'Early Boomer' cohort where at least one household member was aged 51–56 in 2004, and the 'original HRS' cohort who were aged 51–56 in 1992.[2] By comparing cohorts of the same age but in different time periods (2004 vs. 1992), we can assess how being born in a different time and having lived in different economic conditions affects financial behavior.[3]

The Early Boomers are particularly important to study as they represent the leading edge of a large generation on the brink of retirement. To carry out the comparison between this cohort and its predecessor, we construct from the surveys variables that are comparable across years. Specifically, the measure of total net worth includes cash, checking, savings, mutual funds and brokerage accounts, bonds, stocks, IRAs, net housing equity, other real estate, net value of own businesses, cars and other vehicles minus debts.[4] Total household income is the sum of labor and capital income, government transfer program income, and other income (gifts, lottery, and so on). All values are expressed in $2004 and statistics are weighted.[5] Questions about wealth and income are asked to the most knowledgeable member in the HRS household regarding financial matters; this individual is termed as the financial respondent hereafter.

Comparing the demographic composition of the two cohorts, many have noted that Early Boomers have greater educational attainment than the HRS cohort; not only are they more likely to have a college degree or more than college education, but also they are less likely to be high-school dropouts. Boomers are also less likely to be married and more likely to have experienced a family breakup, so the fraction of families with children decreased over the time period (cf. Iams et al., this volume; Manchester et al., Chapter 6, this volume; Wolfe et al., Chapter 3, this volume). The proportion of Hispanic households rose from 1992 to 2004 while the proportion of Whites declined.[6] Because wealth varies substantially across demographic groups and it is strongly affected by education, marital status, and race, it is important to keep these changes into account when examining household wealth holdings (see also Appendix Table 13A-1).

Of key interest is a comparison of the distribution of total household income between the EBB and the HRS cohort (Table 13-1). Both mean and median income for Early Boomers was higher than for the original HRS respondents; to the extent that more household income is a proxy for higher permanent income, we would expect EBB wealth to have increased as well. Note, however, that below-median Boomer households had less income than their counterparts in the HRS cohort, perhaps as a result of the stagnation in wages for workers without a college degree during

TABLE 13-1 Distribution of Total Household Income
for Original HRS (1992) and Early
Boomer (2004) Respondents

Percentile	Original HRS	Early Boomers
5th	9,129	6,984
10th	15,484	12,000
25th	31,957	30,000
50th	59,242	62,000
75th	93,272	100,480
90th	137,737	175,000
95th	175,032	238,000
Mean	73,592	85,931
SD	76,610	109,144
N	4,577	2,631

Source: Authors' calculations.

Notes: Respondents/spouses aged 51–56; all figures weighted
using household weights ($2004).

the 1990s (Autor and Katz 1999; Autor et al. 2006). The households at
the bottom of the income distribution are also disproportionately those
with low education, unmarried, and Blacks and Hispanics, it might be
anticipated that those groups would face increasing difficulty accumulating
wealth over time.

The distribution of total net worth and nonhousing wealth is displayed
in Table 13-2. For both groups, the distribution of total net worth is quite
dispersed: that is, there are large differences in wealth even within this
narrow age band. Also, for both the mean and upper quartiles, Boomers
have indeed accumulated more wealth than their earlier counterparts, and
the differences are statistically significant. On the other hand, it would
appear that Boomers in the lower quartile of the wealth distribution accumulated less wealth than the earlier cohort (differences are not statistically
significant). Lowest quartile households are also more likely to be in debt,
for the more recent group.

One big difference for the EBBs is that they experienced a large run-
up in housing prices, particularly during 2002 and 2003. Consequently
Panel B in Table 13-2 explores the possibility that improvements in EBB
wealth could be the result of the appreciation in home equity. In fact,
we see that most households hold little beside housing wealth, for both
generations. Also when we subtract housing equity from total net worth,
we confirm that EBB respondents at the bottom of the wealth distribution
and all the way up to the median hold lower nonhousing wealth than the

TABLE 13-2 Comparing Wealth Distributions for
Original HRS (1992) and Early
Boomer (2004) Respondents

Percentile	Original HRS ($)	EBB ($)
A. *Total net worth*		
5th	0	−3,500
10th	1,346	200
25th	40,769	36,500
50th	136,256	153,200
75th	315,058	403,000
90th	700,128	891,700
95th	1,218,493	1,332,000
Mean	327,715	391,959
SD	738,164	969,128
N	4,577	2,631
B. *Total nonhousing net worth*		
5th	−1481	−7,800
10th	0	0
25th	9,425	8,090
50th	54,799	53,000
75th	188,496	224,400
90th	527,789	609,000
95th	962,676	1,000,870
Mean	239,145	264,526
SD	687,774	849,317
N	4,577	2,631

Source: Authors' calculations.

Notes: Respondents/spouses aged 51–56; all figures
weighted using household weights ($2004).

precursor generation. As a result, much of the rise in EBB wealth can
be attributed to housing equity and the result is statistically significant.
There are no significant differences in mean nonhousing wealth between
cohorts.

The distribution of total net worth in the population hides some important differences across demographic groups highlighted in Table 13-3.
Here the least educated Boomers, along with Blacks, are found to have
much less wealth than the original HRS cohort. Only EBB households with
a college degree (or higher degrees) have higher wealth than HRS cohort
with the same educational attainment. Thus there are many differences in
the pattern of wealth, even after controlling for both age and economic

TABLE 13-3 Distribution of Total Net Worth by Demographic Factors for Original HRS (1992) and Early Boomer (2004) Respondents

	Original HRS (1992) Cohort			Early Baby Boomer (2004) Cohort		
	25th %	Median	75th %	25th %	Median	75th %
Education						
< HS	1,346	41,065	118,214	200	22,500	80,000
HS grad	39,719	121,176	256,489	15,500	92,035	243,000
Some coll.	67,051	166,954	352,084	36,500	133,000	326,000
Coll. grad	117,137	257,163	556,467	140,000	302,000	690,000
> College	149,451	291,361	706,860	171,000	365,800	847,500
Race/ethnicity						
White	60,588	166,550	368,241	64,000	199,000	464,000
Black	337	36,487	115,117	3	25,000	118,500
Hispanic	2,693	46,047	126,562	5,000	55,800	200,000
Marital status						
Married	72,840	173,686	376,319	85,300	223,000	498,000
Not married	2,558	51,836	172,339	3,000	53,500	200,000
Sex						
Male	58,568	166,954	368,943	55,960	196,000	490,000
Female	20,869	102,326	250,431	19,800	104,600	297,500

Source: Authors' calculations.

Notes: Respondents/spouses aged 51–56; all figures weighted using household weights ($2004). Number of observations is 4,577 for the 1992 HRS cohort and 2,631 for the 2004 EBB.

status. Below we show how low wealth can be traced to lack of retirement planning.

We turn now to a comparison of the composition of wealth between these two generations, as illustrated in Table 13-4 and Figure 13-1. This is important in view of the large changes in both the stock and housing market during the 1990s, which could have influenced the wealth of EBB. Clearly, one of the most important assets held by both generations is their housing. Not only did home-ownership increase slightly between the two generations (differences are significant at the 10% level of significance), but also home equity accounts for one-third of total net worth among the EBB. The amount of wealth accounted for by total real estate is close to 50 percent for EBB, while it was 44 percent for the HRS cohort. Thus, exposure to the housing market has increased for the EBB compared to the HRS cohort.

Two other important assets in the portfolios of both EBB and the HRS cohort are stocks and IRAs or Keoghs. Figure 13-2 shows that ownership of

TABLE 13-4 Asset Ownership and Percentage of Wealth Accounted for by Each Asset for Original HRS (1992) and Early Boomer (2004) Respondents

	Checking Account	Stock Owner	IRA Owner	Home Owner	Real Estate	Business Owner
Owns that asset (%)						
Orig. HRS	82.8	30.6	40.6	78.6	24.8	19.0
EBB	86.9	31.0	41.6	80.3	17.5	14.8
t-stat. of diff.	*4.79*	*0.42*	*0.90*	*1.73*	*−7.52*	*−4.70*
(*p*-Value)	(0.00)	(0.67)	(0.37)	(0.08)	(0.00)	(0.00)
Proportion of total net worth (%)						
Orig. HRS	5.6	8.3	7.5	27.0	16.8	16.7
EBB	5.1	12.6	10.6	32.5	14.1	10.3

Source: Authors' calculations.

Notes: The top panel indicates the probability of ownership of each asset in the 1992 HRS cohort ($N = 4,577$) and the EBB ($N = 2,631$). The bottom panel reports the proportion of total net worth accounted for by the assets listed in the first row. All figures are weighted using household weights.

these assets increases slightly between the two cohorts (but the differences are not statistically significant). Most households do not hold large amounts of wealth in stocks and IRAs; the share of wealth accounted for by stocks is 13 and 8 percent among EBB and the HRS cohort, respectively. The

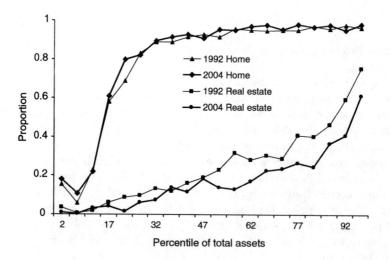

Figure 13-1. Ownership of homes and other real estate for original HRS and Early Boomer Respondents. (*Source*: Authors' calculations.)

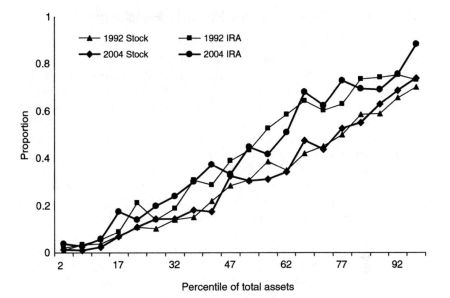

Figure 13-2. Ownership of stocks and IRAs in 1992 and 2004 across the distribution of assets. (*Source*: Authors' calculations.)

share of IRAs or Keoghs is similar but slightly lower in both years. On the assumption that all IRAs were invested in the stock market, more than 23 percent of EBB's wealth would be held in stocks; using similar measures, a lower portion of the HRS cohort's wealth, 156 percent, could have been invested in the stock market. In other words, not only are Early Boomers more concentrated in housing, but also exposure to the stock market has increased compared to the HRS.[7]

In both cohorts, then, a large percentage of households in the lower deciles of the wealth distribution own a home, but stock ownership is high only near the top of the wealth distribution. What this means is that home prices can play a major role in explaining changes in the distribution of wealth between generations. For instance, Lusardi and Mitchell (2006*b*) show that, if home prices by region in 2004 returned to their 2002 levels, which would entail a cut of about 13 percent on average, Boomers would lose approximately 9 percent of total wealth. A similar percentage change in stock prices would have a much smaller impact on Boomer wealth, of only 2 percent (Gustman and Steinmeier 2002). In other words, while Boomers benefited from a remarkable increase in home prices lifting their wealth with respect to the previous generation, they remain vulnerable to housing fluctuations.[8]

Explaining Differences in Wealth Holdings: The Role of Planning

Thus far, we have shown substantial wealth dispersion for both Early Boomers and their HRS precursors, and these wealth patterns persist even for specific demographic groups. Next we ask whether initiatives seeking to foster savings—such as retirement seminars—seem to have any impact on household saving patterns. This question was broached by Lusardi (1999) who pointed out that many households do not plan for retirement, even when they are only a few years from this momentous event. Other studies have confirmed her findings (cf. Yakoboski and Dikemper 1997; Ameriks et al. 2003). And furthermore, Lusardi (1999, 2002, 2003) has demonstrated that *planning* is a powerful determinant of wealth. Specifically, those who report that they do not plan, arrive at retirement with much lower amounts of wealth than those who do.

These issues can be addressed using responses to questions posed in the HRS about retirement planning,[9] comparing self-reported planning efforts across cohorts. We can then link these answers to household wealth. Table 13-5 reports the extent to which people in the two cohorts indicate they have planned for retirement, and the associated levels of wealth they have. We see, first, the proportion of nonplanners (those who have thought about retirement 'hardly at all') fell among Early Boomers, as compared to the original HRS, and this change is statistically significant. Nonetheless, a large fraction of EBB (28 percent) still has not given much thought to

TABLE 13-5 Planning and Total Net Worth for Original HRS (1992) and Early Boomer (2004) Respondents ($2004)

Group	Sample %	25th Percentile ($)	Median ($)	75th Percentile ($)	Mean ($)
A. *Original HRS response to planning question*					
Hardly at all	32.0	10,098	76,906	200,613	224,311
A little	14.3	37,699	126,562	290,149	343,145
Some	24.8	72,032	173,753	367,298	340,681
A lot	28.9	71,393	173,686	356,796	353,523
B. *EBB respondents response to planning question*					
Hardly at all	27.5	9,100	80,000	271,000	315,644
A little	17.0	63,500	173,400	392,000	364,464
Some	27.9	53,000	189,000	447,200	366,074
A lot	27.6	54,000	201,700	470,900	513,211

Source: Authors' calculations.

Notes: Percentages of respondent in each planning group are conditional on being asked the planning question. Respondents/spouses aged 51–56; all figures weighted using household weights ($2004).

retirement; even respondents are rapidly nearing this life change. Second, we note that planning appears to be strongly and positively correlated with wealth holdings: that is, those who plan accumulate much larger amounts of wealth than nonplanners. Overall planners have accumulated up to seven times the amount of wealth of nonplanners. The median planner holds double the amount of wealth than the nonplanner, and differences are even larger at the first quartile of the wealth distribution. Evidently for many, lack of planning is tantamount to lack of saving. Note, however, that there is not much difference in mean net worth between planning categories. This is because there are several extremely wealthy households who have not given any thought to retirement. Later we examine the impact of these households on estimates of the effect of planning. Finally, the planning effect appears strikingly similar, if we compare the two cohorts. In other words, the relationship between planning and wealth does not seem to have been much influenced by changes in home prices, changes in stock prices, or increases in financial education during the 1990s.

Which households are more likely to be planners? Figure 13-3 reports the proportion of planner types across education, sex, race, and cohort. The large majority of those with less than a high-school education are nonplanners. This is the case not only in the HRS cohort but also among EBB. The proportion of nonplanners decreases at higher education levels, but the share of nonplanners across education groups is very similar between the two cohorts. This means that planning is strongly linked to more education, although there is also a sizable fraction of nonplanners among those with college and higher degrees. Since educational attainment has increased during the 1990s, this may explain why the fraction of nonplanners has decreased in the same time period. Similarly, while financial education programs have been undertaken during the 1990s, many low income and minority workers were not exposed to such programs (Lusardi 2004). This may explain why lack of planning tends to persist among these groups over time.

The figure also confirms that planning is also strongly correlated with race/ethnicity: nonplanners are disproportionately concentrated among Blacks and Hispanics. But it is encouraging to see that the proportion of nonplanners among Blacks and Hispanics falls for the later cohort. There are also differences in planning between women and men; women are more likely to be nonplanners in both years. Lusardi and Mitchell (2006a, 20006b) further show that planning is strongly correlated with financial literacy; those who can do simple calculations and understand the working of inflation, interest compounding, and risk diversification, are also more likely to plan.

Do the large differences in wealth across planning type persist when we account for demographic characteristics and income? Has the effect of planning changed over time? To address these questions, we next turn to

A. Planning by education and cohort

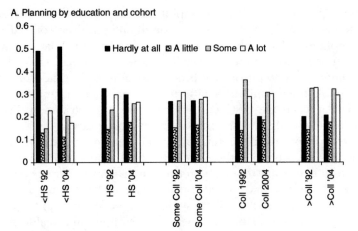

B. Planning by sex and cohort

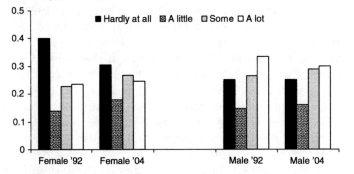

C. Planning by race/ethnicity and cohort

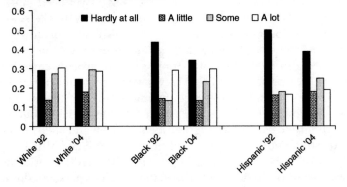

Figure 13-3. Prevalence of retirement planning by demographic characteristics. (*Source*: Authors' calculations.)

a multivariate analysis of the effects of planning on wealth.[10] We perform regressions for each cohort and in the pooled sample, where we combine the data between years.[11] The analysis is structured as follows: we first construct a simple indicator variable indicating 'lack of planning' (called *No planning*), which takes the value 1 when households report they have given 'hardly any thought' to retirement. The models also control for other determinants of wealth including age (and age squared), number of children, marital status, education, sex, race/ethnicity, and whether the financial respondent is partially or fully retired. In addition, we include total household income.[12] Together with race and education, income serves as a proxy for permanent income, that is, lifetime income. Because the distribution of wealth is skewed to the right, we perform quartile regressions rather than Ordinary Least Square (OLS) regressions.

Empirical estimates appear in Table 13-6, where the coefficient on lack of planning is always negative and statistically significant—for each of the three wealth quartiles and in the pooled sample. Estimates are not only sizable but also very similar between cohorts (in the pooled sample, the interaction term between no planning and the 2004 year dummy is mostly not statistically significant). Evidently, lack of planning sharply reduces wealth, even after accounting for demographic characteristics and income. Looking at medians, nonplanners accumulate from $17,000 to $20,000 less wealth than those who do some (a little/a lot) planning, about 20 percent less wealth. Our findings are therefore consistent with previous studies which also show that lack of planning has an effect on wealth (Lusardi 1999, 2003; Ameriks et al. 2003). They are also consistent with other analysis of the 2004 HRS using different measures of planning (Lusardi and Mitchell 2006a).

Other variables in Table 13-6 also have signs consistent with expectations. For example, education and wealth are positively associated, and in particular, in 2004, wealth is concentrated among those with college or higher degrees. Blacks and Hispanics accumulate less wealth than Whites, but the effect is particularly pronounced among Blacks. Family breakups such as divorce and separation are also detrimental to wealth accumulation. The effect of divorce in both the median and third quartile estimates is much larger among the EBB than the previous generation. Having more children also leads to lower wealth holdings.

We also examine a different measure of wealth in Table 13-7, namely total nonhousing wealth.[13] Lack of planning continues to be statistically significant and negative both across years and in the pooled sample. In other words, planning affects other components of wealth beyond housing equity. This result is to be expected, as the effect of planning is similar between cohorts while housing equity increased substantially before 2004.

TABLE 13-6 Quantile Regressions of Net Worth on Planning for Original HRS (1992) and Early Boomer (2004) Respondents

	25th % Orig. HRS	25th % EBB	Median Orig. HRS	Median EBB	75th % Orig. HRS	75th % EBB
A. Two cohorts treated separately						
No planning	−12.495 (3.563)***	−14.390 (4.022)***	−17.233 (4.391)***	−20.025 (8.818)**	−42.059 (7.450)***	−47.362 (21.751)**
High school graduate	13.241 (4.297)***	−5.192 (6.220)	21.493 (5.151)***	2.733 (13.753)	31.133 (8.563)***	9.228 (31.611)
Some college	19.963 (5.101)***	−4.127 (6.403)	38.655 (6.150)***	20.278 (14.134)	73.552 (10.406)***	44.360 (32.831)
College graduate	46.990 (6.344)***	51.527 (7.382)***	83.054 (7.691)***	113.995 (16.195)***	188.936 (13.229)***	237.035 (38.294)***
More than college	70.954 (6.847)***	62.327 (7.966)***	121.807 (8.318)***	169.988 (17.136)***	252.906 (14.153)***	441.711 (40.818)***
Hispanic	−10.389 (5.125)**	−13.237 (6.040)**	−13.289 (6.290)**	−18.879 (13.226)	−25.028 (10.651)**	−45.239 (30.783)
Black	−23.053 (4.058)***	−22.463 (4.656)***	−33.550 (4.875)***	−33.360 (10.032)***	−74.087 (8.062)***	−71.828 (24.231)***
Divorced	−31.876 (4.821)***	−28.229 (4.727)***	−41.669 (5.820)***	−53.389 (10.372)***	−47.224 (9.912)***	−91.769 (25.910)***
Separated	−19.096 (8.528)**	−28.862 (9.091)***	−31.846 (9.942)***	−43.898 (18.951)**	−7.757 (16.231)	−80.357 (44.329)*
Widowed	−13.250 (6.799)*	−18.524 (8.414)**	−25.976 (8.313)***	−21.952 (18.043)	10.445 (14.764)	57.775 (48.528)
Never married	−33.322 (8.055)***	−26.127 (7.075)***	−44.268 (9.714)***	−52.984 (15.418)***	−41.714 (16.204)**	−105.520 (39.251)***
Female	1.985 (3.384)	−9.671 (3.748)***	12.805 (4.171)***	−10.073 (8.174)	23.687 (7.184)***	−13.595 (19.895)
Log of income	31.160 (1.891)***	30.540 (1.449)***	45.063 (2.577)***	46.719 (3.854)***	61.048 (5.283)***	61.415 (13.278)***
Adjusted R^2	0.12	0.11	0.15	0.15	0.17	0.17

	25th %	Median	75th %
B. Pooled Sample			
No planning	−11.034 (3.168)***	−11.334 (5.959)*	−30.007 (10.772)***
Year 2004	3.006 (2.836)	13.864 (5.358)***	37.596 (9.680)***
No Plan Year 2004*	−2.689 (5.108)	−16.019 (9.578)*	−20.723 (16.943)
High school graduate	3.737 (3.722)	10.749 (7.082)	23.326 (11.644)**
Some college	4.879 (4.171)	23.152 (7.903)***	58.355 (13.313)***
College graduate	50.173 (5.072)***	104.611 (9.543)***	240.050 (16.590)***
More than college	66.139 (5.588)***	144.543 (10.270)***	384.486 (17.962)***
Hispanic	−10.526 (4.320)**	−16.305 (7.975)**	−40.647 (13.421)***
Black	−24.279 (3.475)***	−36.609 (6.397)***	−76.166 (11.062)***
Divorced	−29.716 (3.791)***	−46.909 (6.954)***	−78.468 (12.459)***
Separated	−21.814 (6.858)***	−33.786 (12.223)***	−56.986 (19.582)***
Widowed	−14.713 (5.918)**	−16.569 (10.908)	20.426 (20.844)
Never married	−27.867 (5.943)***	−48.068 (11.058)***	−85.901 (19.394)***
Female	−4.104 (2.860)	−3.584 (5.256)	5.403 (9.225)
Log of income	31.750 (1.245)***	45.898 (2.779)***	56.276 (6.740)***
Adjusted R^2	0.11	0.15	0.17

* Significant at 10%; ** Significant at 5%; *** Significant at 1%.

Source: Authors' calculations.

Notes: This table reports quantile regressions of total net worth on planning and other determinants of wealth. Net worth is divided by 1,000 and all monetary values are reported in $2004. Regressions include dummies for retirement status (fully and partially retired), number of children, age, and age squared. The total number of observations is 3,727 in 1992 and 2,156 in 2004. Business owners and the top and bottom 1% of the wealth distribution are excluded. Standard errors in parentheses.

TABLE 13-7 Median Regression of Nonhousing Wealth on Planning for Original
HRS (1992) and Early Boomer (2004) Respondents ($2004)

	Orig. HRS	EBB	Pooled Sample
No planning	−9.904 (3.046)***	−9.709 (3.809)**	−4.320 (2.437)*
Year 2004			9.903 (2.197)***
No plan Year 2004*			−7.546 (3.912)*
Adjusted R^2	0.10	0.09	0.13

* Significant at 10%; ** Significant at 5%; *** Significant at 1%.

Source: Authors' calculations.

Notes: This table reports median regressions of nonhousing net worth on planning and other determinants of wealth. Nonhousing wealth is divided by 1,000; all monetary values in $2004. Regressions include all the same explanatory variables as in Table 13.6. The total number of observations is 3,727 in 1992 and 2,156 in 2004. Business owners and the top and bottom 1% of the wealth distribution are excluded. Standard errors in parentheses.

Interpreting the Effect of Planning

The previous estimates show that the effect of planning on wealth is sizable. How do we interpret the effect of lack of planning on wealth? To better understand this effect, Table 13-8 reports median and OLS estimates of lack of planning on net worth. For brevity, only pooled sample results are reported and only for the key variables of interest. It is very interesting that the OLS estimates of lack of planning are barely significant, indicating that the choice of estimation technique is critical to assess the effect of planning and, most importantly, that at high levels of wealth, planning may cease to matter.

TABLE 13-8 OLS and Median Regressions of Net Worth on Planning in Pooled
Sample ($2004)

	OLS	Median
No planning	−5.054 (16.362)	−11.334 (5.959)*
Year 2004	61.832 (11.080)***	13.864 (5.358)***
No plan year 2004*	−29.273 (20.472)	−16.019 (9.578)*
Adjusted R^2	0.20	0.15

* Significant at 10%; ** Significant at 5%; *** Significant at 1%.

Source: Authors' calculations.

Notes: This table reports OLS and median regressions of total net worth on planning and other determinants of wealth in the pooled sample. Net worth is divided by 1,000 and monetary values reported in $2004. Regressions include all the same explanatory variables as in Table 13-6. The total number of observations is 5,883. Business owners and the top and bottom 1% of the wealth distribution in each year are excluded. Standard errors in parentheses.

To understand this finding further, Figure 13-4 provides a graphic of the prevalence of nonplanning by wealth percentile; the figure reports both the point estimates and 95 percent confidence intervals. Note that, up to the 80th percentile of the wealth distribution, estimates are negative; that is, lack of planning leads to lower wealth; and the confidence intervals are narrow enough to make the estimates statistically significant. The downside range of outcomes becomes more negative as we move to higher values of wealth: for households in the HRS cohort in the third decile of wealth, lack of planning is associated with a 30 percent reduction in wealth, while lack

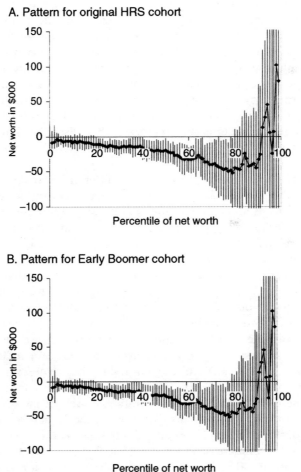

A. Pattern for original HRS cohort

B. Pattern for Early Boomer cohort

Figure 13-4. Estimates of the effect of 'not planning' on net worth by percentile of the wealth distribution. (*Source:* Authors' calculations.)

of planning in the sixth decile is associated with 13 percent lower wealth. Estimates are even stronger for the EBB: lack of planning in the third decile is linked to 45 percent less wealth holdings, while lack of planning in the sixth decile is linked to 25 percent less wealth. The effect of lack of planning reverses as we move close to the top of the wealth distribution. Among EBB, as we move past the third quartile of wealth, the effect of lack of planning first becomes insignificant and then positive rather than negative. The same is true for the HRS cohort, even though the effect happens at higher percentiles of the wealth distribution.[14]

Our next goal is to illustrate that planning actually has an identifiable influence on wealth. In other words, we seek to go beyond correlation to directional causation: if someone were to begin planning tomorrow, would he end up with larger net worth because of it? The difficulty is that planning is potentially endogenous, in which case wealth could also influence planning through reverse causality. One reason reverse causality is a concern is that wealthy individuals may plan more because they have more to gain from planning, driving the significance of the coefficient in the OLS and quantile regressions. There may also be a positive link between planning on wealth due to some unobserved factor such as discipline, impatience, or cognitive ability, which is responsible for the observed correlation between planning and wealth.[15]

For all of these reasons, we require a different estimation technique to test for the causal relationship of interest. One way to account for reverse causality is to use an instrumental variable technique, which poses instruments for planning (Ameriks et al. 2003; Lusardi 2003). By contrast, here we develop a test to examine directly whether reverse causality exists, by instrumenting wealth. The instrument must first provide an exogenous change in wealth, one outside the control of the individual and uncorrelated with his or her preferences. If this exogenous change in wealth is uncorrelated with planning after accounting for all controls, then it allows us to test for reverse causality. Specifically, we run a regression where the dependent variable is lack of planning, and regressors include net worth and all of the demographic variables considered before, including income. Our estimates (Table 13-9) indicate only mild evidence of reverse causality: specifically, the effect of wealth is negative—suggesting that higher wealth tends to increase planning—but the estimate are not always statistically significant (in 2004 they are only significant at the 10 percent level). Most importantly, the estimates are economically small in the separate and the pooled samples; an increase in wealth of $10,000 decreases the probability of not planning 0.4–0.5 percentage points. Given that wealth estimates may be affected by influential observations, we also used a cubic transformation of wealth, but results are similar.[16]

We next undertake Instrumental Variables (IV) estimation, recognizing that net worth is clearly an endogenous variable. The instrument which

TABLE 13-9 OLS Regression of Planning on Total Net Worth ($2004)

	Orig. HRS	EBB	Pooled Sample
Net worth	−0.000054 (0.000027)**	−0.000045 (0.000024)*	−0.000043 (0.000016)***
Year 2004			−0.016 (0.012)
High school grad	−0.080 (0.020)***	−0.117 (0.036)***	−0.107 (0.019)***
Some college	−0.114 (0.024)***	−0.119 (0.036)***	−0.123 (0.020)***
College grad	−0.117 (0.029)***	−0.167 (0.041)***	−0.158 (0.023)***
More than college	−0.103 (0.032)***	−0.134 (0.043)***	−0.127 (0.025)***
Hispanic	0.094 (0.026)***	0.023 (0.037)	0.058 (0.022)***
Black	0.036 (0.023)	0.022 (0.029)	0.027 (0.018)
Divorced	−0.010 (0.021)	0.051 (0.024)**	0.037 (0.015)**
Separated	0.070 (0.039)*	0.053 (0.051)	0.069 (0.031)**
Widowed	0.035 (0.031)	0.056 (0.043)	0.056 (0.025)**
Never married	0.044 (0.036)	0.067 (0.039)*	0.064 (0.025)**
Female	0.087 (0.016)***	0.004 (0.020)	0.038 (0.012)***
Log of income	−0.075 (0.010)***	−0.009 (0.010)	−0.026 (0.006)***
R^2	0.11	0.06	0.07

* Significant at 10%; ** Significant at 5%; *** Significant at 1%.

Source: Authors' calculations.

Notes: This table reports OLS regressions of not planning on total net worth. Net worth is divided by 1,000 and all monetary values are in $2004. Regressions include dummies for retirement status (fully and partially retired), number of children, age, and age squared. The total number of observations is 3,727 in 1992, 2,156 in 2004, and 5,883 in the pooled sample. Business owners and the top and bottom 1% of the wealth distribution in each year are excluded. Standard errors in parentheses.

we argue influences net worth but is unrelated to planning is the recent regional change in house prices, a measure that should be strongly correlated with wealth because housing is a large component of total net worth for both cohorts. We exploit variation by region and not at the individual level, so these price changes are not likely to be correlated with the individual propensity to plan except through the channel of net worth. As mentioned before, the EBB enjoyed a sharp increase in home prices both before and during 2004. However, there is wide variation in home prices across regions in the United States. For example, while the Pacific region experienced an increase of 10.3 percent in 2003, the southeast region experienced an increase of 3.6 percent in 2003. The HRS cohort had the opposite experience; during 1990 and 1991 the housing market experienced a bust, which was particularly pronounced in specific regions of the United States such as New England. We use the change in home prices in the previous year (i.e. the changes between 2004 and 2003 for EBB and the changes between 1992 and 1991 for the HRS cohort) across regions as an instrument for wealth.[17]

TABLE 13-10   First Stage Regressions of IV Estimation of Total Net Worth on Housing Price Increases

	Orig. HRS	EBB	Pooled Sample
Percentage increase	−4.988 (2.121)**	16.757 (3.239)***	10.911 (1.885)***
Year 2004			1.023 (13.363)
High school graduate	13.335 (12.481)	−10.745 (30.827)	−0.105 (14.806)
Some college	49.170 (14.651)***	1.236 (31.173)	14.734 (15.770)
College graduate	96.897 (17.986)***	168.292 (35.201)***	150.764 (18.320)***
More than college	164.724 (19.304)***	242.018 (37.028)***	226.037 (19.454)***
Hispanic	−40.042 (16.332)**	−68.629 (31.973)**	−55.268 (17.069)***
Black	−75.006 (14.207)***	−84.326 (25.246)***	−81.589 (14.096)***
Divorced	−51.387 (13.185)***	−63.436 (21.029)***	−59.194 (12.149)***
Separated	−41.291 (23.928)*	−34.927 (45.006)	−32.472 (24.560)
Widowed	−24.493 (18.949)	124.459 (37.443)***	64.629 (20.031)***
Never married	−60.063 (22.460)***	−64.316 (33.540)*	−61.223 (19.738)***
Female	29.290 (9.745)***	−39.638 (17.105)**	−14.117 (9.579)
Log of income	83.800 (5.997)***	84.658 (8.322)***	86.004 (4.989)***
R^2	0.19	0.22	0.21

* Significant at 10%; ** Significant at 5%: *** Significant at 1%.

Source: Authors' calculations.

Notes: This table reports OLS regressions of total net worth on the percentage increase in housing prices by region in the previous year. Net worth is divided by 1,000 and all monetary values are in $2004. Regressions include dummies for retirement status (fully and partially retired), number of children, age, and age squared. The total number of observations is 3,727 in 1992, 2,156 in 2004, and 5,883 in the pooled sample. Business owners and the top and bottom 1% of the wealth distribution in each year are excluded. Standard errors in parentheses.

As the first-stage regressions reported in Table 13-10 show, changes in regional prices are strong predictors of wealth. In particular, a 1 percent increase in home prices increases wealth by more than $16,000among EBB, while a 1 percent decrease in prices during the early 1990s increased wealth by close to $5,000, perhaps a result of the fact that home prices had decreased sharply before that period and, consequently, had already depressed the value of wealth.[18] In the pooled sample, the increase in wealth following a change in home prices is also positive. The IV estimates reported in Table 13-11 show that the effect of wealth, instrumented by changes in home prices, on lack of planning is either not statistically significant or positive. In addition, in both 1992 and 2004, the positive IV estimates are significantly different than the negative OLS point estimates; for both cohorts, exogenous increases in wealth tend to *reduce* the propensity to plan.[19] What this suggests is that lack of planning is positively influenced by wealth, so the OLS estimates are biased and represent an underestimate of the effect of planning, compatible with what Lusardi (2003) finds. The IV estimates of lack of planning on wealth are much larger than the OLS estimates, a result also consistent with Ameriks et al. (2003) who use a different

TABLE 13-11 Instrumental Variables (IV) Estimation of 'Not Planning' on Net Worth

	Orig. HRS	*EBB*	*Pooled Sample*
OLS	−0.000054	−0.000045	−0.000043
	(0.000027)**	(0.000024)*	(0.000016)***
IV	0.00287	0.000387	0.000135
	(0.00142)**	(0.00024)	(0.000225)
Hausman test	13.283	2.951	0.279
(*p*-Value)	(0.0003)***	(0.085)*	(0.597)

* Significant at 10%; ** Significant at 5%; *** Significant at 1%.

Source: Authors' calculations.

Notes: This table reports IV regressions of not planning on total net worth. Net worth is divided by 1,000 and all monetary values are in $2004. Regressions include all the same explanatory variables as in Table 13-6. The total number of observations is 3,727 in 1992, 2,156 in 2004, and 5,883 in the pooled sample. Business owners and the top and bottom 1% of the wealth distribution in each year are excluded. Standard errors in parenthesis with p-value in parentheses for Hausman test.

data-set and use propensity to plan for a vacation and mathematical abilities as instruments for planning.

To summarize: Planning is an important determinant of wealth and an important reason for why many families arrive close to retirement with little or no wealth. Both the quantile estimates and the IV exercise show that planning has a powerful effect on wealth. The IV estimation shows that reverse causality is not driving the significant relationship between wealth and lack of planning. In fact, reverse causality tends to result in an underestimation of the effect of planning. Thus, the effect of planning is even stronger than the OLS and quantile estimates report. Moreover and most importantly, the effect of planning has remained unchanged between years. Thus, while the increase in home prices has lifted the wealth of many Early Boomers, lack of planning has the same effect between cohorts: it sharply reduces wealth.

Discussion and Conclusion

As the Baby Boomers stand on the verge of retirement, along many dimensions they appear better prepared than their precursor counterparts; for instance, many have accumulated larger amounts of wealth in 2004. Yet this is not the case for all cohort members, since Blacks and the least educated accumulated less wealth than the previous generation. Moreover, a larger proportion of Boomer wealth is exposed to fluctuations in asset prices, particularly housing prices; accordingly a fall in housing values could undermine their retirement preparedness.

It is interesting that many Boomers have still not devoted much thought to their retirement prospects, even when retirement is only a few years away. Close to 30 percent of respondents gave no thought to retirement, which leads to little saving. The effect of planning is found to be strong and positively associated with retirement wealth, and the impact is remarkably stable across cohorts. Thus, nonplanners have not been much affected by the changes in the economy between 1992 and 2004, including the financial education initiatives undertaken during the 1990s. One reason is that they have not devoted much energy to retirement planning, even though planning is a crucial determinant of household wealth. Specifically, those who fail to plan have accumulated much less wealth than those who did some planning, and this finding is strikingly similar across cohorts. Nonplanners are disproportionately those with low education, low income, and Blacks/Hispanics. These households were largely unaffected by financial education programs instituted during the 1990s. In general, policies which stimulate saving might be best targeted to those groups least likely to plan.

Acknowledgments

The authors thank Patricia Anderson, Mark Christman, Olivia S. Mitchell, Douglas Staiger, and Steven Venti for suggestions and comments. Financial support from the Social Security Administration via a grant from the Michigan Retirement Research Center is gratefully acknowledged.

Notes

[1] By comparing two generations at different points in time, we cannot distinguish between 'time' and 'cohort' effect. We will use the term cohort/time interchangeably. For more discussion, see Kapteyn et al. (2005).

[2] We also delete a handful of observations with missing information about demographic variables such as age, sex, marital status, number of children, and race and ethnicity; moreover, we also delete observations with zero income as they are likely to be the result of measurement error. The final sample size for analysis is 2,631 EBBs and 4,577 in the HRS cohort.

[3] Earlier studies on Boomers' saving patterns are mixed; cf. Bernheim (1993) versus the Congressional Budget Office (1993). Research on the effects of retirement seminars during the 1990s has also reported mixed results estimates (for a review, see Lusardi 2004).

[4] Our measure differs from total net nonpension wealth used in other papers in this volume as it includes IRAs and Keoghs.

[5] We use preliminary weights provided by the HRS for 2004 and the final weights for 1992. In both 1992 and 2004, the HRS sample is not representative of the population in that age group due to sample attrition.

[6] Because race and ethnicity is not exclusive and Hispanics can also report being White, Black, or Other Race, in addition to being Hispanic, the percentages in

Table 13-1 sum to more than 100. However, the same definition is used in both years.

[7] We must also note that the analysis includes IRAs and Keoghs but excludes company pensions and Social Security wealth. As Gustman and Steinmeier (1999) show, pension and Social Security wealth can account for as much as half of total wealth. Unfortunately, the HRS has not yet provided accurate measures of these values for the EBB cohort. It is also worth noting that, as Cunningham et al. (Chapter 10, this volume) showed, calculations of pension wealth are difficult to compute very precisely.

[8] Another asset that merits consideration is business equity. While business owners account for a small fraction of the population, they account for a sizable amount of total wealth (Gentry and Hubbard 2004; Hurst and Lusardi 2006). For example, while close to 15 percent of EBB are business owners, wealth they hold in business equity is as large as all the IRA wealth (even though 42% of Early Boomers hold IRAs). In other words, Business owners are disproportionately located at the top of the wealth distribution; Hurst and Lusardi (2006) show that over 80 percent of the richest 3 percent of households are business owners. The percentage of business owners has decreased between cohorts and so has the share of total wealth invested in business equity. Unfortunately, we lack all the needed information to account for differences between business owners and other households, so we exclude business owners from further analysis.

[9] For a detailed discussion of the findings in the module on planning and financial literacy, see Lusardi and Mitchell (2006a).

[10] As noted above, we delete business owners from the analysis since business owners display different motives to save than other households (cf. Hurst and Lusardi 2004, 2006; Hurst et al. 2005). Moreover, there are several measurement issues in assessing correctly their income, as they have a clear incentive to underreport earnings. For a good discussion of this issue, see Hurst et al. (2005).

[11] We trim the top and the bottom 1 percent of the wealth distribution to avoid outliers in the empirical work.

[12] To limit the effect of outliers, we take the log of income. This empirical specification is similar to the specification used in most saving studies (Lusardi 2002, 2003).

[13] For brevity, we only report median rather than other quantile estimates, but planning has an effect across the wealth distribution. For a discussion of the role of housing wealth on retirement savings, see Venti and Wise (1990, 1991).

[14] As there are some very high network households at the top of the wealth distribution, they become influential in the OLS estimates; researchers must take care in assessing the empirical estimates of lack of planning on wealth.

[15] However, it is also possible that extremely wealthy individuals plan less because they do not need to plan in order to build wealth, biasing the coefficient in the previous regressions toward 0.

[16] We cannot take the log of wealth as many households have negative wealth particularly in 2004; for a similar approach, see Haliassos and Bertaut (1995).

[17] Hurst and Lusardi (2004) have used similar instruments for wealth to be able to assess the effect of wealth on business start-ups.

[18] We have also considered other time periods. For example, we consider price changes in the previous two years and we consider price changes in a ten-year

period. In both case, we find that price changes are good predictor of wealth. We report the estimates of the one-year price change only because they are the strongest predictor of wealth. The IV estimates in the other two cases are similar.

[19] Given the importance of housing equity in the measure of total net worth, these estimates may simply show that planning has an effect on housing wealth. Nevertheless, it is difficult to find instruments that predict nonhousing wealth, so we restrict the IV estimation to only one measure of household wealth.

Appendix

TABLE 13A-1 Demographic Characteristics of the Sample: Original HRS and Early Boomers (EBB)

Cohort	Orig. HRS	EBB
Age		
Average age	53.7	53.7
Education (%)		
Less than high school	18.6	9.2
High school graduate	38.5	28.4
Some college	21.1	29.0
College graduate	11.4	18.2
More than college	10.4	15.2
Race/ethnicity (%)		
White	85.9	80.8
Black	10.2	11.7
Hispanic	7.6	8.7
Other	2.9	7.5
Marital status (%)		
Married	71.4	62.8
Divorced	14.8	21.6
Separated	3.4	3.3
Widowed	5.5	4.9
Never married	4.3	7.2
Children (% in sample)		
No children	8.8	17.2
Have children	91.2	82.8
Sex (% in sample)		
Male	55.7	54.4
Female	44.3	45.6

Source: Authors' calculations.

Notes: Number of observations is 4,577 for the 1992 HRS cohort and 2,631 for the 2004 EBB. At least respondent or spouse is 51–56-year old. All figures are weighted using household weights.

TABLE 13A-2 Percentage of Net Worth Accounted for by Not Planning, by Wealth Decile ($2004)

Decile (%)	Estimate	Net Worth	Percentage
A. Original HRS cohort			
10th	−5.90	0	NA
20th	−11.94	6.92	172.57
30th	−9.27	31	29.90
40th	−10.77	60	17.95
50th	−17.23	104	16.57
60th	−20.92	161	13.00
70th	−33.81	229.4	14.74
80th	−55.61	357.61	15.55
90th	−74.08	611.6	12.11
B. EBB cohort			
10th	−8.21	0	NA
20th	−10.78	10.77	100.04
30th	−15.83	35.01	45.22
40th	−16.08	60.59	26.54
50th	−20.03	92.90	21.56
60th	−32.88	131.95	24.92
70th	−40.17	181.44	22.14
80th	−44.68	258.18	17.30
90th	−33.12	420.08	7.88

Source: Authors' calculations.

References

Ameriks, J., Caplin, A., and Leah, J. (2003). 'Wealth Accumulation and the Propensity to Plan', *Quarterly Journal of Economics*, 68: 1007–47.

Autor, D. and Katz, L. (1999). 'Changes in the Wage Structure and Earnings Inequality', in O. Ashenfelter and D. Card (eds.), *Handbook of Labor Economics*. Amsterdam: North-Holland, pp. 1463–555.

—— —— and Kearney, M. (2006). 'The Polarization of the US Labor Market'. *American Economic Review Papers and Proceedings*, 96: 189–94.

Bernheim, D. (1993). *Is the Baby Boom Generation Preparing Adequately for Retirement?* Report to Merrill Lynch, Princeton, NJ.

Congressional Budget Office (1993). *Baby Boomers in Retirement: An Early Perspective.* Washington, DC: US GPO.

Cunningham, C., Engelhardt, G., and Kumar, A. (this volume). 'Measuring Pension Wealth'.

Gentry, W. M. and Hubbard, G. (2004). 'Entrepreneurship and Household Saving', *Advances in Economics Analysis and Policy*, 4 (Issue 1): Article 8.

Gustman, A. and Steinmeier, T. (1999). 'Effects of Pensions on Saving: Analysis with Data from the Health and Retirement Study', *Carnegie-Rochester Conference Series*, 50: 271–336.

—— —— (2002). 'Retirement and the Stock Market Bubble', NBER Working Paper No. 9404, December.

Haliassos, M. and Bertaut, C. (1995). 'Why Do So Few Hold Stocks?', *Economic Journal*, 105: 1110–29.

Hurst, E. and Lusardi, A. (2004). 'Liquidity Constraints, Household Wealth and Entrepreneurship', *Journal of Political Economy*, 112: 319–47.

—— —— (2006). 'Do Household Savings Encourage Entrepreneurship? Household Wealthy, Parental Wealth and the Transition In and Out of Entrepreneurship', Working Paper, Dartmouth College and University of Chicago Graduate School of Business.

—— —— Kennickell, A., and Torralba, F. (2005). 'Precautionary Savings and the Importance of Business Owners'. NBER Working Paper 11731.

Kapteyn, A., Alessie, R., and Lusardi, A. (2005). 'Explaining the Wealth of Different Cohorts: Productivity Growth and Social Security', *European Economic Review*, 49: 1361–81.

Iams, H., Butrica, B., and Smith, K. (this volume). 'It is All Relative. Understanding the Retirement Prospects of Baby Boomers'.

Lusardi, A. (1999). 'Information, Expectations, and Savings for Retirement', in H. Aaron (ed.), *Behavioral Dimensions of Retirement Economics*. Washington, DC: Brookings Institution Press and Russell Sage Foundation, pp. 81–115.

—— (2002). 'Preparing for Retirement: The Importance of Planning Costs', *National Tax Association Proceedings* 2002: 148–54.

—— (2003). 'Planning and Saving for Retirement', Working Paper, Dartmouth College.

—— (2004). 'Savings and the Effectiveness of Financial Education', in O. Mitchell and S. Utkus (eds.), *Pension Design and Structure: New Lessons from Behavioral Finance*. Oxford: Oxford University Press, pp. 157–84.

—— and Olivia S. Mitchell (2006*a*). 'Financial Literacy and Planning: Implications for Retirement Wellbeing', Pension Research Council Working Paper, The Wharton School.

—— —— (2006*b*). 'Baby Boomer Retirement Security: The Role of Planning, Financial Literacy and Housing Wealth', Presented at the Carnegie-Rochester Conference on Public Policy, April.

Manchester, J., Weaver, D., and Whitman, K. (this volume). 'Changes in Economic Well-Being and Health Status'.

Office of Federal Housing Enterprise Oversight (2005). *House Price Index*. http://www.ofheo.gov/HPIRegion.asp

Venti, S. and Wise, D. (1990). 'But They Don't Want to Reduce Housing Equity', in D. Wise (ed.), *Issues in the Economics of Aging*. Chicago, IL: University of Chicago Press, pp. 13–32.

—— —— (1991). 'Aging and the Income Value of Housing Wealth', *Journal of Public Economics*, 44: 371–95.

Wolfe B., Haveman, R., Holden, K., and Romanov, A. (this volume). 'The Sufficiency of Retirement Savings: A Comparison of Two Cohorts of Retired Workers
at the Time of Retirement'.

Yakoboski, P. and Dickemper, J. (1997). *Increased Saving but Little Planning. Results
of the 1997 Retirement Confidence Survey.* EBRI Issue Brief 191. Washington, DC:
EBRI.

Chapter 14

Retiring on the House?
Cross-Cohort Differences
in Housing Wealth

Julia L. Coronado, Dean Maki, and Ben Weitzer

As the leading edge of the Baby Boom generation turns 60, there is growing interest in how well this large group has prepared for retirement and how it will manage its assets in later life. There has been concern among the popular media, policymakers, and academic economists that Boomers have not saved enough for retirement, and indeed Figure 14-1 indicates a precipitous decline in the personal saving rate as Boomers have moved through adulthood.

This chapter evaluates the role of housing wealth in Baby Boomers' retirement prospects to determine what role housing wealth will play in their retirement well-being. Our approach compares the wealth position of the leading edge of the Boomers with that of the generation immediately preceding it, in the years just prior to retirement. We rely on the Health and Retirement Survey (HRS) and compare persons aged 51–61 in 1992, whom we refer to as the original HRS cohort, with the Early Baby Boomers (EBBs) interviewed at age 51–56 in 2004. We conclude that Boomers do have more valuable homes, but they have also borrowed more against these. As a result, they have a similar fraction of assets allocated to home equity as their predecessors. On net, however, the median EBB member had similar home equity and net worth compared to previous retirees at the same age. When we assess how the original HRS respondents have managed their home equity over the period 1992–2004, we find that—unlike prior studies—people do view housing as a source of wealth that can help them finance their retirement needs. Indeed, a substantial fraction of older households do move; and in the process, they appear to liquidate some home equity which they convert to financial assets. Consequently, some of the home equity extraction observed in recent years may be related to the aging of the population, rather than a cyclical response to rapid house appreciation.

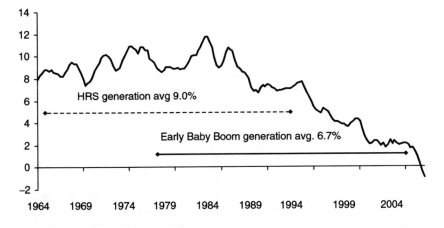

Figure 14-1. Personal saving as a percentage of disposable income between the ages of 28 and 51. (*Source*: US Bureau of Economic Analysis (various years); Haver Analytics (various years).)

Comparing Early Baby Boomers with Their Predecessors

Previous research that has evaluated Boomers' retirement prospects has generally taken one of two approaches.[1] One compares Boomers' finances with those of previous generations at a similar age. As we show below, these studies have typically concluded that Baby Boomer households have higher incomes and are accumulating wealth at a similar or greater pace than previous generations. So in an absolute sense, Boomers, on average, are doing as well or better than their parents. Indeed, though aggregate saving rates have declined, this is partly a response to capital gains on assets which have led households in the aggregate to accumulate significantly more wealth as shown in Figure 14-2. That said, increasing inequality has also been noted: the lowest income households among Boomers appear to be worse off economically than previous generations (Butrica et al., this volume; Manchester et al., this volume).

A second set of studies evaluates the retirement preparedness of Baby Boomers by asking whether they have accumulated enough wealth to sustain their standard of living through retirement (Moore and Mitchell 2000). Their higher real household incomes, combined with static retirement timing, would imply that they need to accumulate more wealth in order to maintain the higher consumption through retirement. This second literature is far from uniform in its conclusions, in part because authors differ in their economic assumptions and definitions of wealth.

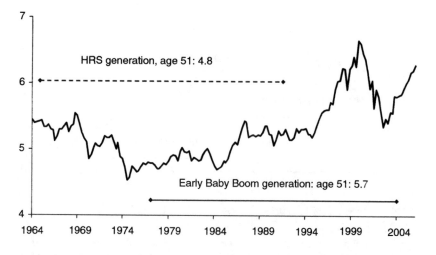

Figure 14-2. The ratio of net worth to disposable income between the ages of 28 and 51. (*Source*: US Bureau of Economic Analysis (various years); Haver Analytics (various years).)

A main bone of contention has been the question of whether home equity should be included as a retirement asset. In our view, it seems unreasonable to exclude housing wealth when evaluating retirement preparedness, inasmuch as home equity accounts for 43 percent of net worth for the median household and more than one-third of aggregate household wealth.[2] It is true that, in the past, there were only limited ways for retirees to tap home equity, short of selling their homes. It is also true that elderly persons appeared to be reluctant to sell their homes unless confronted with the death of a spouse or a serious illness.[3] Thus housing wealth appeared to serve as insurance against adverse events, but not as a source of wealth to finance general consumption needs other than shelter. Nevertheless, the fact that housing satisfies the need for shelter would seem to necessitate its inclusion in evaluating retirement preparedness. Shelter accounts for between 15 and 33 percent of total consumption needs.[4] And not surprisingly, if home equity is included as an asset, this produces a more favorable assessment of Boomers' preparedness for retirement. In any case, the question remains open as to whether households are tapping into their home equity appropriately for two reasons. First, Boomers are beginning to transition into retirement with a great deal of home equity. Second, markets have developed for tapping into home equity; indeed, home equity loans now account for 12 percent of all mortgage debt. In addition, the size of the reverse mortgage market, where older households can obtain an annuity stream of income from their home equity, has doubled in each of the past

Table 14-1 Comparing the Wealth and Home Equity Position of the
Original HRS and Early Baby Boomers at Age 51–56

	Original HRS	EBB
1. Year surveyed	1992	2004
2. Number of respondents	5,722	4,330
3. Married	77.9%	70.3%
4. Some college education or higher	42.1%	57.3%
5. Retired	11.5%	12.1%
6. Has DB pension	64.1%	54.7%
7. Home ownership	80.3%	82.9%
8. Median net worth ($)	153,444	155,000
9. Median net worth per capita ($)	83,116	90,250
10. Net worth/household income	2.40	2.13
11. Median home value ($)	100,950	140,000
12. Median equity in home	84.0%	65.9%
13. Median home equity/net worth	44.0%	43.8%

Source: Authors' calculations.

Note: Dollar amounts in $2004.

five years. In 2005, roughly $3.6 billion in reverse mortgages was issued
against homes valued at $11 billion.[5] This market remains small compared
to the over $1 trillion mortgage market that year; it does appear that older
households can increasingly use their home equity to finance retirement
needs.

Table 14-1 permits an assessment of the comparative economic positions
of the original HRS and EBB cohorts (all dollar figures are in $2004).
We focus on persons aged 51–56 in 2004 and 1992. As others have noted,
Boomers are less likely to be married, are better educated, and are less likely
to be covered by a defined benefit (DB) pension than the HRS generation.
Both generations had similarly low rates of retirement in their early 50s and
remarkably similar median net worth, though the EBB cohort had higher
per capita net worth and a lower ratio of net worth to household income
owing to the smaller household size and higher household incomes.

Turning to housing wealth, we note that the Early Boomers had a slightly
higher rate of home ownership, and they owned homes worth nearly
40 percent more than the HRS cohort. This is not terribly surprising given
that the EBB group was interviewed in 2004 after a housing boom that, as
shown in Figure 14-3, had lasted nearly a decade. The EBB group is indeed
more leveraged with only 66 percent equity versus 84 percent for the HRS
cohort (equity in home is calculated as market value of the home minus
all mortgage debt as a fraction of home value). But because the Boomers'
homes are more valuable, the percentage of their portfolio devoted to

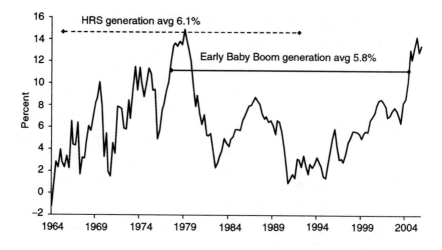

Figure 14-3. Real home price appreciation between the ages of 28 and 51 (% change, year on year). (*Source*: OFHEO (various years); Haver Analytics (various years).)

home equity is nearly identical to the HRS generation. In other words, the two groups had very similar percentage allocations to housing and financial assets, as they approached retirement. Subsequently, the portfolio of the HRS group then experienced the boom and bust of the equity markets, as well as the housing market boom; nonetheless, the two groups were quite similarly situated prior to retirement.

More detail on the distribution of housing wealth across the two generations is provided in Table 14-2. Here households are divided into quintiles of household income, and the picture painted by the aggregate statistics holds up in this more disaggregated view. Increasing home ownership is evident for the younger EBB cohort, and home ownership rates and median home values were higher for every quintile of the EBB generation. Likewise, the data are consistent with more liberal credit markets across the income spectrum, as each EBB quintile had greater leverage (evidenced by the lower median equity in their homes). The share of home equity in total net worth is basically similar across generations by quintile; it is a touch higher for lower HRS quintiles and a bit lower for upper income groups. The ratio of net worth to income is higher for the HRS group in all but the middle income quintile.

In other words, the evidence suggests that, despite higher leverage, the Early Boomers were similarly positioned to the prior generation, just before retirement. Some of the EBBs' increased leverage can thus be viewed as an asset allocation move to keep their portfolio from being overweighed in home equity after an extended period of appreciation in home values. This

TABLE 14-2 Comparison of Home Ownership and Values for the HRS and Early
Baby Boom Generations at Age 51–56, by Household Income
Quintile

	First	Second	Third	Fourth	Fifth
Original HRS					
1. Home ownership	51.5%	74.4%	84.2%	89.5%	97.1%
2. Median home value ($)	13,460	74,030	94,220	134,600	235,550
3. Median equity in home	56.0%	73.1%	81.5%	85.0%	100%
4. Median home equity/net worth	0	59.5%	52.3%	47.0%	28.5%
5. Net worth/household income	0.5	1.58	2.07	3.4	7.69
Early Baby Boomers					
1. Home ownership	60.1%	80.4%	86.3%	91.7%	95.2%
2. Median home value ($)	30,000	95,000	145,000	200,000	375,000
3. Median equity in home	42.2%	58.0%	64.2%	66.6%	78.6%
4. Median home equity/net worth	0	57.8%	54.9%	51.5%	33.8%
5. Net worth/household income	0.4	1.4	2.3	3.0	7.1

Source: Authors' calculations.

Note: Dollar amounts in $2004.

portfolio shifting view is also quite consistent with aggregate data. Many
observers, including former Federal Reserve Chairman Greenspan, credited the extraction of home equity with supporting consumption spending
through the most recent economic downturn (Figure 14-4). But the flows
of money out of home equity through increased leverage have roughly
paralleled the flows of funds into financial assets.

Clearly retirement preparedness rests on more than housing, and
Boomers face lower levels of DB pension coverage, longer life spans, and
looming Social Security and Medicare deficits. Consequently, Boomers may
not be able to retire at the same age and maintain their standard of living
during retirement if they continue to retire early. Yet estimates of saving adequacy respond dramatically to assumptions about retirement ages.
Moore and Mitchell (1997) show how required saving rates are cut in half,
if retirement is delayed from 62 to 65. And there is at least a suggestion that
Boomers may retire later than their predecessors (Maestas, this volume).

Housing Wealth and Retirement Needs: A Focus on the HRS Cohort

Next we assess how the HRS generation has managed its housing investments, as it has moved through retirement. Specifically, we evaluate the

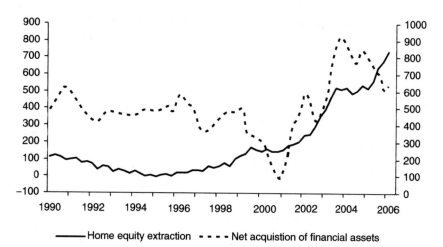

Figure 14-4. Home equity appears to be moving into financial assets ($ billions, 4-quarter moving average). (*Source*: Federal Reserve Board of Governors (various years); Haver Analytics (various years).)

extent to which the HRS generation has drawn down its home equity to finance its retirement needs. This may offer insights into how the EBB generation will manage its housing investments going forward.

The periods during which we observe the HRS cohort are the years between 1992 and 2004. This was a time characterized by first booming, and then falling, equity markets, and then a surging housing market. As Figure 14-2 indicated, on balance, this was a time when net worth grew rapidly relative to disposable income. Since rates of appreciation in both of these asset classes were well beyond their historical norms, at least some portion of this appreciation likely came as a surprise, particularly to the HRS generation who had already reached its peak saving period. This makes it a difficult period to assess the degree and patterns of wealth drawdown.

Some of the same questions are evaluated by Venti and Wise (2001), who ask whether people give up their homes in later life and whether the amount invested in home equity declines with age. They concluded that retirees do not view their home equity as an asset available to finance retirement needs. We approach this question somewhat differently, since in our view, giving up home ownership is a crude way for older persons to access home equity. Furthermore, the fact that the housing market was booming over this period implies that it is unlikely to observe outright declines in the value of home equity. Instead, we explore changes in the share of home equity in retirees' total portfolios, how this share changed

TABLE 14-3 Comparison of Housing and Wealth Measures for the HRS Generation as They Transitioned into Retirement

Year	1992	2004
1. Age of primary respondent	51–56	63–68
2. Number of respondents	5,722	4,127
3. Married	77.9%	68.7%
5. Retired	11.5%	62.1%
6. Has DB pension	64.1%	71.9%
7. Home ownership	80.3%	85.1%
8. Median net worth ($)	153,444	207,000
9. Median net worth per capita ($)	83,116	123,000
10. Net worth/household income	2.40	4.43
11. Median home value ($)	100,950	133,000
12. Median equity in home	84%	95%
13. Median home equity/net worth	44.0%	44.5%

Source: Authors' calculations.

Note: Dollar amounts in $2004.

over this period, and whether those who moved were more likely to tap into this source of wealth, either for rebalancing into financial assets or to finance consumption needs. Accordingly, an examination of movers' choices can shed light on what the unconstrained choices of retirees might look like.

Table 14-3 reports key aspects of the HRS cohort in 1992 and again in 2004. Just under two-thirds of the sample were retired by 2004 (when they were aged 63–68). Some respondents are lost owing to death and nonresponse, and there is a decline in the marriage rate mainly to widowhood (and some divorce). The rate of people indicating they were covered by a DB pension increased significantly due to either pension vesting or lack of awareness of these benefits prior to retirement. Given financial market conditions, both real median net worth and the ratio of net worth to income rose substantially over the period. The rate of home ownership actually rose, as did median home value and equity in the home. In the aggregate, the median fraction of the portfolio allocated to home equity changed little over this time frame.

The same data movers and nonmovers are shown in Table 14-4. Roughly a one quarter of all households moved over this eleven-year period. Movers started the period with greater net worth, higher incomes, and more valuable homes in 1992, though they had slightly less equity in their homes; health, marital status, and retirement were also similar. Then between 1992 and 2004, both movers and nonmovers increased their net worth

TABLE 14-4 Comparing Changes in Housing and Wealth Variables for Original HRS Cohort: Movers versus Nonmovers

	Movers			Nonmovers		
	1992	2004	Difference	1992	2004	Difference
1. Median net worth ($)	205,938	242,000	36,062	188,440	298,000	109,560
2. Median household income ($)	71,338	46,500	−24,838	63,531	45,180	−18,351
3. Median net worth/ household income	2.82	4.70	1.88	2.96	5.99	3.03
4. Median house value ($)	148,060	165,000	16,940	121,000	153,000	31,860
5. Median home equity/net worth	51.7%	37.9%	−13.7%	55.0%	52.7%	−2.4%
6. Good health or better	89.4%	80.8%	− 8.6%	87.3%	77.7%	−9.6%
7. Married	85.5%	67.9%	−15.6%	85.8%	77.8%	−17.6%
8. Retired	11.5%	62.3%	50.8%	11.5%	63.2%	51.8%

Source: Authors' calculations.

Note: Dollar amounts in $2004.

and decreased their income, though movers had a significantly smaller rise in net worth and a larger decline in income. Median home values also increased for both groups, though the increase was much larger for the nonmovers, and the fraction of net worth allocated to home equity declined substantially more for movers while it only edged down for nonmovers. Both groups became less healthy, and retired at a similar pace.

The fact that movers started the sample better-off but saw smaller increases in wealth and significantly reduced their allocation to home equity suggests that movers may have used some of their wealth gains for spending purposes and reallocated some housing wealth to financial assets. Another possibility is that those households who moved suffered some type of health shock or death in the family that precipitated their move and reallocation of wealth. We are interested in distinguishing between the use of home equity as an insurance policy and the use of home equity for more general retirement needs. For this reason, we estimate a multivariate regression model linking the change in the share of net worth allocated to home equity between 1992 and 2004, using movers as

TABLE 14-5 The Impact of Moving on Home Equity Extraction: Evidence of a
Regression of Home Equity Shares Using Movers as a Control Group

Independent Variable	Dependent Variable: Change in the Ratio of Home Equity to Net Worth, 2004–1992		
	(A)	(B)	(C)
Moved	−0.13 (0.011)	−0.10 (0.012)	−0.07 (0.013)
Changed marital status		0.10 (0.021)	0.08 (0.021)
Moved*changed marital status		−0.17 (0.029)	−0.16 (0.031)
Change in health status		0.06 (0.031)	0.02 (0.017)
Moved*change in health status			−0.07 (0.031)
Log of household income			−0.03 (0.006)
Education: < high school			0.12 (0.021)
Education: high school diploma			0.05 (0.017)
Education: some college			0.05 (0.018)
Education: college degree			0.00 (0.021)
Covered by DB pension			0.04 (0.012)
Constant	0.52 (0.006)	0.50 (0.007)	0.79 (0.073)
Adjusted R^2	0.05	0.06	0.09

Source: Authors' calculations.

Notes: Regressions estimated using weighted ordinary least squares. Estimated coefficients shown with standard errors in parentheses. All variables are significant at the 95% confidence level with the exceptions of change in health status and college degree in the specification presented in column (C).

a control group; we also include variables to capture the effect of adverse events.

We estimate the change in home equity by taking the position in 2004 and subtracting the 1992 allocation, so that on average the change will be negative. Results appear in Table 14-5, where the first column shows the results of regression the change in home equity on only an indicator variable indicating whether the household moved. The coefficient indicates that movers reduced their allocation to home equity 13 percentage points over this period relative to nonmovers, highly significant and close to Table 14-4. The second column also controls for whether there was a change in marital status (including widowhood or divorce), change in health status, and an interaction term between change in marital status and moving. The results indicate that households who moved with no change in marital status or health shock reduced their home equity 10 percentage points, relative to nonmovers. This result is highly significant and represents an indication of the magnitude of home equity liquidated through a move *not* accompanied by a health or marital shock, possibly for general retirement purposes. The interaction between moving and marital status suggests that households who moved *and* had a marital status shock reduced their home equity a further 17 percentage points beyond movers without such an event, as their home equity served as a source of insurance.

The third column adds other general controls for education, household income, and whether the household is covered by a DB pension, as well as an interaction between a change in health status and moving. All variables are significant at the 95 percent confidence level with the exception of change in health status and having a college education. The results indicate that movers with no health or marital shock reduced their home equity by 7 percentage points, relative to nonmovers, while those with a marital shock reduced their allocations an additional 16 percentage points; those with a health shock reduced their home equity 7 percentage points relative to movers without adverse marital and health changes.

Discussion and Conclusions

This chapter compares the economic position of Baby Boomers with that of current retirees, both during their preretirement years. We note that Boomers have similar levels of net worth, and a comparable fraction of their net worth invested in equity of their homes. Yet their homes are more valuable, and they hold more mortgage debt against that value. Overall, Boomers have higher rates of home ownership and greater leverage against their homes across the income spectrum. Next we assessed how HRS retirees tapped into their housing wealth, as they transitioned into retirement. This analysis is confounded by a sustained above-trend boom in asset markets, yet we do find that more than a quarter of households in this cohort moved between their early 50s and mid-60s. Further, they used the move as an opportunity to tap into their home equity and reallocate some of this wealth to financial assets. Home equity also serves as an insurance policy in the event of shock such as the death of a house or deterioration in health.

We conclude from this analysis that the recent surge in home equity extraction is more of a trend than a cyclical phenomenon. As indicated in Figure 14-5, this is not inconsistent with the aggregate data which show no sign of slowing in the growth of home equity extraction relative to income, even as the housing market has slowed. While Boomers are more leveraged than their predecessors, they still have considerable equity in their homes. Accordingly, we would expect the trend toward home equity extraction to continue as this cohort ages.

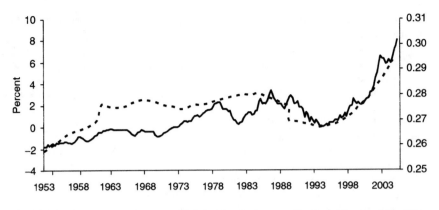

Figure 14-5. Home equity extraction: trend rather than cyclical phenomenon. *Note*: Home equity extraction is measured as net borrowing minus net residential investment in primary residences by households as a percentage of disposable personal income. (*Source*: Federal Reserve Board of Governors (various years); Bureau of Economic Analysis (various years); Haver Analytics (various years).)

Notes

[1] A comprehensive and useful review of studies on this issue is available from the Congressional Budget Office (November 2003).

[2] These figures are taken from Federal Reserve Board of Governors (various years) *Survey of Consumer Finances* and *Flow of Funds*, respectively.

[3] Some notable examples of this work include Sheiner and Weil (1993) and Venti and Wise (1991).

[4] The lower figure is the weight of shelter in consumer spending according to the National Income and Product Accounts published by the US Bureau of Economic Analysis (various years), while the larger number is the weight of shelter in the Consumer Price Index published by the US Bureau of Labor Statistics (various years).

[5] Data on home equity debt come from the Federal Reserve Board of Governors (various years). Figures on reverse mortgages come from IndyMac Bank (2005), OFHEO (various years), and our own calculations.

References

Bureau of Economic Analysis (various years). *National Income and Product Accounts*, US Department of Commerce. Washington, DC: http://www.bea.gov/

Butrica, B. A., Iams, H. M. S., and Smith, K. E. (Chapter 4). 'Understanding Baby Boomers' Retirement Prospects'.

Congressional Budget Office (November 2003). *Baby Boomers Retirement Prospects: An Overview.* Washington, DC: US GPO.

Federal Reserve Board of Governors (various years). *Flow of Funds Accounts of the United States.* Washington, DC: Federal Reserve Board: http://www.federalreserve.gov/

Haver Analytics (various years). *Economic and Financial Databases.* http://www.haver.com/

IndyMac Bank (2005). *Annual Report.* http://phx.corporateir.net/phoenix.zhtml?c=118924&p=irol-reportsAnnual

Maestas, Nicole (Chapter 2). 'Cross-Cohort Differences in Retirement Expectations and Realizations'.

Manchester, J., Weaver, D., and Whitman, K. (Chapter 6). 'Baby Boomers versus Their Parents: Economic Well-Being and Health Status'.

Moore, J. and Mitchell, O. S. (2000). 'Projected Retirement Wealth and Saving Adequacy', in O. Mitchell, B. Hammond, and A. Rappaport (eds.), *Forecasting Retirement Needs and Retirement Wealth.* Philadelphia, PA: University of Pennsylvania Press, pp. 68–94.

Office of Federal Housing Enterprise Oversight (OFHEO) (various years). *House Price Indexes.* http://www.ofheo.gov/

Sheiner, L. and Weil, D. (1993). 'The Housing Wealth of the Aged', NBER Working Paper No. 4115.

US Bureau of Economic Analysis (various years). *National Income and Product Accounts.* Washington, DC: http://internationalecon.com/v1.0/Finance/ch5/5c010.html

US Bureau of Labor Statistics (various years). *Employment Situation.* Washington, DC: http://www.bls.gov/news.release/empsit.nr0.htm

Venti, S. F. and Wise, D. A. (1991). 'Aging and the Income Value of Housing Wealth', *Journal of Public Economics*, 44: 371–97.

—— —— (2001). 'Aging and Housing Equity', in Z. Bodie, B. Hammond, and O. Mitchell (eds.), *Innovations for Financing Retirement.* Philadelphia, PA: University of Pennsylvania Press, pp. 50–76.

Index

AARP (Association for the Advancement of
    Retired Persons) 31
ability to work 100, 102
    see also inability to work
adequacy targets 5
ADLs (activities of daily living) 96–7, 99
    see also IADLs
ADRs (American Depositary Receipts) 253
age-education-pension coverage 41
age profiles/age-earnings profiles 22–7, 71
agility 154
alcoholism screening 144
Ameriks, J. 278, 288–9
annuities 241, 242, 243
ANOVA (analysis of variance) 141
ANW (annuitized net wealth) 4, 36, 37, 41, 43,
    47
    estimates of 51–4
    higher/lower 58
    minimum value of 50
    ratio to poverty line 55, 58, 61, 62
    rising dispersion in 50
arthritis 103, 141
Asians 15, 120
    replacement rates 84
asset allocation 58, 119, 190, 242–3, 252–3
asset information 45
asset-tested public transfers 114
asthma 141
'at retirement' comparisons 21–2
attachment 153
attitudes toward work 4

Baby Boomer Retirement Index
    (Bernheim) 37
background risk 183, 185
bankruptcy 171
bear markets 251
Beeler, Jason 9
Behavioral Risk Factor Surveillance Survey 115
behavioral theory 248
Benítez-Silva, H. 187
Bergstresser, D. 184, 186, 197
Bernheim, B. D. 37, 63, 113
birth cohort dummies 28
Blacks 9, 10, 273
    less likely to invest in stock market 199
    more likely to be poor 74

nondisabled 115
nonplanners 279
non-Hispanic, replacement rates 84
    predicted health index score 149
    retirees more likely than current retirees to
        be 74
    wealth 274, 281
blood pressure 108
BMI (Body Mass Index) 5–6, 102–3
body weight 115
bonds 184, 190, 218
    long-term 219
boom and bust 300
borrowing constraints 185
Bound, J. 95
bubble era 261
buffer stock behavior 114
bull markets 251
Burtless, G. 70
Butrica, Barbara 5, 42, 70, 113, 114, 132, 297

CAGE index 144, 152
cancer 141
capital market risk 7
    undiversifiable 183
CBO (Congressional Budget Office) 125
cerebrovascular disease 141
Chan, S. 191
Chan, Y. L. 185
charity care 7
childhood health 144, 153
cholesterol 108
chronic conditions 6, 10, 108, 141, 152, 153,
    155
    multiple 145
    potentially fatal 149
church attendance 103
CODA (Children of the Depression Age) 14,
    22, 44, 46
chance of working in the future 31
cognitive impairment 145
cognitive measures 141
cognitive tasks 95
Coile, C. 187
college graduates/degrees 81, 84, 165, 272, 274
complete retirement 19
    many ways to define 14
    transition to partial retirement 21

concentration curves/index values 130–2
Congressional Budget Office 113
consumption 8, 36, 99, 298, 301
  behavioral features known to affect 114
  fixed 3
  lower needs in retirement 42
  maintaining desired levels in retirement 159
  marginal utility of 41, 113
  measured 113
  minimum-acceptable adequacy 43
  optimal 41, 42, 114
  potential 41, 43, 47
  smoothing 41, 113
  social minimum 55
  volatility 187
Coronado, Julia 9, 124, 187
counterfactual experiment 266–8
CPS (Current Population Survey) 114, 159, 160–1
Crimmins, E. M. 126
crisis 10
Cunningham, Chris 8, 224, 231
current retirees 72, 85, 86, 87, 132
  characteristics of 73–4
  economic well-being 75–81
  preretirement living standards 113
  replacement rates 81, 84
Currie, J. 95

DB (defined benefit) plans 85, 120, 179, 180, 181, 184, 193, 199, 213, 234, 237, 239, 240, 241, 299, 303
  401(k) participants with 186
  annuitized income 192, 238, 242, 243
  background risk 183
  benefits 77
  changes in the prevalence of 43
  coverage plummeting for young workers 181
  currently received and expected 45
  declining role of pension benefits 79
  defined payout at retirement 182
  EBBs less likely to participate in 28
  effects of tenure in 203
  employer shift to DC 271
  erosion of 71
  falling importance of 86
  future income flows from 241
  income from 119
  increased prevalence and use of 124
  likelihood of stock market investment 202
  long-term shift from 7
  lower levels of 301
  nonlinearities in entitlements 242
  people richer than those with 196

  primary 15
  risks and opportunities 183, 187, 189, 203–4
  safe 185
  spouse income 77
  uncertainty regarding future of 5
  underfunding of 190
DC (defined contribution) plans 7, 8, 77, 85, 120, 179, 180, 181–2, 189, 193, 197, 235, 237, 238, 239, 240, 241, 242
  account balances of 119
  background risk 183
  balance at quit date 215
  contributions defined frequently as percentage of pay 218
  coverage risen 15
  effects of tenure in 203
  emergence of 71
  employer shift from DB to 271
  endogenous sorting or immediate learning effect from 199
  equity held outside of pensions 186
  estimates based on administrative earnings data 224–8
  estimates of wealth 218
  expected present value of wealth 218
  important role that voluntary saving plays in 221
  investment choices 184, 191
  methodology for generating pension wealth for participants 212–14
  modeling strategy for calculating wealth 213
  national 248
  people richer than those with 196
  quit date balances 224
  researchers' ability to model 211–12
  respondent-reported wealth 213
  risks and opportunities 185, 187, 188
  stock market investment 160, 187–8, 199, 202, 248
  thrift or savings 213
  unannuitized lump-sum payouts 192
  uncertainties tied to growth in financial assets of 43
  value of all pension accounts 45
  voluntary participation 189
death:
  average age of 127
  family 301
  leading but preventable cause of 145
  spouse 166
debt:
  uninsured individuals 169
  unsecured 120

decision-making:
  financial 179
  risky choices 266
Delorme, L. 43
demographic characteristics 14, 28, 31, 281
  cross-cohort comparison of 15
  investors 257
  salient historic trends likely to influence
    70
demographic variables 27, 149, 192, 286
demographics 120
  adjusting for expected changes 72
  comparing composition of cohorts 272
  differences across groups 115
  documented trends 144
  individual status 253
  investor 252
  lifetime 70
  wealth varies across groups 272
dependent variables 28, 61
depression 106
DI (disability insurance) programs 72, 96,
  118
  receipt of 126–7, 130, 132
diabetes 6, 103, 106, 141
  treatments for 108
Dickemper, J. 278
disability 6, 10, 101
  association between obesity and 115
  job left because of 204
  measuring 115
  more severe definition of 99
  objective 100
  rates increasing 127
  reported 115
  work 96
disadvantaged groups 55
discount rate 47
  nominal 46
disease:
  chronic 108, 141, 152
  people survive longer with 115
  respiratory 141
divorce 58, 71, 74, 86, 166, 281, 303
  Boomers have higher percentages of 120
  higher probability of men remarrying
    144
  replacement rates 84
drinking 6, 141
  heavy 154
drinking problems 10, 144, 155
  persons who acknowledge 152
  screening for 144–5
DYNASIM model 114

early retirement 13, 44, 301
  increasing trend in 18
  Social Security age 25–6
  transitions 18
earnings 81
  accrued 221
  actual, information on 114
  administrative 224–8
  annual 212
  average 5, 118, 119, 123, 132
  average household 5
  distribution of 72, 75, 114
  future, uncertain 183
  household 5, 114
  inequality 75, 123
  lifetime 117, 211
  low 84
  postretirement 71
  preretirement 42, 43, 114
  respondent-reported 214
  shared, wage-indexed 74
  Social Security 225
  spouse with higher 192
  women 71
  see also income; lifetime earnings
Easterlin, R. A. 139
EBBs (Early Baby Boomers) 5, 8, 9, 14, 18, 19,
  116, 138, 141, 153, 190, 234, 241, 243, 244
  binary variables for 149
  coefficient on cohort dummy for 28
  comparing with predecessors 297–301
  education 15, 144, 272
  ethnic diversity 15
  health 101–2, 104, 108
  health insurance 159, 161, 164, 167
  higher participation rates 24
  home ownership rates 300
  home prices 287
  net worth 299
  nonplanners 278–9
  partial retirement rates lower for 25
  physical tasks 143
  retiring later 17
  wealth 273, 275, 277, 286, 288, 289
  women's risk of having ever smoked 145
EBRI (Employee Benefit Research
  Institute) 119
economic downturn 301
economic prosperity 71
  lifetime 10
economic well-being 6, 36, 71, 72
  current retirees 75
  future retirees 70, 74, 75
  health status and 112–37

economic well-being (*cont.*)
  high replacement rates do not ensure 86
  relative, various subgroups 81
education 74
  college 80, 152, 272, 306
  EBBs 15, 164–5
  financial 184, 279
  health and 106–8, 117, 149, 152, 153
  high school 149–52
  low 271, 273
  mean years of 15
  parental 120, 152
  persons with less/least 5, 9, 10, 166, 274
  wealth strongly affected by 272
emphysema 141
employer-sponsored health insurance 159, 168
employment problems 128
endogeneity issue 261–6
endogenous variables 286
Engelhardt, Gary 8, 214. 218, 224
Engen, E. M. 41, 42–3, 113, 114
Enron 181
ENTERAFTER 257
ENTERSIM 255, 257
ER (employer-reported) pension data 191, 193, 202
ESOP (employee stock ownership plan) 213
ethnic minorities 15, 74
EXITAFTER 257
EXITSIM 257
exogenous retirement 185
expectations:
  cohort differences in 13–35
  longer work lives 6
  realistic, about earnings 114
  survival 104
  working into retirement 10
expected retirement age:
  HRS-Early members 19
  HRS-Late members 19
  WBs 19
expected retirement income 70, 71
  average 41
expense flows 42
explanatory variables 261, 268
extractions 237–8, 239, 240
  predicting future 241–4

family breakups 272, 281
family income 72, 78, 87, 119
  average 81, 84–5
  below absolute minimum level 75
  chance to double 191

less than household-size-adjusted poverty
  threshold 120
  per capita 5
  projected 75
  ratio to family poverty threshold 121
  relative 81
  share from nonretirement income 5
family size 55, 119
  fallen overall 50
financial assets 9, 42, 43, 190, 301
  housing wealth reallocated to 304
  nonpension 188
financial capital 3, 5
financial incentives 13
financial markets:
  positive image of investing in 251
  unequal distribution of gains 41
financial wealth 37
  average 51
  distribution of 124
  increased inequality in 50
  net 119, 120, 129, 130
  nonpension 45, 132, 197
  privately accumulated 36
  rising 51
Fisher, G. D. 95
fixed-effect models 138, 140, 149–55
Flavin, M. 185
Fonda, S. 95
FRA (full retirement age) 17
Freedman, V. A. 106
Friedberg, Leora 7, 192
full retirement rates/patterns 14, 25–6
full-time work 22–4
  higher probabilities of 17
  highest fraction of 18
functioning loss 115
future retirees:
  characteristics of 73–4
  economic well-being 75–9
  replacement rates 81–4
future work likelihood 26–7

Gale, W. G. 113
gender differences 149
gender-specific life tables 46
generational changes 116, 119
Gini coefficients 122, 123, 124, 125
Goldman, D. 187
graded-response model 146
Great Depression 10, 71
Greenspan, Alan 301
Gustman, A. L. 37, 187, 191

hard-coding 215, 218
Haveman, Robert 4, 5
health 9, 14, 28, 31
  cross-cohort differences on verge of
    retirement 138–58
  gender 115
  self-perceived 7
  see also poor health; *also under following
    headings prefixed* 'health'
health capital 3, 10
  why stocks differ across cohorts on verge of
    retirement 138
health care:
  employer-provided 50
  uncertainty regarding costs of 5
  unprecedented effects on 3
health conditions:
  major 15, 19
  spouse 58
health index 141, 152, 153
  see also Summary Health Index
health indicators 144, 145, 149
health insurance 3, 7, 93–175
  see also private health insurance
health problems 128, 130
  ability to work limited by 100, 102
  chronic 144, 154
  low income and 131
  multiple objective 100
  negative influence of 61
  parents' generation with 118, 129
  proximate cause of bankruptcy 171
health status 6, 192
  changing 93–175
  economic well-being and 112–37
  interaction between moving house and 306
  poor 19
heart disease 106, 108, 141
Heckman-type probit selection model 257
hedging demand 185
HEK 2000 (Swedish household economics
    report) 253
hereditary advantage 153
Herzog, A. R. 95
high-school dropouts 79, 86, 272
  incomes for 81, 85
  replacement rates 84
Hispanics 9, 10, 15, 86, 149, 273
  less likely to invest in stock market 199
  nonplanners 279
  poverty rates 74, 79
  rapid growth of retirees 120
  wealth 281
historic events 139

Holden, Karen 4
home equity 9, 119, 120, 298, 299, 304
  appreciation in 273
  distribution 125
  flows of money out of 301
  percentage of portfolio devoted to 299–300
  whether amount invested declines with
    age 302
home prices 277, 279, 287, 288
hospitalization 7
  older households 170
  probability of 160
  spouse 170
  uninsured 160, 170, 171
hours of work 187
household income 15, 85, 272, 299, 306
  real, higher 297
household wealth 37, 42, 114, 211, 272, 278
  financial, nonpension 197
  uninsured 168–9
households:
  access to health insurance 116
  barriers to stock market participation 180
  company pensions 42
  health problems as proximate cause of
    bankruptcy 171
  major decisions 192
  moved 304–6
  nest egg loss as result of hospital stay 160
  pension characteristics 211
  realistic expectations about earnings 114
  replacement rates 42
  retirement nest egg 159
  stock market participation 179
  up-front cost of learning how to invest 184
housing 45, 275
  fluctuations 277
  investment in 58
  market booming 302
  market bust 287
  recent market trends 124
housing equity 4, 7, 274
  appreciation in 271
housing wealth 9, 37, 124, 125, 169, 273
  cross-cohort differences 296–308
HRS (Health and Retirement Study) 4, 5, 6, 7,
    9, 10, 13, 36, 37, 41, 42, 44–5, 46, 58, 61,
    96, 107, 116, 179, 186, 211, 215, 221, 234,
    239, 242
  age of entry into 138
  association between obesity and
    disability 115
  characteristics of later samples 47–51
  conceived to address key questions 95

HRS... (*cont.*)
  DC/401(k) Calculator 211–12, 214–15, 218, 219
  depression measure used in 106
  error terms correlated at household level 140
  health indicators derive from self-reports 141
  higher education categories 50
  household income distribution between EBBs and 272
  housing market 287
  measures not consistent across waves 103
  original 14, 140, 144, 145, 149, 152, 153, 160, 161, 162, 165, 170, 190, 212, 228, 239, 241, 244, 271, 272, 274
  partially retired in first wave of 15
  pensions data 189, 190, 191
  portfolios 300
  raised holdings of equity in 187
  research on respondents' plan reports 213
  retirement planning 278
  right-censored workers 242
  risk-taking 187, 188
  SPD match rates for later waves of 237
  statistical equations estimated from 117
  uninsured cohort members 160
  wealth 8, 114, 189, 277, 285–6, 301–6
  younger half of first cohort 159
HRS-Early cohort 14, 19, 21, 22, 24, 28, 104
  chance of working in the future 31
  full retirement rates 26
  nonworkers 22
HRS-Late cohort 14, 15, 17, 18, 19, 21, 24, 28
  full retirement rates 26
  nonworkers 22
human capital 36, 54, 55
Hurd, Michael 8, 187
hypertension 6, 103, 141
  treatments for 108

IADLs (instrumental activities of daily living) 96–7
Iams, Howard M. 5, 70, 272
Ibbotson Associates 219, 226
ICC (intraclass correlation coefficient) 154
ICI (Investment Company Institute) 119
inability to work 98, 100
  very high likelihood of 97
income:
  adequacy of 70
  asset 5, 75, 119
  coresident 77, 79
  future 42, 241
  health and 131

low 9, 121–2, 131
  measured 113
  never-married women 85
  noncapital 192
  nonfinancial 187
  nonretirement 8, 78
  parents' generation, median per capita 123
  pension-based 251
  projected 75–9, 81
  relative 81, 118–19
  rental 72, 77, 79
  unequal 132
  uninsurability of 42
  see also family income; household income; labor income; real income; retirement income
income distribution 5, 122, 124, 125, 132
  changes in 123
  household 272–3
inequality:
  earnings 75, 123
  health 131
  income 75, 122–3
inequality indices 122
inflation 46, 47, 132
  expected 119
  time-varying 214
instrumental variables 104, 261, 286–7, 288, 289
insulin 108
interaction terms 149, 153
interest rate 47
investment:
  choices 179–210
  long-term, invaluable rewards from 10
  personal accounts 8–9
  stock market 7
involuntary job loss 204
IoF 2000 (Swedish report on individual and household measures of income) 253
IRAs (Individual Retirement Accounts) 45, 71, 77, 85, 190, 193, 239, 275, 276, 277
IRS (Internal Revenue Service) 219
IRT (Item Response Theory) 6, 138, 145, 153
  generalization of the two-parameter model 146
Italian data 187

justification bias 96

Karlsson, Anders 8
Keogh/401k plans 45, 71, 77, 85, 119, 120, 179, 186, 190, 193, 211–12, 213, 221, 228, 275, 277

Kimball, M. 185
knowledge-based jobs 10
Koo, H. K. 185
Kumar, Anil 8

labor force 24, 70
    exits for older Americans 96
    poor health linked to withdrawal 95
    prospects of never-married women 58
    rising experience across cohorts 74
    shifting composition of 19
labor force attachment 97
    EBBs 28
    links to age and functional status 97
    low(er) 36, 55
    strong(est) 54, 81
    weak 79, 84, 86
labor force participation 13
    HRS-Late 22
    most impaired 98
    older women 13
    women with children 50
labor income 15, 31, 183, 185
    self-insured 187
labor supply:
    allowed to vary endogenously 185
    postretirement 22
Late Boomers 5, 116
later-life employment 4
leading Boomers 72, 74, 75, 79, 81
    health trajectories 109
learning effect 261, 266
leverage 301
Levine, P. 187
Levy, Helen G. 7, 116
life-cycle and lifestyle factors 138, 152, 153,
    185, 192
life expectancy 4, 19, 37, 101, 127, 129, 192
    active 99
    important input into retirement planning 17
    improvement in 128
    longer 9, 43
    persistent differences in 144
    pessimism about 6
    systematical underestimate of 18
    uncertainty regarding 42
life table probabilities 22
lifetime earnings 71, 74
    lowest 86
    shared 75, 79, 80, 84
lifetime utility 41
linear probability model 31
liquid assets 190
liquidity constraints 184

living well longer 95–111
'long reach of childhood' 153
longevity risk 7
lump sums 192, 236, 237, 238, 241, 242,
    243
lung disease 103
Lusardi, Annamaria 9, 277, 278, 279

McCabe, John 6
macroeconomic variables 46
Madrian, B. 95
Maestas, Nicole 4, 109, 187, 301
Maki, Dean 9
Manchester, Joyce 6, 123, 272, 297
marginal utility 41
marital status 144
    gender groups 54
    interaction between moving and 306
    transitions 166–7
    wealth strongly affected by 272
market capitalization 253
Marmot, M. 152
marriage:
    historical trends 73
    prevalence among parents' generation
        120
married couples 45
    accumulated retirement saving 43
    health statistically significant only for 58
    lifetime utility 41
    mean ANW 50
    median target wealth/earnings ratio 42
    spouse and survivor benefits 46
Martin, L. G. 106
Massa, Massimo 8
Master Beneficiary File 46
Mayfield, D. 152
measurement error 104, 213
Medicaid 234
Medicare 116, 159, 165, 167, 234
    eligibility for 160, 161, 170
    looming deficits 301
    policies to supplement 187
medications:
    improved 108, 126
    psychotropic 145
Medigap policies 187
mental accounting 248
mental health 106
microsimulation models 86
    see also MINT
middle age 71
    late 109
    receipt of DI after 118

middle Boomers 116
midlife health 152, 153
minority groups 120, 271
  shift in representation 74
MINT (Social Security Model of Income
  in the Near Term) 5, 6, 42, 70, 72,
  112, 117–18, 119, 120, 122, 124,
  126–32
  projection methods in 116
Mitchell, Olivia S. 6, 37, 42, 277, 279, 301
Mitchell Social Security Wealth estimates 46
mobility 103, 154
  endogenous 189, 196
  job 8
  physical 148
Montalto, C. P. 41
Moore, J. 37, 42, 301
mortality 115, 117, 118, 152
  lower 103
  persistent male disadvantage 144
  positive change in 128
mortgages 45, 87
  mortgages reserve 9
  reverse 299
multiple funds 261
multivariate estimates 50, 197
multivariate regression models 27–31, 104,
  281, 304
Munnell, A. H. 42, 71, 85

Nagi, S. 96
narrow framing 248
National Academy of Sciences Panel on Poverty
  Measurement 4
National Center for Health Statistics 115
National Health Interview Survey data 126
Native Americans:
  rapid growth of retirees 120
  replacement rates 84
NBS (New Beneficiary Survey) 4, 36, 41, 43–4,
  44–5, 46, 58, 61
  characteristics of early samples 47–51
NDC (Swedish Notional Defined Contribution)
  plan 249
near-poverty standard 43, 55
near-retirees 14, 19–21, 72, 74, 75, 79
  health insurance patterns 161–9
nearest-neighbor approach 116
net worth 272, 273, 274, 275, 279, 284, 286–7,
  299, 302, 303–4
never-married men 86
  poverty rates highest for 79
never-married persons 71, 74
  Boomers have higher percentages of 120

never-married women 79, 81
  incomes 85
  labor force prospects 58
  poverty rates highest for 79
  replacement rates 84
New England 287
NHANES (National Health and Nutrition
  Examination Study) 141
NIA (National Institute on Aging) 140
NLTCS (National Long-Term Care Survey)
  115
non-Hispanic whites 81
  replacement rates 84
nonmarried persons 10, 15, 74
  current retirees 73
nonplanners 9
nontrivial underestimate 18
nonwhites 5, 50
  household financial wealth 51
  negative effect on ANW 61
  vulnerability to poverty higher for 58
  wealth advantage for whites relative to 54
nonworking persons 19
  Early Boomers 26

obesity 5, 109
  commonly defined 103
  dangers of 10
  disability and 115
  rise in 102, 108, 115
objective information 14
O'Brien, R. M. 139
OCACT (SSA Office of the Chief Actuary) 118
older investors 255
older workers 13
OLS (ordinary least squares) regression 28,
  281, 284, 286, 288, 289
  fixed-effect specification 149
ordered polytomous variables 146
'other race' respondents 149
outcome variables 28
overweight persons 5

pain 10, 154, 155
  frequent 104, 144
  joint 103
  mild/moderate 148
  regular 145
  self-reported 6, 103
  severe 141, 144, 145, 148
parents 6, 144
  Boomers versus 112–37
  Social Security regimes 71
part-time working 15, 18, 22

partial retirement 13, 18, 22
  many ways to define 14
  near doubling of rates 25
  patterns 24–5
  steady rise over time 19
  transition from complete retirement to 21
  transition from full-time work to 21
Past Stock Market Participation Dummy 258
Pattison, D. 114
PBGC (Pension Benefit Guaranty
    Corporation) 203, 206
pension plans 189
  employer-provided 211, 212, 213–14,
    229
  portfolio choice and menu exposure
    248–70
  see also DB; DC; SPDs
pension wealth 7, 46, 47, 51, 191, 197
  accruals 8, 181–2, 183, 203
  discounted 238
  employer-provided 192
  measuring 211–33
pensions 114
  company 42, 234
  impact on nonpension investment
    choices 179–210
  innovative systems 10–11
  overall coverage 15
  private schemes 13, 58
  shift in structure that 8
  trends in values around retirement 234–47
  way in which new global economy is
    remaking 3
PEP (Pension Estimation Program) 8, 46, 213,
    214–15, 218, 219, 224, 225, 228, 229
Perozek, M. 187
physical activity 103
physical limitations 97–8, 99, 102, 104, 106
  severe 101
physical problems 128
physical tasks 95, 141–3
  degree of difficulty in performing 141
  everyday, difficulty with 155
poor health 15, 100, 116, 125, 128, 130, 131,
    145, 146, 148
  childhood 153
  job left because of 204
  linked to labor force withdrawal 95
  low economic status and 129
  low income and 118
  lower incidences of 126
  not increasingly concentrated across
    generations 133
  probability of 159

population characteristics 50
portfolio allocation 181, 184, 186, 188,
    196
  sensible patterns 3
portfolio choice 185, 187, 188, 191, 192
  and menu exposure 248–70
  optimal 181, 183–4
postretirement group 14
  comparisons 22
Poterba, J. 123–4, 184, 186, 197
poverty 85, 120, 130
  declining 114, 121
  female rates 74
  future retiree population face risk of 74
  high(est) rates 74, 128
  lower/lowest 5, 42, 80, 132
  national standard 43
  parents' generation 121
  policies aimed at preventing 160
  projected 79–80, 121
  vulnerability to 58
poverty line 4
  absolute 65
  expected retirement income below 41
  ratio of ANW to 55, 58, 61, 62
  US standard 6
poverty threshold 4, 62, 119, 122
  ability to generate income above 43
  family, ratio of family income to 121
  family-size-conditioned 55
  household-size-adjusted 120
  near 36
  official 75
PPM (Swedish premium pension system)
    248, 249, 268, 269
  campaigns encouraging individuals to
    make active choice in 251–2
  investment patterns in 255–67
preparedness for retirement 9, 113, 297,
    301
  evaluating 298
  model to compute 41
preretirees/preretirement 14, 15–18
  pay 43
  well-being 81
pre-tax deferrals 212, 224
price changes 119
private health insurance coverage 50, 58, 61
privation 10
Probit estimates 197
progressive income tax 114
property 45
PSID (Panel Study of Income Dynamics)
    116

psychiatric problems 6–7, 10, 145, 152–3, 155
  history of 154
psychological benefit 153
psychotropic medications 145

racial issues 54, 74
  current retirees 74
  health 115
  life tables 46, 47
  wealth strongly affected by 272
random error term 28
rates of return 119, 149, 180, 184
  real 218
  stochastic 187
  time-varying 212, 214, 218–19
real income 79
  higher 42, 132, 297
  rising 114, 132
real wage growth 114
  projected 121
replacement rates:
  evolution of 42
  higher than average 86
  lower 132
  median 5
  never-married women 84
  nominal 41
  non-Hispanic blacks 84
  projected 81–5
  widowed men 84
resource adequacy:
  available 36
  correlates of 55–61
  likely 37
  modest problem 41
  newly retired workers 54–5
  standard against which to judge 37
resources 45
  coping, few 10
  financial 115, 234
  inadequate 4, 36, 43
  insufficient, new retirees 41
  limited 130
  needed to maintain standards of living 114
respiratory diseases 141
Reti M. 187
retirement adequacy 5
retirement assets:
  effective way to add to and preserve 10
  new roles for 3, 177–308
  persons with very little in the way of 10
  understanding 7–9

retirement definitions 14–15
retirement income 77, 79, 112
  inadequate 85
  modest improvements in 125
  see also expected retirement income
retirement planning 9, 271–95
  implications for 18
  important input into 17
  lack of 10
reverse causality 106, 286, 289
Reynolds, S. L. 126
risk 249–51
  diversification benefit 181
  exposure to 160
  financial 8
  greater preferences for 7
  health 141, 159
  income 185, 187
  investment 185
  long-term 159
  longevity 11
  management of 10
  pension 180, 181–3, 187, 188–9, 203–4
  realization of 160
  stock market 187, 266
  tolerance for 189
  uninsured 165–8
risk aversion 183, 191, 197
  highest degree of 196
risk factors 104
risk preferences 189, 192
Rohwedder, Susann 8, 214, 218
Romanov, Andrei 4
Rural South 153
Ryder, Norman 139

Sabelhaus, J. 123
safety nets 10
Saito, Y. 126
Samwick, A. 186
Sapolsky, R. 128
savings 42, 159
  life-cycle decisions 179
  low rates 271
  optimal 41, 114
  peak 190
  precautionary 114
  reluctance to part with 10
  role of planning 271–95
  sufficiency of 36–69
  voluntary 8, 221
savings adequacy 8, 43, 113, 301
  anticipated 62
  estimates of 301

methodology for measuring 113–14
wide heterogeneity in 43
SCF (Survey of Consumer Finances) 119, 180,
    186
Scholz, J. K. 42, 114
security 4, 70
    financial 171, 211
Security Register Center (Sweden) 253
self-care 115
self-employment 185
self-reports 96, 100, 148
    chronic diseases 141
    health indicators 141
    labor income risk 187
    pain 6, 103
    planning efforts 278
    prior psychiatric problems 145
    see also SR pension type
separation 281
SES (socioeconomic status) 4, 28, 31, 144
    changes in 14
    childhood 153
    gradient in dimensions of health 106,
        152
SES variables 27, 28
Sevak, P. 187
Seventh Swedish Pension Fund 251
sex-specific life tables 47
shelter 298
shocks:
    earnings 114
    health 159, 170–1, 304, 305
    labor income 185
    marital 305, 306
    medical 114
    old-age 10
    spouse 170
short planning horizon 18
Simonov, Andrei 8
single individuals 36, 50
    accumulated retirement saving 43
    ANW less than poverty line among men 61
SIPP (US Census Bureau Survey of Income and
    Program Participation) 72, 116–17,
    117–18, 119
SIS Ägarservice AB 253
Smith, Karen E. 5, 70
smoking 6, 109, 141, 154
    decline of 102
    disease highly sensitive to 103
    enduring negative effect on health 152
    leading but preventable cause of death 145
    less common than for predecessors 5
    lifetime prevalence of 145

social acceptance 145
social adequacy targets 36
Social Security 41, 42, 58, 71, 114, 234
    benefits provide base level of support 36
    differences in normal retirement age 17
    different regimes compared to parents 71
    disability benefits 126
    early retirement age 25–6
    earnings histories and W-2s linked to
        surveys 225
    earnings records 114
    eligibility of nonwhite population 50
    expansion of coverage to federal
        employment 58
    first receipt of benefits 43, 44, 45, 50, 72
    looming deficits 301
    new retired-worker beneficiaries 47
    pension scheme 13
    progressive payment formula 84, 85
    replacing a portion of benefits with personal
        accounts 181
    significance of benefits 79
    simulated target level of savings minus 37
    spouse benefits 77, 79
    uncertainty regarding the future of 5
    see also SSA; SSI
societal trends 115
socioeconomic variables 117, 118
socioeconomics 72
Soldo, Beth J. 6, 15
Soto, M. 42
Souleles, N. 187
SPDs (Summary Plan Descriptions) 211, 213,
    214, 219, 221, 225, 228, 229, 237, 242
spending patterns 10
spouses:
    death of 166
    health 50, 58
    higher earnings 81, 192
    hospitalized 170
    income 77
    schooling of 61
    SSI benefits 75, 79
SR (self-reported) pension type 193, 197, 202,
    234–5, 241
    and pension wealth 191, 213
SRH (self-reported health) status 127, 141,
    154, 155
    five-level 146
SSA (Social Security Administration) 4, 214
    administrative records 116, 118, 132, 225
    lifetime earnings records 211
    Office of the Chief Actuary 118
    see also MINT

SSI (Supplemental Security Income) 71, 72, 77, 119
  spouse benefits 75, 79
standard deviation 50, 55, 251, 258
standard errors 50, 140, 203
standard of living 132, 301
  maintaining 113, 114
  preretirement 81, 85
statistical significance 25, 28, 58, 117, 191, 203, 255, 274
Statistics Sweden 252, 253
Steinmeier, T. L. 37, 187, 191
Stevens, A. H. 191
stochastic life-cycle model 41, 42, 113, 114
stock market investment/participation 7, 190, 196, 268, 277
  barriers to 180, 186, 203
  DC plans may have helped boost 187–8
  decision to enter 258
  decision to enter 261
  decision to exit 266
  exit rates 257
  funded retirement system affects 248
  holdings and investor demographics 252
  household 179
  impact of recent fluctuations on retirement 187
  likelihood of 199, 202
  nonpension financial wealth in 197
  peak and fall 251
  pension choice and 257–67
  probability of 255, 258–60, 261
  reduced share of assets in 187
  significantly higher 189
  volatility 160, 203
  women with influence 192
stress 106
stroke 6, 141
  treatment of survivors 108
Sturm, R. 115
subjective information 14
Sullivan, D. F. 99
Summary Health Index 145–9, 152, 153, 155
SUN 2000 (Swedish educational status report) 253
Sundin, A. 253
Sundqvist, S.-I. 253
Surveys of Consumer Finance 41
survival:
  expectations 103–4
  probabilities 19, 22, 46, 47, 218, 238
Sweden 8–9, 10–11, 248–70

tax efficiency 197
tax minimization 197
taxes 180, 184, 185, 196–7, 249
  marginal rates 186
Tfaily, Rania 6
TIAs (transient ischemic attacks) 141
time preference 47
Tobit estimates 197, 199
Toder, E. 117, 126
trailing Boomers 72, 74, 75, 77, 79, 81, 86
Treasury bills 190
Type A/Type B pensions 235

Uccello, C. 114, 186
uncertainty 5, 239
  end-of-life 114
  future contingencies 182
  life expectancy 42
  precaution against 41, 113
unemployment 19
uninsured persons 7, 42, 159, 160, 162, 165, 167, 170, 171, 172
  probability of being 166
  wealth at stake 168–9
University of Michigan 8, 213
unmarried persons 5, 45, 273
  relative sizes of groups 120
unretirement 4, 18
  age gradient in 21
  growing trend toward 26
Urban North 153
US Bureau of the Census 72, 75
  poverty thresholds 119
  see also CPS; SIPP
US Decennial Life Tables 47

Van de Ven, W. P. M. M. 257
Van Praag, B. M. S. 257
Venti, S. F. 213, 302
Viceira, L. 185
Vissing-Jørgenson, A. 186, 187
voluntary contributions 184–5, 189
  impact from W-2 data 224
  pre-tax 219–21
  restricted eligibility for 224
  time-varying, individual-specific 214
vulnerability 5

wage growth 119
WBs (War Babies) 8, 14, 15, 17, 19, 26, 28, 140, 141, 154, 159, 190, 192, 212, 225, 228, 234, 242
  binary variables for 149
  education 153, 165

health insurance 161
highest/higher fraction working
    full-time 18, 24
significantly higher partial retirement
    rates 25
wealth 4, 43
    advantage for whites 54
    allocation of 190
    bequeathable 8
    concentration of 36
    differences in holdings 278–84
    estimates of 51–4
    exogenous increases in 288
    low 271, 275
    median 123
    net 45–7, 123; *see also* ANW
    new retiree 36
    nonhousing 271, 273–4
    nonpension 15, 119, 160, 180, 192, 197
    optimal 42, 114
    reallocation of 304
    retirement account 119
    Social Security 41, 45–6, 47, 51
    strong predictors of 288
    variation in holdings 42
    varies across demographic groups 272
    see also financial wealth; household wealth;
        housing wealth; pension wealth
wealth accumulation 43, 61, 112, 123, 180,
    297
    adequate 113
    EBBs 271
    family breakups detrimental to 281
    groups facing increasing difficulty 273
    household 114
    impact of pension structure on 180
    optimal 41
wealth distribution 5, 114, 271, 273, 285,
    286
    home prices play major role in explaining
        changes in 277
    housing 125
    parents' generation 124, 125
Weaver, David 6
Webb, A. 192
Weir, David 5, 6, 144
Weisbenner, S. 184, 188
Weitzer, Ben 9
welfare ratios 119, 121, 122
    median 129, 130

well-being 42, 160
    absolute measures of 75–80,
        85
    financial 170
    physical 6, 127, 128
    primary measure of 47
    relative measures of 80–5
    salient historic trends likely to influence 70
    uninsured elderly 171
    see also economic well-being
Wentworth, S. G. 114
Whitman, Kevin 6
widowhood 46, 58, 81, 303
    replacement rates 84
Wilcoxon test 255
Wise, D. A. 213, 302
Wolfe, Barbara 4, 272
Wolff, E. N. 41, 43, 63, 71, 85
women 5
    career earnings 85
    considered as having a drinking
        problem 144
    divorced at an early age 58
    employer-based pensions 235
    insured for disability benefits 118
    involvement of more in the workforce 127
    less likely to be widowed 74
    lifetime earnings 71
    marrying men about three-years older 144
    more likely to work for pay 71
    older, labor force participation rates 13
    particularly at risk 10
    planning 279
    psychiatric problems often associated
        with 153
    uninsurance 166
    see also never-married women; widowhood
work experience 75, 80, 81
    many years of 84
work flexibility 187
work limitations 10, 100
    percentage without 126
    self-reported 96, 101

Yakoboski, P. 278
Yamashita, T. 185
years-in-plan variables 202
younger investors 255

Zayatz, T. 127